MODERN MULTITHREADING

MODERN MULTITHREADING

Implementing, Testing, and Debugging Multithreaded Java and C++/Pthreads/Win32 Programs

RICHARD H. CARVER
KUO-CHUNG TAI

WILEY-INTERSCIENCE

A JOHN WILEY & SONS, INC., PUBLICATION

Published by John Wiley & Sons, Inc., Hoboken, New Jersey.
Published simultaneously in Canada.

For general information on our other products and services or for technical support, please contact our Customer Care Department within the United States at (800) 762-2974, outside the United States at (317) 572-3993 or fax (317) 572-4002.

Wiley also publishes its books in a variety of electronic formats. Some content that appears in print may not be available in electronic formats. For more information about Wiley products, visit our web site at www.wiley.com.

Library of Congress Cataloging-in-Publication Data:

Carver, Richard H., 1960–
    Modern multithreading: implementing, testing, and debugging multithreaded Java and C++/Pthreads/Win32 programs / by Richard H. Carver and Kuo-Chung Tai.
        p. cm.
    Includes bibliographical references and index.
    ISBN-13 978-0-471-72504-6 (paper)
    ISBN-10 0-471-72504-8 (paper)
    1. Parallel programming (Computer science) 2. Threads (Computer programs) I. Tai, Kuo-Chung. II. Title.

QA76.642.C38 2006
005.1′1–dc22

                                                        2005045775

Printed in the United States of America.

10 9 8 7 6 5 4 3 2

CONTENTS

PREFACE

This is a textbook on multithreaded programming. The objective of this book is to teach students about languages and libraries for multithreaded programming, to help students develop problem-solving and programming skills, and to describe and demonstrate various testing and debugging techniques that have been developed for multithreaded programs over the past 20 years. It covers threads, semaphores, locks, monitors, message passing, and the relevant parts of Java, the POSIX Pthreads library, and the Windows Win32 Application Programming Interface (API).

The book is unique in that it provides in-depth coverage on testing and debugging multithreaded programs, a topic that typically receives little attention. The title *Modern Multithreading* reflects the fact that there are effective and relatively new testing and debugging techniques for multithreaded programs. The material in this book was developed in concurrent programming courses that the authors have taught for 20 years. This material includes results from the authors' research in concurrent programming, emphasizing tools and techniques that are of practical use. A class library has been implemented to provide working examples of all the material that is covered.

Classroom Use

In our experience, students have a hard time learning to write concurrent programs. If they manage to get their programs to run, they usually encounter deadlocks and other intermittent failures, and soon discover how difficult it is to reproduce the failures and locate the cause of the problem. Essentially, they have no way to check the correctness of their programs, which interferes with learning. Instructors face the same problem when grading multithreaded programs. It is tedious, time consuming, and often impossible to assess student programs by hand. The class libraries that we have developed, and the testing techniques they support, can be used to assess student programs. When we assign programming problems in our courses, we also provide test cases that the students must use to assess the correctness of their programs. This is very helpful for the students and the instructors.

This book is designed for upper-level undergraduates and graduate students in computer science. It can be used as a main text in a concurrent programming course or could be used as a supplementary text for an operating systems course or a software engineering course. Since the text emphasizes practical material, provides working code, and addresses testing and debugging problems that receive little or no attention in many other books, we believe that it will also be helpful to programmers in industry.

The text assumes that students have the following background:

- Programming experience as typically gained in CS 1 and CS 2 courses.
- Knowledge of elementary data structures as learned in a CS 2 course.
- An understanding of Java fundamentals. Students should be familiar with object-oriented programming in Java, but no "advanced" knowledge is necessary.
- An understanding of C++ fundamentals. We use only the basic object-oriented programming features of C++.
- A prior course on operating systems is helpful but not required.

We have made an effort to minimize the differences between our Java and C++ programs. We use object-oriented features that are common to both languages, and the class library has been implemented in both languages. Although we don't illustrate every example in both Java and C++, the differences are very minor and it is easy to translate program examples from one language to the other.

Content

The book has seven chapters. Chapter 1 defines operating systems terms such as *process*, *thread*, and *context switch*. It then shows how to create threads, first in Java and then in C++ using both the POSIX Pthreads library and the Win32 API. A C++ *Thread* class is provided to hide the details of thread creation in Pthreads/Win32. C++ programs that use the *Thread* class look remarkably similar to multithreaded Java programs. Fundamental concepts, such as atomicity and nondeterminism, are described using simple program examples. Chapter 1 ends by listing the issues and problems that arise when testing and debugging multithreaded programs. To illustrate the interesting things to come, we present a simple multithreaded C++ program that is capable of tracing and replaying its own executions.

Chapter 2 introduces concurrent programming by describing various solutions to the critical section problem. This problem is easy to understand but hard to solve. The advantage of focusing on this problem is that it can be solved without introducing complicated new programming constructs. Students gain a quick appreciation for the programming skills that they need to acquire. Chapter 2 also demonstrates how to trace and replay Peterson's solution to the critical section problem, which offers a straightforward introduction to several testing and debugging issues. The synchronization library implements the various techniques that are described.

Chapters 3, 4, and 5 cover semaphores, monitors and message passing, respectively. Each chapter describes one of these constructs and shows how to use it to solve programming problems. Semaphore and Lock classes for Java and C++/Win32/Pthreads are presented in Chapter 3. Chapter 4 presents monitor classes for Java and C++/Win32/Pthreads. Chapter 5 presents mailbox classes with send/receive methods and a selective wait statement. These chapters also cover the built-in support that Win32 and Pthreads provide for these constructs, as well as the support provided by J2SE 5.0 (Java 2 Platform, Standard Edition 5.0). Each chapter addresses a particular testing or debugging problem and shows how to solve it. The synchronization library implements the testing and debugging techniques so that students can apply them to their own programs.

Chapter 6 covers message passing in a distributed environment. It presents several Java mailbox classes that hide the details of TCP message passing and shows how to solve several distributed programming problems in Java. It also shows how to test and debug programs in a distributed environment (e.g., accurately tracing program executions by using vector timestamps). This chapter by no means provides complete coverage of distributed programming. Rather, it is meant to introduce students to the difficulty of distributed programming and to show them that the testing and debugging techniques presented in earlier chapters can be extended to work in a distributed environment. The synchronization library implements the various techniques.

Chapter 7 covers concepts that are fundamental to testing and debugging concurrent programs. It defines important terms, presents several test coverage criteria for concurrent programs, and describes the various approaches to testing concurrent programs. This chapter organizes and summarizes the testing and debugging material that is presented in depth in Chapters 2 to 6. This organization provides two paths through the text. Instructors can cover the testing and debugging material in the last sections of Chapters 2 to 6 as they go through those chapters, or they can cover those sections when they cover Chapter 7. Chapter 7 also discusses reachability testing, which offers a bridge between testing and verification, and is implemented in the synchronization library.

Each chapter has exercises at the end. Some of the exercises explore the concepts covered in the chapter, whereas others require a program to be written. In our courses we cover all the chapters and give six homework assignments, two in-class exams, and a project. We usually supplement the text with readings on model checking, process algebra, specification languages, and other research topics.

Online Resources

The home page for this book is located at

> http://www.cs.gmu.edu/~rcarver/ModernMultithreading

This Web site contains the source code for all the listings in the text and for the synchronization libraries. It also contains startup files and test cases for some of the exercises. Solutions to the exercises are available for instructors, as is a copy of our lecture notes. There will also be an errata page.

Acknowledgments

The suggestions we received from the anonymous reviewers were very helpful. The National Science Foundation supported our research through grants CCR-8907807, CCR-9320992, CCR-9309043, and CCR-9804112. We thank our research assistants and the students in our courses at North Carolina State and George Mason University for helping us solve many interesting problems. We also thank Professor Jeff Lei at the University of Texas at Arlington for using early versions of this book in his courses.

My friend, colleague, and coauthor Professor K. C. Tai passed away before we could complete this book. K.C. was an outstanding teacher, a world-class researcher in the areas of software engineering, concurrent systems, programming languages, and compiler construction, and an impeccable and highly respected professional. If the reader finds this book helpful, it is a tribute to K.C.'s many contributions. Certainly, K.C. would have fixed the faults that I failed to find.

RICHARD H. CARVER

Fairfax, Virginia
July 2005
rcarver@cs.gmu.edu

1

INTRODUCTION TO CONCURRENT PROGRAMMING

A concurrent program contains two or more threads that execute concurrently and work together to perform some task. In this chapter we begin with an operating system's view of a concurrent program. The operating system manages the program's use of hardware and software resources and allows the program's threads to share the central processing units (CPUs). We then learn how to define and create threads in Java and also in C++ using the Windows Win32 API and the POSIX Pthreads library. Java provides a *Thread* class, so multithreaded Java programs are object-oriented. Win32 and Pthreads provide a set of function calls for creating and manipulating threads. We wrap a C++ *Thread* class around these functions so that we can write C++/Win32 and C++/Pthreads multithreaded programs that have the same object-oriented structure as Java programs.

All concurrent programs exhibit unpredictable behavior. This creates new challenges for programmers, especially those learning to write concurrent programs. In this chapter we learn the reason for this unpredictable behavior and examine the problems it causes during testing and debugging.

1.1 PROCESSES AND THREADS: AN OPERATING SYSTEM'S VIEW

When a program is executed, the operating system creates a *process* containing the code and data of the program and manages the process until the program terminates. User processes are created for user programs, and system processes are created for system programs. A user process has its own logical address space, separate from the space of other user processes and separate from the space (called the *kernel space*) of the system processes. This means that two processes may reference the same logical address, but this address will be mapped to different physical memory locations. Thus, processes do not share memory unless they make special arrangements with the operating system to do so.

Multiprocessing operating systems enable several programs to execute simultaneously. The operating system is responsible for allocating the computer's resources among competing processes. These shared resources include memory, peripheral devices such as printers, and the CPU(s). The goal of a multiprocessing operating system is to have some process executing at all times in order to maximize CPU utilization.

Within a process, program execution entails initializing and maintaining a great deal of information [Anderson et al. 1989]. For instance:

- The process state (e.g., ready, running, waiting, or stopped)
- The program counter, which contains the address of the next instruction to be executed for this process
- Saved CPU register values
- Memory management information (page tables and swap files), file descriptors, and outstanding input/output (I/O) requests

The volume of this per-process information makes it expensive to create and manage processes.

A *thread* is a unit of control within a process. When a thread runs, it executes a function in the program. The process associated with a running program starts with one running thread, called the *main thread*, which executes the "main" function of the program. In a multithreaded program, the main thread creates other threads, which execute other functions. These other threads can create even more threads, and so on. Threads are created using constructs provided by the programming language or the functions provided by an application programming interface (API).

Each thread has its own stack of activation records and its own copy of the CPU registers, including the stack pointer and the program counter, which together describe the state of the thread's execution. However, the threads in a multithreaded process share the data, code, resources, and address space of their process. The per-process state information listed above is also shared by the threads in the program, which greatly reduces the overhead involved in creating and managing threads. In Win32 a program can create multiple processes or multiple threads. Since thread creation in Win32 has lower overhead, we focus on single-process multithreaded Win32 programs.

The operating system must decide how to allocate the CPUs among the processes and threads in the system. In some systems, the operating system selects a process to run and the process selected chooses which of its threads will execute. Alternatively, the threads are scheduled directly by the operating system. At any given moment, multiple processes, each containing one or more threads, may be executing. However, some threads may not be ready for execution. For example, some threads may be waiting for an I/O request to complete. The scheduling policy determines which of the ready threads is selected for execution.

In general, each ready thread receives a time slice (called a *quantum*) of the CPU. If a thread decides to wait for something, it relinquishes the CPU voluntarily. Otherwise, when a hardware timer determines that a running thread's quantum has completed, an interrupt occurs and the thread is preempted to allow another ready thread to run. If there are multiple CPUs, multiple threads can execute at the same time. On a computer with a single CPU, threads have the appearance of executing simultaneously, although they actually take turns running and they may not receive equal time. Hence, some threads may appear to run at a faster rate than others.

The scheduling policy may also consider a thread's priority and the type of processing that the thread performs, giving some threads preference over others. We assume that the scheduling policy is fair, which means that every ready thread eventually gets a chance to execute. A concurrent program's correctness should not depend on its threads being scheduled in a certain order.

Switching the CPU from one process or thread to another, known as a *context switch*, requires saving the state of the old process or thread and loading the state of the new one. Since there may be several hundred context switches per second, context switches can potentially add significant overhead to an execution.

1.2 ADVANTAGES OF MULTITHREADING

Multithreading allows a process to overlap I/O and computation. One thread can execute while another thread is waiting for an I/O operation to complete. Multithreading makes a GUI (graphical user interface) more responsive. The thread that handles GUI events, such as mouse clicks and button presses, can create additional threads to perform long-running tasks in response to the events. This allows the event handler thread to respond to more GUI events. Multithreading can speed up performance through parallelism. A program that makes full use of two processors may run in close to half the time. However, this level of speedup usually cannot be obtained, due to the communication overhead required for coordinating the threads (see Exercise 1.11).

Multithreading has some advantages over multiple processes. Threads require less overhead to manage than processes, and intraprocess thread communication is less expensive than interprocess communication. Multiprocess concurrent programs do have one advantage: Each process can execute on a different machine (in which case, each process is often a multithreaded program). This type of concurrent program is called a *distributed program*. Examples of distributed programs are file servers (e.g., NFS), file transfer clients and servers (e.g., FTP), remote log-in clients and servers (e.g., Telnet), groupware programs, and Web browsers and servers. The main disadvantage of concurrent programs is that they are extremely difficult to develop. Concurrent programs often contain bugs that are notoriously difficult to find and fix. Once we have examined several concurrent programs, we'll take a closer look at the special problems that arise when we test and debug them.

1.3   THREADS IN JAVA

A Java program has a main thread that executes the *main()* function. In addition, several system threads are started automatically whenever a Java program is executed. Thus, every Java program is a concurrent program, although the programmer may not be aware that multiple threads are running. Java provides a *Thread* class for defining user threads. One way to define a thread is to define a class that extends (i.e., inherits from) the *Thread* class. Class *simpleThread* in Listing 1.1 extends class *Thread*. Method *run()* contains the code that will be executed when a *simpleThread* is started. The default *run()* method inherited from class *Thread* is empty, so a new *run()* method must be defined in *simpleThread* in order for the thread to do something useful.

The *main* thread creates *simpleThreads* named *thread1* and *thread2* and starts them. (These threads continue to run after the *main* thread completes its statements.) Threads *thread1* and *thread2* each display a simple message and terminate. The integer IDs passed as arguments to the *simpleThread* constructor are used to distinguish between the two instances of *simpleThread*.

A second way to define a user thread in Java is to use the *Runnable* interface. Class *simpleRunnable* in Listing 1.2 implements the *Runnable* interface, which means that *simpleRunnable* must provide an implementation of method *run()*. The *main* method creates a *Runnable* instance *r* of class *simpleRunnable*, passes *r* as an argument to the *Thread* class constructor for *thread3*, and starts *thread3*.

Using a *Runnable* object to define the *run()* method offers one advantage over extending class *Thread*. Since class *simpleRunnable* implements interface *Runnable*, it is not required to extend class *Thread*, which means that

```
class simpleThread extends Thread {
    public simpleThread(int ID) {myID = ID;}
    public void run() {System.out.println(''Thread '' + myID + '' is running.'');}
    private int myID;
}
public class javaConcurrentProgram {
    public static void main(String[] args) {
        simpleThread thread1 = new simpleThread(1);
        simpleThread thread2 = new simpleThread(2);
        thread1.start(); thread2.start(); // causes the run() methods to execute
    }
}
```

Listing 1.1   Simple concurrent Java program.

```
class simpleRunnable implements Runnable {
    public simpleRunnable(int ID) {myID = ID;}
    public void run() {System.out.println(''Thread '' + myID + '' is running.'');}
    private int myID;
}
public class javaConcurrentProgram2 {
    public static void main(String[] args) {
        Runnable r = new simpleRunnable(3);
        Thread thread3 = new Thread(r); // thread3 executed r's run() method
        thread3.start();
    }
}
```

Listing 1.2   Java's *Runnable* interface.

simpleRunnable could, if desired, extend some other class. This is important since a Java class cannot extend more than one other class. (A Java class can implement one or more interfaces but can extend only one class.)

The details about how Java threads are scheduled vary from system to system. Java threads can be assigned a priority, which affects how threads are selected for execution. Using method *setPriority()*, a thread T can be assigned a priority in a range from Thread.MIN_PRIORITY (usually, 1) to Thread.MAX_PRIORITY (usually, 10):

```
T.setPriority(6);
```

Higher-priority threads get preference over lower-priority threads, but it is difficult to make more specific scheduling guarantees based only on thread priorities.

We will not be assigning priorities to the threads in this book, which means that user threads will always have the same priority. However, even if all the threads have the same priority, a thread may not be certain to get a chance to run. Consider a thread that is executing the following infinite loop:

```
while (true) { ; }
```

This loop contains no I/O statements or any other statements that require the thread to release the CPU voluntarily. In this case the operating system must preempt the thread to allow other threads to run. Java does not guarantee that the underlying thread scheduling policy is preemptive. Thus, once a thread begins executing this loop, there is no guarantee that any other threads will execute. To be safe, we can add a *sleep* statement to this loop:

```
while (true) {
    try {Thread.sleep(100);}              // delay thread for 100 milliseconds
                                          // (i.e., 0.1 second)
```

```
        catch (InterruptedException e) { }        // InterruptedException must be caught
                                                   // when sleep( ) is called
    }
```

Executing the *sleep( )* statement will force a context switch, giving the other threads a chance to run. In this book we assume that the underlying thread scheduling policy is preemptive, so that *sleep( )* statements are not necessary to ensure fair scheduling. However, since *sleep( )* statements have a dramatic effect on execution, we will see later that they can be very useful during testing.

1.4 THREADS IN Win32

Multithreaded programs in Windows use the functions in the Win32 API. Threads are created by calling function *CreateThread( )* or function *_beginthreadex( )*. If a program needs to use the multithreaded C run-time library, it should use *_beginthreadex( )* to create threads; otherwise, it can use *CreateThread( )*. Whether a program needs to use the multithreaded C run-time library depends on which of the library functions it calls. Some of the functions in the single-threaded run-time library may not work properly in a multithreaded program. This includes functions *malloc( )* and *free( )* (or new and delete in C++), any of the functions in *stdio.h* or *io.h*, and functions such as *asctime( ), strtok( )*, and *rand( )*. For the sake of simplicity and safety, we use only *_beginthreadex( )* in this book. (Since the parameters for *_beginthreadex( )* and *CreateThread( )* are almost identical, we will essentially be learning how to use both functions.) Details about choosing between the single- and multithreaded C run-time libraries can be found in [Beveridge and Wiener 1997].

Function *_beginthreadex( )* takes six parameters and returns a pointer, called a *handle*, to the newly created thread. This handle must be saved so that it can be passed to other Win32 functions that manipulate threads:

```
    unsigned long _beginthreadex(
        void* security,                            // security attribute
        unsigned stackSize,                        // size of the thread's stack
        unsigned ( __stdcall *funcStart ) (void *),  // starting address of the function
                                                   // to run
        void* argList,                             // arguments to be passed to the
                                                   // thread
        unsigned initFlags,                        // initial state of the thread: running
                                                   // or suspended
        unsigned* threadAddr                       // thread ID
    );
```

The parameters of function_*beginthreadex()* are as follows:

- *security*: a security attribute, which in our programs is always the default value NULL.
- *stackSize*: the size, in bytes, of the new thread's stack. We will use the default value 0, which specifies that the stack size defaults to the stack size of the main thread.
- *funcStart*: the (address of a) function that the thread will execute. (This function plays the same role as the *run()* method in Java.)
- *argList*: an argument to be passed to the thread. This is either a 32-bit value or a 32-bit pointer to a data structure. The Win32 type for void* is LPVOID.
- *initFlags*: a value that is either 0 or CREATE_SUSPENDED. The value 0 specifies that the thread should begin execution immediately upon creation. The value CREATE_SUSPENDED specifies that the thread is suspended immediately after it is created and will not run until the Win32 function *ResumeThread*(HANDLE hThread) is called on it.
- *threadAddr*: the address of a memory location that will receive an identifier assigned to the thread by Win32.

If _*beginthreadex()* is successful, it returns a valid thread handle, which must be cast to the Win32 type HANDLE to be used in other functions. It returns 0 if it fails.

The program in Listing 1.3 is a C++/Win32 version of the simple Java program in Listing 1.1. Array *threadArray* stores the handles for the two threads created in *main()*. Each thread executes the code in function *simpleThread()*, which displays the ID assigned by the user and returns the ID. Thread IDs are integers that the user supplies as the fourth argument on the call to function _*beginthreadex()*. Function _*beginthreadex()* forwards the IDs as arguments to thread function *simpleThread()* when the threads are created.

Threads created in *main()* will not continue to run after the *main* thread exits. Thus, the *main* thread must wait for both of the threads it created to complete before it exits the *main()* function. (This behavior is opposite that of Java's *main()* method.) It does this by calling function *WaitForMultipleObjects()*. The second argument to *WaitForMultipleObjects()* is the array that holds the thread handles, and the first argument is the size of this array. The third argument TRUE indicates that the function will wait for *all* of the threads to complete. If FALSE were used instead, the function would wait until any *one* of the threads completed. The fourth argument is a timeout duration in milliseconds. The value INFINITE means that there is no time limit on how long *WaitForMultipleObjects()* should wait for the threads to complete. When both threads have completed, function *GetExitCodeThread()* is used to capture the return values of the threads.

```cpp
#include <iostream>
#include <windows.h>
#include <process.h> // needed for function _beginthreadex( )
void PrintError(LPTSTR lpszFunction,LPSTR fileName, int lineNumber) {
    TCHAR szBuf[256]; LPSTR lpErrorBuf;
    DWORD errorCode = GetLastError();
    FormatMessage( FORMAT_MESSAGE_ALLOCATE_BUFFER |
        FORMAT_MESSAGE_FROM_SYSTEM, NULL, errorCode,
        MAKELANGID(LANG_NEUTRAL,
        SUBLANG_DEFAULT), (LPTSTR) &lpErrorBuf, 0, NULL );
    wsprintf(szBuf, "%s failed at line %d in %s with error %d: %s", lpszFunction,
    lineNumber, fileName, errorCode, lpErrorBuf);
    DWORD numWritten;
    WriteFile(GetStdHandle(STD_ERROR_HANDLE),szBuf,strlen(szBuf),
        &numWritten,FALSE);
    LocalFree(lpErrorBuf);
    exit(errorCode);
}
unsigned WINAPI simpleThread (LPVOID myID) {
// myID receives the 4th argument of _beginthreadex( ).
// Note: "WINAPI" refers to the "__stdcall" calling convention
// API functions, and "LPVOID" is a Win32 data type defined as void*
    std::cout << "Thread " << (unsigned) myID << "is running" << std::endl;
    return (unsigned) myID;
}
int main() {
    const int numThreads = 2;
    HANDLE threadArray[numThreads];  // array of thread handles
    unsigned threadID; // returned by _beginthreadex( ), but not used
    DWORD rc;  // return code; (DWORD is defined in WIN32 as unsigned long)
    // Create two threads and store their handles in array threadArray
    threadArray[0] = (HANDLE) _beginthreadex(NULL, 0, simpleThread,
        (LPVOID) 1U, 0, &threadID);
    if (!threadArray[0])
        PrintError("_beginthreadex failed at ",__FILE__,__LINE__);
    threadArray[1] = (HANDLE) _beginthreadex(NULL, 0, simpleThread,
        (LPVOID) 2U, 0, &threadID);
    if (!threadArray[1])
        PrintError("_beginthreadex failed at ",__FILE__,__LINE__);
    rc = WaitForMultipleObjects(numThreads,threadArray,TRUE,INFINITE);
    //wait for the threads to finish
```

Listing 1.3 Simple concurrent program using C++/Win32.

```
    if (!(rc >= WAIT_OBJECT_0 && rc < WAIT_OBJECT_0+numThreads))
        PrintError("WaitForMultipleObjects failed at ",__FILE__,__LINE__);
    DWORD result1, result2; // these variables will receive the return values
    rc = GetExitCodeThread(threadArray[0],&result1);
    if (!rc) PrintError("GetExitCodeThread failed at ",__FILE__,__LINE__);
    rc = GetExitCodeThread(threadArray[1],&result2);
    if (!rc) PrintError("GetExitCodeThread failed at ",__FILE__,__LINE__);
    std::cout << "thread1:" << result1 << "thread2:" << result2 << std::endl;
    rc = CloseHandle(threadArray[0]);   // release reference to thread when finished
    if (!rc) PrintError("CloseHandle failed at ",__FILE__,__LINE__);
    rc = CloseHandle(threadArray[1]);
    if (!rc) PrintError("CloseHandle failed at ",__FILE__,__LINE__);
    return 0;
}
```

Listing 1.3 (*continued*)

Every Win32 process has at least one thread, which we have been referring to as the *main* thread. Processes can be assigned to a priority class (e.g., High or Low), and the threads within a process can be assigned a priority that is higher or lower than their parent process. The Windows operating system uses preemptive, priority-based scheduling. Threads are scheduled based on their priority levels, giving preference to higher-priority threads. Since we will not be using thread priorities in our Win32 programs, we will assume that the operating system will give a time slice to each program thread, in round-robin fashion. (The threads in a Win32 program will be competing for the CPU with threads in other programs and with system threads, and these other threads may have higher priorities.)

1.5   PTHREADS

A POSIX thread is created by calling function *pthread_create()*:

```
int pthread_create() {
    pthread_t* thread,           // thread ID
    const pthread_attr_t* attr,  // thread attributes
    void* (*start)(void*),       // starting address of the function to run
    void* arg                    // an argument to be passed to the thread
};
```

The parameters for *pthread_create()* are as follows:

- *thread*: the address of a memory location that will receive an identifier assigned to the thread if creation is successful. A thread can get its own identifier by calling *pthread_self()*. Two identifiers can be compared using *pthread_equal(ID1,ID2)*.

- *attr*: the address of a variable of type *pthread_attr_t*, which can be used to specify certain attributes of the thread created.
- *start*: the (address of the) function that the thread will execute. (This function plays the same role as the *run()* method in Java.)
- *arg*: an argument to be passed to the thread.

If *pthread_create()* is successful, it returns 0; otherwise, it returns an error code from the <errno.h> header file. The other Pthreads functions follow the same error-handling scheme.

The program in Listing 1.4 is a C++/Pthreads version of the C++/Win32 program in Listing 1.3. A Pthreads program must include the standard header file *<pthread.h>* for the Pthreads library. Array *threadArray* stores the Pthreads IDs for the two threads created in *main()*. Thread IDs are of type *pthread_t*. Each thread executes the code in function *simpleThread()*, which displays the IDS assigned by the user. The IDS are integers that are supplied as the fourth argument on the call to function *pthread_create()*. Function *pthread_create()* forwards the IDs as arguments to thread function *simpleThread()* when the threads are created.

Threads have attributes that can be set when they are created. These attributes include the size of a thread's stack, its priority, and the policy for scheduling threads. In most cases the default attributes are sufficient. Attributes are set by declaring and initializing an attributes object. Each attribute in the attributes object has a pair of functions for reading (get) and writing (set) its value.

In Listing 1.4, the attribute object *threadAttribute* is initialized by calling *pthread_attr_init()*. The scheduling scope attribute is set to *PTHREAD_SCOPE_SYSTEM* by calling *pthread_attr_setscope()*. This attribute indicates that we want the threads to be scheduled directly by the operating system. The default value for this attribute is *PTHREAD_SCOPE_PROCESS*, which indicates that only the process, not the threads, will be visible to the operating system. When the operating system schedules the process, the scheduling routines in the Pthreads library will choose which thread to run. The address of *threadAttribute* is passed as the second argument on the call to *pthread_create()*.

As in Win32, the main thread must wait for the two threads it created to complete before it exits the *main()* function. It does this by calling function *pthread_join()* twice. The first argument to *pthread_join()* is the thread ID of the thread to wait on. The second argument is the address of a variable that will receive the return value of the thread. In our program, neither thread returns a value, so we use NULL for the second argument. (The value NULL can also be used if there is a return value that we wish to ignore.)

```cpp
#include <iostream>
#include <pthread.h>
#include <errno.h>

void PrintError(char* msg, int status, char* fileName, int lineNumber) {
    std::cout << msg << ' ' << fileName << ":" << lineNumber
            << "- " << strerror(status) << std::endl;
}
void* simpleThread (void* myID) { // myID is the fourth argument of
                                  // pthread_create ()
    std::cout << "Thread " << (long) myID << "is running" << std::endl;
    return NULL;    // implicit call to pthread_exit(NULL);
}

int main() {
    pthread_t threadArray[2];                    // array of thread IDs
    int status;                                  // error code
    pthread_attr_t threadAttribute;              // thread attribute
    status = pthread_attr_init(&threadAttribute);    // initialize attribute object
    if (status != 0) { PrintError("pthread_attr_init failed at", status, __FILE__,
        __LINE__); exit(status);}
    // set the scheduling scope attribute
    status = pthread_attr_setscope(&threadAttribute,
        PTHREAD_SCOPE_SYSTEM);
    if (status != 0) { PrintError("pthread_attr_setscope failed at", status, __FILE__,
        __LINE__); exit(status);}
    // Create two threads and store their IDs in array threadArray
    status = pthread_create(&threadArray[0], &threadAttribute, simpleThread,
        (void*) 1L);
    if (status != 0) { PrintError("pthread_create failed at", status, __FILE__,
        __LINE__); exit(status);}
    status = pthread_create(&threadArray[1], &threadAttribute, simpleThread,
        (void*) 2L);
    if (status != 0) { PrintError("pthread_create failed at", status, __FILE__,
        __LINE__); exit(status);}
    status = pthread_attr_destroy(&threadAttribute); // destroy the attribute object
    if (status != 0) { PrintError("pthread_attr_destroy failed at", status, __FILE__,
        __LINE__); exit(status);}
    status = pthread_join(threadArray[0],NULL); // wait for threads to finish
    if (status != 0) { PrintError("pthread_join failed at", status, __FILE__,
        __LINE__); exit(status);}
    int status = pthread_attr_init(&threadAttribute); // initialize attribute object
    status = pthread_join(threadArray[1],NULL);
    if (status != 0) { PrintError("pthread_join failed at", status, __FILE__,
        __LINE__); exit(status);}
}
```

Listing 1.4   Simple concurrent program using C++/Pthreads.

Suppose that instead of returning NULL, thread function *simpleThread()* returned the value of parameter *myID*:

```
void* simpleThread (void* myID) { // myID was the fourth argument on the call
                                  // to pthread_create ()
   std::cout << "Thread " << (long) myID << "is running" << std::endl;
   return myID; // implicit call to pthread_exit(myID);
}
```

We can use function *pthread_join()* to capture the values returned by the threads:

```
long result1, result2; // these variables will receive the return values
status = pthread_join(threadArray[0],(void**) &result1);
if (status != 0) { /* ... */ }
status = pthread_join(threadArray[1],(void**) &result2);
if (status != 0) { /* ... */ }
std::cout << ''thread1:'' << (long) result1 << '' thread2:'' << (long) result2
   << std::endl;
```

A thread usually terminates by returning from its thread function. What happens after that depends on whether the thread has been *detached*. Threads that are terminated but not detached retain system resources that have been allocated to them. This means that the return values for undetached threads are still available and can be accessed by calling *pthread_join()*. Detaching a thread allows the system to reclaim the resources allocated to that thread. But a detached thread cannot be joined.

You can detach a thread anytime by calling function *pthread_detach()*. For example, the *main* thread can detach the first thread by calling

```
status = pthread_detach(threadArray[0]);
```

Or the first thread can detach itself:

```
status = pthread_detach(pthread_self());
```

Calling *pthread_join*(threadArray[0],NULL) also detaches the first thread. We will typically use *pthread_join()* to detach threads, which will make our Pthreads programs look very similar to Win32 programs.

If you create a thread that definitely will not be joined, you can use an attribute object to ensure that when the thread is created, it is already detached. The code for creating threads in a detached state is shown below. Attribute *detachstate* is set to *PTHREAD_CREATE_DETACHED*. The other possible value for this attribute is *PTHREAD_CREATE_JOINABLE*. (By default, threads are supposed to be created joinable. To ensure that your threads are joinable, you may want to use an attribute object and set the *detachstate* attribute explicitly to *PTHREAD_CREATE_JOINABLE*.)

```
int main() {
    pthread_t threadArray[2];                    // array of thread IDs
    int status;                                  // error code
    pthread_attr_t threadAttribute;              // thread attribute
    status = pthread_attr_init(&threadAttribute);  // initialize the attribute object
    if (status != 0) { /* ... */ }

    // set the detachstate attribute to detached
    status = pthread_attr_setdetachstate(&threadAttribute,
        PTHREAD_CREATE_DETACHED);
    if (status != 0) { /* ... */ }

    // create two threads in the detached state
    status = pthread_create(&threadArray[0], &threadAttribute, simpleThread,
        (void*) 1L);
    if (status != 0) { /* ... */ }
    status = pthread_create(&threadArray[1], &threadAttribute, simpleThread,
        (void*) 2L);
    if (status != 0) { /* ... */ }
    // destroy the attribute object when it is no longer needed
    status = pthread_attr_destroy(&threadAttribute);
    if (status != 0) { /* ... */ }

    // allow all threads to complete
    pthread_exit(NULL);
}
```

When the threads terminate, their resources are reclaimed by the system. This also means that the threads cannot be joined. Later we will learn about several synchronization constructs that can be used to simulate a *join* operation. We can use one of these constructs to create threads in a detached state but still be notified when they have completed their tasks.

Since the threads are created in a detached state, the *main* thread cannot call *pthread_join()* to wait for them to complete. But we still need to ensure that the threads have a chance to complete before the program (i.e., the process) exits. We do this by having the *main* thread call *pthread_exit* at the end of the *main()* function. This allows the *main* thread to terminate but ensures that the program does not terminate until the last thread has terminated. The resulting program behaves similar to the Java versions in Listings 1.1 and 1.2 in that the threads created in *main()* continue to run after the *main* thread completes.

1.6   C++ *THREAD* CLASS

Details about Win32 and POSIX threads can be encapsulated in a C++ *Thread* class. Class *Thread* hides some of the complexity of using the Win32 and POSIX thread functions and allows us to write multithreaded C++ programs that have an object-oriented structure that is almost identical to that of Java programs. Using a *Thread* class will also make it easier for us to provide some of the basic services that are needed for testing and debugging multithreaded programs. The implementation of these services can be hidden inside the *Thread* class, enabling developers to use these services without knowing any details about their implementation.

1.6.1   C++ Class *Thread* for Win32

Listing 1.5 shows C++ classes *Runnable* and *Thread* for Win32. Since Win32 thread functions can return a value, we allow method *run()* to return a value. The return value can be retrieved by using a Pthreads-style call to method *join()*. Class *Runnable* simulates Java's *Runnable* interface. Similar to the way that we created threads in Java, we can write a C++ class that provides a *run()* method and inherits from *Runnable*; create an instance of this class; pass a pointer to that instance as an argument to the *Thread* class constructor; and call *start()* on the *Thread* object. Alternatively, we can write C++ classes that inherit directly from class *Thread* and create instances of these classes on the heap or on the stack. (Java *Thread* objects, like other Java objects, are never created on the stack.) Cass *Thread* also provides a *join()* method that simulates the *pthread_join()* operation. A call to *T.join()* blocks the caller until thread T's *run()* method completes. We usc *T.join()* to ensure that T's *run()* method is completed before *Thread* T is destructed and the *main* thread completes. Method *join()* returns the value that was returned by *run()*.

Java has a built-in *join()* operation. There was no need to call method *join()* in the Java programs in Listings 1.1 and 1.2 since threads created in a Java *main()* method continue to run after the *main* thread completes. Method *join()* is useful in Java when one thread needs to make sure that other threads have completed before, say, accessing their results. As we mentioned earlier, Java's *run()* method cannot return a value (but see Exercise 1.4), so results must be obtained some other way.

The program in Listing 1.6 illustrates the use of C++ classes *Thread* and *Runnable*. It is designed to look like the Java programs in Listings 1.1 and 1.2. [Note that a C-style cast *(int) x* can be written in C++ as *reinterpret_cast <int>(x)*, which is used for converting between unrelated types (as in *void** and *int*).] The

```
class Runnable {
public:
    virtual void* run() = 0;
    virtual~Runnable() = 0;
};
Runnable::~Runnable() { } // function body required for pure virtual destructors

class Thread {
public:
    Thread(std::auto_ptr<Runnable> runnable_);
    Thread();
    virtual~Thread();
    void start();                  // starts a suspended thread
    void* join();                  // wait for thread to complete
private:
    HANDLE hThread;
    unsigned winThreadID;          // Win32 thread ID
    std::auto_ptr<Runnable> runnable;
    Thread(const Thread&);
    const Thread& operator=(const Thread&);
    void setCompleted();           // called when run() completes
    void* result;                  // stores value returned by run()
    virtual void* run() {return 0;}
    static unsigned WINAPI startThreadRunnable(LPVOID pVoid);
    static unsigned WINAPI startThread(LPVOID pVoid);
    void PrintError(LPTSTR lpszFunction,LPSTR fileName, int lineNumber);
};

Thread::Thread(std::auto_ptr<Runnable> runnable_) : runnable(runnable_) {
    if (runnable.get() == NULL)
        PrintError("Thread(std::auto_ptr<Runnable> runnable_) failed at ",
            __FILE__,__LINE__);
    hThread = (HANDLE)_beginthreadex(NULL,0,Thread::startThreadRunnable,
        (LPVOID)this, CREATE_SUSPENDED, &winThreadID );
    if (!hThread) PrintError("_beginthreadex failed at ",__FILE__,__LINE__);
}
Thread::Thread(): runnable(NULL) {
    hThread = (HANDLE)_beginthreadex(NULL,0,Thread::startThread,
        (LPVOID)this, CREATE_SUSPENDED, &winThreadID );
    if (!hThread) PrintError("_beginthreadex failed at ",__FILE__,__LINE__);
}
unsigned WINAPI Thread::startThreadRunnable(LPVOID pVoid){
    Thread* runnableThread = static_cast<Thread*> (pVoid);
```

Listing 1.5   C++/Win32 classes *Runnable* and *Thread*.

```
      runnableThread->result = runnableThread->runnable->run();
      runnableThread->setCompleted();
      return reinterpret_cast<unsigned>(runnableThread->result);
}
unsigned WINAPI Thread::startThread(LPVOID pVoid) {
      Thread* aThread = static_cast<Thread*> (pVoid);
      aThread->result = aThread->run();
      aThread->setCompleted();
      return reinterpret_cast<unsigned>(aThread->result);
}
Thread::~Thread() {
      if (winThreadID != GetCurrentThreadId()) {
         DWORD rc = CloseHandle(hThread);
         if (!rc) PrintError("CloseHandle failed at ",__FILE__,__LINE__);
      }
      // note that the runnable object (if any) is automatically deleted by auto_ptr.
}
void Thread::start() {
      assert(hThread != NULL);
      DWORD rc = ResumeThread(hThread);
      // thread was created in suspended state so this starts it running
      if (!rc) PrintError("ResumeThread failed at ",__FILE__,__LINE__);
}
void* Thread::join() {
      /* a thread calling T.join() waits until thread T completes; see Section 3.7.4.*/
      return result;  // return the void* value that was returned by method run()
}
void Thread::setCompleted() {
/* notify any threads that are waiting in join(); see Section 3.7.4. */
}
void Thread::PrintError(LPTSTR lpszFunction,LPSTR fileName, int lineNumber)
{ /* see Listing 1.3 */}
```

Listing 1.5   (*continued*)

implementation of class *Thread* is not simple. When a C++ *Thred* is created, the corresponding *Thread* constructor calls function *_beginthreadex()* with the following arguments:

- NULL. This is the default value for security attributes.
- 0. This is the default value for stack size.
- The third argument is either *Thread::startThread()* or *Thread::startThread-Runnable()*. Method *startThread()* is the startup method for threads created by inheriting from class *Thread*. Method *startThreadRunnable()* is the startup method for threads created from *Runnable* objects.

```
class simpleRunnable: public Runnable {
public:
    simpleRunnable(int ID) : myID(ID) { }
    virtual void* run() {
        std::cout << "Thread " << myID << "is running" << std::endl;
        return reinterpret_cast<void*>(myID);
    }
private:
    int myID;
};
class simpleThread: public Thread {
public:
    simpleThread (int ID) : myID(ID) { }
    virtual void* run() {
        std::cout << "Thread " << myID << "is running" << std::endl;
        return reinterpret_cast<void*>(myID);
    }
private:
    int myID;
};
int main() {
    std::auto_ptr<Runnable> r(new simpleRunnable(1));
    std::auto_ptr<Thread> thread1(new Thread(r));
    thread1->start();
    std::auto_ptr<simpleThread> thread2(new simpleThread(2));
    thread2->start();
    simpleThread thread3(3);
    thread3.start();
    // thread1 and thread2 are created on the heap; thread3 is created on the stack
    // wait for the threads to finish
    int result1 = reinterpret_cast<int>(thread1->join());
    int result2 = reinterpret_cast<int>(thread2->join());
    int result3 = reinterpret_cast<int>(thread3.join());
    std::cout << result1 << ' ' << result2 << ' ' << result3 << std::endl;
    return 0;
    // the destructors for thread1 and thread2 will automatically delete the
    // pointed-at thread objects
}
```

Listing 1.6   Using C++ classes *Runnable* and *Thread*.

- (LPVOID) this. The fourth argument is a pointer to this *Thread* object,
  which is passed through to method *startThread()* or *startThreadRunnable()*.
  Thus, all threads execute one of the startup methods, but the startup methods
  receive a different *Thread* pointer each time they are executed.

- *CREATE*_SUSPENDED. A Win32 thread is created to execute the startup method, but this thread is created in suspended mode, so the startup method does not begin executing until method *start()* is called on the thread.

Since the Win32 thread is created in suspended mode, the thread is not actually started until method *Thread::start()* is called. Method *Thread::start()* calls Win32 function *ResumeThread()*, which allows the thread to be scheduled and the startup method to begin execution. The startup method is either *startThread()* or *startThreadRunnable()*, depending on which *Thread* constructor was used to create the *Thread* object.

Method *startThread()* casts its void* pointer parameter to *Thread** and then calls the *run()* method of its *Thread** parameter. When the *run()* method returns, *startThread()* calls *setCompleted()* to set the thread's status to completed and to notify any threads waiting in *join()* that the thread has completed. The return value of the *run()* method is saved so that it can be retrieved in method *join()*. Static method *startThreadRunnable()* performs similar steps when threads are created from *Runnable* objects. Method *startThreadRunnable()* calls the *run()* method of the *Runnable* object held by its *Thread** parameter and then calls *setCompleted()*.

In Listing 1.6 we use *auto_ptr <>* objects to manage the destruction of two of the threads and the *Runnable* object *r*. When auto_ptr<> objects *thread1* and thread2 are destroyed automatically at the end of the program, their destructors will invoke `delete` automatically on the pointers with which they were initialized. This is true no matter whether the *main* function exits normally or by means of an exception. Passing an *auto_ptr <Runnable>* object to the *Thread* class constructor passes ownership of the *Runnable* object from the *main* thread to the child thread. The *auto_ptr <Runnable>* object in the child thread that receives this *auto_ptr <Runnable>* object owns the *Runnable* object that it has a pointer to, and will automatically delete the pointed-to object when the child thread is destroyed. When ownership is passed to the thread, the *auto_ptr <Runnable>* object in *main* is set automatically to a null state and can no longer be used to refer to the *Runnable* object. This protects against double deletion by the child thread and the *main* thread. It also prevents *main* from deleting the *Runnable* object before the thread has completed method *run()* and from accessing the *Runnable* object while the thread is accessing it. In general, if one thread passes an object to another thread, it must be clear which thread owns the object and will clean up when the object is no longer needed. This ownership issue is raised again in Chapter 5, where threads communicate by passing message objects instead of accessing global variables.

Note that startup functions *startThreadRunnable()* and *startThread()* are static member functions. To understand why they are static, recall that function *_beginthreadex()* expects to receive the address of a startup function that has a single (*void**) parameter. A nonstatic member function that declares a single parameter actually has *two* parameters. This is because each nonstatic member function has in addition to its declared parameters, a hidden parameter that corresponds to the *this* pointer. (If you execute *myObject.foo(x)*, the value of the *this* pointer in method *foo()* is the address of *myObject*.) Thus, if the startup function is a nonstatic member function, the hidden parameter gets in the way and the call to the startup function fails. Static member functions do not have hidden parameters.

1.6.2   C++ Class *Thread* for Pthreads

Listing 1.7 shows C++ classes *Runnable* and *Thread* for Pthreads. The interfaces for these classes are nearly identical to the Win32 versions. The only difference is that the *Thread* class constructor has a parameter indicating whether or not the thread is to be created in a detached state. The default is undetached. The program in Listing 1.6 can be executed as a Pthreads program without making changes. The main difference in the implementation of the Pthreads *Thread* class is that threads are created in the *start()* method instead of the *Thread* class constructor. This is because threads cannot be created in the suspended state and then later resumed. Thus, we create and start a thread in one step. Note also that calls to method *join()* are simply passed through to method *pthread_join()*.

1.7   THREAD COMMUNICATION

The concurrent programs we have seen so far are not very interesting because the threads they contain do not work together. For threads to work together, they must communicate. One way for threads to communicate is by accessing shared memory. Threads in the same program can reference global variables or call methods on a shared object, subject to the naming and scope rules of the programming language. Threads in different processes can access the same kernel objects by calling kernel routines. It is the programmer's responsibility to define the shared variables and objects that are needed for communication. Forming the necessary connections between the threads and the kernel objects is handled by the compiler and the linker.

Threads can also communicate by sending and receiving messages across communication channels. A channel may be implemented as an object in shared memory, in which case message passing is just a particular style of shared memory communication. A channel might also connect threads in different programs, possibly running on different machines that do not share memory. Forming network connections between programs on different machines requires help from the operating system and brings up distributed programming issues such as how to name and reference channels that span multiple programs, how to resolve program references to objects that exist on different machines, and the reliability of passing messages across a network. Message passing is discussed in Chapters 5 and 6. In this chapter we use simple shared variable communication to introduce the subtleties of concurrent programming.

```
class Runnable {
public:
    virtual void* run() = 0;
    virtual~Runnable() = 0;
};
// a function body is required for pure virtual destructors
Runnable::~Runnable() { }

class Thread {
public:
    Thread(auto_ptr<Runnable> runnable_, bool isDetached = false);
    Thread(bool isDetached = false);
    virtual~Thread();
    void start();
    void* join();
private:
    pthread_t PthreadThreadID;      // thread ID
    bool detached;                  // true if thread created in detached state;
false otherwise
    pthread_attr_t threadAttribute;
    auto_ptr<Runnable> runnable;
    Thread(const Thread&);
    const Thread& operator= (const Thread&);
    void setCompleted();
    void* result;                   // stores return value of run()
    virtual void* run() { }
    static void* startThreadRunnable(void* pVoid);
    static void* startThread(void* pVoid);
    void PrintError(char* msg, int status, char* fileName, int lineNumber);
};
Thread::Thread(auto_ptr<Runnable> runnable_, bool isDetached) :
    runnable(runnable_),detached(isDetached){
    if (runnable.get() == NULL) {
        std::cout << "Thread::Thread(auto_ptr<Runnable> runnable_,
            bool isDetached) failed at " << ' ' << __FILE__ << ":"
            << __LINE__ << "- " << "runnable is NULL " << std::endl; exit(-1);
    }
}
Thread::Thread(bool isDetached) : runnable(NULL), detached(isDetached){ }
void* Thread::startThreadRunnable(void* pVoid){
// thread start function when a Runnable is involved
    Thread* runnableThread = static_cast<Thread*> (pVoid);
    assert(runnableThread);
```

Listing 1.7   C++/Pthreads classes *Runnable* and *Thread*.

```
runnableThread->result = runnableThread->runnable->run();
   runnableThread->setCompleted();
   return runnableThread->result;
}
void* Thread::startThread(void* pVoid) {
   // thread start function when no Runnable is involved
   Thread* aThread = static_cast<Thread*> (pVoid);
   assert(aThread);
   aThread->result = aThread->run();
   aThread->setCompleted();
   return aThread->result;
}
Thread::~Thread() { }
void Thread::start() {
   int status = pthread_attr_init(&threadAttribute); // initialize attribute object
   if (status != 0) { PrintError("pthread_attr_init failed at", status, __FILE__,
      __LINE__); exit(status);}
   status = pthread_attr_setscope(&threadAttribute,
      PTHREAD_SCOPE_SYSTEM);
   if (status != 0) { PrintError("pthread_attr_setscope failed at",
      status, __FILE__, __LINE__); exit(status);}
   if (!detached) {
      if (runnable.get() == NULL) {
         int status = pthread_create(&PthreadThreadID,&threadAttribute,
            Thread::startThread,(void*) this);
         if (status != 0) { PrintError("pthread_create failed at",
            status, __FILE__, __LINE__); exit(status);}
      }
      else {
         int status = pthread_create(&PthreadThreadID,&threadAttribute,
            Thread::startThreadRunnable, (void*)this);
         if (status != 0) {PrintError("pthread_create failed at",
            status, __FILE__, __LINE__); exit(status);}
      }
   }
   else {
      // set the detachstate attribute to detached
      status = pthread_attr_setdetachstate(&threadAttribute,
         PTHREAD_CREATE_DETACHED);
      if (status != 0){
         PrintError("pthread_attr_setdetachstate failed at",
            status,__FILE__,__LINE__);exit(status);
      }
```

Listing 1.7   (*continued*)

```
        if (runnable.get() == NULL) {
            status = pthread_create(&PthreadThreadID,&threadAttribute,
                Thread::startThread, (void*) this);
            if (status != 0) {PrintError("pthread_create failed at",
                status, __FILE__, __LINE__);exit(status);}
        }
        else {
            status = pthread_create(&PthreadThreadID,&threadAttribute,
                Thread::startThreadRunnable, (void*) this);
            if (status != 0) {PrintError("pthread_create failed at",
                status, __FILE__, __LINE__); exit(status);}
        }
    }
    status = pthread_attr_destroy(&threadAttribute);
    if (status != 0) { PrintError("pthread_attr_destroy failed at",
        status, __FILE__, __LINE__); exit(status);}
}
void* Thread::join() {
    int status = pthread_join(PthreadThreadID,NULL);
    // result was already saved by thread start functions
    if (status != 0) { PrintError("pthread_join failed at",
        status, __FILE__, __LINE__); exit(status);}
    return result;
}
void Thread::setCompleted() {/* completion was handled by pthread_join() */}
void Thread::PrintError(char* msg, int status, char* fileName, int lineNumber)
{/*see Listing 1.4 */}
```

Listing 1.7   (*continued*)

Listing 1.8 shows a C++ program in which the *main* thread creates two *communicatingThreads*. Each *communicatingThread* increments the global shared variable *s* 10 million times. The *main* thread uses *join()* to wait for the *communicatingThreads* to complete, then displays the final value of *s*. When you execute the program in Listing 1.8, you might expect the final value of *s* to be 20 million. However, this may not always be what happens. For example, we executed this program 50 times. In 49 of the executions, the value 20000000 was displayed, but the value displayed for one of the executions was 19215861. This example illustrates two important facts of life for concurrent programmers. The first is that the execution of a concurrent program is nondeterministic: Two executions of the *same* program with the *same* input can produce *different* results. This is true even for correct concurrent programs, so nondeterministic behavior should not be equated with incorrect behavior. The second fact is that subtle programming errors involving shared variables can produce unexpected results.

```
int s=0; // shared variable s

class communicatingThread: public Thread {
public:
    communicatingThread (int ID) : myID(ID) { }
    virtual void* run();
private:
    int myID;
};
void* communicatingThread::run() {
    std::cout << "Thread " << myID << "is running" << std::endl;
    for (int i=0; i<10000000; i++) // increment s 10 million times
        s = s + 1;
    return 0;
}

int main() {
    std::auto_ptr<communicatingThread> thread1(new communicatingThread (1));
    std::auto_ptr<communicatingThread> thread2(new communicatingThread (2));
    thread1->start();  thread2->start();
    thread1->join();  thread2->join();
    std::cout << "s: " << s << std::endl; // expected final value of s is 20000000
    return 0;
}
```

Listing 1.8   Shared variable communication.

1.7.1   Nondeterministic Execution Behavior

The following two examples illustrate nondeterministic behavior. In Example 1 each thread executes a single statement, but the order in which the three statements are executed is unpredictable:

Example 1   Assume that integer x is initially 0.

Thread1	Thread2	Thread3
(1) x = 1;	(2) x = 2;	(3) y = x;

The final value of y is unpredictable, but it is expected to be either 0, 1, or 2. Following are some of the possible interleavings of these three statements:

(3), (1), (2) $\Rightarrow$ final value of y is 0
(2), (1), (3) $\Rightarrow$ final value of y is 1
(1), (2), (3) $\Rightarrow$ final value of y is 2

We do not expect y to have the final value 3, which might happen if the assignment statements in *Thread1* and *Thread2* are executed at about the same time and x is assigned some of the bits in the binary representation of 1 and some of the bits in the binary representation of 2. The memory hardware guarantees that this cannot happen by ensuring that read and write operations on integer variables do not overlap. (Below, such operations are called *atomic operations*.)

In the next example, *Thread3* will loop forever if and only if the value of x is 1 whenever the condition ($x == 2$) is evaluated.

Example 2   Assume that x is initially 2.

Thread1	Thread2	Thread3
while (true) {	while (true) {	while (true) {
(1) x = 1;	(2) x = 2;	(3) if (x == 2) exit(0);
}	}	}

Thread3 will never terminate if statements (1), (2), and (3) are interleaved as follows: (2), (1), (3), (2), (1), (3), (2), (1), (3), ... This interleaving is probably not likely to happen, but if it did, it would not be completely unexpected.

In general, nondeterministic execution behavior is caused by one or more of the following:

- The unpredictable rate of progress of threads executing on a single processor (due to context switches between the threads)
- The unpredictable rate of progress of threads executing on different processors (due to differences in processor speeds)
- The use of nondeterministic programming constructs, which make unpredictable selections between two or more possible actions (we look at examples of this in Chapters 5 and 6)

Nondeterministic results do not necessarily indicate the presence of an error. Threads are frequently used to model real-world objects, and the real world is nondeterministic. Furthermore, it can be difficult and unnatural to model nondeterministic behavior with a deterministic program, but this is sometimes done to avoid dealing with nondeterministic executions. Some parallel programs are expected to be deterministic [Empath et al. 1992], but these types of programs do not appear in this book.

Nondeterminism adds flexibility to a design. As an example, consider two robots that are working on an assembly line. Robot 1 produces parts that Robot 2 assembles into some sort of component. To compensate for differences in the rates at which the two robots work, we can place a buffer between the robots. Robot 1 produces parts and deposits them into the buffer, and Robot 2 withdraws the parts and assembles them into finished components. This adds some flexibility to the assembly line, but the order in which parts are deposited and withdraw by the robots may be nondeterministic. If the actions of the robots are controlled by software, using one thread to control each robot and one thread to manage the buffer, the behavior of the threads will also be nondeterministic.

Nondeterminism and concurrency are related concepts. Consider two nonoverlapping events A and B that execute concurrently. The fact that A and B are concurrent means that they can occur in either order. Thus, their concurrency can be modeled as a nondeterministic choice between two interleavings of events: (A followed by B) or (B followed by A). This interleaving model of concurrency is used by certain techniques for building and verifying models of program behavior. But notice that the possible number of interleavings explodes as the number of concurrent events increases, which makes even small programs hard to manage. We quantify this explosion later.

Nondeterminism is an inherent property of concurrent programs. The burden of dealing with nondeterminism falls on the programmer, who must ensure that threads are correctly synchronized without imposing unnecessary constraints that only reduce the level of concurrency. In our assembly line example, the buffer allows the two robots to work concurrently and somewhat independently. However, the buffer has a limited capacity, so the robots and the buffer must be properly synchronized. Namely, it is the programmer's responsibility to ensure that Robot 1 is not allowed to deposit a part when the buffer is completely full. Similarly, Robot 2 must be delayed when the buffer becomes empty. Finally, to avoid collisions, the robots should not be allowed to access the buffer at the same time. Thread synchronization is a major concern of the rest of this book.

Nondeterministic executions create major problems during testing and debugging. Developers rely on repeated, deterministic executions to find and fix programming errors. When we observe a failure in a single-threaded program, we fully expect to be able to reproduce the failure so that we can locate and fix the bug that caused it. If a failure is not reproducible, that tells us something about the problem since only certain types of bugs (e.g., uninitialized variables) cause nondeterministic failures in sequential programs. Concurrent programs, on the other hand, are inherently nondeterministic. Coping successfully with nondeterminism during testing and debugging is essential for concurrent programmers. After we look at some common programming errors, we examine the types of problems that nondeterministic executions cause during testing and debugging.

1.7.2 Atomic Actions

One common source of bugs in concurrent programs is the failure to implement *atomic actions* correctly. An atomic action acts on the state of a program. The program's state contains a value for each variable defined in the program and other implicit variables, such as the program counter. An atomic action transforms the state of the program, and the state transformation is indivisible. For example, suppose that in the initial state of a program the variable x has the value 0. Then after executing an atomic assignment statement that assigns 1 to x, the program will be in a new state in which x has the value 1.

The requirement for state transformations to be indivisible does not necessarily mean that context switches cannot occur in the middle of an atomic action. A state transformation performed during an atomic action is indivisible if other threads can see the program's state as it appears before the action or after the action, but not some intermediate state while the action is occurring. Thus, we can allow a context switch to occur while one thread is performing an atomic action, even if that action involves many variables and possibly multiple assignment statements, as long as we don't allow the other threads to see or interfere with the action while it is in progress. As we will see, this means that we may have to block the other threads until the action is finished.

The execution of a concurrent program results in a sequence of atomic actions for each thread. Since the state transformation caused by an atomic action is indivisible, executing a set of atomic actions concurrently is equivalent to executing them in some sequential order. A particular execution can be characterized as a (nondeterministic) interleaving of the atomic actions performed by the threads. (The relationship between concurrency and nondeterminism was discussed above.) This interleaving determines the result of the execution.

Individual machine instructions such as *load, add, subtract,* and *store* are typically executed atomically; this is guaranteed by the memory hardware. In Java, an assignment of 32 bits or less is guaranteed to be implemented atomically, so an assignment statement such as $x = 1$ for a variable x of type *int* is an atomic action. In general, however, the execution of an assignment statement may not be atomic.

Nonatomic Arithmetic Expressions and Assignment Statements When we write a concurrent program, we might assume that the execution of a single arithmetic expression or assignment statement is an atomic action. However, an arithmetic expression or assignment statement is compiled into several machine instructions, and an interleaving of the machine instructions from two or more expressions or assignment statements may produce unexpected results.

Example 3 Assume that y and z are initially 0.

Thread1	Thread2
x = y + z;	y = 1;
	z = 2;

If we (incorrectly) assume that execution of each assignment statement is an atomic action, the expected final value of x computed by *Thread1* is 0, 1, or 3, representing the sums $0 + 0$, $1 + 0$, and $1 + 2$, respectively. However, the machine instructions for *Thread1* and *Thread2* will look something like the following:

Thread1	Thread2
(1) load r1, y	(4) assign y, 1
(2) add r1, z	(5) assign z, 2
(3) store r1, x	

Below are some of the possible interleavings of these machine instructions. The character * indicates an unexpected result:

(1), (2), (3), (4), (5) ⇒ x is 0
(4), (1), (2), (3), (5) ⇒ x is 1
(1), (4), (5), (2), (3) ⇒ x is 2 *
(4), (5), (1), (2), (3) ⇒ x is 3

Example 4 Assume that the initial value of x is 0.

Thread1	Thread2
x = x + 1;	x = 2;

Again we are assuming incorrectly that the execution of each assignment statement is an atomic action, so the expected final value of x is 2 or 3. The machine instructions for *Thread1* and *Thread2* are

Thread1	Thread2
(1) load r1, x	(4) assign x, 2
(2) add r1, 1	
(3) store r1, x	

Following are some of the possible interleavings of these machine instructions. Once again, the character "*" indicates an unexpected result.

(1), (2), (3), (4) => x is 2
(4), (1), (2), (3) => x is 3
(1), (2), (4), (3) => x is 1 *

As these examples illustrate, since machine instructions are atomic actions, it is the interleaving of the machine instructions, not the interleaving of the statements, that determines the result. If there are n threads ($Thread_1$, $Thread_2$, ..., $Thread_n$) such that $Thread_i$ executes mi atomic actions, the number of possible interleavings of the atomic actions is

$$\frac{(m1 * m2 * ... * mn)!}{(m1! * m2! * ... * mn!)}$$

This formula shows mathematically what concurrent programmers are quick to learn—there is no such thing as a simple concurrent program.

Andrews [2000] defined a condition called *at-most-once* under which expression evaluations and assignments will appear to be atomic. (Our definition of at-most-once is slightly stronger than Andrews's; see Exercise 1.10.) A critical reference in an expression is a reference to a variable that is changed by another thread.

- An assignment statement $x = e$ satisfies the at-most-once property if either:
  (1) e contains at most one critical reference and x is neither read nor written by another thread, or
  (2) e contains no critical references, in which case x may be read or written by other threads.
- An expression that is not in an assignment satisfies at-most-once if it contains no more than one critical reference.

This condition is called at-most-once because there can be at most one shared variable, and the shared variable can be referenced at most one time. Assignment statements that satisfy at-most-once *appear* to execute atomically even though they are not atomic. That is, we would get the same results from executing these assignment statements even if we were to somehow prevent the interleaving of their machine instructions so that the assignment statements were forced to execute atomically. Next, we'll use several examples to illustrate at-most-once.

Consider Example 3 again. The expression in the assignment statement in *Thread1* makes a critical reference to y and a critical reference to z, so the assignment statement in *Thread1* does not satisfy the at-most-once property. The expressions in the assignment statements in *Thread2* contain no critical references, so the assignment statements in *Thread2* satisfy at-most-once.

Example 5   Assume that x and y are initially 0.

Thread1	Thread2
x = y + 1;	y = 1;

Both assignment statements satisfy the at-most-once condition. The expression in *Thread1's* assignment statement references y (one critical reference), but x is not referenced by *Thread2*, and the expression in *Thread2's* assignment statement has no critical references. The final value of x is nondeterministic and is either 1 or 2, as expected.

Nonatomic Groups of Statements   Another type of undesirable nondeterminism in a concurrent program is caused by interleaving groups of statements, even though each statement may be atomic. In the following example, methods *deposit* and *withdraw* are used to manage a linked list implementation of a buffer. One thread calls method *deposit* while another calls method *withdraw*. As shown below, interleaving the statements in methods *deposit* and *withdraw* may produce unexpected results.

Example 6 Variable *first* points to the first *Node* in the list. Assume that the list is not empty

```
class Node {
public:
    valueType value;
    Node* next;
}
Node* first;                          // first points to the first Node in the list;
void deposit(valueType value) {
    Node* p = new Node;               // (1)
    p->value = value;                 // (2)
    p->next = first;                  // (3)
    first = p;                        // (4) insert the new Node at the front of the list
}
valueType withdraw() {
    valueType value = first->value;   // (5) withdraw the first value in the list
    first = first->next;              // (6) remove the first Node from the list
    return value;                     // (7) return the withdrawn value
}
```

If two threads try to *deposit* and *withdraw* a value at the same time, the following interleaving of statements is possible:

```
valueType value = first->value;   // (5) in withdraw
Node* p = new Node();             // (1) in deposit
p->value = value                  // (2) in deposit
p->next = first;                  // (3) in deposit
first = p;                        // (4) in deposit
first = first->next;              // (6) in withdraw
return value;                     // (7) in withdraw
```

At the end of this sequence, the withdrawn item is still pointed to by *first* and the deposited item has been lost. To fix this problem, each of methods *deposit* and *withdraw* must be implemented as an atomic action. Later we will see how to make a statement or a group of statements execute atomically.

1.8 TESTING AND DEBUGGING MULTITHREADED PROGRAMS

Looking back at Listing 1.8, we now know why the program sometimes failed to produce the expected final value 2000000 for *s*. The interleaving of machine instructions for *thread1* and *thread2* sometimes increased the value of *s* by one even though two increments were performed. Failures like this one, which do not occur during every execution, create extra problems during testing and debugging.

- The purpose of testing is to find program failures.

The term *failure* is used when a program produces unintended results.

- A failure is an observed departure of the external result of software operation from software requirements or user expectations [IEEE90].

Failures can be caused by hardware or software faults or by user errors.

- A software *fault* (or defect, or bug) is a defective, missing, or extra instruction or a set of related instructions that is the cause of one or more actual or potential failures [IEEE88].

Software faults are the result of programming errors. For example, an error in writing an `if-else` statement may result in a fault that will cause an execution to take a wrong branch. If the execution produces the wrong result, it is said to fail. (The execution may produce a correct result even though it takes a wrong branch.)

- *Debugging* is the process of locating and correcting faults.

The conventional approach to testing and debugging a program is as follows:

1. Select a set of test inputs.
2. Execute the program once with each input and compare the test results with the intended results.
3. If a test input finds a failure, execute the program *again* with the same input in order to collect debugging information and find the fault that caused the failure.
4. After the fault has been located and corrected, execute the program *again* with each of the test inputs to verify that the fault has been corrected and that, in doing so, no new faults have been introduced. This type of testing, called *regression testing*, is also needed after the program has been modified during the maintenance phase.

This cyclical process of testing, followed by debugging, followed by more testing, is commonly applied to sequential programs. Unfortunately, this process breaks down when it is applied to concurrent programs.

1.8.1 Problems and Issues

Let CP be a concurrent program. Multiple executions of CP with the *same* input may produce *different* results. This nondeterministic execution behavior creates the following problems during the testing and debugging cycle of CP:

Problem 1 When testing CP with input X, a single execution is insufficient to determine the correctness of CP with X. Even if CP with input X has been executed successfully many times, it is possible that a future execution of CP with X will produce an incorrect result.

Problem 2 When debugging a failed execution of CP with input X, there is no guarantee that this execution will be repeated by executing CP with X.

Problem 3 After CP has been modified to correct a fault detected during a failed execution of CP with input X, one or more successful executions of CP with X during regression testing do not imply that the detected fault has been corrected or that no new faults have been introduced.

A major objective of this book is to show that these problems can be solved and that the familiar testing and debugging cycle can be applied effectively to concurrent programs. There are many issues that must be dealt with to solve these problems.

Program Replay Programmers rely on debugging techniques that assume program failures can be reproduced. This assumption of *reproducible testing* does not hold for concurrent programs. Repeating an execution of a concurrent program is called *program replay*. A major issue is how to replay executions of concurrent programs and how to build libraries and tools that support replay.

Program Tracing Before an execution can be replayed it must be traced. But what exactly does it mean to replay an execution? Consider a sequential C++ program that executes in a multiprocessing environment. If the program is executed twice and the inputs and outputs are the same for both executions, are these executions identical? In a multiprocessing environment, context switches will occur during program execution. Furthermore, for two different program executions, the points at which the context switches occur are not likely to be the same. Is this difference important? We assume that context switches are transparent to the execution, so although the executions may not be identical, they appear to be "equivalent". Now consider a concurrent program. Are the context switches among the threads in a program important? Must we somehow trace the points at which the context switches occur and then repeat these switch points during replay?

The questions that need to be answered for tracing are: What should be replayed, and how do we capture the necessary execution information in a trace? The rest of this book answers these questions for various types of programs. In general, an execution trace will contain information about the sequence of actions performed by each thread. An execution trace should contain sufficient information to replay the execution or to perform some other task, but attention must also be paid to the space and time overhead for capturing and storing the trace. In addition, an observability problem occurs in distributed systems, where it is difficult to observe accurately the order in which actions on different computers occur during an execution.

Sequence Feasibility   A sequence of actions that is allowed by a program is said to be a *feasible sequence*. Program replay always involves repeating a feasible sequence of actions. This is because the sequence to be replayed was traced during an actual execution and thus is known to be allowed by the program. Testing, on the other hand, involves determining whether or not a given sequence is feasible or infeasible. "Good" sequences are expected to be feasible, and "bad" sequences are expected to be infeasible.

Selecting effective test sequences is a difficult problem. Perhaps the simplest technique for selecting test sequences is to execute the program under test repeatedly and allow sequences to be exercised nondeterministically. If enough executions are performed, one or more failures may be observed. This type of testing, called *nondeterministic testing*, is easy to carry out, but it can be very inefficient. It is possible that some program behaviors are exercised many times, whereas others are never exercised at all. Also, nondeterministic testing cannot show that bad sequences are infeasible.

An alternative approach is called *deterministic testing*, which attempts to force selected sequences to be exercised. We expect that good sequences can be forced to occur, whereas bad sequences cannot. This approach allows a program to be tested with carefully selected test sequences and can be used to supplement the sequences exercised during nondeterministic testing. However, choosing sequences that are effective for detecting faults is difficult to do. A test coverage criterion can be used to guide the selection of tests and to determine when to stop testing.

The information and the technique used to determine the feasibility of a sequence are different from those used to replay a sequence. In general, different types of execution traces can be defined and used for different purposes. Other purposes include visualizing an execution and checking the validity of an execution.

Sequence Validity   A sequence of actions captured in a trace is definitely feasible, but the sequence may or may not have been intended to be feasible. We assume that each program has a specification that describes the intended behavior of the program. Sequences allowed by the specification (i.e., good sequences) are called *valid sequences*; other sequences are called *invalid sequences*. A major issue is how to check the validity of a sequence captured in a trace. A goal of testing is to find valid sequences that are infeasible and invalid sequences that are feasible; such sequences are evidence of a program failure. In the absence of a complete program specification, a set of valid and invalid sequences can serve as a partial specification.

Probe Effect   Modifying a concurrent program to capture a trace of its execution may interfere with the normal execution of the program [LeDoux and Parker

1985; Gait 1986]. Thus, the program will behave differently after the trace routines have been added. In the worst case, some failures that would have been observed without adding the trace routines will no longer be observed. If the trace routines are eventually removed, additional time should be spent testing the unmodified program to find these failures. In other cases, an incorrect program may stop failing when trace routines are inserted for debugging.

The probe effect is not always negative. There may be failures that cannot be observed without perturbing the executions. Programs may fail when running under abnormal conditions, so checking some abnormal executions is not a bad idea. (We point out that it may be difficult to define "normal" and "abnormal" executions.) If we can create random interference during the executions, we may be able to achieve better test coverage. If a program fails during an early part of the life cycle, when we have tool support for tracing and replaying executions and determining the cause of the failure, we are better off than if it fails later.

One way to address the probe effect is to make sure that every feasible sequence is exercised at least once during testing. A major issue then is how to identify and exercise all of the feasible sequences of a program. One way of doing this, called *reachability testing*, is described in later chapters. However, since the number of sequences required for exhaustive testing may be huge, it might take too much time to exercise all the sequences or too much memory to enumerate them. In that case we can select a subset of sequences that we hope will be effective for detecting faults and use these sequences for deterministic testing.

The probe effect is different from the observability problem mentioned above [Fidge 1996]. The observability problem is concerned with the difficulty of tracing a given execution accurately, whereas the probe effect is concerned with the ability to perform a given execution at all. Both of these problems are different from the *replay problem*, which deals with repeating an execution that has already been observed.

Real Time The probe effect is a major issue for real-time concurrent programs. The correctness of a real-time program depends not only on its logical behavior but also on the time at which its results are produced [Tsai et al. 1996]. A real-time program may have computation deadlines that will be missed if trace functions are added to the program. Instead, tracing can be performed by using special hardware to remove the probe effect or by trying to account for or minimize the probe effect. Real-time programs may also receive sensor inputs that must be captured for replay. Some of the techniques we cover in this book are helpful for testing and debugging the logical behavior of real-time systems, but we will not address the special issues associated with timing correctness.

Tools Solutions to these testing and debugging problems must be supported by tools. Debugging tools that are integrated with compilers and operating systems can accomplish more than tools built from libraries of source code, such as the libraries presented in this book. Access to the underlying virtual machine, compiler, operating system, or run-time system maximizes the ability of a tool to observe and control program executions. On the other hand, this type of low-level access limits the portability of the tool. Also, there is a difference between the system-level events one deals with in an operating system (e.g., interrupts and context switches) and the high-level abstract events that programmers think of when specifying and writing their programs. For example, knowing the number of read and write operations that each thread executes during its time quantum may provide sufficient information for replay, but it will not help with understanding an execution or determining its validity. Different levels of abstraction are appropriate for different activities.

Life-Cycle Issues Typically, a concurrent program, like a sequential program, is subjected to two types of testing during its life cycle. During *black-box testing*, which often occurs during system and user-acceptance testing, access to the program's implementation is not allowed. Thus, only the specification of the program can be used for test generation, and only the result (including the output and termination condition) of each execution can be collected. During *white-box testing*, access to the implementation is allowed. Thus, any desired information about each execution can be collected, and the implementation can be analyzed and used for generating tests. White-box testing gives the programmer unlimited ability to observe and control executions, but it is usually not appropriate during system and acceptance testing. At these later stages of the life cycle, it is often the case that a program's source code cannot be accessed, or it is simply too large and complex to be of practical use. Addressing the problems caused by nondeterminism requires tools that can observe and control executions, but testing techniques that can be used during both white- and black-box testing may be the most useful.

The testing and debugging issues noted above are addressed in this book. We now give a small example of how we handle some of them. We've modified the C++ program in Listing 1.8 so that it can trace and replay its own executions. The new program is shown in Listing 1.9. Classes *TDThread* and *sharedVariable<>* provide functions that are needed for execution tracing and replay. Below we provide a brief description of these classes and preview some of the testing and debugging techniques that are described in detail in later chapters.

1.8.2 Class *TDThread* for Testing and Debugging

Threads in Listing 1.9 are created by inheriting from C++ class *TDThread* instead of class *Thread*. Class *TDThread* provides the same interface as our C++ *Thread* class, plus several additional functions that are used internally during tracing and replay. (We will be using a Java version of *TDThread* in our Java programs.) The main purpose of class *TDThread* is to generate, automatically and unobtrusively, an integer identifier (ID) and a name for each thread. Thread IDs are recorded in execution traces. The name for thread T is based on the name of its parent

```
sharedVariable<int> s(0); // shared variable s
  class communicatingThread: public TDThread {
public:
  communicatingThread(int ID) : myID(ID) { }
  virtual void* run();
private:
  int myID;
};
void* communicatingThread::run() {
  std::cout << "Thread " << myID << "is runnıng" << std::endl;
  for (int i=0; i<2; i++)    // increment s two times (not 10 million times)
    s = s + 1;
  return 0;
}
int main() {
  std::auto_ptr<communicatingThread> thread1(new communicatingThread (1));
  std::auto_ptr<communicatingThread> thread2(new communicatingThread (2));
  thread1->start();  thread2->start();
  thread1->join();  thread2->join();
  std::cout << "s: " << s << std::endl;   // the expected final value of s is 4
  return 0;
}
```

Listing 1.9   Using classes *TDThread* and *sharedVariable* <>.

thread and the order in which *T* and any of its sibling threads are constructed by their parent thread. For example, suppose that we have the following *main()* function, which creates two *creatorThreads*:

```
int main() {
    TDThread* T1 = new creatorThread;
    TDThread* T2 = new creatorThread;
    ...
}
```

Suppose also that the *creatorThread ::run()* method creates two *nestedThreads*:

```
void run() {
    TDThread* TA = new nestedThread;
    TDThread* TB = new nestedThread;
    ...
}
```

The thread names generated for the six threads (two *creatorThreads* and four *nestedThreads*) are as follows:

Thread	Thread Name
creatorThread T1	main_thread1
creatorThread T2	main_thread2
nestedThread TA created by T1	main_thread1_thread1
nestedThread TB created by T1	main_thread1_thread2
nestedThread TA created by T2	main_thread2_thread1
nestedThread TB created by T2	main_thread2_thread2

In general, the name for thread T is generated by concatenating the following values:

The name of T's parent thread + "_thread"

+ a number indicating T's construction order among its siblings.

The *main* thread is not a *TDThread*, so no name is generated for it. *TDThreads* *T1* and *T2* have a parent thread, but it is the *main* thread, which does not have a name that we can access (since *main* is not a *TDThread*). To solve this problem, we let the child threads of *main* use "main" as the default name of their parent thread. For example, thread *T1*'s name is "main_thread1," since its parent is "main" and it is the first thread created in *main()*. Thread *TB* created by *T1* has the name "main_thread1_thread2," since *T1*'s name is "main_thread1" and *TB* is the second thread created by *T1*.

Thread IDs are based on the order in which threads are constructed during execution. (*TDThread*'s constructor calls a method named *getID()*, so it is the order of calls to *getID()* that actually determines the ID values that are generated.) The first thread constructed is assigned ID 1, the second thread is assigned ID 2, and so on. In the example above, *T1*'s ID will be 1. The ID value 2 will be assigned to thread *TA* created by *T1* or to thread *T2*, depending on which thread is constructed first. If both *TA* and *TB* are constructed by *T1* before *T2* is constructed, *T2* will be assigned ID 4.

During tracing, the mapping between thread names and thread IDs is recorded in a file, and this mapping is input at the beginning of replay. Thread names are generated during replay the same way as during tracing. This means that threads will receive the same names and IDs *as long as the thread structure is not changed*. The thread IDs assigned during replay are determined from the mapping, not from the construction order, since the construction order may be different for each execution. Thread ID 0 is reserved for the *main* thread, which is not a *TDThread* and does not have a name. Ensuring that threads have the same ID during tracing and replay is important because thread IDs are recorded in execution traces and then used during replay.

Names such as "main_thread1_thread1" work fine for replay, and they are generated automatically simply by inheriting from *TDThread*, but they are not very descriptive. A more descriptive name can be provided by supplying a name manually to *TDThread's* constructor. For example:

```
class namedThread : public TDThread {
// assigns "namedThread" as the thread name
   namedThread() : TDThread("namedThread") { }
   ...
}
```

User-supplied thread names must be unique or they will be rejected by the ID generator. In the example above, if there were two *namedThreads*, two different thread names would be required, such as "namedThread1" and "namedThread2." This requires extra work on the part of the programmer, and is optional, but having descriptive names is helpful for understanding program traces, so we will often assign names manually.

1.8.3   Tracing and Replaying Executions with Class Template *sharedVariable* < >

Class template *sharedVariable*<> provides functions that allow every shared variable access to be traced and replayed. In Listing 1.9, shared variable *s* is declared as *sharedVariable<int> s*. Class *sharedVariable*<> provides the usual operators $(+, -, =, <$, etc.) for primitive types. It also traces and replays the read and write operations in the implementations of these operators. Details about how class *sharedVariable*<> works are provided in Chapter 2. Here we show what *sharedVariable<int>* does when the program in Listing 1.9 is executed.

The IDs generated by class *TDThread* for threads *thread1* and *thread2* are 1 and 2, respectively. In trace mode, class *sharedVariable<int>* records the order in which these two threads read and write shared variable *s*. Each increment "$s = s + 1$" involves a read of *s* followed by a write of *s*, and each thread increments *s* twice. The final value of *s* is expected to be 4 under the incorrect assumption that the increments are atomic.

A possible trace for Listing 1.9 is shown below. We have added comments to make the trace easier to understand. (The actual format used for execution traces is slightly different, as we will see later.)

```
Read(thread1,s)     // thread1 reads s; s is 0
Read(thread2,s)     // thread2 reads s; s is 0
Write(thread2,s)    // thread2 writes s; s is now 1
Write(thread1,s)    // thread1 writes s; s is now 1
Read(thread1,s)     // thread1 reads s; s is 1
Write(thread1,s)    // thread1 writes s; s is now 2
Read(thread2,s)     // thread2 reads s; s is 2
Write(thread2,s)    // thread2 writes s; s is now 3
```

An execution that produces this trace will display the output 3, not 4. Thus, this trace captures an interleaving of read and write operations that causes an unexpected result. In replay mode, *sharedVariable<int>* forces the threads to execute their read and write operations on *s* in the order recorded in the trace, always producing the output 3.

1.9   THREAD SYNCHRONIZATION

Classes *TDThread* and *sharedVariable<>* allow us to trace and replay executions, which helps us locate and fix bugs in our concurrent programs. The examples in this chapter showed the failures that can occur when accesses to shared variables are not properly synchronized. One type of synchronization is called *mutual exclusion*. Mutual exclusion ensures that a group of atomic actions, called a *critical section*, cannot be executed by more than one thread at a time. That is, a critical section must be executed as an atomic action. The increment statements executed by *thread1* and *thread2* in Listing 1.9 require mutual exclusion to work properly.

Failure to implement critical sections correctly is a fault called a *data race* [Netzer and Miller 1992]. Note that the order in which shared variables and critical sections are accessed usually remains nondeterministic even when critical sections are implemented correctly. Thus, nondeterministic behavior does not necessarily mean that a programming error has been made. We use the term *data race* when a critical section is intended to be executed atomically but it does not.

Another type of synchronization is called *condition synchronization*. Condition synchronization ensures that the state of a program satisfies a particular condition before some action occurs. For the linked list in Example 6, there is a need for both condition synchronization and mutual exclusion. The list must not be in an empty condition when method *withdraw* is allowed to remove an item, and mutual exclusion is required for ensuring that deposited items are not lost and are not withdrawn more than twice.

Mutual exclusion is a common requirement in concurrent programs. In Chapter 2 we take a closer look at programs that contain correct and incorrect attempts to implement critical sections. These programs are small, but they are much more complex than their size indicates and they clearly illustrate the challenges of concurrent programming.

FURTHER READING

Most textbooks on operating systems [Silberschatz et al. 2001; Tannenbaum 2001] and distributed systems [Coulouris et al. 2001] contain basic material on concurrent programming. We assume that many of the readers of this book have taken a course on operating systems.

There are languages besides Java that provide built-in support for concurrent programming, such as C# and Ada. We do not cover these languages in this book, but the concepts that we cover still apply. Some of the end-of-chapter exercises deal with these languages.

There are many books and tutorial articles on Java threads [Hyde 1999; Lea 1999; Lewis and Berg 1999; Oaks and Wong 1999; Holub 2000; Friesen 2002]. Lea [1999] discusses multithreading design principles and patterns and the myriad ways in which objects and threads fit together in Java. Pthreads is described in detail in [Butenhof 1997] and [Lewis and Berg 1997]. Another C++ library is presented in [Schmidt and Huston 2002].

Windows programming, including multithreaded programming, is covered in detail in [Beveridge and Wiener 1997; Petzold 1998; Hart 2000]. More thread classes for Win32/C++ can be found in Cohen and Woodring's [1997] book and in various articles [Kougiouris and Framba 1997; Tennberg 1998; Broadman and Shaw 1999; Harrington 1999; Calkins 2000; Peterson 2000; Huber 2001; Hush 2002; Kempf 2002; Pee 2003].

This book does not cover concurrent real-time programming [Tsai et al. 1996] or parallel programming [Andrews 2000], but many of the testing and debugging concepts that we discuss can be applied in these domains. Some of the testing and debugging problems presented in Section 1.7 were introduced in [Tai 1985].

REFERENCES

Anderson, T. E., E. D. Lazowska, and Henry M. Levy (1989). The performance implications of thread management alternatives for shared-memory multiprocessors. *IEEE Transactions on Computers*, Vol. 38, No. 12, pp. 1631–1644.

Andrews, Gregory R. (2000). *Foundations of Multithreaded, Parallel, and Distributed Programming*. Reading, MA: Addison-Wesley.

Beveridge, Jim, and R. Wiener (1997). *Multithreading Programming Techniques in Win32: The Complete Guide to Threads*. Reading, MA: Addison-Wesley.

Broadman, Allen, and Eric Shaw (1999). Executing a class member in its own thread. *C/C++ Users Journal*, December, pp. 57–62.

Butenhof, David R. (1997). *Programming with POSIX Threads*. Reading, MA: Addison-Wesley.

Calkins, Charles (2000). Integrating threads with template classes. *C/C++ Users Journal*, May, pp. 32–35.

Cohen, A., and M. Woodring (1997). *Win32 Multithreaded Programming*. Sebastopol, CA: O'Reilly & Associates.

Coulouris, George, Jean Dollimore, and Tim Kindberg (2001). *Distributed Systems: Concepts and Design*. Reading, MA: Addison-Wesley.

Empath, P. A., S. Ghosh, and D. A. Padua (1992). Detecting nondeterminacy in parallel programs. *IEEE Software*, Vol. 9, No. 1, pp. 69–77.

Fidge, C. (1996). Fundamentals of distributed system observation. *IEEE Software*, Vol. 13, No. 6, pp. 77–83.

Friesen, Jeff (2002). Achieving strong performance with threads: Parts 1–4. http://www.javaworld.com.

Gait, J. (1986). A probe effect in concurrent programs. *Software: Practice and Experience*, Vol. 16, No. 3, pp. 225–233.

Harrington, John (1999). Win32 multithreading made easy. *C/C++ Users Journal*, August, pp. 48–56.

Hart, Johnson M. (2000). *Win32 System Programming: A Windows 2000 Application Developer's Guide*. Reading, MA: Addison-Wesley.

Holub, Allen (2000). *Taming Java Threads*. Berkely: Apress.

Huber, Andreas (2001). Elegant function call wrappers. *C/C++ Users Journal*, May, pp. 8–16.

Hush, Andy (2002). A template class to encapsulate Win32 threading. *Windows Developer Magazine*, December, pp. 18–25.

Hyde, Paul (1999). *Java Thread Programming*. Howard W. Sams, Indianapolis, IN.

IEEE88 (1988). STD 982.1–1988, *IEEE Standard Dictionary of Measures to Produce Reliable Software*. New York: IEEE Press.

IEEE90 (1990). STD 610.12–1990, *IEEE Standard Glossary of Software Engineering Terminology*. New York: IEEE Press.

Kempf, Bill (2002). The Boost threads library. *C/C++ Users Journal*, May, pp. 6–13.

Kougiouris, Panos, and Marco Framba (1997). A portable multithreading framework. *C/C++ Users Journal*, August, pp. 61–71.

Lea, Doug (1999). *Concurrent Programming in Java*, 2nd ed. Reading, MA: Addison-Wesley.

LeDoux, C. H., and D. Stott Parker (1985). Saving traces for Ada debugging. *Proc. 1985 International Ada Conference*, pp. 97–108.

Lewis, Bill, and Daniel J. Berg (1997). *Multithreaded Programming with PThreads*. Upper Saddle River, NJ: Prentice Hall.

Lewis, Bill, and Daniel J. Berg (1999). *Multithreaded Programming with Java Technology*. Upper Saddle River, NJ: Pearson Education.

Netzer, Robert H. B., and Barton P. Miller (1992). What are race conditions? Some issues and formalizations. *ACM Letters on Programming Languages and Systems*, Vol. 1, No. 1, pp. 74–88.

Oaks, Scott, and Henry Wong (1999). *Java Threads*, 2nd ed. Sebastopol, CA: O'Reilly & Associates.

Pee, James (2003). Multithreaded programming with the command pattern. *Windows Developer Magazine*, January, pp. 20–25.

Peterson, Mark (2000). Self-destructing threads. *C/C++ Users Journal*, December, p. 44.

Petzold, Charles (1998). *Programming Windows*, 5th ed. Redmond, WA: Microsoft Press.

Schmidt, Douglas C., and Stephen D. Huston (2002). *C++ Network Programming: Mastering Complexity Using ACE and Patterns*. Reading, MA: Addison-Wesley.

Silberschatz, Abraham, Peter Baer Galvin, and Greg Gagne (2001). *Operating System Concepts*, 6th ed. New York: Wiley.

Tai, K. C. (1985). On testing concurrent programs. *Proc. COMPSAC'85*, pp. 310–317.

Tannenbaum, Andrew (2001). *Modern Operating Systems*, 2nd ed. Upper Saddle River, NJ: Prentice Hall.

Tennberg, Patrick (1998). Creating active data types via multithreading. *C/C++ Users Journal*, January, pp. 45–47.

Tsai, J., Y. Bi, S. Yang, and R. Smith (1996). *Distributed Real-Time Systems: Monitoring, Debugging, and Visualization*. New York: Wiley.

EXERCISES

1.1. Assume that shared variables y and z are initially 0.

Thread1	Thread2	Thread3
x = y + z;	y = 1;	z = 2;

If the programmer incorrectly assumes that assignment statements are executed atomically, can this program produce unexpected results? Explain.

1.2. Assume that shared variable x is initially 5.

Thread1	Thread2
x = x + 1;	x = x+1;

If the programmer incorrectly assumes that assignment statements are executed atomically, can this program produce unexpected results? Explain.

1.3. Assume that a concurrent program CP contains threads $T_1, T_2, \ldots, T_n$, $n > 1$, which are executed concurrently and access shared variables. Give a sufficient condition for CP to be deterministic (i.e., every execution of CP with input X produces the same result). Assume that there is no mechanism to force a particular sequence of read and write operations to occur. (In your condition, consider the read and write operations performed on the shared variables. What exactly causes nondeterminism?)

1.4. A C++ *Thread* class for Win32 was presented in Section 1.4. This C++ class simulates Java's built-in *Thread* class. Try to construct a Java class named *ThreadWin* that simulates this C++ *Thread* class. Write an interface *RunnableWin* that simulates the C++ *Runnable* class in Section 1.4. Java class *ThreadWin* should create a Java *Thread* that executes the user-defined *run()* method. (Class *ThreadWin* does not extend class *Thread*.) Method *run()* returns an *int* result that can be retrieved after *run()* completes using method *join()*. Test your classes with the following Java program:

```
class simpleRunnable implements RunnableWin {
    public simpleRunnable(int myID) {ID = myID;}
    private int ID;
    public int run() {System.out.println("Thread " + ID + " running");
        return ID;}
}
```

```
class simpleThread extends ThreadWin {
    public simpleThread(int myID) {ID = myID;}
    private int ID;
    public int run() {System.out.println("Thread " + ID + " running");
        return ID;}
}
public class test {
    public static void main(String args[]) {
        ThreadWin thread1 = new simpleThread(1);
        ThreadWin thread2 = new simpleThread(2);
        simpleRunnable r = new simpleRunnable(3);
        ThreadWin thread3 = new ThreadWin(r);
        thread1.start(); thread2.start(); thread3.start();
        int r1=0, r2=0, r3=0;
        try { r1 = t1.join(); r2 = t2.join(); r3 = t3.join();}
        catch (InterruptedException e) {e.printStackTrace();}
        System.out.println("Thread 1 result:" + r1);
        System.out.println("Thread 2 result:" + r2);
        System.out.println("Thread 3 result:" + r3);
    }
}
```

Do your *RunnableWin* and *ThreadWin* classes have any advantages over the built-in Java *Thread* class?

1.5. Implement classes *ThreadWin* and *RunnableWin* from Exercise 1.4, but this time use C#. Test your classes with the following C# program:

```
public class simpleThread : ThreadWin {
    int ID;
    public simpleThread(int ID) {this.ID = ID;}
    public override void run() {Console.WriteLine("Thread "+ID+
        " running");}
}
class simpleRunnable : RunnableWin {
    public simpleRunnable(int ID) {this.ID = ID;}
    private int ID;
    public void run() {Console.WriteLine("Thread " + ID + " running");}
}
public class Test {
    public static void Main(String [] argv){
        ThreadWin thread1 = new simpleThread(1);
        ThreadWin thread2 = new simpleThread(2);
        simpleRunnable r = new simpleRunnable(3);
        ThreadWin thread3 = new ThreadWin(r);
        thread1.start(); thread2.start(); thread3.start();
```

```
        int r1=0, r2=0, r3=0;
        try { r1 = t1.join(); r2 = t2.join(); r3 = t3.join();}
        catch (ThreadInterruptedException e) {
            Console.WriteLine(e.StackTrace);
        }
        Console.WriteLine("Thread 1 result: " + r1);
        Console.WriteLine("Thread 2 result: " + r2);
        Console.WriteLine("Thread 3 result: " + r3); }
    }
}
```

1.6. The following program attempts to make the assignment statement "x = x + 1" atomic by adding statements before and after the assignment to x:

```
// intendsi is true if Thread_i intends to execute its assignment
boolean intends0 = false, intends1 = false;
```

Thread0		Thread1	
while (true) {		while (true) {	
while (intends1) { ; }	(1)	while (intends0) { ; }	(1)
intends0 = true;	(2)	intends1 = true;	(2)
x = x + 1;	(3)	x = x + 1;	(3)
intends0 = false;	(4)	intends1 = false;	(4)
}		}	

Thread0 and Thread1 use variables *intends0 and intends1* to indicate their intention to increment x. A thread will not increment x if the other thread has already signaled that it intends to increment x.

(a) Does the use of variables *intends0 and intends1* guarantee that the assignments to x are executed atomically? Explain.

(b) If your answer to part (a) is "no," try to modify the statements before and after the assignment so that the assignment statement "x = x + 1" executes atomically. Does your solution guarantee that each thread will eventually get a chance to execute its assignment statement?

1.7. If n threads each execute m atomic actions, the number of possible interleavings of the atomic actions is

$$\frac{(n*m)!}{(m!)^n}$$

(a) How many possible interleavings are there for the program in Listing 1.9? Consider only the machine instructions for the assignment statements, not the machine instructions generated for loop or the output statements. (The loop still executes twice.) You can assume that the assignment statement for *s* is translated into a sequence of three machine instructions (i.e., load s; add 1; store s). For your analysis, you can treat *s* like a regular *int* variable.

(b) Assume that some mechanism is used to ensure that each assignment statement in Listing 1.9 is executed atomically. Now how many possible interleavings are there?

1.8. Write a Java version of the program in Listing 1.8 of the notes. When you execute your program, does it always display 20000000? Run your program many times. Increasing the number of iterations may affect the output. Describe your results.

1.9. Section 1.8.3 shows a possible format for tracing read and write operations:

Read(thread1,s)   // thread1 reads shared variable *s*
Write(thread1,s)   // thread1 writes shared variable *s*

A thread may execute many thousands of read and write operations during its time quantum, causing many read and write events to be generated and recorded. Can you suggest a scheme for "compressing" a trace of read and write operations so that fewer events may need to be recorded?

1.10. Condition at-most-once was defined in Section 1.6.2.1. Andrews [2000] defines the first part of condition at-most-once differently:

(Andrews-1) *e* contains at most one critical reference and *x* is not *read* by another thread

This prevents *x* from being read by another thread but allows *x* to be written. The second part of Andrews's condition is the same as the definition in Section 1.7.2.1. Show that (Andrews-1) above is not strong enough by finding an example where (Andrews-1) is satisfied by two assignment statements but the assignments may not appear to execute atomically.

1.11. Amdahl's law estimates the speedup from running a program on multiple processors. It uses the following estimated running times:

- t_s: running time of the serial part of a program (using one processor). The serial part of a program is the part that must run on a single processor.
- $t_p(1)$: running time of the parallel part of the program using one processor.
- $t_p(P)$: running time of the parallel part of the program using P processors. The serial and the parallel programs are required to execute the same number of instructions, so $t_p(P) = t_p(1)/P$ (i.e., the P processors each execute the same number of instructions).
- $T(1)$: total running time of the program, including both the serial and parallel parts using one processor, which equals $t_s + t_p(1)$.

- T(P): total running time of the program, including both the serial and parallel parts using P processors, which equals $t_s + t_p(P) = t_s + [t_p(1)/P]$. From Amdahl's law, we have

$$speedup = T(1)/T(P) = [t_s + t_p(1)]/\{t_s + [t_p(1)/P]\}.$$

Let $P = 10$, $t_p(P) = 4$, and $t_s = 6$. What is the speedup?

2

THE CRITICAL SECTION PROBLEM

As an introduction to concurrent programming, we study a fundamental problem called the *critical section problem* [Dijkstra 1965]. The problem is easy to understand and its solutions are small in terms of the number of statements they contain (usually, fewer than five). However, the critical section problem is not easy to solve, and it illustrates just how difficult it can be to write even small concurrent programs.

A code segment that accesses shared variables (or other shared resources) and that has to be executed as an atomic action is referred to as a *critical section*. The critical section problem involves a number of threads that are each executing the following code:

```
while (true) {
      entry-section
      critical section        // accesses shared variables or other shared resources.
      exit-section
      noncritical section     // a thread may terminate its execution in this section.
}
```

The entry- and exit-sections that surround a critical section must satisfy the following correctness requirements [Silberschatz et al. 1991]:

Modern Multithreading: Implementing, Testing, and Debugging Multithreaded Java and C++/Pthreads/Win32 Programs, By Richard H. Carver and Kuo-Chung Tai
Copyright © 2006 John Wiley & Sons, Inc.

- *Mutual exclusion.* When a thread is executing in its critical section, no other threads can be executing in their critical sections. (If a thread is executing in its critical section when a context switch occurs, the thread is still considered to be in the critical section. With the assumption of fair scheduling, this thread will eventually resume execution and exit the critical section.)

- *Progress.* If no thread is executing in its critical section and there are threads that wish to enter their critical sections, only the threads that are executing in their entry- or exit-sections can participate in the decision about which thread will enter its critical section next, and this decision cannot be postponed indefinitely.

- *Bounded waiting.* After a thread makes a request to enter its critical section, there is a bound on the number of times that other threads are allowed to enter their critical sections before this thread's request is granted.

We assume that a thread that enters its critical section will eventually exit its critical section. (If a thread is stuck in an infinite loop inside its critical section, or the thread terminates in its critical section, other threads waiting to enter their critical sections will wait forever.) The noncritical section may contain a statement that terminates a thread's execution.

If the threads are being time-sliced on a single processor, one simple solution to the critical section problem is for each thread to disable interrupts before it enters its critical section:

```
disableInterrupts();    // disable all interrupts
critical section
enableInterrupts();     // enable all interrupts
```

This disables interrupts from the interval timer that is used for time slicing and prevents any other thread from running until interrupts are enabled again. However, commands for disabling and enabling interrupts are not always available to user code. Also, this solution does not work on systems with multiple CPUs when a thread on one processor is not able to disable interrupts on another processor.

In this chapter we present low-level software and hardware solutions to the critical section problem. In Chapters 3 and 4 we show a number of solutions that use high-level synchronization constructs.

2.1   SOFTWARE SOLUTIONS TO THE TWO-THREAD CRITICAL SECTION PROBLEM

We first consider the case where there are only two threads T0 and T1 that are attempting to enter their critical sections. Threads T0 and T1 may be executing in their entry-sections at the same time. Informally, the entry-section of thread T0 should enforce the following rules (thread T1's entry- and exit-sections mirror those of T0):

- If thread T1 is in its critical section, thread T0 must wait in its entry-section.
- If thread T1 is not its critical section and does not want to enter its critical section, thread T0 should be allowed to enter its critical section.
- When both threads want to enter their critical sections, only one of them should be allowed to enter.

The exit-section of thread T0 should do the following:

- If thread T1 is waiting to enter its critical sections, allow T1 to enter.

The derivation of correct entry- and exit-sections is not a trivial problem. It is difficult to find a solution that satisfies all three correctness properties. The solutions we examine do not use any special programming constructs; they use global variables, arrays, loops, and if-statements, all of which are found in sequential programming languages. This allows us to study a difficult concurrent programming problem without introducing new programming language constructs.

Although shared variables are used in the entry- and exit-sections, this will not create another mutual exclusion problem. The entry- and exit-sections will be written carefully so that all assignment statements and expressions involving shared variables are atomic operations and there are no groups of statements that must be executed atomically. Thus, the entry- and exit-sections themselves need not be critical sections.

The solutions below assume that the hardware provides mutual exclusion for individual read and write operations on shared variables. This means that the memory system must implement its own solution to the critical section problem. (Later, we will see a solution that does not require atomic reads and writes of variables.) Our focus here is on condition synchronization (i.e., defining the conditions under which threads can enter their critical sections). As we will see in later chapters, high-level synchronization constructs make it easy to create critical sections, but condition synchronization will always remain difficult to achieve.

We first present a number of incorrect solutions to the critical section problem. Then we show a correct solution.

2.1.1   Incorrect Solution 1

Threads T0 and T1 use variables *intendToEnter0* and *intendToEnter1* to indicate their intention to enter their critical section. A thread will not enter its critical section if the other thread has already signaled its intention to enter.

boolean intendToEnter0=false, intendToEnter1=false;

T0		T1	
while (true) {		while (true) {	
while (intendToEnter1) {;}	(1)	while (intendToEnter0) {;}	(1)
intendToEnter0 = true;	(2)	intendToEnter1 = true;	(2)
critical section	(3)	critical section	(3)
intendToEnter0 = false;	(4)	intendToEnter1 = false;	(4)
noncritical section	(5)	noncritical section	(5)
}		}	

This solution does not guarantee mutual exclusion. The following execution sequence shows a possible interleaving of the statements in T0 and T1 that ends with both T0 and T1 in their critical sections.

T0	T1	Comments
(1)		*T0* exits its `while`-loop
context switch →		
	(1)	*T1* exits its `while`-loop
	(2)	*intendToEnter1* is set to true
	(3)	*T1* enters its critical section
← context switch		
(2)		*intendToEnter0* is set to true
(3)		T0 enters its critical section

2.1.2 Incorrect Solution 2

Global variable *turn* is used to indicate which thread is allowed to enter its critical section (i.e., the threads take turns entering their critical sections). The initial value of *turn* can be 0 or 1.

int turn = 1;

T0		T1	
while (true) {		while (true) {	
while (turn !=0){;}	(1)	while (turn !=1){;}	(1)
critical section	(2)	critical section	(2)
turn = 1;	(3)	turn = 0;	(3)
noncritical section	(4)	noncritical section	(4)
}		}	

This solution forces *T0* and *T1* to alternate their entries into the critical section and thus ensures mutual exclusion and bounded waiting. Assume that the initial value of *turn* is 1 and consider the following execution sequence:

T0	T1	Comments
	(1)	*T1* exits its `while`-loop
	(2)	*T1* enters and exits its critical section
	(3)	*turn* is set to 0
	(4)	*T1* terminates in its noncritical section
← context switch		
(1)		*T0* exits its `while`-loop
(2)		*T0* enters and exits its critical section
(3)		*turn* is set to 1
(4)		*T0* executes its noncritical section
(1)		*T0* repeats (1) forever

Thread *T0* cannot exit the loop in (1) since the value of *turn* is 1 and *turn* will never be changed by T1. Thus, the progress requirement is violated.

2.1.3   Incorrect Solution 3

Solution 3 is a more "polite" version of Solution 1. When one thread finds that the other thread also intends to enter its critical section, it sets its own *intendToEnter* flag to *false* and waits until the other thread exits its critical section.

T0		T1	
while (true) {		while (true) {	
intendToEnter0 = true;	(1)	intendToEnter1 = true;	(1)
while (intendToEnter1) {	(2)	while (intendToEnter0) {	(2)
intendToEnter0 = false;	(3)	intendToEnter1 = false;	(3)
while(intendToEnter1) {;}	(4)	while(intendToEnter0) {;}	(4)
intendToEnter0 = true;	(5)	intendToEnter1 = true;	(5)
}		}	
critical section	(6)	critical section	(6)
intendToEnter0 = false;	(7)	intendToEnter1 = false;	(7)
noncritical section	(8)	noncritical section	(8)
}		}	

This solution ensures that when both *intendToEnter0* and *intendToEnter1* are true, only one of *T0* and *T1* is allowed to enter its critical section. Thus, the mutual exclusion requirement is satisfied. However, there is a problem with this solution, as illustrated by the following execution sequence:

T0	T1	Comments
(1)		*intendToEnter0* is set to true
(2)		*T0* exits the first `while`-loop in the entry section
(6)		*T0* enters its critical section; *intendToEnter0* is true
context switch →		
	(1)	*intendToEnter1* is set to true
	(2)–(3)	*intendToEnter1* is set to false
	(4)	*T1* enters the second `while`-loop in the entry section
← context switch		
(7)		*intendToEnter0* is set to false
(8)		*T0* executes its noncritical section
(1)		*intendToEnter0* is set to true
(2)		*T0* exits the first `while`-loop in the entry section
(6)		*T0* enters its critical section; *intendToEnter0* is true
context switch →		
	(4)	*T1* is still waiting for *intendToEnter0* to be false
← context switch		
(7)		

... repeat infinitely

In this execution sequence, *T0* enters its critical section infinitely often and *T1* waits forever to enter its critical section. Thus, this solution does not guarantee bounded waiting.

The foregoing incorrect solutions to the critical section problem raise the following question: How can we determine whether a solution to the critical section problem is correct? One approach is to use mathematical proofs (see [Andrews 1991]). Another formal approach is to generate all the possible interleavings of the atomic actions in the solution and then check that all the interleavings satisfy the three required correctness properties (see Chapter 7). Next, we suggest an informal approach to checking the correctness of a solution.

When checking a solution to the critical section problem, consider each of these three important cases:

1. Thread T0 intends to enter its critical section and thread T1 is not in its critical section or in its entry-section. In this case, if T0 cannot enter its critical section, the progress requirement is violated.
2. Thread T0 intends to enter its critical section and thread T1 is in its critical section. In this case, if both threads can be in their critical sections, the mutual exclusion requirement is violated.

3. Both threads intend to enter their critical sections (i.e., both threads are in their entry-sections, or one is in its entry-section and one is in its exit-section). This case is difficult to analyze since we have to consider all possible interleavings of statements in the entry- and exit-sections in order to detect violations of the mutual exclusion, progress, and bounded waiting requirements.

Next we show a correct solution to the critical section problem and apply our informal correctness check. We invite the reader to try to solve the critical section problem before looking at the solution!

2.1.4 Peterson's Algorithm

Peterson's algorithm is a combination of solutions 2 and 3. If both threads intend to enter their critical sections, *turn* is used to break the tie.

boolean intendToEnter0 = false, intendToEnter1 = false;
int turn; // no initial value for *turn* is needed.

T0		T1	
while (true) {		while (true) {	
intendToEnter0 = true;	(1)	intendToEnter1 = true;	(1)
turn = 1;	(2)	turn = 0;	(2)
while (intendToEnter1 &&	(3)	while (intendToEnter0 &&	(3)
turn == 1) {;}		turn == 0) {;}	
critical section	(4)	critical section	(4)
intendToEnter0 = false;	(5)	intendToEnter1 = false;	(5)
noncritical section	(6)	noncritical section	(6)
}		}	

A formal proof of Peterson's algorithm is given in [Silberschatz et al. 1991, p. 161]. Here, we show only that the algorithm works in each of three important cases:

1. Assume that thread *T0* intends to enter its critical section and *T1* is not in its critical section or its entry-section. Then *intendToEnter0* is *true* and *intendToEnter1* is *false* so *T0* can enter its critical section.
2. Assume that thread *T0* intends to enter its critical section and *T1* is in its critical section. Since *turn* = 1, *T0* loops at statement (3). After the execution of (5) by *T1*, if *T0* resumes execution before *T1* tries to enter again, then *T0* can enter its critical section; otherwise, see case (3).
3. Assume that both threads intend to enter the critical section (i.e., both threads have set their *intendToEnter* flags to true). The first thread that executes "*turn* = ...;" waits until the other thread executes "*turn* = ...;" and then the first thread enters its critical section. The second thread will

enter after the first thread exits. This case is illustrated by the following execution sequence:

T0	T1	Comments
(1)		*intendToEnter0* set to true
context switch →		
	(1)	*intendToEnter1* is set to true
	(2)	*turn* is set to 0
	(3)	*T1* enters its while-loop
← context switch		
(2)		*turn* is set to 1
(3)		*T0* enters its while-loop
context switch →		
	(3)	*T1* exits its while-loop
	(4)	*T1* enters and exits its critical section
	(5)	*intendToEnter1* is set to false
	(6)	*T1* executes its noncritical section
	(1)	*intendToEnter1* is set to true
	(2)	*turn* is set to 0
	(3)	*T1* enters its while-loop
← context switch		
(3)		*T0* exits its while-loop
(4)		*T0* enters and exits its critical section
(5)		*intendToEnter0* is set to false
(6)		*T0* executes its noncritical section
context switch →		
	(3)	*T1* exits its while-loop
	(4)	*T1* enters its critical section

Peterson's algorithm is often called the *tie-breaker algorithm*, referring to the way in which variable *turn* is used when both threads want to enter their critical sections.

2.1.5 Using the `volatile` Modifier

As presented above, Peterson's algorithm may not work in the presence of certain compiler and hardware optimizations that are safe for single-threaded programs but unsafe for multithreaded programs. For example, to optimize speed, the compiler may allow each thread to keep private copies of shared variables *intendToEnter0, intendToEnter1*, and *turn*. If this optimization is performed, updates made to these variables by one thread will be made to that thread's private copies and thus will not be visible to the other thread. This potential inconsistency causes an obvious problem in Peterson's algorithm (see also Exercise 2.12).

In Java, the solution to this problem is to declare shared variables (that are not also declared as `double` or `long`) as `volatile`:

volatile boolean intendToEnter0 = false; volatile boolean intendToEnter1 = false; volatile int turn;

Declaring the variables as `volatile` ensures that consistent memory values will be read by the threads. C++ also allows variables to be declared as `volatile`. (Note that in C++, each element of a `volatile` array is `volatile`. In Java, declaring an array object as `volatile` applies to the array object itself, not its elements.) However, C++ does not make the same strong guarantees that Java does for programs with `volatile` variables and multiple threads. Thus, even if the variables are `volatile`, some hardware optimizations may cause Peterson's algorithm to fail in C++. The general solution to this problem is to add special memory instructions, called *memory barriers*, that constrain the optimizations. In Section 2.6 we discuss shared memory consistency in greater detail.

Peterson's algorithm requires `volatile` variables, but this does not mean that shared variables must always be `volatile` variables. In later chapters we present high-level synchronization constructs that solve the critical section problem and also deal with optimizations so that `volatile` variables are not needed.

2.2   TICKET-BASED SOLUTIONS TO THE n-THREAD CRITICAL SECTION PROBLEM

In the n-thread critical section problem, there are n threads instead of just two. Two correct solutions to this problem are given in this section. Both solutions are based on the use of *tickets*. When a thread wishes to enter a critical section, it requests a ticket. Each ticket has a number on it. Threads are allowed to enter their critical sections in ascending order of their ticket numbers.

The global array *number* is used to hold the ticket numbers for the threads:

volatile int number[n];   // array of ticket numbers where number[i] is the ticket
                          // number for thread Ti

Initially, all elements of array *number* have the value 0. If number[i] $\neq$ 0, then *number[i]* is the ticket number for thread Ti, $0 \leq i \leq n - 1$.

2.2.1   Ticket Algorithm

The *ticket algorithm* uses variables *next* and *permit* and a special atomic operation. When a thread requests a ticket, it is given a ticket with a number equal to the value of variable *next*, and then *next* is incremented by 1. A thread can enter the critical section when it has a ticket number equal to the value of variable *permit*. Variable *permit* is initialized to 1 and is incremented each time a thread enters the critical section.

Many machines provide special hardware instructions that allow us to test and modify a value, or add two values, atomically. These instructions can be used directly or they can be used to implement atomic functions. The Win32 API provides a family of atomic functions called the *Interlocked* functions. Function *InterlockedExchangeAdd* can be used to implement the ticket algorithm. The prototype for this function is

long InterlockedExchangeAdd(long* target, long increment);

A call such as

oldValueOfX = InterlockedExchangeAdd(&x, increment);

atomically adds the value of *increment* to *x* and returns the old value (i.e., before adding *increment*) of *x*. *InterlockedExchangeAdd* is used in the ticket algorithm as follows:

number[i] = InterlockedExchangeAdd(&next, 1).

This is equivalent to the following critical section:

number[i] = next;   // these statements are executed
next = next + 1;   // as a critical section

On Intel processors (starting with the Intel 486 processor), function *InterlockedExchangeAdd* can be implemented using the atomic XADD (Exchange and Add) instruction. The XADD instruction also serves as a memory barrier (see Section 2.5.6) to ensure that threads see consistent values for the shared variables. J2SE 5.0 provides package *java.util.concurrent.atomic*. This package supports operations such as *getAndIncrement()* and *getAndSet()*, which are implemented using the machine-level atomic instructions (such as XADD) that are available on a given processor (see Exercise 2.13).

In the ticket algorithm, each thread T_i, $0 \le i \le n - 1$, executes the following code:

```
volatile long next = 1;     // next ticket number to be issued to a thread
volatile long permit =1;    // ticket number permitted to enter critical section
while (true) {
    number[i] = InterlockedExchangeAdd(&next,1);   (1)
    while (number[i] != permit) {;}                (2)
    critical section                               (3)
    ++permit;                                      (4)
    noncritical section                            (5)
}
```

This algorithm is very simple, but it requires special machine instructions to implement *InterlockedExchangeAdd* or a similar atomic function. Another shortcoming of this algorithm is that the values of *permit* and *next* grow without bounds.

2.2.2 Bakery Algorithm

As in the ticket algorithm, the *bakery algorithm* [Lamport 1974] allows threads to enter their critical sections in ascending order of their ticket numbers. But unlike the ticket algorithm, it does not require special hardware instructions. The tickets in the bakery algorithm are a bit more complicated. Each thread T_i, $0 \le i \le n - 1$, gets a ticket with a pair of values (*number*[i],i) on it. The value *number*[i] is the ticket number, and i is the ID of the thread. Since each ticket contains a pair of values, a special comparison is used to order the tickets. If two threads have the same ticket numbers, the IDs are used to break the tie. That is, for two tickets (a,b) and (c,d), define

Ticket (a,b) < Ticket (c,d) if a < c or (a == c and b < d).

First, we show a simpler, but incorrect version of the Bakery algorithm to explain the basic ideas. Each thread T_i, $0 \le i \le n - 1$, executes the code below. Initially, all elements of array *number* have the value 0.

```
while (true) {
        number[i] = max(number) + 1;                (1)
        for(int j=0; j<n; j++ )                       (2)
        while (j != i && number[j] != 0 &&          (3)
              (number[j],j) < (number[i],i) ) {;}    (4)
        critical section                              (5)
        number[i] = 0;                               (6)
        noncritical section                          (7)
}
```

In statement (1), the call to max(*number*) returns the maximum value in array *number*. This maximum value is incremented by 1, and the result is used as the ticket number. Since different threads may execute (1) at the same time, thread T_i may obtain the same ticket number as another thread. As we mentioned above, thread IDs are used to break ties when the ticket numbers are the same.

In the for-loop, thread T_i compares its ticket with the ticket of each of the other threads. If some other thread T_j intends to enter its critical section and it has a ticket with a value that is less than T_i's ticket, T_i waits until T_j exits its critical section. (If T_j tries to enter its critical section again, its new ticket will have a value higher than T_i's ticket and thus T_j will have to wait.) When T_i completes the loops in (2) and (3), no other thread is in its critical section. Also, thread T_i

is the only thread that can enter its critical section since any other threads that are in their entry-sections will have higher ticket numbers.

This algorithm does not satisfy the mutual exclusion requirement, as illustrated by the following sequence:

T0	T1	Comments
(1)		T_0 evaluates max(*number*) + 1, which is 1, but a context switch occurs *before* assigning 1 to number[0]
context switch →		
	(1)	T_1 sets *number*[1] to max(*number*) + 1, which is 1
	(2)	T_1 starts its `for`-loop
	(3)	T_1 exits its `while` and `for`-loops
	(4)	T_1 enters its critical section
← context switch		
(1)		T_0 assigns 1 (*not 2*) to *number*[0].
(2)		T_0 starts its `for`-loop
(3)		T_0 exits its `while`- and `for`-loops since *number*[0] == *number*[1] == 1, and (*number*[0],1) < (*number*[1],2)
(4)		T_0 enters its critical section while T_1 is in its critical section

To fix this problem, once thread T_i, $i > 0$, starts executing statement (1), *number*[i] should not be accessed by other threads during their execution of statement (3) until T_i finishes executing statement (1).

The complete bakery algorithm is given below. It uses the following global array:

    volatile bool choosing[n];

Initially, all elements of *choosing* have the value *false*. If *choosing[i]* is true, thread T_i is in the process of choosing its ticket number at statement (2):

```
while (true) {
    choosing[i] = true;                      (1)
    number[i] = max(number)+1;               (2)
    choosing[i] = false;                     (3)
    for (int j=0; j<n; j++) {                (4)
    while (choosing[j]) {;}                   (5)
    while ( j != i && number[j] !=0 &&       (6)
        (number[j],j) < (number[i],i) ) {;}
    }
```

```
    critical section                          (7)
    number[i] = 0;                            (8)
    noncritical section                       (9)
}
```

A formal proof of the bakery algorithm is given in [Lamport 1974]. Here we consider three important cases:

1. Assume that one thread, say T_i, intends to enter its critical section and no other thread is in its critical section or entry-section. Then $number[i]$ is 1 and $number[j]$, where $j \neq i$, is 0. Thus, T_i enters its critical section immediately.

2. Assume that one thread, say T_i, intends to enter its critical section and T_k, $k \neq i$, is in its critical section. Then at statement (6), $number[k]$!=0 and $number[k] < number[i]$. Thus, T_i is delayed at (6) until T_k executes statement (8).

3. Two or more threads intend to enter their critical sections and no other thread is in its critical section. Assume that T_k and T_m, where $k < m$, intend to enter. Consider the possible relationships between $number[k]$ and $number[m]$:

   - $number[k] < number[m]$. T_k enters its critical section since $(number[k],k) < (number[m],m)$.
   - $number[k] == number[m]$. T_k enters its critical section since $(number[k],k) < (number[m],m)$.
   - $number[k] > number[m]$. T_m enters its critical section since $(number[m],m) < (number[k],k)$.

   Thus, array *choosing* solves the problem that stems from the nonatomic arithmetic expression in statement (2).

The bakery algorithm satisfies the mutual exclusion, progress, and bounded waiting requirements. However, the values in *number* grow without bound. Lamport [1974] showed how a practical upper bound can be placed on these values. He also showed that the bakery algorithm can be made to work even when read and write operations are not atomic (i.e., when the read and write operations on a variable may overlap).

2.3   HARDWARE SOLUTIONS TO THE n-THREAD CRITICAL SECTION PROBLEM

In this section we show how to use Win32 function *InterlockedExchange* to solve the n-process critical section problem. Here is the function prototype for the Win32 function *InterlockedExchange*:

```
long InterlockedExchange(long* target, long newValue);
```

The *InterlockedExchange* function atomically exchanges a pair of 32-bit values and behaves like the following atomic function:

```
long InterLockedExchange(long* target, long newValue) { // executed atomically
    long temp = *target; *target = newValue; return temp;
}
```

Like *InterlockedExchangeAdd()*, this function also generates a memory barrier instruction.

2.3.1   Partial Solution

This solution uses *InterlockedExchange* to guarantee mutual exclusion and progress but not bounded waiting. Shared variable *lock* is initialized to 0:

```
volatile long lock = 0;
```

Each thread executes

```
while (true) {
    while (InterlockedExchange(const_cast<long*>(&lock), 1) == 1) {;}     (1)
    critical section                                                     (2)
    lock = 0;                                                            (3)
    noncritical section                                                  (4)
}
```

If the value of *lock* is 0 when *InterlockedExchange* is called, *lock* is set to 1 and *InterlockedExchange* returns 0. This allows the calling thread to drop out of its `while`-loop and enter its critical section. While this thread is in its critical section, calls to *InterlockedExchange* will return the value 1, keeping the calling threads delayed in their `while`-loops.

When a thread exits its critical section, it sets *lock* to 0. This allows one of the delayed threads to get a 0 back in exchange for a 1. This lucky thread drops out of its `while`-loop and enter its critical section. Theoretically, an unlucky thread could be delayed forever from entering its critical section. However, if critical sections are small and contention among threads for the critical sections is low, unbounded waiting is not a real problem.

2.3.2   Complete Solution

This solution to the n-process critical section satisfies all three correctness requirements. The global array *waiting* is used to indicate that a thread is waiting to enter its critical section.

```
volatile bool waiting[n];
```

Initially, all elements of *waiting* are *false*. If *waiting*[i] is true, thread T_i, $0 \le i \le n-1$, is waiting to enter its critical section. Each thread T_i executes the following code:

```
volatile bool waiting[n];    // initialized to false
volatile long lock, key;     // initialized to 0
while (true) {
    waiting[i] = true;                                          (1)
    key = 1;                                                    (2)
    while (waiting[i] && key) {                                 (3)
        key = InterlockedExchange(const_cast<long*>(&lock), 1); (4)
    }                                                           (5)
    waiting[i] = false;                                         (6)
    critical section                                            (7)
    j = (i+1) % n;                                              (8)
    while ((j != i) && !waiting[j]) { j = (j+1) % n; }          (9)
    if (j == i)                                                 (10)
        lock = 0;                                               (11)
    else                                                        (12)
        waiting[j] = false;                                     (13)
    noncritical section                                         (14)
}
```

In statement (1), thread T_i sets *waiting*[i] to *true* to indicate that it is waiting to enter its critical section. Thread T_i then stays in the while-loop until either *InterlockedExchange* returns 0 or *waiting*[i] is set to 0 by another thread when that thread exits its critical section.

When thread T_i exits its critical section, it uses the while-loop in statement (9) to search for a waiting thread. Thread T_i starts its search by examining *waiting[i+1]*. If the while-loop terminates with $j == i$, no waiting threads exist; otherwise, thread T_j is a waiting thread and *waiting*[j] is set to 0 to let T_j exit the while-loop at statement (3) and enter its critical section.

2.3.3 Note on Busy-Waiting

All of the solutions to the critical section problem that we have seen so far use *busy-waiting*—a waiting thread executes a loop that maintains its hold on the CPU. Busy-waiting wastes CPU cycles. To reduce the amount of busy-waiting, some type of sleep instruction can be used. In Win32, execution of

Sleep(time);

releases the CPU and blocks the executing thread for *time* in milliseconds. In Java, a thread sleeps by executing Thread.sleep(time) for *time* in milliseconds, while Pthreads uses sleep(time) for *time* in seconds. Executing a sleep statement results in a context switch that allows another thread to execute. (We use the term *blocked* to describe a thread that is waiting for some event to occur, such as the expiration of a timer or the completion of an I/O statement. Such a thread is not running and will not run until the target event occurs and the operating system schedules the thread to run.) The amount of busy waiting in the while-loop in statement (3) of the complete solution can be reduced as follows:

```
while (waiting[i] && key) {
    Sleep(100); // release the CPU
    key = InterlockedExchange(const_cast<long*>(&lock), 1);
}
```

If contention among threads for the critical section is low and critical sections are small, there may be little chance that a thread will execute the while-loop for more than a few iterations. In such cases it may be more efficient to use busy-waiting and avoid the time-consuming context switch caused by executing a sleep statement.

A slightly different version of this code can be used to solve a potential performance problem on multiprocessor systems with private caches and cache-coherence protocols that allow shared writable data to exist in multiple caches. For example, consider the case where two processors are busy-waiting on the value of *lock* in the complete solution above. When a waiting processor modifies *lock* in statement (4), it causes the modified *lock* to be invalidated in the other processor's cache. As a result, the value of *lock* can bounce repeatedly from one cache to the other [Dubois et al. 1988].

Instead of looping on the call to *InterlockedExchange* in (3), which causes the ping-pong effect, we can use a simpler loop that waits for *lock* to become 0:

```
while (waiting[i] && key) {                                    (3)
    while (lock) {;} // wait for lock to be released           (4)
    // try to grab lock                                        (5)
    key = InterlockedExchange(const_cast<long*>(&lock), 1);
}
```

When a processor wants to acquire the lock, it spins locally in its cache without modifying and invalidating the *lock* variable. When the lock is eventually released, the function *InterlockedExchange* is still used, but only to attempt to change the value of *lock* from 0 to 1. If another thread happens to "steal" the lock between statements (4) and (5), looping will continue at statement (3).

In general, the performance of busy-waiting algorithms depends on the number of processors, the size of the critical section, and the architecture of the system. Mellor-Crummey and Scott [1991] described many ways to fine-tune the performance of busy-waiting algorithms (see Exercise 2.13).

2.4   DEADLOCK, LIVELOCK, AND STARVATION

We have identified three correctness requirements for solutions to the critical section problem: mutual exclusion, progress, and bounded waiting. Different concurrent programming problems have different correctness requirements. However, one general requirement that is often not explicitly stated is the absence of deadlock, livelock, and starvation. In this section we explain this requirement and give examples of programs that violate it. A more formal definition of this requirement is presented in Section 7.3.3.

2.4.1   Deadlock

A deadlock requires one or more threads to be blocked forever. As we mentioned above, a thread is blocked if it is not running and it is waiting for some event to occur. Sleep statements block a thread temporarily, but eventually the thread is allowed to run again. In later chapters we will see other types of statements that can permanently block the threads that execute them. For example, a thread that executes a receive statement to receive a message from another thread will block until the message arrives, but it is possible that a message will never arrive.

Let CP be a concurrent program containing two or more threads. Assume that there is an execution of CP that exercises an execution sequence S, and at the end of S, there exists a thread T that satisfies these conditions:

- T is blocked due to the execution of a synchronization statement (e.g., waiting to receive a message).
- T will remain blocked forever, regardless of what the other threads will do.

Thread T is said to be *deadlocked* at the end of S, and CP is said to have a *deadlock*. A *global deadlock* refers to a deadlock in which all nonterminated threads are deadlocked.

As an example, assume that CP contains threads T1 and T2 and the following execution sequence is possible:

- T1 blocks waiting to receive a message from T2.
- T2 blocks waiting to receive a message from T1.

Both T1 and T2 will remain blocked forever since neither thread is able to send the message for which the other thread is waiting.

2.4.2   Livelock

We assume that some statements in CP are labeled as *progress statements*, indicating that threads are expected eventually to execute these statements. Statements that are likely to be labeled as progress statements include the last statement of a thread, the first statement of a critical section, or the statement immediately following a loop. If a thread executes a progress statement, it is considered to be *making progress*.

Assume that there is an execution of CP that exercises an execution sequence S, and at the end of S there exists a thread T that satisfies the following conditions, regardless of what the other threads will do:

- T will not terminate or deadlock.
- T will never make progress.

Thread T is said to be *livelocked* at the end of S, and CP is said to have a *livelock*. Livelock is the busy-waiting analog of deadlock. A livelocked thread is running, not blocked, but it will never make progress.

Incorrect solution 2 in Section 2.1.2 has an execution sequence that results in a violation of the progress requirement for solutions to the critical section problem. (This progress requirement should not be confused with the general requirement to make progress. The latter is used to indicate the absence of livelock and can be required for solutions to any problem.) Below is a prefix of this execution sequence:

- T0 executes (1), (2), (3), and (4). Now *turn* is 1.
- T1 executes (1), (2), and (3) and then terminates in its noncritical section. Now *turn* is 0.
- T0 executes (1), (2), (3), and (4), making *turn* 1, and executes its `while`-loop at (1).

At the end this sequence, $T0$ is stuck in a busy-waiting loop at (1) waiting for *turn* to become 0. T0 will never enter its critical section (i.e., make any progress). Thus, $T0$ is livelocked.

2.4.3 Starvation

Assume that CP contains an infinite execution sequence S satisfying the following three properties:

1. S ends with an infinite repetition of a fair cycle of statements. (A cycle of statements in CP is said to be *fair* if each nonterminated thread in CP is either always blocked in the cycle or is executed at least once. Nonfair cycles are not considered here, since such cycles cannot repeat forever when fair scheduling is used.)
2. There exists a nonterminated thread T that does not make progress in the cycle.
3. Thread T is neither deadlocked nor livelocked in the cycle. In other words, when CP reaches the cycle of statements that ends S, CP may instead execute a different sequence S' such that T makes progress or terminates in S'.

Thread T is said to be *starved* in the cycle that ends S, and CP is said to have a *starvation*. When CP reaches the cycle of statements at the end of S, whether thread T will starve depends on how the threads in CP are scheduled. Note that fair scheduling of the threads in CP does not guarantee a starvation-free execution of CP.

Incorrect solution 3 in Section 2.1.3 has an execution sequence that results in a violation of the bounded waiting requirement. Following is that execution sequence:

(a) *T*0 executes (1), (2), and (6). Now *T*0 is in its critical section and *intend-ToEnter*[0] is *true*.

(b) *T*1 executes (1)–(4). Now *intendToEnter* [1] is *false* and *T*1 is waiting for *intendToEnter* [0] to be *false*.

(c) *T*0 executes (7), (8), (1), (2), and (6). Now *T*0 is in its critical section and *intendToEnter* [0] is *true*.

(d) *T*1 resumes execution at (4) and is still waiting for *intendToEnter* [0] to be *false*.

(e) *T*0 executes (7), (8), (1), (2), and (6).

(f) *T*1 resumes execution at (4).

... Infinite repetition of steps (e) and (f) ...

In this sequence, *T*1 never makes progress in the cycle of statements involving (e) and (f). However, when execution reaches step (e), the following sequence may be executed instead:

(e) *T*0 executes (7).

(f) *T*1 resumes execution at (4) and executes (5), (2), (6), and (7).

Thus, *T*1 is not deadlocked or livelocked, but it is starved in the cycle involving (e) and (f).

If contention for a critical section is low, as it is in many cases, starvation is unlikely, and solutions to the critical section problem that theoretically allow starvation may actually be acceptable. This is the case for the partial hardware solution in Section 2.3.1.

2.5 TRACING AND REPLAY FOR SHARED VARIABLES

In this section we show how to trace and replay executions of concurrent programs that read and write shared variables. We present a C++ class that will allow us to demonstrate program tracing and replay and we show how to trace and replay a C++ implementation of Peterson's algorithm. Even though real programs use high-level synchronization constructs to create critical sections, not algorithms like Peterson's, the tracing and replay techniques presented in this section are easy to generalize and can be applied to the high-level constructs introduced in later chapters. Also, the concepts that we introduce here are easier to understand when complicated programming constructs are not involved.

We assume that read and write operations are atomic (i.e., that read and write operations do not overlap), and that the synchronization of read and write operations is provided by the memory system. Thus, each thread issues its read and write operations according to the order in its code, and its operations are serviced by the memory system one at a time. This leads to an interleaving of the read and write operations in different threads, resulting in a total order of memory operations. We also assume that the total order that results is consistent with the (partial) order specified by each thread's code. As we will see in Section 2.5.6, this assumption may not always hold.

We also assume that the interleaving of read and write operations is the only source of nondeterminism. This excludes other sources of nondeterminism, such as uninitialized variables and memory allocation problems. Under these assumptions, an execution of a program with the same input and the same sequence of read and write operations will produce the same result. We first carefully define what a sequence of read and write operations looks like, so that such a sequence can be traced and then replayed.

2.5.1   ReadWrite-Sequences

In general, a thread executes synchronization events on synchronization objects. Each shared object in a concurrent program is associated with a sequence of synchronization events, called a *SYN-sequence*, which consists of the synchronization events that are executed on that object. For the programs that we are considering here, the synchronization objects are simply shared variables, and the synchronization events are read and write operations on the shared variables. (It is often the case that a synchronization event also involves communication. This is certainly the case for read and write operations. We still refer to such events as synchronization events.)

A SYN-sequence of a concurrent program is a collection of the SYN-sequences for its synchronization objects. This type of SYN-sequence is called an *object-based* SYN-sequence. In later chapters we introduce other types of SYN-sequences. For example, we can define a SYN-sequence for each thread instead of each synchronization object. A *thread-based* SYN-sequence may be easier to read and understand, since programmers normally think of a concurrent program's behavior in terms of the behavior of its threads, not its synchronization objects. Object-based sequences turn out to be better suited for the replay solution we have developed.

A SYN-sequence for a shared variable v is a sequence of read and write operations, called a *ReadWrite-sequence* [LeBlanc and Mellor-Crummey 1987]. Each write operation on a shared variable creates a new version of the variable. We give each variable a version number so that we can keep track of its versions. A program trace associates a version number with each read and write operation performed by a thread. An execution can be replayed by ensuring that each thread reads and writes the same versions of variables that were recorded in the execution trace.

During program tracing, we record the following information about each read and write operation. When a thread reads a variable, we record the unique identifier (ID) of that thread and the version of the variable that is read. (As we explained in Chapter 1, threads that are created by inheriting from class *TDThread* receive a unique ID as part of their initialization. *TDThread* IDs start at 1.) The format for a read event is

Read(ID, version)

where *ID* is the identifier of the reader thread and *version* is the version of the variable that was read. Each write operation on a variable creates a new version and thus increases the variable's version number by 1. The format for a write event is

Write(ID, version, total readers)

where *ID* is the identifier of the writer thread, *version* is the old version number (i.e., before the version number was incremented by this write), and *total readers* is the number of readers that read the old version of the variable.

As an example, consider the following three simple threads that access a single shared variable s:

Thread1	Thread2	Thread3
temp = s;	temp = s;	s = s + 1;

Assume that s is initialized to 0. A possible ReadWrite-sequence of s is

Read(3,0)   // Thread3 reads version 0 of s
Read(1,0)   // Thread1 reads version 0 of s
Write(3,0,2)   // Thread3 writes s and increments s' version number to one;
                // 2 readers read version 0 of s
Read(2,1)   // Thread2 reads version 1 of s

From the threads and this sequence, we conclude that Thread1 read the value 0 and Thread2 read the value 1. Notice that Thread1 read s after Thread3 read s but before Thread3 wrote the new value of s.

The information in a ReadWrite-sequence is used to resolve any nondeterministic choices that arise during the replay of an execution. In the example above, Thread3's write operation on variable s could occur either before or after the read operations by Thread1 and Thread2. The ReadWrite-sequence above specifies that during replay Thread3 should write s after Thread1 reads s but before Thread2 reads s.

There are two important points to be made about the definition of ReadWrite-sequences. First, the value read or written by a memory operation is not recorded in a ReadWrite-sequence. If the order of read and write operations is replayed as specified by a ReadWrite-sequence, the values read and written will also be replayed.

The second point is that we do not actually need to label the events in a ReadWrite-sequence as "read" or "write" events. The "Read" and "Write" labels in the sample sequence were added to make the sequence easier to understand. We must identify the thread that executes the event but not the type of event. It is true that the type of an event could easily be identified by its format, since read events have two fields and write events have three fields. However, we are free to add a third field to read events and always give this field a value of 0. This uniform format increases the size of a trace, but it makes it easier to input a ReadWrite-sequence. In fact, we use this input format in the replay tool presented later. The point is that information about event types is not needed when we perform program replay. The type (read or write) of the next operation to be performed by a thread is fixed by its source code, the program input, and the operations that precede it. The source code and input are the same for every replayed execution, and the values read or written by the preceding operations are always replayed, starting with the first operation.

Adding extra information to a trace, such as "read" and "write" labels, and the values that are read and written can certainly make a trace more readable during debugging. However, this information is not needed to perform replay, so we do not include it in ReadWrite-sequences. (Also, any additional debugging information that is needed can be collected during replay.) Different types of traces with different amounts of information can be defined and used for different purposes.

2.5.2   Alternative Definition of ReadWrite-Sequences

It may be possible to decrease the overhead required for tracing and replaying executions if system-level events can be observed and controlled. For example, another way to trace an execution is to record the number of read and write operations that each thread executes during each time quantum that it is scheduled on the CPU [Choi and Srinivasan 1998]. For example, assume that Thread1 executes 50 operations during its time quantum. Instead of recording each of the 50 operations, we can number each read and write operation that gets executed, and record a single event such as (1, 20, 69) to represent the fact that Thread1 executed the (50) operations numbered 20 through 69.

We can apply this same idea to ReadWrite-sequences for shared variables. For each Read or Write operation, we record the ID of the thread that executes the operation. This gives us a simple sequence such as

1, 1, 1, 1, 1, 2, 2, 2

indicating that Thread1 executed five operations and then Thread2 executed three operations. We can "compress" this sequence into

(1, 5), (2, 3).   // the format is (a, b), where a is the thread ID and b is the
                   // number of operations

This indicates that Thread1 executed the first five operations (1, 5), then Thread2 executed the next three (2, 3). Compressing sequences may reduce the amount of space that is required for storing traces.

2.5.3   Tracing and Replaying ReadWrite-Sequences

During program tracing, information is recorded about each read and write operation, and a ReadWrite-sequence is recorded for each shared variable. During program replay, the read and write operations on a shared variable are forced to occur in the order specified by the ReadWrite-sequence recorded during tracing. For tracing and replay, we use our original definition of ReadWrite-sequences, which records ID and version information about each operation. Read and write operations are instrumented by adding routines to control the start and end of the operations:

```
Read(x) {                   Write(x) {
    startRead(x);               startWrite(x);
    read value of x;           write new value of x;
    endRead(x);                endWrite(x);
}                           }
```

Functions *startRead(), endRead(), startWrite(),* and *endWrite()* contain the trace and replay code. Listing 2.1 shows a sketch of these functions. Certain details have been omitted to simplify our discussion. For example, since these functions access shared variables (e.g., *activeReaders, totalReaders*), some synchronization mechanism must be used to create critical sections. Another mechanism is needed so that threads are delayed by blocking them instead of using busy-waiting loops. Both of these mechanisms are easily implemented using constructs that we discuss in later chapters.

In trace mode, *startRead(x)* increments *x.activeReaders* to indicate that another reader has started to read shared variable x. Then the reader thread's ID and variable x's version number are recorded. Writers cannot write while any readers are active [i.e., (*x.activeReaders*>0)]. Readers and writers are serviced in the order of their requests to read and write. If a writer requests to write while one or more readers are reading, the writer will wait until those readers are finished. Readers that request to read while a writer is writing will wait for that writer to finish. Function *endRead(x)* decrements *x.activeReaders* and increments *x.totalReaders*. The latter represents the total number of readers that have read the current version of x.

```
startRead(x) {
    if (mode == trace) {
        ++x.activeReaders; // one more reader is reading x
        ReadWriteSequence.record(ID,x.version);   // record read event for x
    }
    else { // replay mode
        // get next event to be performed by thread ID
        readEvent r = ReadWriteSequence.nextEvent(ID);
        myVersion = r.getVersion(); // find version of x read during tracing
        while (myVersion != x.version) delay; // wait for correct version of x to read
    }
}
endRead(x) {
    ++x.totalReaders; // one more reader has read this version of x
    --x.activeReaders; // one less reader is reading x (ignored in replay mode)
}
startWrite(x) {
    if (mode = trace) {
    // wait for all active readers to finish reading x
    while (x.activeReaders>0) delay;
        // record write event for x
        ReadWriteSequence.record(ID,x.version,x.totalReaders);
    }
    else { // replay mode
        // find version modified during tracing
        writeEvent w = ReadWriteSequence.nextEvent(ID);
        myVersion = w.getVersion();
        // wait for correct version of x to write
        while (myVersion != x.version) delay;
        // find count of readers for previous version
        myTotalReaders = w.getTotalReaders();
        // wait until all readers have read this version of x
        while (x.totalReaders < myTotalReaders) delay;
    }
}
endWrite(x) {
    x.totalReaders = 0;
    ++x.version;                        // increment version number for x
}
```

Listing 2.1   Tracing and replaying a ReadWrite-sequence.

In trace mode, *startWrite(x)* waits for all current readers to finish reading *x*, then it records the writer thread's ID, *x*'s current version number, and the total number of readers for the current version of *x*. Function *endWrite(x)* resets *x.totalReaders* and increments the version number of *x*, as each write operation creates a new version of the variable.

During replay, the read and write operations on a shared variable are controlled so that a ReadWrite-sequence captured in trace mode can be repeated. Writers will repeat the order of their write operations. If two or more readers read a particular version during tracing, they must read the same version during replay, but these reads can be in any order. Thus, reads are only partially ordered with respect to write operations, while writes operations are totally ordered for each shared variable.

This concurrent reading and exclusive writing (CREW) policy increases concurrency and still produces the same result. We could, instead, use a stricter policy that required exclusive reads and writes and a total ordering of all read and write operations, but the result would be the same. (For example, the alternative definition of ReadWrite-sequences in Section 2.5.2 is a total ordering of read and write operations.)

In replay mode, *startRead(x)* delays a thread's read operation until the version number of variable *x* matches the version number recorded during tracing. After the read is performed, *endRead(x)* increments *x.totalReaders* to indicate that one more read operation has been replayed. Write operations are delayed in *startWrite(x)* until the *version* number of *x* matches the *version* number recorded during tracing and until *totalReaders* reaches the same value that it reached during tracing. After the write, *endWrite(x)* resets *x.totalReaders* and increments the *version* number so that the next operation can be replayed.

2.5.4   Class Template *sharedVariable* <>

As we mentioned in Chapter 1, we have written a C++ class template called *sharedVariable* that implements our tracing and replay technique for ReadWrite-sequences. Listing 2.2 shows part of the header file for class *sharedVariable*. We can use class *sharedVariable* to create shared variables that are of primitive types such as *int* and *double*. Class *sharedVariable* provides operators for adding, subtracting, assigning, comparing, and so on, and provides functions for tracing and replaying the read and write operations in the implementations of these operators. It has a member variable of type *T* (the type specified by the template parameter) which holds the actual value of the *sharedVariable*.

The implementations of the operators are straightforward. Each operator calls the appropriate control functions (*startRead()*, *endRead()*, *startWrite()*, and *endWrite()*) for the variables that are read and written. Listing 2.3 shows the implementation of operator+=(). This operation contains two read operations and a write operation. The control functions make sure that these operations are recorded during tracing and controlled during replay.

```
template <class T>
class sharedVariable {
public:
    sharedVariable();
    explicit sharedVariable(const T& v);
    const sharedVariable<T>& operator+=(const sharedVariable<T>& sv);
    const sharedVariable<T>& operator+=(const T& sv);
    sharedVariable<T>& operator=(const sharedVariable<T>& sv);
    sharedVariable<t>& operator=(const T& v);
    /* ... more operations ... */
private:
    T value; // actual value of the shared variable
    void startRead(const sharedVariable<T>& sv) const;
    void endRead(const sharedVariable<T>& sv) const;
    void startWrite(const sharedVariable<T>& sv) const;
    void endWrite(const sharedVariable<T>& sv) const;
};
```

Listing 2.2   C++ class template *sharedVariable<>*.

```
template<class T>
sharedVariable<T>::operator+=(const sharedVariable<T>& sv) const {
// implementation of operation A += B, which is shorthand for A = A + B
    T svTemp, thisTemp;

    startRead(*this);
    thisTemp = value;          // read A
    endRead(*this);
    startRead(sv);
    svTemp = sv.value;         // read B
    endRead(sv);
    startWrite(*this);
    value = thisTemp + svTemp;   // write A
    endWrite(*this);

    return *this;
}
```

Listing 2.3   Implementation of *sharedVariable<T>::operator+=()*.

2.5.5   Putting It All Together

Listing 2.4 shows a C++ implementation of Peterson's algorithm using *shared-Variables*. Each thread enters its critical section twice. When executed in trace mode, the program in Listing 2.4 will produce a ReadWrite-sequence for each

```
sharedVariable<int> intendToEnter1(0), intendToEnter2(0), turn(0);
const int maxEntries = 2;
class Thread1: public TDThread {
private:
    virtual void* run() {
        for (int i=0; i<maxEntries; i++) {
            intendToEnter1 = 1;
            turn = 2;
            while (intendToEnter2 && (turn == 2)) ;
            // critical section
            intendToEnter1 = 0;
        }
        return 0;
    }
};
class Thread2 : public TDThread {
private:
    virtual void* run() {
        for (int i=0; i<maxEntries; i++) {
            intendToEnter2 = 1;
            turn = 1;
            while (intendToEnter1 && (turn == 1)) ;
            // critical section
            intendToEnter2 = 0;
        }
        return 0;
    }
};
int main() {
    std::auto_ptr<Thread1> T1(new Thread1);
    std::auto_ptr<Thread2> T2(new Thread2);
    T1->start();   T2->start();
    T1->join();    T2->join();
    return 0;
}
```

Listing 2.4 Peterson's algorithm using class template *sharedVariable*<>.

of the shared variables *intendtoEnter1, intendToEnter2*, and *turn*. Three such sequences that were produced when we executed the program are shown in Fig. 2.5, which also shows a totally ordered sequence of read and write events that is consistent with the three object-based sequences. This single sequence, which contains all the program events, is easier to follow than are the three object-based sequences. (In the totally ordered sequence, we omitted the actual events and simply showed the sequence of statements that are executed.)

ReadWrite-sequence for *intendToEnter1*:

1 0 0   // T1: intendtoenter1 = 1
2 1   // T2: while(intendtoenter1 ...)–T2 is busy-waiting
1 1 1   // T1: intendtoenter1 = 0
2 2   // T2: while(intendtoenter1 ...)–T2 will enter its critical section
1 2 1   // T1: intendtoenter1 = 1
2 3   // T2: while(intendtoenter1 ...)–T2 is busy-waiting
1 3 1   // T1: intendtoenter1 = 0
2 4   // T2: while(intendtoenter1 ...)–T2 will enter its critical section

ReadWrite-sequence for *intendToEnter2*:

2 0 0   // T2: intendtoenter2 = 1
1 1   // T1: while(intendtoenter2 ...)–T1 will enter its critical section
2 1 1   // T2: intendtoenter2 = 0
2 2 0   // T2: intendtoenter2 = 1
1 3   // T1: while(intendtoenter2 ...)–T1 is busy-waiting
1 3   // T1: while(intendtoenter2 ...)–T1 will enter its critical section
2 3 2   // T2: intendtoenter2 = 0

ReadWrite-sequence for *turn*:

1 0 0   // T1: turn = 2
2 1 0   // T2: turn = 1
1 2   // T1: while(... && turn == 2)–T1 will enter its critical section
2 2   // T2: while(... && turn == 1)–T2 is busy-waiting
2 2   // T2: while(... && turn == 1)–T2 will enter its critical section
1 2 3   // T1: turn = 2
1 3   // T1: while(.. && turn == 2)–T1 is busy-waiting
2 3 1   // T2: turn = 1
1 4   // T1: while(... && turn == 2)–T1 will enter its critical section
2 4   // T2: while(... && turn == 1)–T2 is busy-waiting
2 4   // T2: while(... && turn == 1)–T2 will enter its critical section

A Totally-Ordered Sequence for Peterson's Algorithm:

T1: intendtoenter1 = 1; turn = 2;
T2: intendtoenter2 = 1; turn = 1;
T1: while (intendtoenter2 && turn == 2)–T1 will enter its critical section
T2: while (intendtoenter1 && turn == 1)–T2 is busy-waiting
T1: intendtoenter1 = 0   –T1 has exited its critical section
T2: while (intendtoenter1 && turn == 1)–T2 will enter its critical section
T2: intendtoenter2 = 0   –T2 has exited its critical section
T1: intendtoenter1 = 1; turn = 2
T2: intendtoenter2 = 1

Figure 2.5 ReadWrite-sequences for shared variables *intendtoEnter1*, *intendToEnter2*, and *turn*.

T1: while (intendtoenter2 && turn == 2) −T1 is busy-waiting
T2: turn = 1
T1: while (intendtoenter2 && turn == 2) −T1 will enter its critical section
T2: while (intendtoenter1 && turn == 1) −T2 is busy-waiting
T1: intendtoenter1 = 0   −T1 has exited its critical section
T2: while (intendtoenter1 && turn == 1) −T2 will enter its critical section
T2: intendtoenter2 = 0   −T2 has exited its critical section

Figure 2.5   (*continued*)

Note that it is not possible to construct the totally ordered sequence in Fig. 2.5 from the three object-based sequences without adding or computing some additional information to determine whether one event "happened before" another during the execution (see Chapter 6). Alternatively, we could modify our tracing mechanism so that a single totally ordered sequence is recorded, but this would create a bottleneck at the tracing module and reduce the amount of concurrency during execution.

The ability to replay an execution of Peterson's algorithm is helpful, but it still leaves the difficult problem of determining whether a given execution of Peterson's algorithm, or of some other solution to the critical section problem, is correct. Expressing the required correctness properties of the execution is difficult in itself. One approach to checking correctness is to generate user-level events representing each thread's entry into, and exit from, its critical section. Then we can systematically generate all possible ReadWrite-sequences of the implementation and check whether these user-level events occur in their proper order. For example, events *enter-1* and *exit-1* can be generated at the beginning and end of Thread1's critical section. Given consecutive *enter-1* and *exit-1* events executed by Thread1, any *enter-2* event executed by Thread2 must happen before *enter-1* or after *exit-1*. Various mechanisms for ordering the events of an execution are described in Chapter 6. This general approach to testing, called *reachability testing*, is overviewed in Chapters 3 through 5 and described in detail in Chapter 7.

2.5.6   Note on Shared Memory Consistency

In the cases outlined above, it may be difficult to determine the actual order of read and write operations on shared variables. We have been assuming that read and write operations are executed in an order that is consistent with the order implied by the source code. This allows read and write operations in different threads to be interleaved but requires operations in the same thread to occur in the order specified by that thread's code. Lamport [1979] formalized this notion when he defined *sequentially consistent multiprocessor systems*: "[A multiprocessor system is sequentially consistent if] the result of any execution is the same as if the operations of all the processors were executed in some sequential order, and the operations of each individual processor appear in this sequence in the order specified by its program."

Note that sequential consistency does not require the actual execution order of operations to be consistent with any *particular* sequential order. In particular, operations of the same processor may be performed in an order that differs from program order as long as both orders give the same result [Anderson 2001]. We use a similar notion of *consistent executions* during program replay. The events exercised during replay may be performed in an order that differs from the original execution as long as both executions give the same result. For example, two concurrent write events on different shared variables can be performed in either order.

Sequential consistency may not hold for several reasons [Adve and Gharachorloo 1995]:

- Due to performance optimizations performed by the compiler or the memory hardware, the actual order of execution of the shared variable read and write operations of a thread may be different from the order specified in the program, and the result of the execution may violate the semantics of sequential consistency.
- If multiple copies of the same shared variable exist, as is the case with cache-based multiprocessor systems and certain compiler optimizations, and if all the copies are not updated at the same time, different threads can individually observe different ReadWrite-sequences during the same execution [Dubois et al. 1988] (see Exercise 2.15).

In such cases, the effects of compiler and hardware optimizations create a larger number of possible interleavings than is implied by the program's source code. More important, the actual order of read and write operations might not be known at the program level; rather, the order may be known only at the hardware level. The result of all this is that the actual SYN-sequence of an execution may involve low-level events such as cache invalidations and therefore may be unobservable and uncontrollable at levels above the hardware. Verifying program correctness then becomes a "monumental task" [Lamport 1979].

Following is a simple example that illustrates the complexity of dealing with shared memory consistency. *Thread1* and *Thread2* communicate using shared variables x and y:

```
int x = 1;
boolean y = false;
```

Thread1	Thread2
x = 0;	if (y)
y = true;	/* what is the value of x? */

If *Thread2* finds that *y* is *true*, *Thread2* might also expect *x* to be 0 since *Thread1* assigns 0 to *x* before it assigns *true* to y. But there are several reasons why this might not be the case:

1. If each thread is allowed to keep a private copy of shared variable *y* in a register in order to speed up access to *y*, the update to *y* by *Thread1* will not be visible to *Thread2*. Thus, *Thread2* will always find that *y* is *false*.

2. Hardware optimizations such as allowing write operations to overlap can result in reorderings of the write operations in *Thread1*. Thus, *y* may be assigned *true* before *x* is assigned 0.

3. A compiler optimization may reorder the assignment statements in *Thread1* so that the assignment to *y* is performed before the assignment to *x*.

Guaranteeing sequential consistency would rule out these and some other optimizations, which would also mean that these optimizations could not be used to speed up individual sequential processors. Instead of slowing down all the processors, programmers are asked to identify the places in the program at which the optimizations should be turned off.

In Section 2.1.5 we saw that one way to turn off optimizations on shared variables is to declare them as `volatile`. Declaring a variable as `volatile` indicates that the value of the variable may be read or written from outside the thread or even outside the program in which the variable appears. For instance, in the example program above, the value of variable *y* in *Thread2* can be changed by *Thread1*. If *y* is declared as `volatile`, the compiler will ensure that updates to *y* by *Thread1* are immediately visible to *Thread2*. As another example, consider a program that used memory-mapped I/O. A variable's memory location may be mapped to a data port for an input device. This allows the program to perform input simply by reading the value of the variable. Since the variable is written by the input device, not by the program, the compiler may assume that the value of the variable never changes and then perform optimizations that are based on this incorrect assumption. Declaring the variable as `volatile` turns these optimizations off for this variable.

In our example Java program we can deal with problem 1 above by declaring *y* to be `volatile`:

```
volatile boolean y = false;
int x = 1;
```

This prohibits the compiler from allocating *y* to a register. However, in versions of Java before J2SE 5.0, problems 2 and 3 remain even when *y* is declared as `volatile`. In these earlier versions, reads and writes of `volatile` variables cannot be reordered with reads and writes of other `volatile` variables, but they can be reordered with reads and writes of non-`volatile` variables. This type of reordering is prohibited in J2SE 5.0. Thus, if *Thread2* reads the value *true* for *y*, it is guaranteed to see the write of 0 to *x* that happened before the write of *true* to *y*, even though *x* is not `volatile`.

The compiler ensures that the reordering rules for `volatile` variables are obeyed by emitting special memory barrier instructions, which control the interactions among the caches, memory, and CPUs. The atomic XADD (Exchange and Add) instruction mentioned in Section 2.2.1 is an example of a memory barrier. Prior to executing an XADD instruction, the processor ensures that all previous read and write operations have been completed.

The semantics of `volatile` variables and other issues related to shared memory consistency in Java are spelled out in the Java Memory Model, which is part of the Java Language Specification. The goal of the Java Memory Model is to ensure that multithreaded Java programs can be implemented correctly on a variety of hardware platforms and with a variety of compiler and hardware optimizations. Programmers can rely on the guarantees provided by the Java Memory Model when they are reasoning about the possible behavior of their programs. The original Java Memory Model had several flaws [Pugh 2000] that were fixed in J2SE 5.0. Since C++ does not have threads built into the language, C++ does not have a memory model like Java's. The reorderings that are permitted in a multithreaded C++ program depend on the compiler, the thread library being used, and the platform on which the program is run [Meyers and Alexandrescu 2004a,b].

In the next two chapters we study higher-level synchronization constructs that are designed to hide some of the complexity we've seen in this chapter. Creating critical sections will be easier with these constructs, as will be execution tracing and replay. As it turns out, critical sections are exactly the place where special care is needed to ensure sequential consistency. Thus, these synchronization constructs are implemented with memory barrier instructions that guarantee sequential consistency as a side effect of using the constructs to create critical sections.

FURTHER READING

Our treatment of the critical section problem in Section 2.1 follows [Silberschatz et al. 1991]. The first solution to the two-process critical section problem was developed in 1962 by Th. J. Dekker [Dijkstra 1968]. Edsger Dijkstra [1965] presented the first solution to the n-process critical section problem. Dijkstra's solution satisfied mutual exclusion but was not starvation free. Knuth's [1966] solution remedied this, and further improvement's in the algorithm's fairness were presented by deBruijn [1967] and Eisenberg and McGuire [1972]. Lamport [1974] pointed out that all of these solutions assumed atomic reads and writes and presented his bakery algorithm (see Section 2.2.2). Anderson [2001] surveys Lamport's other contributions to research on mutual exclusion.

Mellor-Crummey and Scott [1991] analyzed the performance of five hardware-based busy-waiting solutions to the critical section problem for shared-memory multiprocessors. Adve and Gharachorloo [1995] have written a tutorial on shared memory consistency.

REFERENCES

Adve, Sarita V., and K. Gharachorloo (1995). *Shared Memory Consistency Models: A Tutorial*. Western Research Laboratory Research Report 95/7. http://www.research.digital.com/wrl/home.html.

Anderson, J. (2001). Lamport on mutual exclusion: 27 years of planting seeds. *Proc. 20th Annual ACM Symposium on Principles of Distributed Computing*, pp. 3–12.

Andrews, Gregory R. (1991). *Concurrent Programming: Principles and Practice*. Redwood City, CA: Benjamin-Cummings.

Choi, J., and H. Srinivasan (1998). Deterministic replay of Java multithreaded applications. *Proc. ACM Sigmetrics Symposium on Parallel and Distributed Tools*, pp. 48–59.

deBruijn, N. G. (1967). Additional comments on a problem in concurrent programming. *Communications of the ACM*, Vol. 10, No. 3, pp. 137–138.

Dijkstra, Edsger W. (1965). Solution of a problem in concurrent programming control. *Communications of the ACM*, Vol. 8, No. 9 (September), p. 569.

Dijkstra, Edsger W. (1968). Cooperating sequential processes. In F. Genuys (Ed.), *Programming Languages*. New York: Academic Press, pp. 43–112.

Dubois, M., C. Scheurich, and F. A. Briggs (1988). Synchronization, coherence, and event ordering in multiprocessors. *IEEE Computer*, Vol. 21, No. 2, pp. 9–21.

Eisenberg, M. A., and M. R. McGuire (1972). Further comments on Dijkstra's concurrent programming control problem. *Communications of the ACM*, Vol. 15, No. 11 (November), p. 999.

Knuth, D. (1966). Additional comments on a problem in concurrent programming. *Communications of the ACM*, Vol. 9, No. 5 (May), pp. 321–322.

Lamport, L. (1974). A new solution of Dijkstra's concurrent programming problem. *Communications of the ACM*, Vol. 17, No. 8 (August), pp. 453–455.

Lamport, L. (1979). How to make a multiprocessor computer that correctly executes multiprocess programs. *IEEE Transactions on Computers*, Vol. 28, No. 9 (September), pp. 690–691.

LeBlanc, T. J., and J. M. Mellor-Crummey (1987). Debugging parallel programs with Instant Replay. *IEEE Transactions on Computers*, Vol. 36, No. 4 (April), pp. 471–482.

Mellor-Crummey, John M., and Michael L. Scott (1991). Algorithms for scalable synchronization on shared-memory multiprocessors. *ACM Transactions on Computer Systems*, Vol. 9, No. 1 (February), pp. 21–65.

Meyers, Scott, and Andrei Alexandrescu (2004a), C++ and the perils of double-checked locking: Part I. *Dr. Dobb's Journal*, August, pp. 46–49.

Meyers, Scott, and Andrei Alexandrescu (2004b), C++ and the perils of double-checked locking: Part II. *Dr. Dobb's Journal*, September, pp. 57–61.

Pugh, William (2000). The Java memory model is fatally flawed. *Concurrency: Practice and Experience*, Vol. 12, No. 1 (January), pp. 1–11.

Silberschatz, A., J. L. Peterson, and P. Galvin (1991). *Operating Systems Concepts*. Reading, MA: Addison-Wesley.

EXERCISES

2.1. The following solutions are intended to solve the two-thread critical section problem. Thread0 and Thread1 execute the same code, which is shown below. When Thread0 executes the code, *i* is 0 and *j* is 1. When Thread1 executes the code, *i* is 1 and *j* is 0. Variable *turn* can be initialized to 0 or 1. The execution of the break statement inside the first while-loop transfers control to the statement immediately following the loop. For each solution, determine whether it guarantees mutual exclusion. If mutual exclusion is guaranteed, determine whether it guarantees progress. If mutual exclusion and progress are guaranteed, determine whether it guarantees bounded waiting. Justify your answers.

(a)
```
    while (true) {
            flag[i] = true;                    (1)
            while (flag[j]) {                  (2)
                if (turn != i) {               (3)
                    flag[i] = false;           (4)
                    while (turn == j) {;}      (5)
                    flag[i] = true;            (6)
                    break;                     (7)
                }
            }
            critical section
            turn = j;                          (8)
            flag[i] = false;                   (9)
            noncritical section
    }
```

(b)
```
    while (true) {
            flag[i] = true;                    (1)
            while (flag[j]) {                  (2)
                flag[i] = false;               (3)
                while (turn == j) {;}          (4)
                flag[i] = true;                (5)
            }                                  (6)
            critical section
            turn = j;                          (7)
            flag[i] = false;                   (8)
            noncritical section
    }
```

(c)
```
    while (true) {
            flag[i] = true;                    (1)
            turn = j;                          (2)
```

```
        while (flag[j] && turn== i) {;}        (3)
        critical section
        flag[i] = false;                       (4)
        noncritical section
    }
```

2.2. In Peterson's algorithm, is every assignment statement atomic? Explain.

2.3. The "eventual entry" requirement for the critical section problem is as follows: A thread that intends to enter its critical section must eventually succeed.

   (a) If the progress requirement is satisfied, does that necessarily imply that eventual entry is also satisfied? Explain.

   (b) If the bounded waiting requirement is satisfied, does that necessarily imply that eventual entry is also satisfied? Explain.

   (c) If the eventual entry requirement is satisfied, does that necessarily imply that progress and bounded waiting are also satisfied? Explain.

2.4. For Peterson's algorithm, is it necessary to assume that Thread0 and Thread1 have the same priority? Explain.

2.5. Suppose that we switch the order of the first two statements in Peterson's algorithm:

```
boolean intendToEnter0 = false, intendToEnter1 = false;
int turn; // no initial value for turn is needed.
```

T0		T1	
while (true) {		while (true) {	
turn = 1;	(1)	turn = 0;	(1)
intendToEnter0 = true;	(2)	intendToEnter1 = true;	(2)
while (intendToEnter1 &&	(3)	while (intendToEnter0 &&	(3)
turn == 1) {;}		turn == 0) {;}	
critical section	(4)	critical section	(4)
intendToEnter0 = false;	(5)	intendToEnter1 = false;	(5)
noncritical section	(6)	noncritical section	(6)
}		}	

   Does the modified solution guarantee mutual exclusion? Explain. If yes, does the modified solution guarantee progress and bounded waiting? Explain.

2.6. For the bakery algorithm in Section 2.2.2, assume that thread T_i, $i > 0$, has just executed statement (3) and thread T_k, $k \mathrel{!=} i$, is in its critical section. Prove that (number[i],i) > (number[k],k).

2.7. For the bakery algorithm in Section 2.2.2, the value of *number[i]* is not bounded.

(a) Explain how the value of *number[i]* grows without bound.

(b) One suggestion for bounding the value of *number[i]* is to replace the statement

number[i] = max(number) + 1;

with the statement

// *numThreads* is # of threads in the program
number[i] = (max(number) + 1) % numThreads;

Is this suggestion correct? Explain.

2.8. Simplify the bakery algorithm in Section 2.2.2 for the case where there are only two threads, Thread0 and Thread1. Use *turn$_0$* and *turn$_1$* to denote *number[0]* and *number[1]*, respectively. Try to simplify the algorithm as much as possible.

2.9. Suppose that a computer has an atomic *DecrementAndCompare()* function:

```
int DecrementAndCompare (int& v) { // done atomically
    v = v - 1;
    if (v>=0) return 0; else return 1;
}
```

(a) Is the following a correct solution to the n-thread critical section problem?

```
volatile int v = 1;
while (DecrementAndCompare(v)) {v++;}      // entry-section
// Note: Stay in the loop if 1 is returned
critical section
v++;                                        // exit-section
```

(b) How can *DecrementAndCompare()* be used to develop a critical section solution for *n* threads? Your solution does not have to satisfy the bounded waiting requirement.

2.10. Assume that each thread in Peterson's algorithm runs on a separate processor. Also assume that processors use a write buffer with bypassing capability. On a write, a processor inserts the write operation into a write buffer and proceeds without waiting for the write to complete. Subsequent reads are allowed to bypass any previous writes in the write buffer for faster completion. This bypassing is allowed as long as the read address does not match the address of any of the buffered writes (on the same processor). Can Peterson's algorithm fail if write buffers are used?

2.11. The java.concurrent.atomic package introduced in J2SE 5.0 provides class *AtomicBoolean* to store *Boolean* values. Method *set(b)* sets the stored value to *b*, while *getAndSet(b)* atomically replaces the stored value with value *b* and returns the previous value. Thus, *getAndSet()* is equivalent to the *testAndSet* instruction provided by some machines.

   (a) Show how to use *getAndSet()* to solve the critical section problem by writing a solution that is similar to the partial solution in Section 2.3.1.

   (b) Use *getAndSet()* to solve the critical section problem by writing a solution that is similar to the second solution in Section 2.3.3 (i.e., the one that use two loops).

   (c) Fine-tune your solution to part (b) by using the *exponential backoff technique*. If a thread's call to *getAndSet()* fails to acquire the lock, the thread should sleep for some random amount of time between 0 and 32 milliseconds. If the next call to *getAndSet()* also fails, double the maximum sleep time (i.e., the thread should sleep a random amount of time between 0 and 64 milliseconds). Continue doubling the maximum sleep time until it reaches some upper bound, then stop doubling the maximum sleep time if further calls fail. The idea behind this scheme is as follows. If a call to *getAndSet()* fails, threads are contending for the critical section. The contending threads should sleep a random amount of time (i.e., "back off") so that they all don't try to acquire the lock again at the same time. The more times *getAndSet()* fails, the more contention there is and the greater variability there should be in the amount of time threads should sleep before they try again.

2.12. Consider a program such as the following, which is similar to Listing 1.9:

int s = 0;

Thread0	Thread1
for (int i=0; i<2; i++) {	for (int i=0; i<2; i++) {
s = s + 1;	s = s + 1;
}	}

Modify this program so that Thread0 and Thread1 take turns incrementing *s*, starting with Thread0. Use one of the solutions to the critical section problem to create critical sections for Thread0 and Thread1. Then use an integer to keep track of whose turn it is to do the increment. If a thread tries to increment *s* out of turn, it should busy-wait in a loop until its turn arrives.

2.13. Consider the following programs, which are executed concurrently on three processors:

int a, b, c, = 0;

P1	P2	P3
(1) a = 1;	(3) b = 1;	(5) c = 1;
(2) output(bc);	(4) output(ac);	(6) output(ab);

Function *output()* atomically reads and displays the values of the variables passed as arguments. For example, if the statements are executed in the order (1), (2), (3), (4), (5), (6), the program displays 001011.

(a) Assume that the processors execute the statements in program order [i.e., (1) before (2), (3) before (4), and (5) before (6)]. How many possible interleavings of the statements are there?

(b) If processors are allowed to execute the statements out of program order, how many possible interleavings are there?

(c) Is there any interleaving that preserves program order and that produces the output 111111? If so, show an interleaving. You can assume that only a single copy of shared variables a, b, and c, exists (i.e., that shared variables are not cached).

(d) Is there any interleaving, either preserving program order or not preserving program order, that produces the output 011001? If so, show an interleaving. You can assume that only a single copy of shared variables a, b, and c, exists (i.e., that shared variables are not cached).

(e) Repeat part (d), but this time assume that multiple copies of shared variables a, b, and c can exist (as in a cache-based system) and that the copies may not be updated at the same time. This allows different processors to observe different interleavings during the same execution.

3

SEMAPHORES AND LOCKS

Semaphores and locks are synchronization objects. *Semaphores* are used to provide mutual exclusion and condition synchronization. *Locks* provide mutual exclusion and have special properties that make them useful in object-oriented programs. In this chapter we learn how to use semaphores and locks to create critical sections and solve various programming problems. We then see how semaphores and locks are supported in Java, Win32, and Pthreads. Finally, we show how to build custom semaphore and lock classes that support testing and replay.

3.1 COUNTING SEMAPHORES

A *counting semaphore* is a synchronization object that is initialized with an integer value and then accessed through two operations, named *P* and *V* [Dijkstra 1965]. These operations are sometimes called *down* and *up*, *decrement* and *increment*, or *wait* and *signal*, respectively. (The classes in our synchronization library support all these names.) Traditionally, a counting semaphore is defined as a special integer-valued variable that is passed as a parameter to procedures *P()* and *V()*. We use an object-oriented definition in which a counting semaphore is an instance of a class named *countingSemaphore*:

Modern Multithreading: Implementing, Testing, and Debugging Multithreaded Java and C++/Pthreads/Win32 Programs, By Richard H. Carver and Kuo-Chung Tai

```
class countingSemaphore {
    public countingSemaphore(int initialPermits) {permits = initialPermits;}
    public void P() {...};
    public void V() {...};
    private int permits;
}
```

When defining the behavior of methods *P()* and *V()*, it is helpful to interpret a counting semaphore as having a pool of permits. A thread calls method *P()* to request a permit. If the pool is empty, the thread waits until a permit becomes available. A thread calls method *V()* to return a permit to the pool. A counting semaphore *s* is declared and initialized using

countingSemaphore s(1);

The initial value, in this case 1, represents the initial number of permits in the pool.

Here is a sketch of one of the many possible implementations of methods *P()* and *V()*. The private integer variable *permits* holds the current number of permits in the pool:

```
public void P( ) {
    if (permits > 0)
        --permits;         // take a permit from the pool
    else                   // the pool is empty so wait for a permit
        wait until permits becomes positive and then decrement permits by one.
}

public void V( ) {
    ++permits;             // return a permit to the pool
}
```

If a thread calls *P()* when the value of *permits* is zero, it waits until *permits* is positive, decrements *permits*, and then exits *P()*; otherwise, *permits* is positive, so the thread decrements *permits* and exits *P()*. Method *V()* increments *permits* and never blocks the thread that calls it. There may be many threads waiting in *P()* for a permit. The waiting thread that gets a permit as the result of a *V()* operation is not necessarily the thread that has been waiting the longest.

For a counting semaphore *s*, at any time, the following relation holds:

(the initial number of permits) + (the number of completed *s.V()* operations)
≥ (the number of completed *s.P()* operations).

This relation is referred to as the *invariant* for semaphore *s*. Notice that the invariant refers to "completed" *P()* and *V()* operations. A thread that starts a *P()*

operation may be blocked inside *P()*, so the operation may not be completed right away. Thus, the number of completed *P()* operations may be less than the number of started *P()* operations. For a counting semaphore, *V()* operations never block their caller and are always completed immediately.

We will try to avoid referring to the "value of semaphore *s*" when describing the behavior of *s*, since a semaphore's value is not clearly defined. Often, the value of a semaphore is taken to mean the number of available permits, which is expected to be a nonnegative number. In the sample implementation above, the variable *permits* represents the number of available permits, and *permits* is never negative, so variable *permits* could be used as the "value of s." However, this is an implementation detail that may not always hold. In other implementations of *P()* and *V()*, *permits* can have a negative value when threads are waiting for a permit.

Class *countingSemaphore* does not provide any methods for accessing the value of a semaphore; only *P()* and *V()* are provided. Even if the value were available, it would not be useful since the value could be changed by a *P()* or *V()* operation immediately after it was retrieved. Thus, we rely on a semaphore's invariant to define its behavior.

The implementation above defines *P()* and *V()* without specifying any details about how to implement the *wait* operation in *P()* or how to provide mutual exclusion for accessing shared variable *permits*. Later, we discuss these implementation issues and provide Java and C++ implementations of class *countingSemaphore*.

3.2   USING SEMAPHORES

Learning to use semaphores takes practice. There are, however, some common idioms or minipatterns in the way semaphores are used to solve problems. These patterns are described below. Being able to recognize and apply these patterns is a first step toward understanding and writing semaphore-based programs.

3.2.1   Resource Allocation

Consider the problem where three threads are contending for two resources. If neither resource is available, a thread must wait until one of the resources is released by another thread. Listing 3.1 shows a semaphore solution to this problem. The *countingSemaphore s* is initialized to 2, which is the initial number of available resources. Calls to *s.P()* and *s.V()* surround the use of a resource. If two of the threads are using resources, the third thread will be blocked when it executes *s.P()*. A thread executing *s.V()* makes its resource available to the other threads. This means that a thread that is blocked in an *s.P()* operation will be awakened when *s.V()* is performed. The invariant for semaphore *s* and the placement of the *P()* and *V()* operations guarantees that there can be no countingSemaphore s(2); //two resources are available initially

Thread1	Thread2	Thread3
s.P();	s.P();	s.P();
/* use the resource */	/* use the resource */	/* use the resource */
s.V();	s.V();	s.V();

Listing 3.1   Resource allocation using semaphores.

more than two consecutive completed *s.P()* operations without an intervening *s.V()* operation.

Counting semaphores provide a perfect solution to the resource allocation problem. The pool of permits represented by semaphore *s* maps directly to the managed pool of resources. For example, if the value of *s.permits* is 2, two resources are available. Methods *P()* and *V()* do all of the necessary bookkeeping internally: counting resources, checking the number of available resources, and blocking threads when no resources are available. Unfortunately, such a simple solution is not possible for every problem. Some problems require bookkeeping to be done outside methods *P()* and *V()*, and semaphores are used for other things besides managing resources.

3.2.2   More Semaphore Patterns

Listing 3.2 shows an alternative solution to the resource allocation problem. This solution is much more complicated, but it illustrates some commonly used semaphore patterns. In this solution, shared variable *count* tracks the number of resources available. Variable *count* is initialized to 2. When the value of *count* is greater than zero, a resource is available. The value of *count* is decremented when a resource is taken and incremented when a resource is released.

Shared variable *waiting* tracks the number of threads waiting. When a thread wants to use a resource, it checks the value of *count*. If *count* is less than or equal to zero, the thread increments *waiting* and then blocks itself by executing *resourceAvailable.P()*. When a thread releases a resource, it checks the value of *waiting*. If *waiting* is greater than zero, a waiting thread is notified that a resource is available; otherwise, *count* is incremented so that future requests for resources will be granted. Notice that *count* is not incremented when a waiting thread is notified, just as *count* is not decremented after a waiting thread receives a resource. This solution contains several patterns that commonly appear in semaphore-based solutions. These patterns rely on the semaphore invariant and the placement of *P()* and *V()* operations to create the necessary synchronization.

Mutex   Semaphores can be used to solve the critical section problem. A semaphore, typically named *mutex* (for "mutual exclusion") is initialized to 1. A

```
// variables shared by the threads
int count = 2;                          // number of available resources
int waiting = 0;                        // number of waiting threads
// provides mutual exclusion for count and waiting
countingSemaphore mutex = new countingSemaphore(1);
// used as a queue of blocked threads
countingSemaphore resourceAvailable = new countingSemaphore(0);
Thread i { // each thread executes the following code:
mutex.P();                              // enter the critical section

if (count>0) {                          // is a resource available?
   count--;                             // one less resource available
   mutex.V();                           // exit the critical section
}
else {
   waiting++;                           // one more waiting thread
   mutex.V();                           // exit the critical section
   resourceAvailable.P();               // wait for a resource
}
/* use the resource */
mutex.P();                              // enter the critical section
if (waiting>0) {                        // are there waiting threads?
   --waiting;                           // one less waiting thread
   resourceAvailable.V();               // notify a waiting thread
}
else count++;                           // return a resource to the pool
mutex.V();
}
```

Listing 3.2   Alternative solution to the resource allocation problem.

critical section begins with a call to *mutex.P()* and ends with a call to *mutex.V()*:

```
mutex.P()
/* critical section */
mutex.V()
```

The semaphore invariant ensures that the completion of *P()* and *V()* operations alternates, which allows one thread at a time to be inside the critical section. In Listing 3.2, semaphore *mutex* is used to create critical sections for shared variables *count* and *waiting*.

Enter-and-Test   Often, a thread will enter a critical section and then test a condition that involves shared variables. In Listing 3.2, the test for available resources follows the call to *mutex.P()*:

```
mutex.P();
  if (count>0) {            // test for available resources; count is a shared variable
  ...;                      // count>0 means that resource is available
  }
  else {
  ...;
  resourceAvailable.P();   // wait for a resource
  }
```

One of the alternatives of the `if`-statement will contain a *P()* operation so that the thread can block itself until it is notified that the condition is satisfied.

Exit-Before-Wait   A thread executing inside a critical section will exit the critical section before blocking itself on a *P()* operation. *Exit-before-wait* is necessary since a thread that blocks itself in a critical section may create a deadlock. In Listing 3.2, when no resource is available, *mutex.V()* is executed before *resourceAvailable.P()*.

```
mutex.V();                 // exit critical section
resourceAvailable.P();     // wait for a resource
```

If a thread did not call *mutex.V()* to leave the critical section before it called *resourceAvailable.P()*, no other threads would be able to enter the critical section, and no calls to *resourceAvailable.V()* would ever occur. *Exit-before-Wait* is a useful pattern, but it is also the source of subtle programming errors. In Section 3.4 we show one way to make this pattern safer.

Condition Queue   A semaphore can be used as a queue of threads that are waiting for a condition to become true. If the initial value of a semaphore *s* is 0, and the number of started *s.P()* operations is never less than the number of *s.V()* operations completed, the semaphore invariant ensures that every *s.P()* operation is guaranteed to block the calling thread. This indicates that *s* is being used as a queue, not as a resource counter.

In Listing 3.2, semaphore *resourceAvailable* is used as a queue of threads that are waiting for a resource to become available. Semaphore *resourceAvailable* is initialized to 0, and all *resourceAvailable.V()* operations are performed when at least one thread is waiting:

```
if (waiting>0)             // if one or more threads are waiting
  resourceAvailable.V();   // then notify a blocked thread
```

Under these conditions, a call to *resourceAvailable.P()* will always block the calling thread and a call to *resourceAvailable.V()* will always unblock a waiting thread.

These patterns represent the building blocks of semaphore solutions. We will see these patterns and several others used throughout the example programs in Section 3.5.

3.3 BINARY SEMAPHORES AND LOCKS

The *mutex* pattern is the most commonly used semaphore pattern and it deserves a closer look. A semaphore named *mutex* is initialized with the value 1. The calls to *mutex.P()* and *mutex.V()* create a critical section [Dijkstra 1968]:

Thread1	Thread2
mutex.P();	mutex.P();
/* critical section */	/* critical section */
mutex.V();	mutex.V();

Due to the initial value 1 for *mutex* and the placement of *mutex.P()* and *mutex.V()* around the critical section, a *mutex.P()* operation will be completed first, then *mutex.V()*, then *mutex.P()*, and so on. For this pattern, we can let *mutex* be a counting semaphore, or we can use a more restrictive type of semaphore called a *binary semaphore*.

A binary semaphore must be initialized with the value 1 or 0, and the completion of *P()* and *V()* operations must alternate. (Note that *P()* and *V()* operations can be started in any order, but their completions must alternate.) If the initial value of the semaphore is 1, which is the case for critical sections, the first operation completed must be *P()*. If a *V()* operation is attempted first, the *V()* operation will block its caller. Similarly, if the initial value of the semaphore is 0, the first completed operation must be *V()*. Thus, the *P()* and *V()* operations of a binary semaphore may block the calling threads. Recall that counting semaphores have a blocking *P()* operation, but the *V()* operation never blocks the calling thread.

A third type of synchronization object, called a *mutex lock* or simply *lock*, can also be used to solve the critical section problem. (Locks can provide mutual exclusion but not condition synchronization.) The operations on a lock are named *lock()* and *unlock()*. The *Mutex* pattern for locks and semaphores looks the same:

mutexLock mutex;

Thread1	Thread2
mutex.lock();	mutex.lock();
/* critical section */	/* critical section */
mutex.unlock();	mutex.unlock();

Unlike a semaphore, a lock has an owner, and ownership plays an important role in the behavior of a lock:

- A thread requests ownership of lock L by calling *L.lock()*.
- A thread that calls *L.lock()* becomes the owner if no other thread owns the lock; otherwise, the thread is blocked.
- A thread releases its ownership of L by calling *L.unlock()*. If the thread does not own L, the call to *L.unlock()* generates an error.
- A thread that already owns lock L and calls *L.lock()* again is not blocked. In fact, it is common for a thread to request and receive ownership of a lock that it already owns. But the owning thread must call *L.unlock()* the same number of times that it called *L.lock()* before another thread can become L's owner.
- A lock that allows its owning thread to lock it again is called a *recursive* lock.

Locks are commonly used in the methods of classes. This is illustrated by the following class:

```
class lockableObject {
    public void F() {
        mutex.lock();
        ...;
        mutex.unlock();
    }
    public void G() {
        mutex.lock();
        ...; F(); ...;                   // method G() calls method F()
        mutex.unlock();
    }
    private mutexLock mutex;
}
```

Lock *mutex* in class *lockableObject* is used to turn methods $F()$ and $G()$ into critical sections. Thus, only one thread at a time can execute inside a method of a *lockableObject*. When a thread calls method $G()$, the *mutex* is locked. When method $G()$ calls method $F()$, *mutex.lock()* is executed in $F()$, but the calling thread is not blocked since it already owns *mutex*. If *mutex* were a binary semaphore instead of a lock, the call from $G()$ to $F()$ would block the calling thread when *mutex.P()* was executed in $F()$. (Recall that completions of $P()$ and $V()$ operations on a binary semaphore must alternate.) This would create a deadlock since no other threads would be able execute inside $F()$ or $G()$.

There are several differences between locks and binary semaphores:

- For a binary semaphore, if two calls are made to *P()* without any intervening call to *V()*, the second call will block. But a thread that owns a lock and requests ownership again is not blocked. (Beware of the fact that locks are not always recursive, so check the documentation before using a lock.)
- The owner for successive calls to *lock()* and *unlock()* must be the same thread. But successive calls to $P()$ and $V()$ can be made by different threads.

Since locks are more flexible when it comes to calling methods, we will typically use locks instead of semaphores to create lockable objects. However, we will encounter situations where it is not possible to use locks without violating the ownership restriction. In such situations, we use binary or counting semaphores.

3.4   IMPLEMENTING SEMAPHORES

Semaphores can be implemented at the user level, the operating system level, or with hardware support. There are no commercial operating systems or any programming languages that we are aware of that provide semaphores supporting program replay. In this section we discuss how to implement semaphores. Later we present user-level semaphore implementations in Java and C++/Win32/Pthreads. We also show how these implementations can be extended to support execution tracing and replay, as well as an interesting testing technique.

3.4.1   Implementing *P()* and *V()*

Listings 3.3 and 3.4 show several possible implementations of operations *P()* and *V()*. These implementations illustrate various mechanisms for blocking and unblocking threads. Implementations 1 and 2 in Listing 3.3 are for *P()* and *V()* operations on counting semaphores. These implementations differ in how they handle the *wait* operation in *P()*. Implementation 1 uses busy-waiting to delay threads. Notice that when a waiting thread is awakened in *P()*, it must recheck the value of *permits*. It is possible that an awakened thread will always find that the value of *permits* is 0 and will thus never be allowed to complete its *P()* operation. Semaphores with this type of implementation are called *weak semaphores*.

Implementation 2 blocks waiting threads in a queue until they are notified. Blocking the threads avoids wasted CPU cycles but requires support from the underlying language or operating system. When a thread blocked in *P()* is awakened by a *V()* operation, the thread is allowed to complete its *P()* operation. This implements a *strong semaphore*. The Java class *countingSemaphore* presented later is based on Implementation 2.

```
// Implementation 1 uses semi-busy-waiting.
P():        while (permits == 0) {
                    Sleep(..);        // voluntarily relinquish CPU
            }
            permits = permits - 1;
V():        permits = permits + 1;
```

```
// Implementation 2 uses a queue of blocked threads; permits may be negative.
P():        permits = permits - 1;
            if (permits < 0) wait on a queue of blocked threads until notified;
V():        permits = permits + 1;
            if (permits <= 0) notify one waiting thread;
```

Listing 3.3   Implementations of *P()* and *V()* for counting semaphores.

```
//Implementation 3 uses two queues of blocked threads. V() may block calling
//thread.
P():        if (permits == 0)
                    wait in a queue of blocked threads until notified;
            permits = 0;
            if (queue of threads blocked in V() is not empty)
                    notify one blocked thread in V();

V():        if (permits == 1)
                    wait in a queue of blocked threads until notified;
            permits = 1;
            if (queue of threads blocked in P() is not empty)
                    notify one blocked thread in P();
```

Listing 3.4   Implementation of *P()* and *V()* for binary semaphores.

Implementation 3 in Listing 3.4 is for a (strong) binary semaphore. In Implementation 3, a thread executing *s.V()* on a binary semaphore *s* will be blocked if *permits* has the value 1. According to this implementation, the invariant for a binary semaphore *s* is the following:

((the initial value of *s* (which is 0 or 1))

+ (the number of completed *s.V()* operations)

− (the number of completed *s.P()* operations)) = 0 or 1.

Many books that define binary semaphores do not clearly indicate whether the *V()* operation is blocking or nonblocking. In this book we use a blocking *V()* operation. Java class *binarySemaphore* presented later is based on Implementation 3.

An implementation of *P()* and *V()* must ensure that mutual exclusion holds when the shared variables and queues in the implementation are accessed. Consider Implementation 1 in Listing 3.3. Suppose that the value of *permits* is 1. If several threads perform a *P()* operation at about the same time, one of the threads should decrement *permits* to 0 and the other threads should wait. Implementations of *P()* and *V()* can solve this n-thread critical section problem for shared variable *permits* by using one of the software or hardware solutions discussed in Chapter 2:

```
P():    entry-section;
        while (permits == 0) {
            exit-section;
            ;    // null-statement
            entry-section;
        };
        permits = permits - 1;
        exit-section;

V():    entry-section;
        permits = permits + 1;
        exit-section;
```

Operations *P()* and *V()* are now atomic actions.

Other solutions to the critical section problem can be used in the implementation of *P()* and *V()* if they are available. Java provides a construct that is similar to the mutex lock mentioned in Section 3.3. Java locks are used in the Java semaphore implementations presented in Section 3.6. The semaphore implementations that we have seen so far can be implemented at the user level. Semaphores can also be implemented at the operating system level. Listing 3.5 shows implementations of *P()* and *V()* as operations in the kernel of an operating system. Critical sections are created by disabling and enabling interrupts. For a shared-memory multiprocessor machine, disabling interrupts may not work, so atomic hardware instructions like those described in Section 2.3 can be used. [Andrews 2000] describes how to implement semaphores in the kernel.

3.4.2   *VP()* Operation

An additional semaphore operation that we use in this book is the *VP()* operation [Tai and Carver 1996]. Instead of writing

```
s.V();
t.P();
```

P(s):   disable interrupts;
        permits = permits - 1;
        if (permits < 0) {
            add the calling thread to the queue for s and change its state to blocked;
            schedule another thread;
        }
        enable interrupts;

V(s):   disable interrupts;
        permits = permits + 1;
        if (permits <= 0) {
            select a thread from the queue for s; change the thread's state to ready;
        }
        enable interrupts;

Listing 3.5   Implementation of *P()* and *V()* in the kernel of an operating system.

we combine the separate *V()* and *P()* operations into a single atomic *VP()* operation:

t.VP(s);

An execution of *t.VP(s)* is equivalent to *s.V()*; *t.P()*, except that during the execution of *t.VP(s)*, no intervening *P()*, *V()*, or *VP()* operations are allowed to be started on *s* and *t*.

We make the restriction that *t.VP(s)* can only be used in cases where the *V()* operation on *s* cannot block the calling thread. This means that *s* is a counting semaphore, or *s* is or a binary semaphore that is guaranteed to be in a state in which a *V()* operation will not block. We use the *VP()* operation extensively in Chapter 4, where due to the particular way in which we use *VP()*, this restriction is always guaranteed to be satisfied.

Consider the following program fragment:

binarySemaphore t(0);

Thread1	Thread2
s.V();	t.P();
t.P();	

Assume that a context switch occurs immediately after *Thread1* executes the *s.V()* operation. Then it is possible that the *t.P()* operation in *Thread2* will be executed before the *t.P()* in *Thread1* is executed. On the other hand, if *t.VP(s)* is used in *Thread1*, a context switch is still possible after the *s.V()* part of the *VP()* operation, but the *t.P()* part of the *VP()* operation is guaranteed to block *Thread1* before the *t.P()* operation blocks *Thread2*.

A context switch between successive *V()* and *P()* operations is often a source of subtle programming errors. A *V()* operation followed by a *P()* operation appears in the exit-before-wait pattern:

```
mutex.V();            // exit critical section
someCondition.P();    // wait until some condition is true
```

A thread T that executes *mutex.V()* releases mutual exclusion. Thus, other threads may enter their critical sections and perform their *mutex.V()* and *someCondition.P()* operations before thread T has a chance to execute *someCondition.P()*. This can create a problem, which is often in the form of a deadlock. Furthermore, an equivalent solution that does not use the exit-before-wait pattern can be difficult to find. The *VP()* operation removes these types of errors and, as we will see in later chapters, *VP()* will prove to be helpful for building classes that support testing and debugging.

The implementation of *t.VP(s)* is a combination of the implementations of *V()* and P() with one complication: Mutual exclusion must be obtained for both semaphores *s* and *t* when the *VP()* operation starts. This is necessary to prevent any other operations on *s* and *t* from completing while the *VP()* operation is in progress. However, the locking of *s* and *t* must be done carefully to avoid a deadlock. An implementation of *VP()* is presented in Section 3.6.

3.5 SEMAPHORE-BASED SOLUTIONS TO CONCURRENT PROGRAMMING PROBLEMS

In this section we present solutions to various classical synchronization problems. These problems were developed to demonstrate that a particular synchronization construct could be used to solve a commonly occurring synchronization problem.

3.5.1 Event Ordering

Assume that code segment *C1* in *Thread1* has to be executed after code segment *C2* in *Thread2*. Let *s* be a counting or binary semaphore initialized to 0.

Thread1	Thread2
s.P();	C2;
C1;	s.V();

The *s.P()* operation will block *Thread1* until *Thread2* does its *s.V()* operation. This guarantees that code segment *C1* is executed after segment *C2*.

3.5.2 Bounded Buffer

The bounded-buffer problem [Dijkstra 1965] was introduced in Chapter 1. A bounded buffer has *n* slots. Each slot is used to store one item. Items are deposited

```
int buffer[ ] = new int[n];
countingSemaphore emptySlots(n);
countingSemaphore fullSlots(0);

Producer {
    int in = 0;
    int item;

    ...
    /* produce item */
    emptySlots.P();          // wait if there are no empty slots
    buffer[in] = item;       // in is the index for a deposit
    in = (in + 1) % n;       // 0 ≤ in < n; and in = (out+#items in buffer)%n
    fullSlots.V();           // signal that a slot was filled
    ...
}


Consumer {
    int out = 0;
    int item;
    fullSlots.P();           // wait if there are no full slots
    item = buffer[out];      // out is the index for a withdraw
    out = (out + 1) % n;     // 0 ≤ out < n
    emptySlots.V();          // signal that a slot was emptied
    /* consume item */
}
```

Listing 3.6   Bounded buffer using semaphores.

into the buffer by a single producer and withdrawn from the buffer by a single consumer. A producer is not permitted to deposit an item when all the slots are full. A consumer is not permitted to withdraw an item when all the slots are empty.

The solution to the bounded-buffer problem in Listing 3.6 uses two counting semaphores for condition synchronization. Semaphores *fullSlots* and *emptySlots* are used as resource counters, counting the full and empty slots, respectively, in the buffer.

```
countingSemaphore fullSlots = 0;      // the number of full slots
countingSemaphore emptySlots = n;     // the number of empty slots
```

The condition (number of full slots+number of empty slots == n) is true before and after each *deposit* and *withdraw* operation. The producer deposits items into slot *buffer[in]* and the consumer withdraws items from slot *buffer[out]*. Since *in* and *out* cannot have the same value when the buffer is accessed, no critical section is required for accessing the slots in the *buffer*.

3.5.3 Dining Philosophers

There are n philosophers who spend their time eating and thinking [Dijkstra 1971]. They sit at a table with n seats. A bowl of rice sits in the center of the table. There is one chopstick between each pair of philosophers. When a philosopher is hungry, she picks up the two chopsticks that are next to her one at a time. When she gets her chopsticks, she holds them until she is finished eating. Then she puts down her chopsticks one at a time and goes back to thinking.

Solutions to the dining philosophers problem are required to be free from deadlock and starvation. In fact, the dining philosophers problem is the origin of the term *starvation*, which in this case refers to the possibility that a philosopher will literally starve if not allowed to eat. A classical deadlock situation is created in solutions that use a *hold-and-wait policy*. This policy allows a philosopher to hold one chopstick, which she is not willing to relinquish, while waiting on another chopstick.

In general, deadlocks can be avoided by preventing threads from holding some resources while waiting on others. This can be done by making a blocked thread give back its resources so that other threads will have enough, by forcing a thread to request all of its resources at once, or by ordering resource requests in a way that prevents deadlocks from occurring (see Section 3.7.3). Despite our best efforts, deadlocks may still occur, in which case deadlock detection becomes important. In Section 3.8.4 we describe a deadlock detection scheme that is built into our semaphore and lock classes.

An additional property, called *maximal parallelism*, may also be required. This property is satisfied by a solution that allows a philosopher to eat as long as her neighbors are not eating. This requirement is violated in hold-and-wait situations, where neighboring philosophers each hold only one chopstick and cannot eat.

Solution 1 In the solution in Listing 3.7, all n philosophers pick up their chopsticks in the same order. Each chopstick is represented as a binary semaphore, which serves as a simple resource counter that is initialized to 1. Picking up a chopstick is implemented as a *P( )* operation, and releasing a chopstick is implemented as a *V( )* operation.

For a program with five philosophers, the following execution sequence is possible:

- Philosopher 0 completes *chopsticks[0].P( )* and has a context switch.
- Philosopher 1 completes *chopsticks[1].P( )* and has a context switch.
- Philosopher 2 completes *chopsticks[2].P( )* and has a context switch.
- Philosopher 3 completes *chopsticks[3].P( )* and has a context switch.
- Philosopher 4 completes *chopsticks[4].P( )* and is blocked at *chopstick[0].P( )*.
- Each of philosophers 0, 1, 2, and 3 resumes execution and is blocked on her next *P( )* operation.

Now all five philosophers are blocked. A global deadlock occurs since each philosopher holds her left chopstick and waits forever for her right chopstick.

```
binarySemaphore chopsticks[ ] = new binarySemaphore[n];
for (int j = 0; j < n; j++) chopsticks[j] = new binarySemaphore(1);

philosopher(int i /* 0..n-1 */) {
    while (true) {
        /* think */
        chopsticks[i].P();                  // pick up left chopstick
        chopsticks[(i+1) % n].P();          // pick up right chopstick
        /* eat */
        chopsticks[i].V();                  // put down left chopstick
        chopsticks[(i+1) % n].V();          // put down right chopstick
    }
}
```

Listing 3.7   Dining philosophers using semaphores: Solution 1.

Solution 2   This solution is the same as Solution 1 except that only $(n - 1)$ philosophers are allowed to sit at a table that has n seats. A semaphore *seats* with initial value $(n - 1)$ is used as a resource counter to count the number of seats available. Each philosopher executes *seats.P()* before she picks up her left chopstick and *seats.V()* after she puts down her right chopstick. This solution does not satisfy maximal parallelism since it is possible that two neighboring philosophers hold a single chopstick but are unwilling to let each other eat. (There are enough chopsticks for every other philosopher to eat but only one actually does.) This solution is deadlock-free. If semaphores with first-come-first-serve (FCFS) *P()* and *V()* operations are used (see Section 3.6), this solution is also starvation free.

Solution 3   This solution is the same as Solution 1 except that one philosopher is designated as the "odd" philosopher. The odd philosopher picks up her right chopstick first (instead of her left chopstick). This solution is deadlock-free, and it is starvation free if semaphores with FCFS *P()* and *V()* operations are used. This solution does not satisfy maximal-parallelism.

Solution 4   In the solution in Listing 3.8, a philosopher picks up two chopsticks only if both of them are available. Each philosopher has three possible states: thinking, hungry, and eating. A hungry philosopher can eat if her two neighbors are not eating. After eating, a philosopher unblocks a hungry neighbor who is able to eat. This solution is deadlock-free and it satisfies maximal parallelism, but it is not starvation-free. A hungry philosopher will starve if whenever one of her neighbors puts her chopstick down the neighbor on her other side is eating. This scheme can be extended to prevent starvation even if the semaphores are not FCFS (see Section 4.2.3).

The key to this solution is the *self[k].V()* operation in function *test()*. Array *self[ ]* is an array of semaphores used to block philosophers who are unable to eat.

```
final int thinking = 0; final int hungry = 1; final int eating = 2;
int state[] = new int[n];
for (int j = 0; j < n; j++) state[j] = thinking;
// mutex provides mutual exclusion for accessing state[].
binarySemaphore mutex = new binarySemaphore(1);
// philosopher i blocks herself on self[i] when she is hungry but unable to eat
binarySemaphore self[] = new binarySemaphore[n];
for (int j = 0; j < n; j++) self[j] = new binarySemaphore(0);


philosopher(int i /* 0..n-1 */) {
    while (true) {
        /* think */
        mutex.P()
        state[i] = hungry;
        test(i);                // performs self[i].V() if philosopher i can eat
        mutex.V();
        self[i].P();            // self[i].P() will not block if self[i].V() was
        /* eat */               //     performed during call to test(i)
        mutex.P();
        state[i] = thinking;
        test((n + i - 1) %n);   // unblock left neighbor if she is hungry and can eat
        test((i +1) %n);        // unblock right neighbor if she is hungry and can eat
        mutex.V();
    }
}
void test(int k /* 0..n-1 */) {
// philosopher i calls test(i) to check whether she can eat.
// philosopher i calls test ((n + i - 1) % n) when she is finished eating to
// unblock a hungry left neighbor.
// philosopher i calls test((i + 1) % n) when she is finished eating to
// unblock a hungry right neighbor.
    if ((state[k] == hungry) && (state[(k+n-1) % n)] != eating) &&
        (state[(k+1) % n] != eating)) {
        state[k] = eating;
        self[k].V();     // unblock philosopher i's neighbor, or guarantee
    }                    // that philosopher i will not block on self[i].P().
}
```

Listing 3.8 Dining philosophers using semaphores: Solution 4.

Philosopher i blocks itself on semaphore *self[i]* when she is hungry but unable to eat. Philosopher i's first call to *test()* is to check whether her neighbors are eating:

- If neither neighbor is eating, Philosopher i executes *self[i].V()* in function *test()*. Since only Philosopher i executes a *P()* operation on *self[i]*, and since Philosopher *i* is obviously not blocked on semaphore *self[i]* at the time she executes *self[i].V()*, no thread is unblocked by this *V()* operation. Furthermore, since *self[i]* is initialized to 0, this *V()* operation does not block and Philosopher *i* is allowed to continue. The purpose of this *V()* operation is not clear until we notice that Philosopher *i* immediately thereafter executes *self[i].P()*, which, thanks to the *V()* operation just performed, is guaranteed not to block.

- If one or both of Philosopher *i*'s neighbors are eating when *test(i)* is called, *self[i].V()* is not executed, causing Philosopher *i* to be blocked when she executes *self[i].P()*.

The other two calls to *test()* that Philosopher *i* makes are to unblock hungry neighbors that are able to eat when Philosopher *i* finishes eating.

3.5.4   Readers and Writers

Data is shared by multiple threads [Courtois et al. 1971]. When a thread reads (writes) the shared data, it is considered to be a reader (writer). Readers may access the shared data concurrently, but a writer always has exclusive access. Table 3.1 shows six different strategies for controlling how readers and writers access the shared data. These strategies fall into one of three categories based on whether readers or writers get priority when they both wish to access the data:

1. R=W: readers and writers have equal priority and are served together in FCFS order.
2. R>W: readers generally have a higher priority than writers.
3. R<W: readers generally have a lower priority than writers.

Several strategies exist within each category due to changing priorities in specific situations. The strategies differ in the conditions under which permission

TABLE 3.1   Strategies for the Readers and Writers Problem

Access Strategy	Description
R=W.1	One reader or one writer with equal priority
R=W.2	Many readers or one writer with equal priority
R>W.1	Many readers or one writer, with readers having a higher priority
R>W.2	Same as R>W.1 except that when a reader arrives, if no other reader is reading or waiting, it waits until all writers that arrived earlier have finished
R<W.1	Many readers or one writer, with writers having a higher priority
R<W.2	Same as R<W.1 except that when a writer arrives, if no other writer is writing or waiting, the arriving writer waits until all readers that arrived earlier have finished

to read or write will be granted and, in some cases, permission may never be granted:

- In strategies R>W.1 and R>W.2, writers will starve if before a group of readers finishes reading there is always another reader requesting to read.
- In strategies R<W.1 and R<W.2, readers will starve if before a writer finishes writing there is always another writer requesting to write.
- In strategies R=W.1 and R=W.2, no readers or writers will starve.

Figure 3.9 compares strategies R<W.1 and R<W.2. This scenario contains events for two readers and two writers. In the shaded part at the top, Reader 1, Reader 2, and Writer 2 issue a request after Writer 1 finishes writing. Below the dashed line, the scenario is completed using the two different strategies. For strategy R<W.1, Writer 2 writes before the readers read. For strategy R<W.2, both readers are allowed to read before Writer 2 writes. Strategy R<W.2 requires Writer 2 to wait until the readers that arrived earlier have finished since Writer 2 requested to write when no other writer was writing or waiting. We are assuming that multiple request events can occur before a decision is made as to whether to allow a reader or writer to start. This assumption is important in order to distinguish between the various strategies.

Figure 3.10 compares strategies R>W.1 and R>W.2. This scenario contains events for three writers and one reader. In the shaded part at the top, Reader 1, Writer 2, and Writer 3 issue a request while Writer 1 is writing. For strategy R>W.1, Reader 1 reads before the writers write. For strategy R>W.2, both writers are allowed to write before Reader 1 reads. This is because Reader 1 requested to read when no other reader was reading or waiting, so Reader 1 must wait until the writers who arrived earlier have finished.

In our solutions to the readers and writers problem, threads execute *Read()* and *Write()* operations of the following form:

```
Read() {              Write() {
   entry-section         entry-section
   read                  write
   exit-section          exit-section
}                     }
```

The entry- and exit-sections implement one of the strategies in Table 3.1. Below, we show implementations for three of the strategies. The reader will surely agree that these implementations offer a terrific test of one's proficiency with semaphores.

R>W.1   This strategy gives readers a higher priority than writers and may cause waiting writers to starve. In Listing 3.11, semaphore *mutex* provides mutual exclusion for the *Read()* and *Write()* operations, while semaphores *readers_que* and *writers_que* implement the *Condition Queue* pattern from Section 3.2.2. In

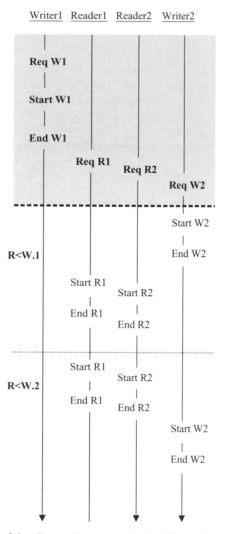

Figure 3.9   Comparing strategies R<W.1 and R<W.2.

operation *Write()*, a writer can write if no readers are reading and no writers are writing. Otherwise, the writer releases mutual exclusion and blocks itself by executing *writers_que.P()* The *VP()* operation ensures that delayed writers enter the *writer_que* in the same order that they entered operation *Write()*.

In operation *Read()*, readers can read if no writers are writing; otherwise, readers block themselves by executing *readers_que.P()*. At the end of the read operation, a reader checks to see if any other readers are still reading. If not, it signals a writer blocked on *writers_que*. A continuous stream of readers will cause waiting writers to starve.

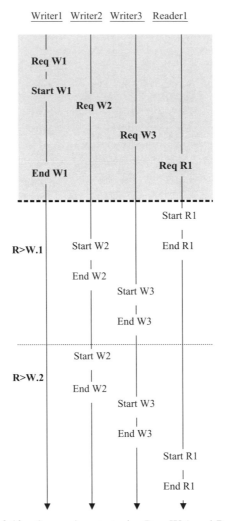

Figure 3.10 Comparing strategies R > W.1 and R > W.2.

At the end of a write operation, waiting readers have priority. If readers are waiting in the *readers_que*, one of them is signaled. This first reader checks to see if any more readers are waiting. If so, it signals the second reader, which signals the third, and so on. This cascaded wakeup continues until no more readers are waiting. If no readers are waiting when a writer finishes, a waiting writer is signaled.

This implementation illustrates another important semaphore pattern, called *passing-the-baton* [Andrews 2000]. Notice that delayed readers and writers exit their critical sections before they block themselves on *readers_que.P()* or *writers_que.P()*. This is part of the exit-before-wait pattern mentioned earlier.

```
int activeReaders = 0;                    // number of active readers
int activeWriters = 0;                    // number of active writers
int waitingWriters = 0;                   // number of waiting writers
int waitingReaders = 0;                   // number of waiting readers
binarySemaphore mutex = new binarySemaphore(1);        // exclusion
binarySemaphore readers_que = new binarySemaphore(0);  // waiting readers
binarySemaphore writers_que = new binarySemaphore(0);  // waiting writers
sharedData x ... ;                        // x is shared data
```

```
    Read() {                              Write() {
        mutex.P();                            mutex.P();
        if (activeWriters > 0) {              if (activeReaders > 0 ||
                                                 activeWriters > 0 ) {
            waitingReaders++;                     waitingWriters++;
            readers_que.VP(mutex);                writers_que.VP(mutex);
        }                                     }
        activeReaders++;                      activeWriters++;
        if (waitingReaders > 0) {             mutex.V();
            waitingReaders--;
            readers_que.V();                  /* write x */
        }
        else                                  mutex.P();
            mutex.V();                        activeWriters--;
                                              if (waitingReaders > 0) {
        /* read x */                              waitingReaders--;
                                                  readers_que.V();
        mutex.P();                            }
        activeReaders--;                      else if (waitingWriters > 0) {
        if (activeReaders == 0 &&                 waitingWriters--;
            waitingWriters > 0) {                 writers_que.V();
                waitingWriters--;             }
                writers_que.V();              else
        }                                         mutex.V();
        else                              }
            mutex.V();
    }
```

Listing 3.11   Strategy R>W.1.

However, after these delayed threads are signaled, they never execute *mutex.P()* to reenter the critical section. That is, we expect to see readers executing

```
readers_que.VP(mutex);    // exit the critical section
                          // (mutex.V()) and (readers_que.P())
mutex.P();                // reenter the critical section before continuing
```

but the *mutex.P( )* operation is missing. To understand why this operation is not needed, it helps to think of mutual exclusion as a baton that is passed from thread to thread. When a waiting thread is signaled, it receives the baton from the signaling thread. Possession of the baton gives the thread permission to execute in its critical section. When that thread signals another waiting thread, the baton is passed again. When there are no more waiting threads to signal, a *mutex.V( )* operation is performed to release mutual exclusion. This will allow some thread to complete a future *mutex.P( )* operation and enter its critical section for the first time.

This technique is implemented using an `if`-statement, such as the one used in the cascaded wakeup of readers:

```
if (waitingReaders > 0) {      // if another reader is waiting
     waitingReaders--;
     readers_que.V();          // then pass the baton to a reader (i.e., do not
                               // release mutual exclusion)
}
else
     mutex.V();                // else release mutual exclusion
```

When a waiting reader is awakened, it receives mutual exclusion for accessing shared variables *activeReaders* and *waitingReaders*. If another reader is waiting, the baton is passed to that reader. If no more readers are waiting, mutual exclusion is released by executing *mutex.V( )*. Andrews [1989] shows how to apply passing-the-baton to a wide variety of synchronization problems.

R>W.2   This strategy allows concurrent reading and generally gives readers a higher priority than writers. Writers have priority in the following situation: When a reader requests to read, if it is a *lead reader* (i.e., no other reader is reading or waiting), it waits until all writers that arrived earlier have finished writing. This strategy may cause waiting writers to starve.

In Listing 3.12, when a reader R executes *Read( )*:

- If one or more other readers are reading, R starts reading immediately.
- If one or more other readers are waiting for writers to finish, R is blocked on *mutex*.
- If no reader is reading or waiting, R is a lead reader, so R executes *writers_r_que.P( )*. If a writer is writing, R will be blocked on *writers_r_que* behind any waiting writers that arrived before R. (Writers that arrived before R executed *writers_r_que.P( )* before R did.) Otherwise, R can start reading, and writers will be blocked when they execute *writers_r_que.P( )*.

When a *Write( )* operation ends, semaphore *writers_r_que* is signaled. Waiting writers that arrived before a lead reader will be ahead of the reader in the queue

```
int activeReaders = 0;                    // number of active readers
mutexLock mutex = new mutexLock();   // mutual exclusion for activeReaders
// condition queue for waiting writers and the first waiting reader
binarySemaphore writers_r_que = new binarySemaphore(1);
sharedData x ... ;                        // x is shared data

Read() {
    mutex.lock();      // block readers if lead reader waiting in writers_r_que
    ++activeReaders;
    if (activeReaders == 1)
        writers_r_que.P();                // block lead reader if a writer is writing
    mutex.unlock();

    /* read x */

    mutex.lock();
    --activeReaders;
    if (activeReaders == 0)
        writers_r_que.V();                // allow waiting writers, if any, to write
    mutex.unlock();
}

Write() {
    writers_r_que.P();    // block until no readers are reading or waiting and
    /* write x */         //    no writers are writing
    writers_r_que.V();    // signal lead reader or a writer at the front of the queue
}
```

Listing 3.12   Strategy R>W.2.

for *writers_r_que*; thus, the lead reader will have to wait for these writers to finish writing.

This solution is interesting because it violates the exit-before-wait pattern described earlier. As a rule, a thread will exit a critical section before blocking itself on a *P()* operation. However, lead readers violate this rule when they execute *writers_r_que.P()* without first executing *mutex.V()* to exit the critical section. This is a key part of the solution. Only a lead reader (i.e., when *activeReaders* == 1) can enter the queue for *writers_r_que* since any other readers are blocked by *mutex.P()* at the beginning of the read operation. When the lead reader is released by *writers_r_que.V()*, the lead reader allows the other waiting readers to enter the critical section by signaling *mutex.V()*. These other readers will not execute *writers_r_que.P()* since (*activeReaders* == 1) is true only for the lead reader. (Note that the name of the semaphore *writers_r_que* indicates that multiple writers but only one reader may be blocked on the semaphore.)

R<W.2 This strategy allows concurrent reading and generally gives writers a higher priority than readers. Readers have priority in the following situation: When a writer requests to write, if it is a lead writer (i.e., no other writer is writing or waiting), it waits until all readers that arrived earlier have finished reading. This strategy and strategy R>W.2 are symmetrical. The solution in Listing 3.13 for R<W.2 differs from the solution in Listing 3.12 for R>W.2 as follows:

- Semaphore *readers_w_que* is used to allow a lead writer to block readers. Only one writer (a lead writer) can be blocked in this queue.
- Semaphore *writers_r_que* is renamed *writers_que*, since readers are never blocked in this queue. (When a reader executes *writers_que.P()* in its entry-section, it will never block; why? See Exercise 3.3.)
- Variable *waitingOrWritingWriters* is used to count the number of waiting or writing writers. At the end of a write operation, readers are permitted to read only if there are no waiting or writing writers.

When a writer W executes *Write()*:

- If one or more other writers are waiting for readers to finish, W is blocked on *mutex_w*.
- If no writer is writing or waiting, W is a lead writer, so W executes *readers_w_que.P()*. (If a writer is writing, *waitingOrWritingWriters* will be greater than 1 after it is incremented by W, so W will not execute *readers_w_que.P()*.) If a reader is reading, W will be blocked on *readers_w_que* behind any waiting readers; otherwise, W can start writing, and readers will be blocked when they execute *readers_w_que.P()*.
- W can be followed by a stream of writers. When the last of these writers finishes, it executes *readers_w_que.V()* to signal waiting readers. If a finishing writer always finds that another writer is waiting, readers will starve.

The use of *readers_w_que* ensures that readers that arrive before a lead writer have a higher priority. This is because readers and lead writers both call *readers_w_que.P()*, and they are served in FCFS order. When a reader blocked in *readers_w_que* is given permission to read, it executes *readers_w_que.V()* to signal the next waiting reader, who executes *readers_w_que.V()* to signal the next waiting reader, and so on. This cascaded wakeup continues until there are no more waiting readers or until the *readers_w_que.V()* operation wakes up a lead writer. The lead writer executes *writers_que.P()* to block itself until the readers have finished. The last reader executes *writers_que.V()* to signal the lead writer that readers have finished.

3.5.5 Simulating Counting Semaphores

Suppose that a system provides binary semaphores but not counting semaphores. Listing 3.14 shows how to use binary semaphores to implement the *P()* and

```
int activeReaders = 0;                    // number of active readers
int waitingOrWritingWriters = 0;          // number of writers waiting or writing
mutexLock mutex_r = new mutexLock();      // exclusion for activeReaders
// exclusion for waitingOrWritingWriters
mutexLock mutex_w = new mutexLock();
binarySemaphore writers_que = new binarySemaphore(1);    // waiting writers
// condition queue for waiting readers and the first waiting writer
binarySemaphore readers_w_que = new binarySemaphore(1);
sharedData x ... ;                         // x is shared data

    Read() {
        readers_w_que.P();      // serve waiting readers and lead writer FCFS
        mutex_r.lock();
        ++activeReaders;
        if (activeReaders == 1)
            writers_que.P();    // block writers reads are occurring
        mutex_r.unlock();
        readers_w_que.V();      // signal the next waiting reader or a lead writer

        /* read x */

        mutex_r.lock();
        --activeReaders;
        if (activeReaders == 0)
            writers_que.V();    // allow writing
        mutex_r.unlock();
    }


    Write () {
        // if a lead writer is waiting in readers_w_que, this blocks other writers
        mutex_w.lock();
        ++waitingOrWritingWriters;
        if (waitingOrWritingWriters == 1)   // true if this is a lead writer
            readers_w_que.P();  // block lead writer if there are waiting readers
        mutex_w.unlock();
        writers_que.P();        // block if a writer is writing or a reader is reading

        /* write x */

        writers_que.V();  // signal writing is over; wakes up waiting writer (if any)
        mutex_w.lock();
        -- waitingOrWritingWriters;
        if (waitingOrWritingWriters == 0)   // no writers are waiting or writing
            readers_w_que.V();              // so allow reading
        mutex_w.unlock();
    }
```

Listing 3.13   Strategy R<W.2.

```
class countingSemaphore {
    private int permits = 0;
    // provides mutual exclusion for permits
    private binarySemaphore mutex = new binarySemaphore(1);
    // condition queue for threads blocked in P
    private binarySemaphore delayQ = new binarySemaphore(0);
    public void P() {
        mutex.P();
        --permits;
        if (permits < 0){
            mutex.V();
            delayQ.P();
        }
        else
            mutex.V();
    }
    public void V() {
        mutex.P();
        ++permits;
        if (permits <= 0)
            delayQ.V();
        mutex.V();
    }
}
```

Listing 3.14 Implementing counting semaphores by using *P()* and *V()* operations on binary semaphores.

V() operations in a *countingSemaphore* class. Here is a possible execution scenario for four threads T1, T2, T3, and T4 that are using a *countingSemaphore s* initialized to 0:

1. T1 executes $s.P()$: T1 decrements *permits* to -1 and has a context switch immediately after completing the *mutex.V()* operation but before it executes *delayQ.P()*.

2. T2 executes $s.P()$: T2 decrements *permits* to -2 and has a context switch immediately after completing the *mutex.V()* operation but before it executes *delayQ.P()*.

3. T3 executes $s.V()$: T3 increments *permits* to -1 and executes *delayQ.V()*.

4. T4 executes $s.V()$: T4 increments *permits* to 0 and executes *delayQ.V()*. Since T3 just previously completed an $s.V()$ operation in which the value of *delayQ* was incremented to 1, T4 is blocked at *delayQ.V()*.

5. T1 resumes execution, completes *delayQ.P()*, and then completes its $s.P()$ operation.

6. T4 resumes execution and completes its *delayQ.V()* operation.

7. T2 resumes execution, completes *delayQ.P()*, and then completes its *s.P()* operation.

In step 4, T4 executes *s.V()* and is blocked by the *delayQ.V()* operation. If *V()* operations for binary semaphores are redefined so that they never block the calling thread, this scenario would not execute correctly (see Exercise 3.5).

3.6   SEMAPHORES AND LOCKS IN JAVA

The Java language does not provide a semaphore construct, but Java's built-in synchronization constructs can be used to simulate counting and binary semaphores. First, we describe how to create user-level semaphore and lock classes. Later, we extend them with the functions that are needed for testing and debugging. J2SE 5.0 (Java 2 Platform, Standard Edition 5.0) introduces package *java.util.concurrent*, which contains a collection of synchronization classes, including classes *Semaphore* and *ReentrantLock*. We also describe how to use these classes.

Following is an abstract class named *semaphore*:

```
public abstract class semaphore {
    protected abstract void P();
    protected abstract void V();
    protected semaphore(int initialPermits) {permits = initialPermits;}
    protected int permits;
}
```

Next we show a Java *countingSemaphore* class that extends class *semaphore* and provides implementations for methods *P()* and *V()*.

3.6.1   Class *countingSemaphore*

The implementations of methods *P()* and *V()* in class *countingSemaphore* are based on Implementation 2 in Listing 3.3, which is reproduced here:

```
// Implementation 2 uses a queue of blocked threads. The value of permits may be
// negative.
P(): permits = permits - 1;
     if (permits < 0) wait on a queue of blocked threads

V(): permits = permits + 1;
     if (permits <= 0) notify one waiting thread;
```

To complete this implementation, we need to provide mutual exclusion for accessing shared variable *permits* and implementations for the wait and notify operations. Java's built-in synchronization constructs, which include operations `wait` and `notify`, make this easy to do.

Each Java object is associated with a built-in lock. If a thread calls a method on an object, and the method is declared with the `synchronized` modifier, the calling thread must wait until it acquires the object's lock. Here are the declarations of synchronized methods *P()* and *V()* in class *countingSemaphore*:

```
public synchronized void P() {...};
public synchronized void V() {...};
```

Only one thread at a time can execute in the `synchronized` methods of an object. Java's implementation of a `synchronized` method ensures that the object's lock is properly acquired and released. If an object's data members are only accessed in `synchronized` methods, the thread that owns the object's lock has exclusive access to the object's data members.

We can use Java's `wait` operation to complete the implementation of *P()*. A thread must hold an object's lock before it can execute a `wait` operation. (The use of `synchronized` ensures that this restriction is satisfied.) When a thread executes `wait`, it releases the object's lock and waits in a *wait set* that is associated with the object. The thread waits until it is notified or interrupted. (A thread T is interrupted when another thread calls *T.interrupt().*) Here is the implementation of method *P()*:

```
synchronized public void P() {
  permit--;
  if (permit<0)
    try { wait(); }                          // same as this.wait();
  catch (InterruptedException e) {}
}
```

If a thread is interrupted before it is notified, the thread returns from `wait` by throwing *InterruptedException*. This is why `wait` usually appears in a `try`-`catch` block. Since none of our programs use interrupts, we have elected to catch *InterruptedException* with an empty `catch` block instead of adding the clause "*throws InterruptedException*" to the header of method *P()*. Threads that call *P()* are thus not required to handle *InterruptedException*, which is convenient, but unsafe if interrupts are possible. We discuss interrupts again in Chapter 4.

A `notify` operation notifies one of the waiting threads, but not necessarily the one that has been waiting the longest or the one with the highest priority. If no threads are waiting, a `notify` operation does nothing. Here is method *V()* using Java's `notify` operation:

```
synchronized public void V() {
  ++permits;
  if (permits <= 0)
    notify();                                // same as this.notify()
}
```

```
public final class countingSemaphore extends semaphore {
    public countingSemaphore(int initialPermits) {super(initialPermits);}
    synchronized public void P() {
        permits--;
        if (permits<0)
            try { wait(); } catch (InterruptedException e) {}
    }
    synchronized public void V() {
        ++permits;
        if (permits <=0)
            notify();
    }
}
```

Listing 3.15 Java class *countingSemaphore*.

A notified thread must reacquire the lock before it can begin executing in the method. Furthermore, notified threads that are trying to reacquire an object's lock compete with threads that have called a method of the object and are trying to acquire the lock for the first time. The order in which these notified and calling threads obtain the lock is unpredictable.

The complete implementation of class *countingSemaphore* is shown in Listing 3.15. Notice that this implementation does not allow threads that call *P()* to barge ahead of waiting threads and "steal" permits. When a waiting thread is notified, it may compete with other threads for the object's lock, but when it eventually reacquires the lock, it will not execute wait again. Instead, it will start executing in *P()* after the wait operation, which means that it will definitely be allowed to complete its *P()* operation.

This Java implementation of *countingSemaphore* does not guarantee a FCFS notification policy among waiting threads. That is, the order in which threads are notified is not necessarily the same order in which the threads waited. In Chapter 4 we discuss more details about Java's wait and notify operations and present semaphore implementations that guarantee a FCFS notification policy for waiting threads. These implementations are needed to build the testing and debugging tools described later.

We should also point out that Java implementations are permitted to perform *spurious wakeups* (i.e., wakeup threads without there having been any explicit Java instructions to do so). If spurious wakeups occur, class *countingSemaphore* may fail (see Exercise 3.18). A *countingSemaphore* implementation that deals with spurious wakeups and interrupts is given in Chapter 4.

3.6.2 Class *mutexLock*

Listing 3.16 shows Java class *mutexlock*. Class *mutexlock* is more flexible than the built-in Java locks obtained through the synchronized keyword. A

```java
public final class mutexLock {
    private Thread owner = null;   // owner of this lock
    private int waiting = 0;       // number of threads waiting for this lock
    private int count = 0;         // number of times mutexLock has been locked
    private boolean free = true;   // true if lock is free; false otherwise

    public synchronized void lock() {
        if (free) {
            count = 1; free = false;
            owner = Thread.currentThread();
        }
        else if (owner == Thread.currentThread()) {
            ++count;
        }
        else {
            ++waiting;
            while (count > 0)
                try {wait();} catch (InterruptedException ex) {}
                count = 1;
                owner = Thread.currentThread();
            }
    }

    public synchronized void unlock() {
        if (owner != null) {
            if (owner == Thread.currentThread()) {
                --count;
                if (count == 0) {
                    owner = null;
                    if (waiting > 0) {
                        --waiting;
                        notify(); // free remains false
                    }
                    else {free = true;}
                        return;
                    }
                else {
                    return;
                }
            }
        }
        throw new ownerException();
    }
}
```

Listing 3.16   Java class *mutexLock*.

mutexlock object can be locked in one method and unlocked in another, and one method can contain multiple calls to *lock()* and *unlock()*. On the other hand, calls to *lock()* and *unlock()* are not made automatically on method entry and exit as they are in synchronized methods.

Member variable *owner* holds a reference to the current owner of the lock. This reference is obtained by calling *Thread.currentThread()*, which returns the thread that is currently executing method *lock()*. The value of member variable *free* is *true* if the lock is not owned currently. A thread that calls *lock()* becomes the owner if the lock is free; otherwise, the calling thread increments *waiting* and blocks itself by executing *wait()*. When a thread calls *unlock()*, if there are any waiting threads, *waiting* is decremented and one of the waiting threads is notified. The notified thread is guaranteed to become the new owner, since any threads that barge ahead of the notified thread will find that the lock is not free and will block themselves on *wait()*. Member *count* tracks the number of times that the owning thread has called *lock()*. The owning thread must call *unlock()* the same number of times that it called *lock()* before another thread can become the owner of the lock.

3.6.3 Class *Semaphore*

Package *java.util.concurrent* contains class *Semaphore*. Class *Semaphore* is a counting semaphore with operations *acquire()* and *release()* instead of *P()* and *V()*. The constructor for class *Semaphore* optionally accepts a fairness parameter. When this fairness parameter is false, class *Semaphore* makes no guarantees about the order in which threads acquire permits, as barging is permitted. When the fairness parameter is set to true, the semaphore guarantees that threads invoking *acquire()* obtain permits in FCFS order.

Semaphore mutex = new Semaphore(1,true); // *mutex* is a FCFS semaphore
// initialized to 1

Thread1	Thread2
mutex.acquire();	mutex.acquire();
/* critical section */	/* critical section */
mutex.release();	mutex.release();

Class *Semaphore* also provides method *tryAcquire()*, which acquires a permit only if one is available at the time of invocation. Method *tryAcquire()* returns true if a permit was acquired and false otherwise.

if (mutex.tryAcquire()) { ... }

A limit can be placed on the amount of time that a thread will wait for a permit:

if (mutex.tryAcquire(50L, TimeUnit.MILLISECONDS)) {...}

This call to *tryAcquire()* acquires a permit from semaphore *mutex* if one becomes available within 50 milliseconds and the current thread has not been interrupted. Note that a call to the (untimed) *tryAcquire()* method does not honor the fairness setting. Even when a semaphore has been set to use a fair ordering policy, a call to *tryAcquire()* will immediately acquire a permit if one is available, whether or not other threads are currently waiting.

3.6.4   Class *ReentrantLock*

Package *java.util.concurrent.locks* provides a mutex lock class called *Rentrant-Lock* with methods *lock()* and *unlock()*. Class *ReentrantLock* has the same behavior and semantics as the implicit monitor lock accessed using synchro-nized methods and statements. Like class *Semaphore*, the constructor for class *ReentrantLock* accepts an optional fairness parameter. When set to true, priority is given to the longest-waiting thread. Class *ReentrantLock* also provides untimed and timed *tryLock()* methods that behave the same as the untimed and timed *tryAcquire()* methods of class *Semaphore*.

It is recommended that a call to *lock()* be followed immediately by a try block:

```
class illustrateTryBlock {
    private final ReentrantLock mutex = new ReentrantLock();
    public void foo() {
        mutex.lock();
        try {
            /* body of method foo() */
        } finally { // ensures that unlock() is executed
            mutex.unlock()
        }
    }
}
```

3.6.5   Example: Java Bounded Buffer

Listing 3.17 is a Java solution to the bounded buffer problem for two producers and two consumers. This solution is based on the solution in Listing 3.6. Since there are multiple producers and consumers, two *mutexLocks* are used. Lock *mutexD* provides mutual exclusion among the *Producers* and lock *mutexW* provides mutual exclusion among the *Consumers*. (No mutual exclusion is needed between *Producers* and *Consumers* since a *Producer* and a *Consumer* can never access the same slot simultaneously.)

A better programming style would be to move the four semaphores and the *P()* and *V()* operations that are executed on them into the methods of the *Buffer* class. We will save this step until Chapter 4, where we present a synchroniza-tion construct that better supports the concepts of encapsulation and information hiding.

```
public final class boundedBuffer {
    public static void main (String args[]) {
        final int size = 3;
        Buffer b = new Buffer(size);
        mutexLock mutexD = new mutexLock();      // exclusion for Producers
        mutexLock mutexW = new mutexLock();      // exclusion for Consumers
        countingSemaphore emptySlots = new countingSemaphore(size);
        countingSemaphore fullSlots = new countingSemaphore(0);
        Producer p1 = new Producer (b,emptySlots,fullSlots,mutexD,1);
        Producer p2 = new Producer (b,emptySlots,fullSlots,mutexD,2);
        Consumer c1 = new Consumer (b,emptySlots,fullSlots,mutexW,1);
        Consumer c2 = new Consumer (b,emptySlots,fullSlots,mutexW,2);
        p1.start(); c1.start();
        p2.start(); c2.start();
    }
}
final class Producer extends Thread {
    private Buffer b = null;
    private int num;
    private countingSemaphore emptySlots;
    private countingSemaphore fullSlots;
    private mutexLock mutexD;
    Producer (Buffer b, countingSemaphore emptySlots,
            countingSemaphore fullSlots, mutexLock mutexD, int num) {
        this.b = b; this.num = num;
        this.emptySlots = emptySlots; this.fullSlots = fullSlots;
        this.mutexD = mutexD;
    }
    public void run () {
        System.out.println ("Producer Running");
        for (int i = 0; i < 3; i++) {
            emptySlots.P();
            mutexD.lock();
            b.deposit(i);
            System.out.println ("Producer # "+ num + "deposited "+ i);
            System.out.flush();
            mutexD.unlock();
            fullSlots.V();
        }
    }
}
```

Listing 3.17 Java bounded buffer using semaphores and locks.

```
final class Consumer extends Thread {
    private Buffer b;
    private int num;
    private countingSemaphore emptySlots;
    private countingSemaphore fullSlots;
    private mutexLock mutexW;
    Consumer (Buffer b, countingSemaphore emptySlots,
            countingSemaphore fullSlots, mutexLock mutexW, int num) {
        this.b = b; this.num = num;
        this.emptySlots = emptySlots; this.fullSlots = fullSlots;
        this.mutexW = mutexW;
    }
    public void run () {
            System.out.println ("Consumer running");
            int value = 0;
            for (int i = 0; i < 3; i++) {
                fullSlots.P();
                mutexW.lock();
                value = b.withdraw();
                System.out.println ("Consumer # "+ num + "withdrew "+ value);
                System.out.flush();
                mutexW.unlock();
                emptySlots.V();
            }
    }
}
final class Buffer {
    private int[] buffer = null;
    private int in = 0, out = 0;
    private int capacity;
    public Buffer(int capacity) {
        this.capacity = capacity;
        buffer = new int[capacity];
    }
    public int withdraw () {
        int value = buffer[out];
        out = (out + 1) % capacity; // out is shared by consumers
        return value;
    }
    public void deposit (int value) {
        buffer[in] = value;
        in = (in + 1) % capacity; // in is shared by producers
    }
}
```

Listing 3.17   (*continued*)

3.7 SEMAPHORES AND LOCKS IN Win32

Win32 provides four types of objects that can be used for thread synchronization:

- Mutex
- CRITICAL_SECTION
- Semaphore
- Event

Mutex and CRITICAL_SECTION objects are Win32 versions of the lock objects we have been using, while Win32 Semaphores are counting semaphores. (Unfortunately, Win32 uses "CRITICAL_SECTION" as the name of the lock instead of the name of the code segment that the lock protects.) Semaphore, Event, and Mutex objects can be used to synchronize threads in different processes or threads in the same process, but CRITICAL_SECTION objects can only be used to synchronize threads in the same process.

3.7.1 CRITICAL_SECTION

A CRITICAL_SECTION is a lock object that can be used to synchronize threads in a single process. A CRITICAL_SECTION is essentially a Win32 version of the recursive *mutexLock* object described in Section 3.3:

- A thread that calls *EnterCriticalSection()* is granted access if no other thread owns the CRITICAL_SECTION; otherwise, the thread is blocked.
- A thread releases its ownership by calling *LeaveCriticalSection()*. A thread calling *LeaveCriticalSection()* must be the owner of the CRITICAL_SECTION. If a thread calls *LeaveCriticalSection()* when it does not have ownership of the CRITICAL_SECTION, an error occurs that may cause another thread using *EnterCriticalSection()* to wait indefinitely.
- A thread that owns a CRITICAL_SECTION and requests access again is granted access immediately. An owning thread must release a CRITICAL_SECTION the same number of times that it requested ownership before another thread can become the owner.

Listing 3.18 shows how to use a CRITICAL_SECTION. A CRITICAL_SECTION object must be initialized before it is used and deleted when it is no longer needed. Listing 3.19 shows class *win32Critical_Section*, which is a wrapper for CRITICAL_SECTION objects. Class *win32Critical_Section* hides the details of using CRITICAL_SECTIONs. The methods of *win32Critical_Section* simply forward their calls to the corresponding CRITICAL_SECTION functions. The CRITICAL_SECTION member *cs* is initialized when a *win32Critical_Section* object is constructed and deleted when the object is destructed.

```
CRITICAL_SECTION cs;        // global CRITICAL_SECTION
unsigned WINAPI Thread1(LPVOID lpvThreadParm) {
    EnterCriticalSection(&cs);
    // access critical section
    LeaveCriticalSection(&cs);
    return 0;
}
unsigned WINAPI Thread2(LPVOID lpvThreadParm) {
    EnterCriticalSection(&cs);
    // access critical section
    LeaveCriticalSection(&cs);
    return 0;
}
int main() {
    HANDLE threadArray[2];
    unsigned winThreadID;
    InitializeCriticalSection(&cs);
    threadArray[0]= (HANDLE)_beginthreadex(NULL,0, Thread1, NULL,0,
        &winThreadID );
    threadArray[1]= (HANDLE)_beginthreadex(NULL,0, Thread2, NULL,0,
        &winThreadID );
    WaitForMultipleObjects(2,threadArray,TRUE,INFINITE);
    CloseHandle(threadArray[0]);
    CloseHandle(threadArray[1]);
    DeleteCriticalSection(&cs);
    return 0;
}
```

Listing 3.18   Using a Win32 CRITICAL_SECTION.

```
class win32Critical_Section {
// simple class to wrap a CRITICAL_SECTION object with lock/unlock
operations
private:
    CRITICAL_SECTION cs;
public:
    win32Critical_Section () { InitializeCriticalSection(&cs); }
    ~win32Critical_Section () { DeleteCriticalSection(&cs);}
    void lock() { EnterCriticalSection(&cs);}
    void unlock() { LeaveCriticalSection(&cs);}
};
```

Listing 3.19   C++ class *win32Critical_Section*.

Class *win32Critical_Section* can be used to create lockable objects as shown in Section 3.3:

```
class lockableObject {
public:
   void F() {
      mutex.lock();
      ...;
      mutex.unlock();
   }
   void G() {
      mutex.lock();
      ...; F(); ...;        // method G() calls method F()
      mutex.unlock();
   }
private:
   ...
   win32Critical_Section mutex;
};
```

A better approach to creating lockable objects is to take advantage of C++ semantics for constructing and destructing the local (automatic) variables of a method. Listing 3.20 shows class template *mutexLocker<>* whose type parameter *lockable* specifies the type of lock (e.g., *win32Critical_Section*) that will be used to create a lockable object. The constructor and destructor for *mutexLocker* are responsible for locking and unlocking the *lockable* object that is stored as data member *aLockable*.

To make a method a critical section, begin the method by creating a *mutexLocker* object. A new *lockableObject* class is shown below. Methods *F()* and *G()* begin by constructing a *mutexLocker* object called *locker*, passing *locker* a *win32Critical_Section* lock named *mutex* to manage:

```
class lockableObject {
public:
   void F() {
      mutexLocker< win32Critical_Section > locker(mutex);
      ...
   }
   void G() {
      mutexLocker< win32Critical_Section > locker(mutex);
      ...; F(); ...;                // this call to F() is inside a critical section
   }
private:
   ...
   win32Critical_Section mutex;
};
```

```
template<class lockable> class mutexLocker {
public:
    mutexLocker(lockable& aLockable_) : aLockable(aLockable_) {lock();}
    ~mutexLocker() { unlock();}
    void lock() {aLockable.lock();}
    void unlock() {aLockable.unlock();}
private:
    lockable& aLockable;
};
```

Listing 3.20   C++ class template *mutexLocker*.

The locking and unlocking of *mutex* will occur automatically as part of the normal allocation and deallocation of local variable *locker*. When *locker* is constructed, *mute.lock()* is called. When *locker* is destructed, *mutex.unlock()* is called. It is now impossible to forget to unlock the critical section when leaving *F()* or *G()*. Furthermore, the destructor for *locker* will be called even if an exception is raised.

3.7.2   Mutex

A Mutex is a recursive lock with behavior similar to that of a CRITICAL_ SECTION. Operations W*aitForSingleObject()* and *ReleaseMutex()* are analogous to *EnterCriticalSection()* and *LeaveCriticalSection()*, respectively:

- A thread that calls W*aitForSingleObject()* on a Mutex is granted access to the Mutex if no other thread owns the Mutex; otherwise, the thread is blocked.
- A thread that calls W*aitForSingleObject()* on a Mutex and is granted access to the Mutex becomes the owner of the Mutex.
- A thread releases its ownership by calling *ReleaseMutex()*. A thread calling *ReleaseMutex()* must be the owner of the Mutex.
- A thread that owns a Mutex and requests access again is immediately granted access. An owning thread must release a Mutex the same number of times that it requested ownership, before another thread can become the owner.

Mutex objects have the following additional features:

- A timeout can be specified on the request to access a Mutex.
- When the Mutex is created, there is an argument that specifies whether the thread that creates the Mutex object is to be considered as the initial owner of the object.

Listing 3.21 shows how to use a Mutex object. You create a Mutex by calling the *CreateMutex()* function. The second parameter indicates whether the thread creating the Mutex is to be considered the initial owner of the Mutex. The last parameter is a name that is assigned to the Mutex.

```
HANDLE hMutex = NULL;                    // global mutex

unsigned WINAPI Thread1(LPVOID lpvThreadParm) {
    // Request ownership of mutex.
    DWORD rc =::WaitForSingleObject(
        hMutex,                          // handle to the mutex
        INFINITE);                       // wait forever (no timeout)
    switch(rc) {
        case    WAIT_OBJECT_0:           // wait completed successfully
                break;                   // received ownership
        case    WAIT_FAILED:             // wait failed
                // received ownership but the program's state is unknown
        case    WAIT_ABANDONED:
        case    WAIT_TIMEOUT: // timeouts impossible since INFINITE used
                PrintError("WaitForSingleObject failed at ",__FILE__,__LINE__);
                // see Listing 1.3 for PrintError().
                break;
    }

    // Release ownership of mutex
    rc = ::ReleaseMutex(hMutex);
    if (!rc) PrintError("ReleaseMutex failed at ",__FILE__,__LINE__);

    return 0;
}

unsigned WINAPI Thread2(LPVOID lpvThreadParm) {
    /* same as Thread1 */
}

int main() {
HANDLE threadArray[2];
    unsigned threadID;
    hMutex = CreateMutex(
        NULL,    // no security attributes
        FALSE,   // this mutex is not initially owned by the creating thread
        NULL);   // unnamed mutex that will not be shared across processes
    threadArray[0]= (HANDLE)_beginthreadex(NULL,0, Thread1, NULL,0,
        &threadID );
    threadArray[1]= (HANDLE)_beginthreadex(NULL,0, Thread2, NULL,0,
        &threadID );
    WaitForMultipleObjects(2,threadArray,TRUE,INFINITE);
    CloseHandle(threadArray[0]);   // release references when finished with them
    CloseHandle(threadArray[1]);
    CloseHandle(hMutex);
    return 0;
}
```

Listing 3.21   Using Win32 Mutex objects.

Unlike a CRITICAL_SECTION, a Mutex object is a kernel object that can be shared across processes. A Mutex's name can be used in other processes to get the handle of the Mutex by calling *CreateMutex()* or *OpenMutex()*. The fact that Mutex objects are kernel objects means that CRITICAL_SECTIONS may be faster than Mutexes. If a thread executes *EnterCriticalSection()* on a CRITICAL_SECTION when the CRITICAL_SECTION is not owned, an atomic *interlocked* test is performed (see Sections 2.2.1 and 2.3) and the thread continues without entering the kernel. If the CRITICAL_SECTION is already owned by a different thread, the thread enters the kernel and blocks. A call to *WaitForSingleObject()* on a Mutex always enters the kernel. In practice, the relative performance of CRITICAL_SECTIONS and Mutexes depends on several factors [Hart 2000b].

If a thread terminates while owning a Mutex, the Mutex is considered to be *abandoned*. When this happens, the system will grant ownership of the Mutex to a waiting thread. The thread that becomes the new owner receives a return code of WAIT_ABANDONED.

We can wrap a Mutex object inside a C++ class, just as we did for CRITICAL_SECTION objects. Instead of showing wrapper class *win32Mutex*, later we present a C++/Win32/Pthreads version of Java class *mutexLock*. This custom class guarantees FCFS notifications and can be extended to support tracing, testing, and replay.

3.7.3 Semaphore

Win32 Semaphores are counting semaphores. Operations *WaitForSingleObject()* and *ReleaseSemaphore()* are analogous to *P()* and *V()*, respectively. When a Semaphore is created, the initial and maximum values of the Semaphore are specified. The initial value must be greater than or equal to zero and less than or equal to the maximum value. The maximum value must be greater than zero. The value of the Semaphore can never be less than zero or greater than the maximum value specified.

```
HANDLE hSemaphore;
hSemaphore = CreateSemaphore(
    NULL,        // no security attributes
    1L,          // initial count
    LONG_MAX,    // maximum count (defined in C++ as at least 2147483647)
    NULL);       // unnamed semaphore
if (!hSemaphore)
    PrintError("CreateSemaphore",__FILE__,__LINE__);
```

The last parameter of *CreateSemaphore()* is a name that is assigned to the Semaphore. Other processes can use this name to get the handle of the Semaphore by calling *CreateSemaphore()* or *OpenSemaphore()*. A Semaphore is not considered to be owned by a thread—one thread can execute *WaitForSingleObject()* on a Semaphore and another thread can call *ReleaseSemaphore()*.

```
DWORD rc = WaitForSingleObject(
  hSemaphore,        // handle to Semaphore
  INFINITE);         // no timeout
switch(rc) {
  case      WAIT_OBJECT_0:
            break;                      // wait completed successfully
  case      WAIT_FAILED:
  case      WAIT_TIMEOUT:     // no timeouts possible since INFINITE used
            PrintError("WaitForSingleObject failed at ",__FILE__,__LINE__);
            break;
}


rc = ReleaseSemaphore(
  hSemaphore,        // handle to Semaphore
  1,                 // increase count by one
  NULL);             // not interested in previous count
if (!rc) PrintError("Release Semaphore failed at ",__FILE__,__LINE__);
```

The second argument for *ReleaseSemaphore()* specifies how much to increment the value of the Semaphore. Thus, many threads can be unblocked by a single call to *ReleaseSemaphore()*. The increment amount must be greater than zero. If the amount specified would cause the Semaphore's value to exceed the maximum value that was specified when the Semaphore was created, the value is not changed and the function returns FALSE. The last argument for *ReleaseSemaphore()* is the address of a long value that will receive the value of the Semaphore's count *before* incrementing the count.

When you are finished with the Semaphore, call *CloseHandle()* to release your reference to it:

```
CloseHandle(hSemaphore);
```

A simple C++ wrapper class called *win32Semaphore* is shown in Listing 3.22. The methods of class *win32Semaphore* forward their calls through to the corresponding Win32 Semaphore functions. To assist with testing and debugging, we'll need user-level lock and Semaphore classes. We can use *win32Semaphore* to implement both of these classes.

Class mutexLock   Class *mutexLock* in Listing 3.23 guarantees FCFS notifications. This C++ class is similar to the Java version of *mutexLock* in Listing 3.16 except for the way in which threads are blocked. The Java version blocks threads on calls to *wait()*. Here we block threads by calling a *P()* operation on a *win32Semaphore*. When a thread needs to wait in method *lock()*, it acquires a *win32Semaphore* from a pool of available Semaphores, inserts the Semaphore into a FCFS queue, and executes a *P()* operation on the Semaphore. In method

```cpp
#include <windows.h>
#include <limits.h>

const int maxDefault = LONG_MAX; //defined in C++ as at least 2147483647
class win32Semaphore {
private:
    HANDLE hSemaphore;
    int initialValue;
    int maxValue;
public:
    void P();
    DWORD P(long timeout);
    void V();
    win32Semaphore(int initial);
    win32Semaphore(int initial, int max);
    ~win32Semaphore();
};
win32Semaphore :: win32Semaphore(int initial) : initialValue(initial),
maxValue(maxDefault) {
    hSemaphore = CreateSemaphore(
        NULL,            // no security attributes
        initial,         // initial count
        maxValue,        // maximum count
        NULL);           // unnamed semaphore
    if (!hSemaphore)
        PrintError("CreateSemaphore",__FILE__,__LINE__);
}
win32Semaphore :: win32Semaphore(int initial, int max) : initialValue(initial),
        maxValue(max) {
    hSemaphore = CreateSemaphore(
        NULL,            // no security attributes
        initial,         // initial count
        maxValue,        // maximum count
        NULL);           // unnamed semaphore
    if (!hSemaphore)
        PrintError("CreateSemaphore",__FILE__,__LINE__);
}
win32Semaphore :: ~win32Semaphore() {
    DWORD rc = CloseHandle(hSemaphore);
    if (!rc)
        PrintError("CloseHandle",__FILE__,__LINE__);
}
```

Listing 3.22   Class *win32Semaphore*.

```
void win32Semaphore :: P() {
    DWORD rc = WaitForSingleObject(
    hSemaphore,          // handle to semaphore
    INFINITE);           // no timeout
    if (!rc)
      PrintError("WaitForSingleObject",__FILE__,__LINE__);
}
DWORD win32Semaphore :: P(long timeout) {
    DWORD rc = WaitForSingleObject(
    hSemaphore,          // handle to semaphore
    timeout);            // no timeout
    if (!(rc==WAIT_OBJECT_0)||(rc==WAIT_TIMEOUT))
      PrintError("WaitForSingleObject failed at ",__FILE__,__LINE__);
    return rc;
}
void win32Semaphore :: V() {
    DWORD rc = ReleaseSemaphore(
    hSemaphore,          // handle to semaphore
    1,                   // increase count by one
    NULL);               // not interested in previous count
    if (!rc)
      PrintError("ReleaseSemaphore failed at ",__FILE__,__LINE__);
}
```

Listing 3.22   (*continued*)

unlock(), ownership of the *mutexLock* is passed to a waiting thread by performing a *V()* operation on the Semaphore at the front of the queue. The unblocked
thread returns its *win32Semaphore* to the pool by calling *release()*.

The FCFS queue of Semaphores maintained by class *mutexLock* guarantees FCFS notifications for *mutexLock* objects. Each thread that is blocked in
method *lock()* is blocked on a *win32Semaphore* in the queue. The *unlock()*
operation unblocks the thread that has been blocked the longest. As we mentioned, *win32Semaphores* are acquired from a Semaphore pool and then returned
to the pool when they are no longer needed. This makes it possible to reuse
win32Semaphores instead of creating a new one each time a thread blocks. The
Semaphore pool initially contains a single Semaphore. If an attempt is made
to acquire a Semaphore when the pool is empty, the *acquire()* method creates
another Semaphore and adds it to the pool. This type of *resource pooling* is
commonly used for resources that are expensive to create.

Class countingSemaphore   Class *countingSemaphore* in Listing 3.24 uses a
FCFS queue of *win32Semaphores* to implement FCFS notifications just as
mutexLock did. Class *countingSemaphore* also provides an implementation of the
VP() operation. An execution of *t.VP(s)* performs a *V()* operation on *s* followed

```
class mutexLock {
// A FCFS mutex lock
private:
    semaphorePool pool;                          // pool of semaphores
    std::queue<win32Semaphore*> waitingLock;  // threads blocked in lock()
    unsigned long owner;
    int count;
    win32Semaphore mutex;      // mutual exclusion for lock() and unlock()
public:
    void lock();
    void unlock();
    mutexLock();
    ~mutexLock();
};
mutexLock::mutexLock(): owner(0), count(0), mutex(1) { }
mutexLock::~mutexLock() { }
void mutexLock::lock() {
    mutex.P();
    if (count == 0) { count = 1; owner = GetCurrentThreadId(); }
    else if (owner == GetCurrentThreadId()) {++count;}
    else  { // block threads
        win32Semaphore* s = pool.acquire();
        waitingLock.push(s);       // otherwise append semaphore
        mutex.V();                 // release mutual exclusion before blocking
        s->P(); // call to P() returns holding mutex since unlock() doesn't release it
        count = 1;
        owner = GetCurrentThreadId();
        pool.release(s);
    }
    mutex.V();
}

void mutexLock::unlock() {
    mutex.P();
    if (owner != 0) {
        if (owner == GetCurrentThreadId()) {
            --count;
            if (count == 0) {
                owner = 0;
                if (!waitingLock.empty()) { // any threads waiting for the lock?
                    // wakeup longest waiting thread
                    win32Semaphore* oldest = waitingLock.front();
```

Listing 3.23 Class *mutexLock*.

```
                        waitingLock.pop();
                        oldest->V();
                        // mutex not released so oldest thread completes P() next
                        return;
                    }
                else { mutex.V(); return; }
            }
            else { mutex.V(); return; }
        }
        else {
            std::cout << "unlock failed at line " << __LINE__ << " in "
            << __FILE__ << " with error: Calling thread is not the owner."
            << std::endl; exit(1);
        }
    }
    else {
        std::cout << "unlock failed at line " << __LINE__ << " in " << __FILE__
        << " with error: Calling thread is not the owner."<< std::endl;
        exit(1);
    }
}
```

Listing 3.23   (*continued*)

by a *P()* operation on *t*. The *VP()* operation must lock both Semaphores before either operation is begun. This locking must be done carefully. Consider the case where two threads are performing a *VP()* operation on the same two Semaphores:

Thread1	Thread2
t.VP(s);	s.VP(t);

If thread1 succeeds in locking *s* while thread2 succeeds in locking *t*, neither thread will be able to lock its other Semaphore, resulting in a deadlock. To prevent this circular waiting condition from occurring, the locks for the two Semaphores are always acquired in the same order. This is accomplished by giving each Semaphore a unique ID and forcing the *VP()* operation to lock the Semaphore with the lowest ID first.

The *V()* part of a *VP()* operation must satisfy the requirement that it will not block. This is checked by *VP()*. If a *V()* is attempted on a binary Semaphore whose *permits* value is 1, the *VP()* operation fails. If the *P()* part of the operation is required to block, *VP()* releases both Semaphore locks and blocks the calling thread.

```
class countingSemaphore : public semaphore {
// a countingSemaphore with FCFS notifications
private:
    std::queue<win32Semaphore*> waitingP;    // queue of threads blocked on P
    bool doP();
    semaphorePool pool;                      // pool of semaphores
    virtual bool isBinary() {return false;}
public:
    countingSemaphore(int initialPermits);
    void P();
    void V();
    void VP(semaphore* vSem);
};

countingSemaphore::countingSemaphore(int initialPermits) :
semaphore(initialPermits) {}

void countingSemaphore::P() {
    lock();                        // lock is inherited from class Semaphore
    --permits;
    if (permits>=0) {unlock(); return; }
    // each thread blocks on its own semaphore
    win32Semaphore* s = pool.acquire();
    waitingP.push(s);                         // append the semaphore
    unlock();
    s->P();                                   // block on the semaphore
    pool.release(s);
}

void countingSemaphore::V() {
// each thread blocks on its own semaphore
    lock(); // lock semaphore
    ++permits;
    if (permits>0) { unlock(); return; }
    win32Semaphore* oldest = waitingP.front();
    waitingP.pop();
    oldest->V();
    unlock(); // end synchronized(this) to avoid doing s.P() while
}               // holding the lock on this semaphore

bool countingSemaphore::doP() {
// Called by VP() operation; checks permits and returns true if P() should block;
// false otherwise.
    --permits;
```

Listing 3.24   C++/Win32 class *countingSemaphore*.

```
      if (permits>=0)
         return false;      // P() does not block
      else
         return true;       // P() does block
}

void countingSemaphore::VP(semaphore* vSem) {
// Execute {vSem->V(); this->P();} without any intervening P() or V() operations
// on this or vSem. Return 0 if this operation fails.
// Lock the semaphores in ascending order of IDs to prevent circular deadlock (i.e.,
// T1 holds the lock of this and waits for vSem's lock while T2 holds vSem's lock
// and waits for the lock of this)
      semaphore* first = this;
      semaphore* second = vSem;
      if (this->getSemaphoreID() > vSem->getSemaphoreID()) {
         first = vSem;
         second = this;
      }
      first->lock();
      second->lock();
      //vSem.V() must not block
      if (vSem->permits==1 && vSem->isBinarySemaphore()) {
        // method isBinarySemaphore() is inherited from class semaphore
         std::cout << "VP failed at line " << __LINE__ << " in " << __FILE__
            << " with error: V operation will block." << std::endl;
         exit(1);
      }
      // perform vSem.V()
      vSem->V(); // okay to already hold vSem's lock (which is first or second)
                 //    since it is a recursive lock
      // perform this->P()
      bool blockingP = doP();
      if (!blockingP) {
         second->unlock();
         first->unlock();
      }
      // each thread blocks on own semaphore
      win32Semaphore* s = pool.acquire();
      waitingP.push(s);                        // otherwise append blocked thread
      second->unlock();                        // unlock semaphores before blocking
      first->unlock();
      s->P();                   // s is already in waitingP so FCFS is enforced
      pool.release(s);
}
```

Listing 3.24   (*continued*)

3.7.4 Events

One thread can signal the occurrence of an activity or event to one or more other threads using a Win32 Event object. An Event can be either a manual-reset or auto-reset Event. The state of an Event is either *signaled* or *nonsignaled*. When an Event is created, the initial state (signaled or nonsignaled) and the type (manual-reset or auto-reset) is specified. When the state of a manual-reset Event object is set to signaled, it remains signaled until it is explicitly reset to nonsignaled by the *ResetEvent()* function. Any number of waiting threads, or threads that subsequently begin wait operations for the Event object specified, can be released while the object's state is signaled. When the state of an auto-reset Event object is set to signaled, it remains signaled until a single waiting thread is released; the system then automatically resets the state to nonsignaled.

The state of an Event is changed using operations *SetEvent()*, *ResetEvent()*, or *PulseEvent()*:

- For an auto-reset Event, *SetEvent()* sets the state to signaled until one waiting thread is released. That is, if one or more threads are waiting, one will be released and the state will be reset to nonsignaled. If no threads are waiting, the state will stay signaled until one thread waits, at which time the waiting thread will be released and the state will be returned to nonsignaled. For a manual-reset Event, all waiting threads are released and the state remains signaled until it is reset by *ResetEvent()*. Setting an Event that is already in the signaled state has no effect.
- *ResetEvent()* sets the state to nonsignaled (for both manual-reset and auto-reset Events). Resetting an Event that is already in the nonsignaled state has no effect.
- For a manual-reset Event, *PulseEvent()* sets the state to signaled, wakes up all waiting threads, then returns the state to nonsignaled. For an auto-reset Event, *PulseEvent()* sets the state to signaled, wakes up a single waiting thread (if one is waiting), then returns the state to nonsignaled. If no threads are waiting, *PulseEvent()* simply sets the state to nonsignaled and returns.

We used a manual-reset Event in the implementation of the C++/Win32 *Thread* class from Chapter 1. Listing 3.25 shows several methods of class *Thread*. Recall from Chapter 1 that the *Thread* class constructor calls Win32 function *_beginthreadex()* to create a new Win32 thread. Several arguments are passed to *_beginthreadex()*, including:

- Thread::*startThread()*: the startup method for the Win32 thread.
- (LPVOID) this: a pointer to the *Thread* object that is being constructed. This pointer is forwarded to method *startThread()*.

Method *startThread()* casts its void* pointer parameter to *Thread** and then calls the *run()* method of the *Thread*. When *run()* returns, *startThread()* calls

```
Thread::Thread(std::auto_ptr<Runnable> runnable_) : runnable(runnable_) {
    if (runnable.get() == NULL)
        PrintError("Thread(std::auto_ptr<Runnable> runnable_) failed at ",
            __FILE__,__LINE__);
    completionEvent = CreateEvent(
        NULL,           // no security attributes
        1,              // manual reset Event
        0,              // initially nonsignaled
        NULL);          // unnamed event

    hThread = (HANDLE)_beginthreadex(NULL,0, Thread::startThreadRunnable,
        (LPVOID)this, CREATE_SUSPENDED, &winThreadID );
    if (!hThread)
        PrintError("_beginthreadex failed at ",__FILE__,__LINE__);
}

unsigned WINAPI Thread::startThread(LPVOID pVoid) {
    Thread* aThread = static_cast<Thread*> (pVoid);
    assert(aThread);
    aThread->result = aThread->run();
    aThread->setCompleted();
    return reinterpret_cast<unsigned>(aThread->result);
}

void* Thread::join() {
    DWORD rc = WaitForSingleObject(
        completionEvent,     // handle to event
        INFINITE);           // no timeout
    if (!(rc==WAIT_OBJECT_0))
        PrintError("WaitForSingleObject failed at ",__FILE__,__LINE__);
    return result;
}

void Thread::setCompleted() {
    DWORD rc = SetEvent(completionEvent);
    if (!rc)
        PrintError("SetEvent failed at ",__FILE__,__LINE__);
}
```

Listing 3.25 Event object in the Win32 *Thread* class.

setCompleted() to set the thread's status to completed and to notify any threads waiting in *join()* that the thread has completed. Methods *setCompleted()* and *join()* are implemented using an Event called *completionEvent* that is created in the *Thread* class constructor. A thread calling *T.join()* is blocked on *completionEvent* if T has not yet completed. The call to *setCompleted()* releases all threads that are blocked on *completionEvent* and leaves *completionEvent* in the signaled state. Since the *completionEvent* is never reset, threads that call *join()* after *setCompleted()* is called are not blocked.

If *completionEvent* were an auto-reset Event, a call to *setCompleted()* would release all the waiting threads and reset *completionEvent* to the nonsignaled state. This would cause a problem since any threads that then called T.*join()* would be blocked forever even though thread T had already completed.

3.7.5 Other Synchronization Functions

The *WaitForMultipleObjects()* function was described in Section 1.4, where it was used in the main thread to wait for child threads to finish. Threads are kernel objects and thus are either in the signaled or nonsignaled state. When a thread is created and running, its state is nonsignaled. When the thread terminates, it becomes signaled.

The *SignalObjectAndWait()* function allows the caller to signal an object atomically and wait on another object. When used with semaphores, it is equivalent to the *VP()* operation defined in Section 3.4.2.

```
DWORD SignalObjectAndWait(
    HANDLE                          // handle to object for signal
    HANDLE                          // handle to object for wait
    DWORD                           // timeout interval
    BOOL                            // alertable option: specifies whether the
                                    // wait state can be aborted
);
```

Function *SignalObjectAndWait()* is available in Windows NT/2000 4.0 and higher. It is not supported in Windows 95/98.

3.7.6 Example: C++/Win32 Bounded Buffer

Listing 3.26 is a Win32 solution to the bounded buffer problem that is based on the Java version in Listing 3.17. Notice that Semaphores *fullSlots* and *emptySlots* and locks *mutexD* and *mutexW*, which protect the Buffer, are declared outside the *Buffer* class. A better design would be to encapsulate the Semaphores within class *Buffer*. We will save this improvement for Chapter 4, where we also address some of the difficulties of programming with Semaphores.

3.8 SEMAPHORES AND LOCKS IN PTHREADS

Mutex locks are part of the Pthreads (POSIX1.c) standard. Semaphores are not a part of Pthreads, but are in POSIX1.b.

```cpp
const int capacity = 3;
class Buffer {
private:
    int buffer[capacity];
    int count, in, out;
public:
    Buffer() : in(0), out(0), count(0) {  }
    int size() { return count;}
    int withdraw () {
        int value = 0;
        value = buffer[out];      // out is shared by Consumers
        out = (out + 1) % capacity;
        count--;
        return value;
    }
    void deposit (int value) {
        buffer[in] = value;       // in is shared by Producers
        in = (in + 1) % capacity;
        count++;
    }
};
Buffer sharedBuffer;      // 3-slot buffer
mutexLock mutexD, mutexW;
countingSemaphore emptySlots(capacity);
countingSemaphore fullSlots(0);
class Producer : public Thread {
public:
    virtual void* run () {
        int i;
        std::cout << "producer running" << std::endl;
        for (i=0; i<2; i++) {
            emptySlots.P();
            mutexD.lock();
            sharedBuffer.deposit(i);
            std::cout << "Produced: " << i << std::endl;
            mutexD.unlock();
            fullSlots.V();
        }
        return 0;
    }
};
```

Listing 3.26 Win32 bounded buffer using *countingSemaphores* and *mutexLocks*.

```
class Consumer : public Thread {
public:
    virtual void* run () {
        int result;
        std::cout << "consumer running" << std::endl;
        for (int i=0; i<2; i++) {
            fullSlots.P();
            mutexW.lock();
            result = sharedBuffer.withdraw();
            mutexW.unlock();
            std::cout << "Consumed: " << result << std::endl;
            emptySlots.V();
        }
        return 0;
    }
};
int main() {
    std::auto_ptr<Producer> p1(new Producer);
    std::auto_ptr<Producer> p2(new Producer);
    std::auto_ptr<Consumer> c1(new Consumer);
    std::auto_ptr<Consumer> c2(new Consumer);
    p1->start();c1->start(); p2->start();c2->start();
    p1->join(); p2->join(); c1->join(); c2->join();
    return(0);
}
```

Listing 3.26 (*continued*)

3.8.1 Mutex

A Pthreads *mutex* is a lock with behavior similar to that of a Win32 CRITICAL_ SECTION. Operations *pthread_mutex_lock()* and *pthread_mutex_unlock()* are analogous to *EnterCriticalSection()* and *LeaveCriticalSection()*, respectively:

- A thread that calls *pthread_mutex_lock()* on a *mutex* is granted access to the *mutex* if no other thread owns the *mutex*; otherwise, the thread is blocked.

- A thread that calls *pthread_mutex_lock()* on a *mutex* and is granted access to the *mutex* becomes the owner of the *mutex*.

- A thread releases its ownership by calling *pthread_mutex_unlock()*. A thread calling *pthread_mutex_unlock()* must be the owner of the mutex.

- There is a conditional wait operation *pthread_mutex_trylock* (pthread_mutex_ t* mutex) that will never block the calling thread. If the mutex is currently locked, the operation returns immediately with the error code EBUSY. Otherwise, the calling thread becomes the owner.

Listing 3.27 shows how to use a Pthreads *mutex*. You initialize a *mutex* by calling the *pthread_mutex_init()* function. The first parameter is the address of the *mutex*. If you need to initialize a *mutex* with nondefault attributes, the second parameter can specify the address of an attribute object. When the *mutex* is no longer needed, it is destroyed by calling *pthread_mutex_destroy()*.

When you declare a static *mutex* with default attributes, you can use the PTHREAD_MUTEX_INITIALIZER macro instead of calling *pthread_mutex_int()*. In Listing 3.27, we could have written

```
pthread_mutex_t mutex = PTHREAD_MUTEX_INITIALIZER;
```

You do not need to destroy a *mutex* that was initialized using the *PTHREAD_MUTEX_INITIALIZER* macro.

By default, a Pthreads *mutex* is not recursive, which means that a thread should not try to lock a *mutex* that it already owns. However, the POSIX 1003.1 2001 standard allows a *mutex*'s type attribute to be set to recursive:

```
pthread_mutex_t mutex;
pthread_mutexattr_t mutexAttribute;
int status = pthread_mutexattr_init (&mutexAttribute);
if (status !=0) { /* ... */ }
status = pthread_mutexattr_settype(&mutexAttribute,
    PTHREAD_MUTEX_RECURSIVE);
if (status != 0) { /* ... */}
status = pthread_mutex_init(&mutex,&mutexAttribute);
if (status != 0) { /* ... */ }
```

If a thread that owns a recursive *mutex* tries to lock the *mutex* again, the thread is granted access immediately. Before another thread can become the owner, an owning thread must release a recursive *mutex* the same number of times that it requested ownership.

3.8.2 Semaphore

POSIX semaphores are counting semaphores. Operations *sem_wait()* and *sem_post()* are equivalent to *P()* and *V()*, respectively. POSIX semaphores have the following properties:

- A semaphore is not considered to be owned by a thread—one thread can execute *sem_wait()* on a semaphore and another thread can execute *sem_post()*.
- When a semaphore is created, the initial value of the semaphore is specified. The initial value must be greater than or equal to zero and less than or equal to the value SEM_VALUE_MAX.

```
#include <pthread.h>
pthread_mutex_t mutex;

void* Thread1(void* arg) {
   pthread_mutex_lock(&mutex);
   /* critical section */
   pthread_mutex_unlock(&mutex);
   return NULL;
}

void* Thread2(void* arg) {
   pthread_mutex_lock(&mutex);
   /* critical section */
   pthread_mutex_unlock(&mutex);
   return NULL;
}

int main() {
   pthread_t threadArray[2];        // array of thread IDs
   int status;                      // error code
   pthread_attr_t threadAttribute;  // thread attribute

   // initialize mutex
   status = pthread_mutex_init(&mutex,NULL);
   if (status != 0) { /* See Listing 1.4 for error handling */ }
   // initialize the thread attribute object
   status = pthread_attr_init(&threadAttribute);
   if (status != 0) { /* ... */}
   // set the scheduling scope attribute
   status = pthread_attr_setscope(&threadAttribute,
        PTHREAD_SCOPE_SYSTEM);
   if (status != 0) { /* ... */}

   // Create two threads and store their IDs in array threadArray
   status = pthread_create(&threadArray[0], &threadAttribute, Thread1,
        (void*) 1L);
   if (status != 0) { /* ... */}
   status = pthread_create(&threadArray[1], &threadAttribute, Thread2,
        (void*) 2L);
   if (status != 0) { /* ... */}
   status = pthread_attr_destroy(&threadAttribute); // destroy attribute object
   if (status != 0) { /* ... */}
```

Listing 3.27   Using Pthreads *mutex* objects.

```
// Wait for threads to finish
status = pthread_join(threadArray[0],NULL);
if (status != 0) { /* ... */}
status = pthread_join(threadArray[1],NULL);
if (status != 0) { /* ... */}

// Destroy mutex
status = pthread_mutex_destroy(&mutex);
if (status != 0) { /* ... */ }
}
```

Listing 3.27   (*continued*)

- Semaphore operations follow a different convention for reporting errors. They return 0 for success. On failure, they return a value of -1 and store the appropriate error number into *errno*. We use the C function perror(const char* string) to transcribe the value of *errno* into a string and print that string to *stderr*.
- There is a conditional wait operation *sem_trywait*(sem_t* sem) that will never block the calling thread. If the semaphore value is greater than 0, the value is decremented and the operation returns immediately. Otherwise, the operation returns immediately with the error code EAGAIN indicating that the semaphore value was not greater than 0.

Listing 3.28 shows how Pthreads semaphore objects are used. Header file <semaphore.h> must be included to use the semaphore operations. Semaphores are of the type *sem_t*. A semaphore is created by calling the *sem_init()* function. The first argument is the address of the semaphore. If the second argument has a nonzero value, the semaphore can be shared between processes. With a zero value, it can be shared only between threads in the same process. The third argument is the initial value. When the semaphore is no longer needed, it is destroyed by calling *sem_destroy()*.

We can create a simple C++ class that wraps POSIX semaphores, just as we did with Win32 semaphores. Listing 3.29 shows wrapper class *POSIXSemaphore*. The methods of *PthreadSemaphore* forward calls to the corresponding POSIX semaphore functions. To assist with testing and debugging, we'll need user-level lock and semaphore classes like the ones we developed for Win32. We can use *POSIXSemaphore* to implement both of these classes. The code for C++/Pthreads classes *mutexLock* and *countingSemaphore* is identical to the code in Listings 3.23 and 3.24, respectively, except that class *win32Semaphore* should be replaced by class *POSIXSemaphore*. The difference between Win32 and POSIX is encapsulated in the semaphore classes.

```cpp
#include <pthread.h>
#include <semaphore.h>
#include <stdio.h>

sem_t s;

void* Thread1(void* arg) {
    int status;
    status = sem_wait(&s);
    if (status !=0) {
        std::cout << __FILE__ << ":" << __LINE__ << "- " << flush;
        perror("sem_wait failed"); exit(status);
    }
    /* critical section */
    status = sem_post(&s);
    if (status !=0) {
        std::cout << __FILE__ << ":" << __LINE__ << "- " << flush;
        perror("sem_post failed"); exit(status);
    }
    return NULL; // implicit call to pthread_exit(NULL);
}
void* Thread2(void* arg) {
    int status;
    status = sem_wait(&s);
    if (status !=0) {
        std::cout << __FILE__ << ":" << __LINE__ << "- " << flush;
        perror("sem_wait failed"); exit(status);
    }
    /* critical section */
    status = sem_post(&s);
    if (status !=0) {
        std::cout << __FILE__ << ":" << __LINE__ << "- " << flush;
        perror("sem_post failed"); exit(status);
    }
    return NULL; // implicit call to pthread_exit(NULL);
}

int main() {
    pthread_t threadArray[2];        // array of thread IDs
    int status;                      // error code
    pthread_attr_t threadAttribute;  // thread attribute
```

Listing 3.28   Using POSIX semaphore objects.

```
// initialize semaphore s
status = sem_init(&s,0,1);
if (status !=0) {
    std::cout << __FILE__ << ":" << __LINE__ << "- " << flush;
    perror("sem_init failed"); exit(status);
}
// initialize the thread attribute object
status = pthread_attr_init(&threadAttribute);
if (status != 0) { /* see Listing 1.4 for Pthreads error handling */}
// set the scheduling scope attribute
status = pthread_attr_setscope(&threadAttribute,
    PTHREAD_SCOPE_SYSTEM);
if (status != 0) { /* ... */}

// Create two threads and store their IDs in array threadArray
status = pthread_create(&threadArray[0], &threadAttribute, Thread1,
    (void*) 1L);
if (status != 0) { /* ... */}
status = pthread_create(&threadArray[1], &threadAttribute, Thread2,
    (void*) 2L);
if (status != 0) { /* ... */}
status = pthread_attr_destroy(&threadAttribute); // destroy the attribute object
if (status != 0) { /* ... */}

// Wait for threads to finish
status = pthread_join(threadArray[0],NULL);
if (status != 0) { /* ... */}
status = pthread_join(threadArray[1],NULL);
if (status != 0) { /* ... */}

// Destroy semaphore s
status = sem_destroy(&s);
if (status !=0) {
    std::cout << __FILE__ << ":" << __LINE__ << "- " << flush;
    perror("sem_destroy failed"); exit(status);
}
}
```

Listing 3.28   (*continued*)

3.9 ANOTHER NOTE ON SHARED MEMORY CONSISTENCY

Recall from Section 2.5.6 the issues surrounding shared memory consistency. Compiler and hardware optimizations may reorder read and write operations on shared variables, making it difficult to reason about the behavior of multithreaded

```cpp
#include <pthread.h>
#include <semaphore.h>
#include <stdio.h>
#include <iostream>

const int maxDefault = 999;
class POSIXSemaphore {
private:
    sem_t s;
    int permits;
public:
    void P();
    void V();
    POSIXSemaphore(int initial);
    ~POSIXSemaphore();
};

POSIXSemaphore::POSIXSemaphore (int initial) : permits(initial) {
    // assume semaphore is accessed by the threads in a single process
    int status = sem_init(&s, 0, initial);
    if (status !=0) {
        std::cout << __FILE__ << ":" << __LINE__ << "- " << flush;
        perror("sem_init failed"); exit(status);
    }
}
POSIXSemaphore:: ~ POSIXSemaphore () {
    int status = sem_destroy(&s);
    if (status !=0) {
        std::cout << __FILE__ << ":" << __LINE__ << "- " << flush;
        perror("sem_destroy failed"); exit(status);
    }
}
void POSIXSemaphore::P() {
    int status = sem_wait(&s);
    if (status !=0) {
        std::cout << __FILE__ << ":" << __LINE__ << "- " << flush;
        perror("sem_wait failed"); exit(status);
    }
}
void POSIXSemaphore::V() {
    int status = sem_post(&s);
    if (status !=0) {
        std::cout << __FILE__ << ":" << __LINE__ << "- " << flush;
        perror("sem_post failed"); exit(status);
    }
}
```

Listing 3.29   Class *POSIXSemaphore*.

programs. Fortunately, critical sections created using Java's built-in synchronization operations or the operations in the Win32 or Pthreads library provide mutual exclusion and also protect against unwanted reorderings.

These synchronization operations in Java and in the thread libraries interact with the memory system to ensure that shared variables accessed in critical sections have values that are consistent across threads. For example, the shared variable values that a thread can see when it unlocks a mutex can also be seen by any thread that later locks the *same* mutex. Thus, an execution in which shared variables are correctly protected by locks or semaphores is guaranteed to be sequentially consistent. This guarantee allows us to ignore shared memory consistency issues when we use locks and semaphores to create critical sections in our programs. For this reason, we make it a rule always to access shared variables inside critical sections. Next we will see that this rule also simplifies testing and debugging.

3.10 TRACING, TESTING, AND REPLAY FOR SEMAPHORES AND LOCKS

In this section we address two testing and debugging issues for programs that use semaphores and locks. First, we describe a special testing technique for detecting violations of mutual exclusion. Then we show how to trace and replay program executions during debugging.

3.10.1 Nondeterministic Testing with the Lockset Algorithm

A concurrent program that uses semaphores and locks can be tested for data races. Recall from Chapter 1 that a data race is a failure to correctly implement critical sections for nonatomic shared variable accesses. The approach we will use to detect data races is to monitor shared variable accesses and make sure that each variable has been properly locked before it is accessed. Since program executions are nondeterministic, we will need to execute the program several times with the same test input in order to increase our chances of finding data races. This type of testing is called *nondeterministic testing*.

Nondeterministic testing of a concurrent program CP involves the following steps:

1. Select a set of inputs for CP.
2. For each input X selected, execute CP with X many times and examine the result of each execution.

Multiple, nondeterministic executions of CP with input X may exercise different behaviors of CP and thus may detect more failures than a single execution of CP with input X.

The purpose of nondeterministic testing is to exercise as many distinct program behaviors as possible. Unfortunately, experiments have shown that repeated executions of a concurrent program are not likely to execute different behaviors [Hwang et al. 1995]. In the absence of significant variations in I/O delays or network delays, or significant changes in the system load, programs tend to exhibit the same behavior from execution to execution. Furthermore, the probe effect (see Section 1.7), which occurs when programs are instrumented with debugging code, may make it impossible for some failures to be observed.

There are several techniques we can use to increase the likelihood of exercising different behaviors. One is to change the scheduling algorithm used by the operating system (e.g., change the value of the time quantum that is used for round-robin scheduling). However, in many commercial operating systems this is simply not an option. The second technique is to insert `Sleep(t)` statements into the program with the sleep amount t randomly chosen. Executing a `Sleep` statement forces a context switch and thus indirectly affects thread scheduling. We have implemented this second technique as an execution option for programs that use the *binarySemaphore, countingSemaphore*, and *mutexLock* classes in our synchronization library. When this option is specified, `Sleep` statements are executed at the beginning of methods *P()*, *V()*, *lock()*, and *unlock()*. The `Sleep` time is randomly chosen within a programmable range. The random delays can be used in conjunction with the tracing and replay functions so that any failures that are observed can also be replayed.

To detect data races, we combine nondeterministic testing with the lockset algorithm [Savage et al. 1997]. The lockset algorithm checks that all shared variables follow a consistent locking discipline in which every shared variable is protected by a lock. Since there is no way of knowing which locks are intended to protect which variables, we must monitor the executions and try to infer a relationship between the locks and variables. For each variable, we determine if there is some lock that is always held whenever the variable is accessed.

For shared variable v, let the set *CandidateLocks(v)* be those locks that have protected v during the execution so far. Thus, a lock l is in *CandidateLocks(v)* if, during the execution so far, every thread that has accessed v was holding l at the moment of the access. *CandidateLocks(v)* is computed as follows:

- When a new variable v is initialized, its candidate set is considered to hold all possible locks.
- When v is accessed on a read or write operation by T, *CandidateLocks(v)* is refined. The new value of *CandidateLocks(v)* is the intersection of *CandidateLocks(v)* and the set of locks held by thread T.

Based on this refinement algorithm, if some lock l protects v consistently, it will remain in *CandidateLocks(v)* as *CandidateLocks(v)* is refined. If *CandidateLocks(v)* becomes empty, it indicates that there is no lock that protects v consistently. Following is the *lockset algorithm*:

Thread1	LocksHeld(Thread1)	CandidateLocks(s)
	{ }	{mutex1,mutex2}
mutex1.lock();	{mutex1}	{mutex1,mutex2}
s = s+1;	{mutex1}	{mutex1}
mutex1.unlock();	{ }	{mutex1}
mutex2.lock();	{mutex2}	{mutex1}
s = s+1;	{mutex2}	{ }
mutex2.unlock();	{ }	{ }

Figure 3.30   Lockset algorithm.

// Let *LocksHeld(T)* denote the set of locks currently held by thread *T*
For each shared variable *v*, initialize *CandidateLocks(v)* to the set of all locks.
On each read or write access to *v* by thread *T*:
    CandidateLocks(v) = *CandidateLocks(v)* ∩ LocksHeld(T);
if (*CandidateLocks(v)* == { }) issue a warning;

For example, in Fig. 3.30, *Thread1*'s access of shared variable *s* is protected first by *mutex1* then by *mutex2*. This is a violation of mutual exclusion that can be detected by the lockset algorithm. *CandidateLocks(s)* is initialized to {*mutex1, mutex2*} and is refined as *s* is accessed. When *Thread1* locks *mutex1*, *LocksHeld(Thread1)* becomes {*mutex1*}. When *s* is accessed in the first assignment statement, *CandidateLocks(s)* becomes *mutex1*, which is the intersection of sets *CandidateLocks(s)* and *LocksHeld(Thread1)*. When the second assignment statement is executed, *Thread1* holds lock *mutex2* and the only candidate lock of *s* is *mutex1*. After the intersection of *CandidateLocks(s)* and *LocksHeld(Thread1)*, *CandidateLocks(s)* becomes empty. The lockset algorithm has detected that no lock protects shared variable *s* consistently.

We have implemented the lockset algorithm in the *mutexLock* class and in the C++ *sharedVariable* class template that was presented in Chapter 2:

- We assume that threads can access a *sharedVariable* only after it is initialized. Thus, no refinement is performed during initialization (i.e., in the constructor of *sharedVariable*).
- Read-only variables can be accessed without locking. This means that warnings are issued only after a variable has been initialized and has been accessed by at least one write operation.
- The refinement algorithm can be turned off to eliminate false alarms. For example, the bounded-buffer program in Listing 3.26 can be modified to use a buffer of *sharedVariables*. These variables are shared by the *Producer* and *Consumer* threads, but no locks are needed. Even so, when this program is executed, a warning will be issued by the lockset algorithm. When it is determined that the warning can safely be ignored, the lockset algorithm can be disabled for these variables. Alternatively, the buffer can be implemented without using *sharedVariables*.

The lockset algorithm was originally implemented in a testing tool called Eraser [Savage et al. 1997]. It has also been implemented as part of a Java virtual machine called Java Pathfinder [Havelund and Pressburger 2000]. The lockset algorithm has been shown to be a practical technique for detecting data races in programs that protect shared variables with locks. However, programs that use semaphores for mutual exclusion, with patterns like passing-the-baton, will generate false alarms. As shown above for the bounded buffer program, lockset can produce false alarms even if locks are used. The number of false alarms can be reduced by allowing users to turn off the detection algorithm for regions of code or to provide the detection algorithm with extra information. As a nondeterministic testing technique, the lockset algorithm cannot prove that a program is free from data races. Still, knowing that a particular execution contains no data races can be helpful during tracing and replay, as we will see next.

3.10.2 Simple SYN-Sequences for Semaphores and Locks

In general, we can characterize an execution of a concurrent program as a sequence of synchronization events on synchronization objects. A sequence of synchronization events is called a SYN-sequence. First we define the types of synchronization events and synchronization objects that occur in programs containing semaphores and locks. Then we show how to collect and replay SYN-sequences of these programs. These two steps are not independent. There are several ways to define a SYN-sequence, and the definition of a SYN-sequence has an effect on the design of a replay solution, and vice versa.

Let CP be a concurrent program that uses shared variables, semaphores, and locks. The result of executing CP with a given input depends on the (unpredictable) order in which the shared variables, semaphores, and locks in CP are accessed. The semaphores are accessed using P and V operations, the locks are accessed using *lock* and *unlock* operations, and the shared variables are accessed using *read* and *write* operations. Thus, the synchronization objects in CP are its shared variables, semaphores, and locks. The synchronization events in CP are executions of *read/write*, P/V, and *lock/unlock* operations on these objects.

We point out that there may be shared variables that are accessed in the implementations of the P/V and *lock/unlock* operations. In fact, these shared variables may be accessed a large number of times, due to busy waiting loops. However, we will not trace the read and write operations on these shared variables. Since P/V and *lock/unlock* operations are atomic operations; we will consider them to be operating on a single (shared) semaphore or lock variable. This abstraction decreases the number of operations that need to be traced during execution.

A SYN-sequence for a shared variable v is a sequence of *read* and *write* operations on v. ReadWrite-sequences for shared variables were defined in Chapter 2. A SYN-sequence for a *binarySemaphore* or *countingSemaphore s* is a sequence of events of the following types:

- Completion of a P operation
- Completion of a V operation

```
binarySemaphore mutex(1);
Thread1                      Thread2
mutex.P();                   mutex.P();
x = 1;                       x = 2;
mutex.V();                   mutex.P(); // error: should be mutex.V();
```

Listing 3.31 ReadWrite-sequences and PV-sequences.

- Start of a P operation that is never completed due to a deadlock or an exception
- Start of a V operation that is never completed due to a deadlock or an exception

We refer to such a sequence as a *PV-sequence* of s. An event in a PV-sequence is denoted by the identifier (ID) of the thread that executed the P or V operation. The order in which threads complete their P and V operations is not necessarily the same as the order in which they call P and V or even the same as the order in which the P and V operations start. For operations that are completed, it is their order of completion that must be replayed, since this order determines the result of the execution. We also replay the starts of operations that do not complete, so that the same events, exceptions, and deadlocks will occur during replay.

A SYN-sequence for a *mutexLock l* is a sequence of events of the following types:

- Completion of a *lock* operation
- Completion of an *unlock* operation
- Start of a *lock* operation that is never completed due to a deadlock or an exception
- Start of an *unlock* operation that is never completed due to a deadlock or an exception

We refer to such a sequence as a *LockUnlock-sequence* of l. An event in a LockUnlock-sequence is denoted by the identifier (ID) of the thread that executed the *lock* or *unlock* operation. To illustrate these definitions, consider the simple program in Listing 3.31. The final value of shared variable x is either 1 or 2.

A possible ReadWrite-sequence of shared variable x is

(1, 0, 0), (2, 1, 0).   // from Chapter 2, the event format is (thread ID, version
                           // number, total readers)

This denotes that x was first accessed by Thread1 and then by Thread2. Since Thread1 accessed x first, the PV-sequence for *mutex* must be

1, 1, 2, 2

indicating that Thread1 performed its P and V operations before Thread2. The second P operation in Thread2 is an error. This P operation will start but not complete and should be a V operation instead.

A SYN-sequence for concurrent program CP is a collection of ReadWrite-sequences, PV-sequences, and LockUnlock-sequences. There is one sequence for each shared variable, semaphore, and lock in the program. A SYN-sequence for the program in Listing 3.31 contains a ReadWrite-sequence for x and a PV-sequence for *mutex*:

((ReadWrite-sequence of x: (1, 0, 0), (2, 1, 0); PV-sequence of *mutex*: (1, 1, 2, 2)).

This is a partial ordering of the synchronization events in the program. That is, the events on a single object are (totally) ordered, but the order of events among different objects is not specified. Alternatively, we can define a SYN-sequence of a program as a single totally ordered sequence of synchronization events over all the synchronization objects. A totally ordered sequence of events that is consistent with the partially ordered sequence above is

1, (1, 0, 0), 1, 2, (2, 1, 0), 2.

In general, there may be two or more totally ordered sequences that are consistent with a given partial ordering since two concurrent events can appear in the total ordering in either order.

The definition of a SYN-sequence is intended to capture what it means for one execution to replay another. Suppose that when the program above is executed, Thread2 executes *mutex.P()* and blocks because Thread1 is already in its critical section. During the replay of this execution, assume that Thread2 executes its first *mutex.P()* operation without blocking, because Thread1 has already executed its *mutex.P()* and *mutex.V()* operations. These two executions are not identical. However, in both executions:

- The sequence of *completed* $P()$ and $V()$ operations is the same.
- The final value of x is 2.

Thus, we consider the second execution to replay the first. Although we could include events such as "*call V()*" or "*block in P()*" in the SYN-sequence of a semaphore object, we are not required to trace these events in order to do a successful replay, so we omit them. The events that we ignore during replay may be important when we are doing other things. Thus, we define different types of SYN-sequences for the different activities that occur during testing and debugging. Since the SYN-sequences that we use for replay tend to be much simpler than the other types of SYN-sequences, we use the term *simple SYN-sequences* to refer to the SYN-sequences that are used for replay.

According to the foregoing definition of a simple SYN-sequence for CP, we must be prepared to record and replay arbitrary interleavings of read and write operations on shared variables. This is a general replay solution, which can be applied to programs that use shared variables and constructs other than semaphores and locks. However, this general solution may not be easy to implement. Controlling read and write operations during replay adds a significant amount of execution overhead and requires access to the implementation of CP. Hence, we examine some alternative solutions.

In Listing 3.31, observe that the simple ReadWrite-sequence for shared variable x is completely determined by the simple PV-sequence of *mutex*. That is, if we replay the PV-sequence for *mutex*, we will, with no additional effort, also replay the ReadWrite-sequence for x. This is an important observation, for it means that if we assume that shared variables are always safely accessed within critical sections, we can develop a simpler and more efficient solution.

Of course, in general, we cannot assume that mutual exclusion holds when shared variables are accessed. A programmer may make an error when writing the program, or even violate mutual exclusion on purpose. If mutual exclusion for a particular shared variable is not critical to a program's correctness, a critical section can be eliminated to eliminate the overhead of acquiring a lock. Also, a statement accessing a shared variable need not occur within a critical section if the execution of the statement is atomic. (But remember that accessing a shared variable outside a critical section raises the shared memory consistency issues discussed in Section 3.9.)

Our observation about critical sections does not lead to a better replay solution. It does, however, highlight the importance of mutual exclusion and the need for synchronization constructs that aid in implementing mutual exclusion correctly. The monitor construct in Chapter 4 is such a construct. Using monitors greatly improves the chances that shared variables are accessed inside critical sections and, as we will see, makes it easier to replay executions.

For now, we will try to improve our replay solution by using the lockset algorithm in concert with replay. During replay, we will assume that shared variables are accessed inside critical sections that are implemented with *mutexLocks* that are being used as locks. This allows us to ignore read and write operations on shared variables. During tracing, we will use the lockset algorithm to validate our assumption. The lockset algorithm will tell us when replay may fail.

As we mentioned earlier, in cases where a shared variable can safely be accessed outside a critical section, the lockset algorithm can be turned off for that variable so that no warnings will be issued. However, this may create a problem for replay since we depend on each shared variable to be accessed inside a critical section so that each shared variable access is represented by a *lock()* or *P()* operation in the execution trace. In these cases, locks can be used to create critical sections, at least temporarily, so that replay can be performed. Designing a program so that it will be easier to test and debug increases the *testability* of the program.

Let CP be a concurrent program containing mutex locks, binary semaphores, and counting semaphores. Assume that shared variables are correctly accessed inside critical sections:

- Each semaphore and lock in CP is a synchronization object.
- The synchronization events in a simple PV-sequence for a semaphore are the four types of events defined above.
- The synchronization events in a simple LockUnlock-sequence for a mutex lock are the four types of events defined above.
- Each synchronization event is denoted by the identifier of the thread that executed the event.

To replay an execution of CP, we must replay the simple PV-sequences for the semaphores in CP and the simple LockUnlock-sequences for the locks in CP. In the next section we show how to do this.

3.10.3 Tracing and Replaying Simple PV-Sequences and LockUnlock-Sequences

We now show how to modify the semaphore and lock classes so that they can trace and replay simple PV-sequences and LockUnlock-sequences.

Modifying Methods P() and V() The implementations of methods *P()* and *V()* in classes *binarySemaphore* and *countingSemaphore* can be modified so that simple PV-sequences can be collected and replayed. Collecting a PV-sequence for a semaphore *s* is simple. During execution, the identifier of the thread that completes a call to method *s.P()* or *s.V()* is recorded and saved to a trace file for *s*. Methods *P()* and *V()* can easily be modified (see below) to collect these events.

For the purpose of explaining our replay method, we assume that each semaphore has a permit, called a *PV-permit*. A thread must hold a semaphore's PV-permit before it executes a *P()* or *V()* operation on that semaphore. The order in which threads receive a semaphore's PV-permit is based on the PV-sequence that is being replayed. A thread requests and releases a semaphore's PV-permit by calling methods *requestPermit()* and *releasePermit()*. These calls are added to the implementations of methods *P()* and *V()*. Method *P()* becomes

```
void P() {
    if (replayMode)
        control.requestPermit(ID);

    // code to lock this semaphore appears here

    if (replayMode)
        control.releasePermit();
```

```
        /* rest of body of P() */

        if (traceMode)
            control.traceCompleteP(ID);

        // code to unlock this semaphore appears here
    }
```

Method *V( )* becomes:

```
    public final void V() {
        if (replayMode)
            control.requestPermit(ID);

        // code to lock this semaphore appears here

        if (replayMode)
            control.releasePermit();

        /* rest of body of V() */

        if (traceMode)
            control.traceCompleteV(ID);

        // code to unlock this semaphore appears here
    }
```

We assume that the implementations of *P( )* and *V( )* contain critical sections for accessing the variables that they share. We have indicated this with comments referring to the lock and unlock operations that create these critical sections. Calls to *requestPermit( ), releasePermit( ), traceCompleteP( )*, and *traceCompleteV( )* must be positioned correctly with respect to the critical sections in *P( )* and *V( )*. The call to *requestPermit( )* appears before the lock operation, and the call to *releasePermit( )* appears right after the lock operation. The calls to *traceCompleteP( )* and *traceCompleteV( )* both appear inside the critical section. This ensures that events are recorded in the execution trace in the order in which they actually occur. If the calls to the *trace* function are made outside the critical section, the order of the calls may not be consistent with the order in which threads actually complete their *P( )* and *V( )* operations.

Modifying Methods lock() and unlock()   The implementations of methods *lock( )* and *unlock( )* in class *mutexLock* are modified just like methods *P( )* and *V( )*. Class *mutexLock* contains calls to *requestPermit( )* and *releasePermit( )* before and after, respectively, the lock operation in *mutexLock*. Calls to *traceCompleteLock( )* and *traceCompleteUnlock( )* appear at the end of their respective critical sections.

To simplify tracing and replay, we do not trace events that represent the start of a *P*, *V*, *lock*, or *unlock* operation that never completes due to a deadlock or exception. Thus, when deadlock-producing operations are replayed, the calling threads will not be blocked inside the body of the operation; rather, they will be blocked forever on the call to *requestPermit()* before the operation. Since in either case the thread will be blocked forever, the effect of replay is the same. Similarly, events involving exceptions that occur during the execution of a *P*, *V*, *lock*, or *unlock* operation will not be replayed. But the trace would indicate that the execution of these operations would raise an error, which probably provides enough help to debug the program. Our solution can be extended so that incomplete events are actually executed.

Class Control   Each semaphore and lock is associated with a control object. In replay mode, the control object inputs the simple SYN-sequence of the semaphore or lock and handles the calls to *requestPermit()* and *releasePermit()*. In trace mode, the control object collects the synchronization events that occur and records them in a trace file. When a thread calls *requestPermit()* or one of the *trace* methods, it passes its identifier (ID). We assume that all threads are instances of class *TDThread*, which was described in Chapter 1. *TDThread* handles the creation of unique thread IDs.

A C++ *control* class is shown in Listing 3.32. Consider a semaphore *s* and a simple PV-sequence for *s* that was recorded during a previous execution. When the control object for *s* is created, it reads the simple PV-sequence for *s* into vector *SYNsequence*. Assume that the first $j - 1$, $j > 0$, operations of *SYNsequence* have been completed (i.e., *index* == j) and the value of *SYNsequence*[j] is k, which means that thread T_k is required to execute the next event. When thread T_i, $i <> k$, calls method *requestPermit()*, it blocks itself by executing *Threads[i].P()*. When thread T_k calls *requestPermit()*, it is allowed to return from the call (i.e., it receives the PV-permit). Thread T_k then starts the jth operation on *s*. Assume that this operation is a completed *P()* or *V()* operation. After completing this operation, thread T_k calls method *releasePermit()* to increment *index* to $j + 1$ and allow the next operation in the *SYNsequence*. The ID of the thread that is to execute the next operation is the value *SYNsequence[index]*. If this thread was previously blocked by a *P()* operation in method *requestPermit()*, method *releasePermit()* performs operation *threads[SYNsequence[index]].V()* to unblock this thread. Otherwise, when the next thread eventually calls *requestPermit()*, it will not block itself since its ID will match the next ID in the *SYNsequence*.

To illustrate the operation of the controller, consider a corrected version of the simple program in Listing 3.31. In this version, Thread2 calls *mutex.P()* followed by *mutex.V()*. Assume that the PV-sequence traced during an execution of this program is

1, 1, 2, 2

which indicates that Thread1 entered its critical section first. During replay, the controller will guarantee that Thread1 will be the first thread to enter its

```
class control {
public:
    control() {
        /* input integer IDs into SYNsequence; initialize arrays threads and
        hasRequested */
    }
    void requestPermit(int ID) {
        mutex.lock();
        if (ID != SYNsequence[index]){ // thread ID should execute next event?
            hasRequested[ID] = true;    // No; set flag to remember ID's request
            mutex.unlock();
            threads[ID].P();            //    wait for permission
            hasRequested[ID] = false;   //    reset flag and exit requestPermit
        }
        else mutex.unlock();            // Yes; exit requestPermit
    }
    void releasePermit() {
        mutex.lock();
        ++index;
        if (index < SYNsequence.size()) {    // Are there more events to replay?
            // Has the next thread already requested permission?
            if (hasRequested[SYNsequence[index]])
                threads[SYNsequence[index]].V(); // Yes; wake it up.
        }
        mutex.unlock();
    }
    void traceCompleteP(int ID) {...} // record integer ID
    void traceCompleteV(ID) {...}    // record integer ID
private:
    // PV-sequence or LockUnlock-sequence; a sequence of integer IDs
    vector SYNsequence;
    binarySemaphore* threads; // all semaphores are initialized to 0
    // hasRequested[i] is true if Thread i is delayed in requestPermit(); init to false
    bool* hasRequested;
    int index = 0; // SYNsequence[index] is ID of next thread to execute an event
    mutexLock mutex; // note: no tracing or replay is performed for this lock
}
```

Listing 3.32 C++ class *control* for replaying PV-sequences and LockUnlock-sequences.

critical section. Suppose, however, that Thread2 tries to execute *mutex.P()* first and thus calls *requestPermit(2)* before Thread1 *calls requestPermit(1)*. Since the value of *index* is 0 and the value of *SYNsequence[index]* is 1, not 2, Thread2 blocks itself in *requestPermit()* by executing *Threads[2].P()*. When Thread1 eventually calls *requestPermit(1)*, it will be allowed to exit *requestPemit()* and execute its *mutex.P()* operation. Thread1 will then call *releasePermit()*. Method *releasePermit()* increments *index* to 1 and checks whether the thread that is to execute the next *P/V* operation has already called *requestPermit()*. The next thread is *SYNsequence[1]*, which is 1. Thread1 has not called *requestPermit()* for the next operation, so nothing further happens in *releasePermit()*. Eventually, Thread1 calls *requestPermit(1)* to request permission to execute its *mutex.V()* operation. Thread1 receives permission, executes *mutex.V()*, and calls *releasePermit()*. Method *releasePermit()* increments *index* to 2 and finds that the thread to execute the next *P/V* operation is Thread2. Thread2, having already called *requestPermit()*, is still blocked on its call to *Threads[2].P()*. This is indicated by the value of *hasRequested[2]*, which is *true*. Thus, *releasePermit()* calls *Threads[2].V()*. This allows Thread2 to exit *requestPermit()* and perform its *mutex.P()* operation. Thread2 will eventually request and receive permission for its *mutex.V()* operation, completing the replay.

3.10.4 Deadlock Detection

Deadlock is a major problem, especially for concurrent programming novices. In Chapter 2 we defined a deadlock as a situation in which one or more threads become blocked forever. In this chapter, we learned that threads may be blocked forever when they call *P()*, *V()*, or *lock()* operations. Let CP be a concurrent program containing threads that use semaphores and locks for synchronization. Assume that there is an execution of CP that exercises a SYN-sequence S, and at the end of S, there exists a thread T that satisfies these conditions:

- T is blocked due to the execution of a *P()*, *V()*, or *lock()* statement.
- T will remain blocked forever, regardless of what the other threads will do.

Thread T is said to be *deadlocked* at the end of S, and CP is said to have a *deadlock*. A deadlock in CP is a *global deadlock* if every thread in CP is either blocked or completed; otherwise, it is a *local deadlock*.

Programmers typically become aware of a deadlock when their programs don't terminate; however, there is usually no indication about how the deadlock was created. Below, we describe a deadlock detection method that we have built into our synchronization classes. When a deadlock is detected, the threads and synchronization operations that are involved in the deadlock are displayed.

Deadlock prevention, avoidance, and detection algorithms are covered in most operating system textbooks. In operating systems, processes request resources (e.g., printers and files) and enter a wait-state if the resources are held by other processes. If the resources requested can never become available, the processes can never leave their wait-state and a deadlock occurs. The information about which process is waiting for a resource held by which other process can be represented by a *wait-for graph*. An edge in a wait-for graph from node P_i to

P_j indicates that process P_i is waiting for process P_j to release a resource that P_i needs [Silberschatz et al. 2001]. A deadlock exists in the system if and only if the wait-for graph contains a cycle. To detect deadlocks, the operating system maintains a wait-for graph and periodically invokes an algorithm that searches for cycles in the wait-for graph.

Deadlock detection using wait-for graphs is not always applicable to concurrent programs. A thread blocked in a *P( )* operation, for example, does not know which of the other threads can unblock it, and thus the wait-for relation among the threads is unknown. We use a different approach, which assumes that a deadlock occurs if all the threads in a program are permanently blocked [Feitelson 1991]. We also assume that all of the threads are expected to terminate. To detect deadlocks, we maintain a count of the threads that have not completed their *run( )* methods, and a count of the blocked threads, and compare the two counts:

- The *numThreads* counter is incremented when a thread starts its *run( )* method and decremented when a thread completes its *run( )* method.
- The *blockedThreads* counter is incremented when a thread blocks in a *P( )*, *V( )*, or *lock( )* operation, and is decremented when a thread is unblocked during a *V( )* or *unlock( )* operation. The *blockedThreads* counter should also be maintained in other blocking methods, such as *join( )*.
- If the *numThreads* and *blockedThreads* counters are ever equal (and nonzero), all of the threads are blocked and we assume that a deadlock has occurred.

This approach can be used to detect global deadlocks, but not local deadlocks, since it requires all nondeadlocked threads to be completed. Implementation of this approach in our synchronization classes is simple but incomplete. For example, we do not modify the *blockedThreads* counter inside the *join( )* method. Also, we do not modify the *numThreads* counter when the *main* thread starts and completes, simply because there is no convenient and transparent way to do so. Since we do not include the *main* thread in *numThreads* and we do not know the status of the *main* thread, it is possible for the *numThreads* and *blockedThreads* counters temporarily to become equal (indicating that a deadlock has occurred) and then for more threads to be created and start running. Thus, we cannot be certain that a deadlock has occurred when the counters are equal.

Despite these shortcomings, our implementation handles successfully both the example programs in this book and programs written to solve end-of-chapter programming exercises. This makes deadlock detection easy to use and helpful for students, which is our main objective. Typically, these programs have a simple *main* method that creates several threads and then completes; thus, the *main* thread does not need to be included in the deadlock analysis.

There are several ways to handle the uncertainty about whether a deadlock has truly occurred. One way is to compare the *numThreads* and *blockedThreads* counters after some initial waiting period and then periodically (e.g., every 2 seconds), which gives plenty of time for all the threads to be created. Another way is to let the trace and replay *control* object check for deadlocks while it is tracing the program's execution. The *control* object can compare the *numThreads* and *blockedThreads* counters after it observes that no synchronization events have been generated for some period of time, indicating that all the threads are blocked or completed, or that running threads are stuck in infinite loops (i.e., livelocked). This is exactly what our *control* object does.

To aid in understanding why a deadlock has occurred, we maintain a list of blocked threads along with a reason why each thread is blocked. This status information is displayed when a deadlock is detected. The events leading to a deadlock can be traced and replayed using the methods described earlier. As an example, here is the output for a deadlock detected in Solution 1 of the dining philosophers problem from Section 3.5:

Deadlock detected:
- philosopher3 blocked on operation P() of semaphore chopstick[4]
- philosopher2 blocked on operation P() of semaphore chopstick[3]
- philosopher4 blocked on operation P() of semaphore chopstick[0]
- philosopher1 blocked on operation P() of semaphore chopstick[2]
- philosopher0 blocked on operation P() of semaphore chopstick[1]

Some wait-for relations among threads can be captured by wait-for graphs. For example, a thread blocked in a *lock()* operation knows that the thread that owns the lock can unblock it. Thus, the wait-for relation among threads and locks is known. When one thread tries to lock two locks in one order while another thread tries to lock them in reverse order, a deadlock may occur. (This situation is discussed in Section 3.7.3.) Such a deadlock will be indicated by a cycle in the wait-for graph. Wait-for graphs can be used to detect both local and global deadlocks, and local deadlocks can be detected and reported as soon as they occur. Other wait-for relations, like the relation between threads and semaphores, can be approximated by using information extracted from the source code. This allows wait-for graphs to be used to detect other deadlock situations. However, the approximation can introduce a delay between the time local deadlocks occur and the time they are reported [Nonaka et al. 2001].

A deadlock detection utility has been incorporated into the Java HotSpot VM [Sun Microsystems 2002]. This utility is invoked by typing Ctrl+ (for Linux or the Solaris Operating Environment) or Ctrl-Pause/Break (for Microsoft Windows) on the command line while an application is running. The utility displays a description of any deadlocks it detects. If the application is deadlocked because two or more threads are involved in a cycle to acquire locks, the list of threads involved in the deadlock is displayed. This utility will not find deadlocks involving one or more threads that are permanently blocked in a monitor (see Chapter 4) waiting for a notification that never comes, which is similar to the situation where a thread is blocked in a *P()* operation waiting for a *V()* operation that will never come.

3.10.5   Reachability Testing for Semaphores and Locks

The testing and debugging tools that we have seen so far are very helpful during nondeterministic testing. If a program failure such as a deadlock occurs, the program can be debugged by replaying the execution repeatedly and collecting debugging information until the fault is located. Although this process is easy to carry out, it can be very inefficient. It is possible that some behaviors will be exercised many times, while others will not be exercised at all. For example, we performed 100 executions of Solution 1 for the dining philosophers problem with five philosophers and no deadlock was detected. After inserting random delays, deadlocks were detected in 18 of 100 executions. When we doubled the number of philosophers to 10, deadlocks were detected in only 4 of 100 executions. As the number of threads increases and thus the total number of possible behaviors increases, it apparently becomes more difficult to detect deadlocks with nondeterministic testing.

In general, nondeterministic testing may or may not uncover an existing fault. Furthermore, the instrumentation added to perform tracing and deadlock detection may create a probe effect that prevents some failures from being observed. What is needed is a testing technique that allows us to examine all the behaviors of a program, or at least as many different behaviors as is practical, in a systematic manner. By *systematic* we mean that there is an attempt to execute a given STN-sequence only once and it is possible to know when all the SYN-sequences have been exercised. Reachability testing is such a technique.

Reachability testing combines nondeterministic testing and program replay. During reachability testing, the SYN-sequence exercised by a nondeterministic execution is traced as usual. The execution trace captures the behavior that actually happened. But if the trace is defined carefully, it can also capture alternative behaviors that could have happened, but didn't, due to the way in which race conditions were arbitrarily resolved during execution. These alternative behaviors are called *race variants* of the trace. Replaying a race variant ensures that a different behavior is observed during the next test execution.

Identifying race conditions and race variants is the key challenge for reachability testing. Figure 3.33a shows a portion of an execution trace for the dining philosophers program. The diagram visually represents an execution in which Philosopher$_1$ picks up its left and right chopsticks before Philosopher$_2$ can pick up its left chopstick. (Philosopher$_1$ and Philosopher$_2$ share chopstick[2], which lies between them.) A labeled arrow from a philosopher to a semaphore represents a $P()$ or $V()$ operation that the philosopher called and completed on the semaphore. In the trace in Fig. 3.33a, Philosopher$_1$ and Philosopher$_2$ race to pick up chopstick$_2$, with Philosopher$_1$ completing its $P()$ operation on chopstick[2] before Philosopher$_2$ can complete its $P()$ operation.

In general, there is a race between calls to $P()$ or $V()$ operations on the same semaphore if these calls could be completed in a different order during another execution (with the same input). Figure 3.33b shows a race variant of the execution in Fig. 3.33a. In this race variant, Philosopher$_2$ wins the race to chopstick[2]

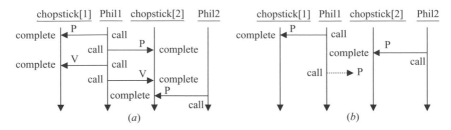

Figure 3.33   Execution trace and a race variant.

and picks it up before Philosopher₁ can grab it. The dashed arrow indicates that Philosopher₁'s *P( )* operation on chopstick[2] was called but not completed in the race variant. As we explain next, this call will be completed in an execution that replays the variant.

In general, a race variant represents the beginning portion of a SYN-sequence. Reachability testing uses replay to make sure that the events in the race variant are exercised and then lets the execution continue nondeterministically so that a complete sequence can be traced. Note that there may be many complete SYN-sequences that have a given race variant at the beginning. One of these sequences will be captured in the nondeterministic portion of the execution. The complete traced sequence can then be analyzed to derive more race variants, which can be used to generate more traces, and so on. When replay is applied to the race variant in Fig. 3.33*b*, Philosopher₁ and Philosopher₂ will both pick up their left chopsticks, which is part of the deadlock scenario in which all the philosophers hold their left chopstick and are waiting for their right. Although the complete deadlock scenario may not occur immediately, reachability testing ensures that every possible PV-sequence of the dining philosophers program will eventually be exercised and thus that the deadlock will eventually be detected.

In addition to the information required for replay, reachability testing requires execution traces to have sufficient information for identifying races. Also, algorithms are needed for race analysis and race variant generation. We describe these details in Chapter 7. Here, we mention the results of applying reachability testing to three of the example programs in Section 3.5.

The three Java programs and the reachability testing results are shown in Table 3.2. The first column shows the names of the programs. Program BB is the bounded buffer program from Listing 3.6, modified to allow multiple producers and consumers. Programs DP1 and DP4 are solutions 1 and 4 of the dining philosophers problem in Listings 3.7 and 3.8, respectively. (Recall that program DP1 has a deadlock.) Program RW is the readers and writers program from Listing 3.11. The second column shows the configuration of each program. For BB it indicates the number of producers (P), the number of consumers (C), and the number of slots (S) in the buffer. For RW it indicates the number of readers (R) and the number of writers (W). For DP, it indicates the number of philosophers (P).

TABLE 3.2 Reachability Testing for the Example Programs in Section 3.5

Program	Configuration	No. Seqs.
BB	1P+1C+2S	1
BB	2P+2C+2S	132
BB	3P+3C+2S	9252
RW	2R+2W	608
RW	2R+3W	12816
RW	3R+2W	21744
DP1	5P/10P	31/1023
DP4	4P	720
DP4	5P	22300

The threads in these programs deposit, withdraw, read, write, or eat one time. The third column shows the number of PV-sequences generated during reachability testing. To shed some light on the total time needed to execute these sequences, we observe that, for instance, the total reachability testing time for the DP4 program with five philosophers is 10 minutes on a 1.6-GHz PC with 512 MB of random access memory.

Following are several observations about the results in Table 3.2:

1. There is only one possible sequence for program BB with one producer and one consumer. We might expect more sequences to be possible since there are six $P()$ and $V()$ operations exercised during an execution of BB. There are two reasons why this is not the case. First, reachability testing exercises all of the partially ordered PV-sequences of BB, not all of the totally ordered sequences. That is, in a given execution trace, if events E1 and E2 are concurrent and E1 appears before E2, no race variant is generated to cover the case where the order of E1 and E2 is reversed. This creates a considerable reduction in the number of sequences. Second, reachability testing considers only sequences of *completed* $P()$ and $V()$ operations. Although there are many different orders in which the producer and consumer threads can *start* their $P()$ and $V()$ operations, there is only one order in which they can *complete* these operations.

2. Program DP1, with five philosophers, has a total of 31 sequences, one of which results in a deadlock. For DP1 with 10 philosophers, there is one deadlock sequence in 1023 possible sequences.

3. The ability to exercise all of the behaviors of a program maximizes test coverage. Notice, however, that in Table 3.2 the number of sequences exercised during reachability testing grows quickly as the number of threads increases. Thus, it may be impractical to exercise all of the sequences, let alone to inspect manually the output of all the test executions. At present, deadlocks can be detected and assertion can be checked automatically during reachability testing, but additional tool support is needed

to help programmers analyze test results. Also, reachability testing does not have to be applied exhaustively; rather, it can stop when a selected coverage criterion is satisfied.

4. Exercising and examining every PV-sequence may be more effort than is really required. Consider program BB again. There is an execution of BB with two producers in which Producer$_1$ executes *fullSlots.V()* followed immediately by Producer$_2$ executing *fullSlots.V()*. A race variant of this execution can be created simply by reversing the order of these two *V()* operations. But this variant is not very interesting since the order of the *V()* operations has no effect on the rest of the execution. In fact, if you use the semantics of *P()* and *V()* operations to ignore these types of variants, the number of sequences for BB with three Producers and three Consumers drops from 9252 to 36. For two Producers and two Consumers, the number of sequences drops from 132 to 4. The remaining sequences may still be more than what is needed. For example, reachability testing with three Producers will exercise all the possible orders in which the three Producers can deposit their items: (Producer$_1$, Producer$_2$, Producer$_3$), (Producer$_2$, Producer$_1$, Producer$_3$), (Producer$_3$, Producer$_2$, Producer$_1$), and so on. But the Producers all execute the same code and their behavior is independent of their IDs, so this batch of variants is not very interesting. If you use the symmetry of the threads to ignore these types of variants, the number of sequences for BB with three Producers and three Consumers drops from 36 to 4. For two Producers and two Consumers, the number of sequences drops from four to two [or perhaps even lower (see Exercise 7.5)]. These numbers are in line with the numbers we would probably come up with if we tried to generate sequences manually. Obviously, we need to think carefully about the types of sequences and the coverage criteria that we use for reachability testing.

We examine these issues in more detail in Chapter 7.

3.10.6 Putting It All Together

We have implemented these tracing, testing, and replay techniques in our semaphore and lock classes for C++/Win32/Pthreads and Java.

Tracing and Replaying C++/Win32/Pthreads Programs   To trace and replay executions of the C++/Win32/Pthreads bounded buffer program in Listing 3.26, class *Buffer* is modified to use *sharedVariables* and to turn tracing and race analysis off for the *sharedVariables* in the *buffer* array:

```
const int capacity = 3;
class Buffer {
private:
    sharedVariable<int> buffer[capacity];
```

```
        sharedVariable<int> count, in, out;
public:
    Buffer() : in(0), out(0), count(0) {
        for (int i=0; i<capacity; i++) {
        // Turn tracing and race analysis off
        // for the sharedVariables in array buffer
            buffer[i].setTrace(sharedVariable<int>::traceOff);
            buffer[i].setAnalysis(sharedVariable<int>::analysisOff);
        }
    }
    int size() { return count;}
    int withdraw () {
        int value = 0;
        value = buffer[out];
        out = (out + 1) %capacity;
        count--;
        return value;
    }
    void deposit (int value) {
        buffer[in] = value;
        in = (in + 1) %capacity;
        count++;
    }
};
```

Class *TDThread* ensures that the Producer and Consumer threads receive unique thread IDs, which in this case are 1 and 2, respectively. Tracing, replay, and analysis are controlled through the values of environment variables MODE and RACEANALYSIS. To set tracing *on* in Windows, execute the command

set MODE=TRACE   // Unix: setenv MODE TRACE

before executing the program. To execute random delays during TRACE mode, execute the command

set RANDOMDELAY=ON   // Unix: setenv RANDOMDELAY ON

This will enable the execution of *Sleep* statements at the beginning of methods *P()*, *V()*, *lock()*, and *unlock()*. The command "set RANDOMDELAY=OFF" will turn off random delays, and OFF is the default value. To turn on deadlock detection during trace mode, execute the command

 set DEADLOCKDETECTION=ON
 // Unix: setenv DEADLOCKDETECTION ON

The command "set DEADLOCKDETECTION=OFF" will turn off deadlock detection, and OFF is the default value. Data race detection using the lockset algorithm is enabled by

set DATARACEDETECTION=ON
// Unix: setenv DATARACEDETECTION ON

The command "set DATARACEDETECTION=OFF" will turn off data race detection, and OFF is the default value.

Environment variable CONTROLLERS is used to determine the number of trace files that will be created. The value SINGLE causes one controller and one trace file to be created:

set CONTROLLERS=SINGLE   // Unix: setenv CONTROLLERS SINGLE

The trace file semaphores-replay.txt will contain a totally ordered sequence of events for the two *countingSemaphore* objects and the two *mutexLock* objects. To create a separate controller for each object, which results in a separate trace file for each object's SYN-sequence, use the value MULTIPLE:

set CONTROLLERS=MULTIPLE
// Unix setenv CONTROLLERS MULTIPLE

The default value for the number of controllers is SINGLE. When the bounded-buffer program is executed, no races will be reported for the *sharedVariables* of *Buffer* since race analysis was turned off for each variable.

An execution is replayed by setting the MODE to REPLAY and executing the program:

set MODE=REPLAY   // Unix: setenv MODE REPLAY

The value of CONTROLLERS must be the same during tracing and replay. No data race detection or random delays are performed during replay.

Finally, reachability testing is performed on *Buffer* by setting the MODE to RT and customizing the driver process in file *RTDriver*.cpp, which is part of the synchronization library. Directions for customizing the driver process are in the file.

Tracing and Replaying Java Programs   For Java programs, tracing and replay are controlled using a property named *mode*. An execution of a Java version of *Buffer* is traced using the command

java–Dmode=trace–DrandomDelay=on–Dcontrollers=single Buffer

This executes the program Buffer with random delays and creates a single controller and a trace file named semaphores-replay.txt. The trace file will contain a totally ordered sequence of events for the two *countingSemaphore* objects and the two *mutexLock* objects. To create a separate controller for each synchronization object and a separate file for each object's SYN-sequence, set the value of the *controllers* property to *multiple*:

    -Dcontrollers=multiple

The default value for property *controllers* is *single* and the default value for property *randomDelay* is *off*. To turn on deadlock detection during trace mode, specify −DdeadlockDetection=on. The default value for property *deadlockDetection* is *off*.

An execution is replayed by setting the *mode* property to *replay*:

    java −Dmode=replay Buffer

The value of CONTROLLERS must be the same during tracing and replay. No random delays are performed during replay.

Finally, reachability testing is performed on *Buffer* by setting the *mode* property to *rt* and executing a driver process named *RTDriver* that is part of the synchronization library:

    java −Dmode=rt RTDriver Buffer

The class name *Buffer* is passed as a command-line parameter to driver process *RTDriver*, which carries out the reachability testing process.

FURTHER READING

Andrews [1989] describes a systematic method for using semaphores to solve synchronization problems. Starting with an assertion that specifies a desired synchronization invariant, a sequence of steps is followed to derive a correct program that maintains this invariant. He also illustrates passing-the-baton and other semaphore patterns.

Details about using Win32 CRITICAL_SECTION, Semaphore, Mutex, and Event objects can be found in [Beveridge and Wiener 1997; Petzold 1998; Hart 2000a]. Hart [2000b] compares the performance of these objects. Ringle [1999a,b] discusses issues related to creating singleton objects in multithreaded C++/Win32 programs. He presents a lock class that avoids certain construction order problems inherent with static lock objects. More information on C++ and Win32 synchronization can be found in various articles [Becker 1999; Manley 1999; Kleber 2000; Lowy 2000; Abramson 2002, 2003; Chaudry 2002; Khamsi 2003; LaPlante 2003].

The VP operation was introduced in [Tai and Carver 1996]. Howard [2000] illustrates the use of Win32's *SignalObjectAndWait()* operation, which when applied to semaphores is equivalent to *VP()*. Pugh [1999] describes some potential problems with certain programming idioms that are commonly used with

Java threads. One of these idioms, called *double-checked locking*, has been the subject of a tremendous amount of discussion [Goetz 2001; Meyers and Alexandrescu 2004a,b]. Reading about problems with double-checked locking is a good way to learn more about volatile variables and shared memory consistency. Courtois et al. [1971] introduced the readers and writers problem. The tracing and replay techniques in Section 3.8 are from [Carver 1985; Carver and Tai 1986, 1991].

REFERENCES

Abramson, Tomer (2002). Performing multiple read/write locks. *C/C++ Users Journal*, May, pp. 25–27.

Abramson, Tomer (2003). Detecting deadlocks in C++ using a locks monitor. *Windows Developer Magazine*, April, pp. 32–37.

Andrews, Gregory R. (1989). A method for solving synchronization problems. *Science of Computer Programming*, Vol. 13, No. 1 (January), pp. 1–21.

Andrews, Gregory R. (2000). *Foundations of Multithreaded, Parallel, and Distributed Programming*. Reading, MA: Addison-Wesley.

Becker, Thomas (1999). A semaphore with priorities for Win32. *C/C++ Users Journal*, August, pp. 18–30.

Beveridge, Jim, and R. Wiener (1997). *Multithreading Programming Techniques in Win32: The Complete Guide to Threads*. Reading, MA: Addison-Wesley.

Carver, Richard H. (1985). *Reproducible testing of concurrent programs based on shared variables*. Master's thesis, Computer Science Department, North Carolina State University, Raleigh, NC.

Carver, Richard H., and K. C. Tai (1986). Reproducible testing of concurrent programs based on shared variables. *Proc. 6th International Conference on Distributed Computing Systems*, pp. 428–433.

Carver, R. H., and K. C. Tai (1991). Replay and testing for concurrent programs. *IEEE Software*, Vol. 8, No. 2, pp. 66–74.

Chaudry, Puneesh (2002). A per-thread singleton class. *C/C++ Users Journal*, May, pp. 14–19.

Courtois, P. J., F. Heymans, and D. L. Parnas (1971). Concurrent control with readers and writers. *Communications of the ACM*, Vol. 14, No. 10 (October), pp. 667–668.

Dijkstra, Edsger W. (1965). Solution of a problem in concurrent programming control. *Communications of the ACM*, Vol. 8, No. 9 (September), p. 569.

Dijkstra, Edsger W. (1968). Cooperating sequential processes. In F. Genuys (Ed.), *Programming Languages*. New York: Academic Press, pp. 43–112.

Dijkstra, Edsger W. (1971). Hierarchical ordering of sequential processes. *Acta Informatica*, Vol. 1, pp. 115–138.

Feitelson, D. G. (1991). Deadlock detection without wait-for graphs. *Parallel Computing*, Vol. 17, No. 12 (December), pp. 1377–1383.

Goetz, Brian (2001). Double-checked locking: clever, but broken. http://www.javaworld.com/javaworld/jw-02-2001/jw-0209-double.html.

Hart, Johnson M. (2000a). *Win32 System Programming: A Windows 2000 Application Developer's Guide*, 2nd ed. Reading, MA: Addison-Wesley.

Hart, Johnson M. (2000b). Online supplement to *Win32 System Programming: A Windows 2000 Application Developer's Guide*, 2nd ed. Reading, MA: Addison-Wesley, http://world.std.com/~jmhart/csmutx.htm.

Havelund, K., and T. Pressburger (2000). Model checking Java programs using Java PathFinder. *International Journal on Software Tools for Technology Transfer*, Vol. 2, No. 4 (April), pp. 366–381.

Howard, David M. (2000). Using predicates with Win32 threads. *C/C++ Users Journal*, May, pp. 18–30.

Hwang, Gwan-Hwan, Kuo-Chung Tai, and Ting-Lu Huang (1995). Reachability testing: an approach to testing concurrent software. *International Journal of Software Engineering and Knowledge Engineering*, Vol. 5, No. 4, pp. 493–510.

Khamsi, Sarir (2003). A class for handling shared memory under Win32. *C/C++ Users Journal*, May, p. 34.

Kleber, Jeff (2000). Thread-safe access to collections. *C/C++ Users Journal*, May, pp. 36–39.

LaPlante, John (2003). Efficient thread coordination. *C/C++ Users Journal*, May, pp. 6–19.

Lowy, Juval (2000). Making primitive objects thread safe. *C/C++ Users Journal*, March, pp. 85–86.

Manley, Kevin (1999). Improving performance with thread-private heaps. *C/C++ Users Journal*, September, pp. 50–62.

Meyers, Scott, and Andrei Alexandrescu (2004a). C++ and the perils of double-checked locking: Part I. *Dr. Dobb's Journal*, August, pp. 46–49.

Meyers, Scott, and Andrei Alexandrescu (2004b). C++ and the perils of double-checked locking: Part II. *Dr. Dobb's Journal*, September, pp. 57–61.

Nonaka, Yusuka, Kazuo Ushijima, Hibiki Serizawa, Shigeru Murata, and Jingde Cheng (2001). A run-time deadlock detector for concurrent Java programs. *Proc. 8th Asia-Pacific Software Engineering Conference (APSEC'01)*, pp. 45–52.

Petzold, Charles (1998). *Programming Windows*, 5th ed. Redmond, WA: Microsoft Press.

Pugh, William (1999). Fixing the Java memory model. *Proc. ACM Java Grande Conference*, pp. 89–98.

Ringle, Jon (1999a). Singleton creation: the thread-safe way. *C/C++ Users Journal*, October, pp. 43–49.

Ringle, Jon (1999b). We Have Mail: letter. *C/C++ Users Journal*, December.

Savage, S., M. Burrows, G. Nelson, P. Sobalvarro, and T. E. Anderson (1997). Eraser: a dynamic data race detector for multithreaded programs. *ACM Transactions on Computer Systems*, Vol. 15, No. 4 (April), pp. 391–411.

Silberschatz, Abraham, Peter Baer Galvin, and Greg Gagne (2001). *Operating System Concepts*, 6th ed. New York: Wiley.

Sun Microsystems (2002). Java virtual machines. http://java.sun.com/j2se/1.4.2/docs/guide/vm.

Tai, K. C., and R. H. Carver (1996). VP: a new operation for semaphores. *ACM Operating Systems Review*, Vol. 30, No. 3, pp. 5–11.

EXERCISES

3.1. Can the bounded-buffer solution in Section 3.5 be used with multiple producers and consumers? If not, modify it to produce a correct solution.

3.2. Section 3.4 defined *strong* and *weak* semaphores. Assume that semaphore
mutex is initialized to 1 and that each thread executes:

```
mutex.P();
/* critical section */
mutex.V();
```

    (a) Suppose that there are two threads and *mutex* is a weak semaphore. Is
the critical section problem solved?

    (b) Suppose there are three threads and *mutex* is a strong semaphore. Is
the critical section problem solved?

    (c) Is class *countingSemaphore* in Listing 3.15 a strong or weak
semaphore?

3.3. Consider the semaphore-based solution to strategy R<W.2 in Section 3.5.4.

    (a) Is it possible that a writer waits on *readers_w_que.P()*? Explain.

    (b) Is it possible that a reader waits on *writers_que.P()*? Explain.

3.4. The *InterlockedExchange* function was described in Section 2.3. It has two
parameters and behaves like the following atomic function:

```
LONG InterlockedExchange (LONG* target, LONG newValue) {
    LONG temp = *target; *target = newValue; return temp;
}
```

The following is an implementation of a *countingSemaphore* using *Inter-
lockedExchange()*:

```
class countingSemaphore {
private:
    volatile int permits;
    volatile LONG mutex;      // provides mutual exclusion for permits
    volatile LONG block;      // used to delay threads waiting on permits
public:
    countingSemaphore(int init) : permits(init), mutex(0), block(1) { }
    voidP() {
        while (InterlockedExchange(const_cast<LONG*>(&mutex),true))
            {Sleep(0);}
        permits = permits - 1 ;
        if (permits < 0) {
            mutex = false;
```

```
        while (InterlockedExchange(const_cast<LONG*>(&block),true))
          {Sleep(0);}
      }
      else
        mutex = false;
    }
  void V() {
      while (InterlockedExchange(const_cast<LONG*>(&mutex),true))
          {Sleep(0);};
      permits = permits + 1 ;
      if (permits <= 0) {
        while (!block) {Sleep(0);};
        block = false;
      }
      mutex = false;
    }
};
```

Statements

```
while (InterlockedExchange(const_cast<LONG*>(&mutex),true))
    {Sleep(0);};
```

and

```
mutex = false;
```

are used to enforce mutual exclusion for *permits*. In the *P()* operation, the statement

```
while (InterlockedExchange(const_cast<LONG*>(&block),true))
    {Sleep(0);}
```

is used to delay threads that are waiting to be awakened by *V()* operations. In the *V()* operation, the statement

```
while (!block) {Sleep(0);};
```

is used to make sure that *block* is set to false only when it is true. The initial value of *block* is true. *Block* is set to false in order to awaken a delayed thread. After *block* is set to false, it remains false until a delayed thread executes InterlockedExchange(const_cast<LONG*> (&block),true). (Then the delayed thread becomes awakened.) If *block* is false when *V()* is executed, the previous *V()* operation has not yet awakened a delayed thread.

(a) Show that the deletion of while (!block) {Sleep(0);} in *V()* can create an error.

(b) Can the implementation of *V()* be replaced by the following?

```
public void V(int s) {
    while (InterlockedExchange(const_cast<LONG*>(&mutex),true))
        {Sleep(0);};
    permits = permits + 1;
    if (permits <= 0) {
        mutex = false;
        while (!block) {Sleep 0;};
        block = false;
    }
    else
        mutex = false;
}
```

3.5. Section 3.5.5 shows how to use binary semaphores to implement *P()* and *V()* operations for a *countingSemaphore* class. Suppose that binary semaphores are redefined so that a *V()* operation never blocks the calling thread. That is, if the value of a binary semaphore is 1 when a *V()* operation is called, the value is not modified and the calling thread simply completes the operations and returns.

(a) Are the implementations of *P()* and *V()* still correct if these new binary semaphores are used? Explain.

(b) If not, suppose that we replace the statements

```
mutex.V();
delayQ.P();
```

with the single statement

```
delayQ.VP(mutex);
```

Is this new implementation correct? Explain.

3.6. In Section 3.5.4 a semaphore-based solution to strategy R<W.2 for the readers and writers problem is given.

(a) Below is a revised version of the read operation, in which semaphore *mutex_r* is deleted and semaphore *readers_w_que* is used to provide mutual exclusion for accessing *activeReaders* and for synchronization between readers and writers. Does the revised solution still implement strategy R<W.2? Explain.

```
Read() {
    readers_w_que.P();        // readers may be blocked by a writer
    ++activeReaderCount;
    if (activeReaderCount = 1) writer_que.P()
```

```
    readers_w_que.V();
    /* read x */
    readers_w_que.P();
    --activeReaderCount;
    if (activeReaderCount = 0) writer_que.V();
    readers_w_que.V();
  }
```

(b) Below is a revised version of the read operation in which the last two
statements have been reversed. Does the revised solution still implement strategy R<W.2? Explain.

```
Read() {
    readers_w_que.P();
    mutex_r.lock();
    ++activeReaders;
    if (activeReaders == 1) writers_que.P();
    mutex_r.unlock();
    readers_w_que.V();
    /* read x */
    mutex_r.lock();
    --activeReaders;
    mutex_r.V();                              // ***** these two statements
    if (activeReaders == 0) writers_que.V();  // ***** were reversed
  }
```

3.7. *The unisex bathroom* [Andrews 2000]. This problem is similar to the readers and writers problem. Suppose that there is one bathroom in your office.
It can be used by both men and women, but not by both at the same time.

(a) Develop a semaphore solution that allows any number of men or any
number of women (but not both) in the bathroom at the same time. Your
solution should ensure the required exclusion and avoid deadlock, but it
need not be fair (i.e., some people may never get to use the bathroom).

(b) Modify your solution to part (a) to ensure that at most four people are
in the bathroom at the same time.

(c) Develop a semaphore solution that ensures fairness:

- All men and women eventually get to use the bathroom.
- When the last man in the bathroom exits, all women that are currently
  waiting are allowed to enter the bathroom.
- When the last woman in the bathroom exits, all men that are currently
  waiting are allowed to enter the bathroom.
- If men are in the bathroom, another man cannot enter the bathroom
  if women are waiting.
- If women are in the bathroom, another women cannot enter the bathroom if men are waiting.

3.8. Write a semaphore implementation of an Event object that is similar to the Event object in Win32. Event objects have operations *block()* and *set()*. A call to *block()* always blocks the caller. A call to *set()* awakens every thread that has called *block()* since the last time *set()* was called. Use *P()* and *V()* (but no *VP()*) operations on semaphores. Declare and initialize any variables and semaphores that you use.

3.9. Are the following busy-waiting definitions of operations *P()* and *V()* for a counting semaphore *s* correct?

P(): permits = permits-1; while (permits < 0) {;}
V(): permits = permits + 1;

3.10. Solution 4 of the dining philosophers problem allows a philosopher to starve. Show an execution sequence in which a philosopher starves.

3.11. Below is a proposed implementation of operations *P()* and *V()* in class *BinarySemaphore*. Is this implementation correct? Explain.

```
public synchronized void P() {
    while (value==0)    try { wait(); } catch ( InterruptedException e) { }
    value=0;
    notify();
}
public synchronized void V() {
    while (value==1)    try { wait(); }catch ( InterruptedException e) { }
    value=1;
    notify();
}
```

3.12. Many problems require iterative solutions. In these solutions, *n* threads are created at the beginning of execution. Each thread performs some subtask on each iteration. All *n* threads synchronize at the end of each iteration:

```
Worker Thread i {
    while (true) {
        perform thread i's task;
        wait for all n threads to complete;
    }
}
```

This is called *barrier synchronization*, because the *wait* at the end of each iteration represents a barrier that all threads have to arrive at before any are allowed to pass. Notice that the same barrier is reused at the end of each iteration.

Use semaphores to implement a reusable barrier for *n* threads. A template for class *Barrier* is given below.

```
class Barrier {
    private int count = 0;          // count of waiting threads
    private int n = 0;              // number of threads
    private binarySemaphore mutex(1); // provides mutual exclusion
    private binarySemaphore go(0);    // a queue for threads to wait in until
                                      // they are permitted to go
    public Barrier (int n) {this.n = n);
    public void waitB() {             // call b.waitB() to wait on Barrier b
        /* implement this method */
    }
}
```

Complete the template. You can assume that the semaphores are FCFS semaphores.

3.13. *The bear and the honeybees* [Andrews 2000]. There are *n* bees and one bear who share a pot of honey. The pot is initially empty; its capacity is H portions of honey, where H ¡= *n*.

- The bee threads repeatedly put one portion of honey in the pot (i.e., pot++); the bee who fills the pot awakens the bear. When the pot is full, bees must wait until the bear eats all the honey.
- The bear thread sleeps until the pot is full (i.e., pot == H), then eats all the honey and goes back to sleep.

  The pot is a shared resource (implemented as a variable), so at most one bee or the bear can access it at a time. Write implementations of bee and bear threads using *P()* and *V()* operations on semaphores.

3.14. *Message exchange* [Carr et al. 2001]. There are two groups of threads. Threads from group A wish to exchange integer messages with threads in group B. Group A threads execute method *exchangeWithB()* while group B threads execute method *exchangeWithA()*:

```
void exchangeWithB() {              void exchangeWithA {
    while (true) {                      while (true) {
        msgA = "A message";                 msgB = "B message";
        /* exchange message */              /* exchange message */
        // now msgA is "B message"          // now msgB is "A message"
    }                                   }
}                                   }
```

There are two constraints:

- Once a thread T_A from group A makes a message available, T_A can continue only if it receives a message from a thread T_B in group B that has successfully retrieved T_A's message. Similarly, thread T_B can continue only if it receives a massage from T_A rather than from some other thread in group A.

- Once a thread T_A from group A makes its message available, another thread in group A should not be allowed to overwrite T_A's message before the message is retrieved by a thread in group B.

For each solution below, state whether the solution is correct or incorrect. If the solution is incorrect, describe a scenario that illustrates the error.

(a) countingSemaphore A(0), B(0);77
     int bufferA, bufferB;

```
void exchangeWithB() {     void exchangeWithA() {
    int msgA;                  int msgB;
    while (true) {             while (true) {
        // create the messages that will be exchanged
        msgA = ...;                msgB = ...;
        // signal the other thread that you are ready
        B.V();                     A.V();
        // wait for signal from the other thread
        A.P();                     B.P();
        // make a copy of message for the other thread
        bufferA = msgA;            bufferB = msgB;
        // swap copies; now msgB contains A's message
        msgA = bufferB;            msgB = bufferA;
        // and msgA contains B's message
        ...;                       ...;
    }                          }
}                          }
```

(b) binarySemaphore mutex(1); countingSemaphore A(0), B(0); int bufferA, bufferB;

```
void exchangeWithB() {     void exchangeWithA() {
    int msgA;                  int msgB;
    while (true) {             while (true) {
        // create the messages that will be exchanged
        msgA = ...;                msgB = ...;
        // signal the other thread you are ready
        B.V();                     A.V();
        // wait forsignal from the other thread
        A.P();                     B.P();
        // critical section start
        mutex.P();                 mutex.P();
        // make copy for the other thread
        bufferA = msgA;            bufferB = msgB;
        // critical section end
        mutex.V();                 mutex.V();
```

```
                  // signal ready to swap
                  B.V();                          A.V();
                  // wait for signal from the other thread
                  A.P();                          B.P();
                  // critical section start
                  mutex.P();                      mutex.P();
                  // swap copies
                  msgA = bufferB;                 msgB = bufferA;
                  // critical section end
                  mutex.V();                      mutex.V();
                  // now msgB contains A's message
                  ...;                            ...;
                  // and msgA contains B's message
              }                               }
          }                               }
```

(c) binarySemaphore Aready(1), Bready(1); countingSemaphore Adone(0),
      Bdone(0);
      int bufferA, bufferB;

```
      void exchangeWithB() {   void exchangeWithA() {
          int msgA;                int msgB;
          while (true) {           while (true) {
              // create the messages that will be exchanged
              msgA = ...;              msgB = ...;
              // critical section start
              Aready.P();              Bready.P();
              // make a copy of message for the other thread
              bufferA = msgA;          bufferB = msgB;
              // signal ready to swap
              Adone.V();               Bdone.V();
              // wait for signal from the other thread
              Bdone.P();               Adone.P();
              // swap copies
              msgA = bufferB;          msgB = bufferA;
              // critical section end
              Aready.V();              Bready.V();
              // now msgB contains A's message
              ...;                     ...;
              // and msgA contains B's message
          }                        }
      }                        }
```

(d) binarySemaphore Aready(1), Bready(1); countingSemaphore Adone(0),
      Bdone(0);
      int bufferA, bufferB;

```
      void exchangeWithB() {    void exchangeWithA() {
         int msgA;                 int msgB;
         while (true) {            while (true) {
            // create the messages that will be exchanged
            msgA = ...;               msgB = ...;
            // critical section start
            Bready.P();               Aready.P();
            // make copy for the other thread
            bufferA = msgA;           bufferB = msgB;
            // signal ready to swap
            Adone.V();                Bdone.V();
            // wait for signal from the other thread
            Bdone.P();                Adone.P();
            // swap copies
            msgA = bufferB;           msgB = bufferA;
            // critical section end and signal other ...;
            Aready.V();               Bready.V();
            // now msgB contains A's message
            ...;                      ...;
            // and msgA contains B's message
         }                         }
      }                         }
```

(e) binarySemaphore Amutex(1), Bmutex(1);
     binarySemaphore notFullA(1), notFullB(1), notEmptyA(1),
        notEmptyB(0);

```
      void exchangeWithB() {    void exchangeWithA() {
         int msgA;                 int msgB;
         while (true) {            while (true) {
            // create the messages that will be exchanged
            msgA = ...;               msgB = ...;
            // critical section start
            Amutex.P();               Bmutex.P();
            // wait for previous swap complete
            notFullA.P();             notFullB.P();
            // make copy
            bufferA = msgA;           bufferB = msgB;
            // signal the other thread copy made
            notEmptyA.V();            notEmptyB.V();
            // wait for copy to be made
            notEmptyB.P();            notEmptyA.P();
            // swap
            msgA = bufferB;           msgB = bufferA;
            // signal swap complete
```

```
    noFullB.V();                    notFullA.V();
    // critical section end
    Amutex.V();                     Bmutex.V();
    // now msgB contains A's message
    ...;                            ...;
    // and msgA contains B's message
  }                               }
}                               }
```

(f) binarySemaphore notFull(1), notEmptyA(0), notEmptyB(0);
int shared;

```
void exchangeWithB() {    void exchangeWithA() {
  int msgA;                   int msgB, temp;
  while (true) {              while (true) {
    // create the messages that will be exchanged
    msgA = ...;                   msgB = ...;
    // mutual exclusion for exchange
    notFull.P();
    // A makes copy for B
    shared = msgA;
    // signal copy made for B
    notEmptyA.V();               notEmptyA.P();
    // B gets A's copy
    temp = shared;
    // B makes copy for A
    shared = msgB;
    // signal copy made for A
    notEmptyB.P();               notEmptyB.V();
    // A gets B's copy
    msgA = shared;
    // allow next exchange
    notFull.V();
    // now msgB contains A's message
    ...;                         ...;
    // and msgA contains B's message
  }                            }
}                            }
```

3.15. *Alternating threads* [Reek 2003]. Consider method *alternate()*, which two threads call in order to alternate execution with one another. Each time a thread calls *alternate()*, it signals the other thread and then blocks itself. The signaling thread remains blocked until the other thread calls *alternate()*.

    (a) Is the following implementation of method *alternate()* correct? Explain your answer.

```
boolean isWaiting = false;
binarySemaphore mutex = new binarySemaphore(1);
binarySemaphore block = new binarySemaphore(0);
public void alternate() {
   mutex.P()
   if (isWaiting) {block.V(); block.P();}
   else {isWaiting = true; mutex.V(); block.P();}
   mutex.V();
}
```

(b) If you believe that this solution is incorrect, describe how to fix it without making any major changes. (For example, do not change the number of semaphores.)

(c) Write another solution to this problem. You may add additional semaphores, but you cannot use operation *VP()*.

3.16. Suppose that reachability testing is applied to program CP. Assume that every execution of CP is checked during reachability testing and that all outputs and all sequences are correct. Can we say then that program CP is correct? Explain.

3.17. The number of sequences exercised during reachability testing for the bounded-buffer program in Listing 3.6 is shown in Table 3.2. There are at least two possible ways to modify the program in Listing 3.6 to allow multiple producers and consumers (see Exercise 3.1). Compare the number of sequences exercised by reachability testing for each program. Which program is the best, considering all factors?

3.18. The *countingSemaphore* class in Section 3.6.1 may fail if threads blocked on the `wait` operation in method *P()* can be interrupted or if spurious wakeups can occur. Describe a sequence of *P()* and *V()* operations that leads to a failure if interrupts or spurious wakeups occur. *Hint*: Assume that semaphore *s* is initialized to 1 and consider the value that variable *permits* should have after each *P()* and *V()* operation.

3.19. Figures 3.9 and 3.10 shows scenarios in which multiple readers and writers issue requests before any one of them is allowed to read or write. Consider strategy R>W.2 in Section 3.5.4. Where in the code for readers and writers would you consider a "read request" or "write request" event to occur? After identifying the location, determine whether it is possible to have two successive "read request" events or two successive "write request" events without an intervening read or write event. Can the scenarios in Figs. 3.9 and 3.10 occur in the readers and writers solutions presented in Section 3.5.4?

4

MONITORS

Semaphores were defined before the introduction of programming concepts such as data encapsulation and information hiding. In semaphore-based programs, shared variables and the semaphores that protect them are global variables. This causes shared variable and semaphore operations to be distributed throughout the program. Since P and V operations are used for both mutual exclusion and condition synchronization, it is difficult to determine how a semaphore is being used without examining all the code.

Monitors were invented to overcome these problems. The monitor concept was developed by Tony Hoare and Per Brinch Hansen in the early 1970s. This is the same time period in which the concept of information hiding [Parnas 1972] and the `class` construct [Dahl et al. 1970] originated. Monitors support data encapsulation and information hiding and are adapted easily to an object-oriented environment.

In this chapter we show how to use semaphores to implement monitor classes for C++ and Java. These custom classes support cyclical testing and debugging techniques for monitor-based programs. Even though Java and Pthreads provide built-in support for monitor-like objects, our monitor classes are still useful since it is not easy to test and debug built-in Java or Pthreads monitors. Win32 does not provide monitors, but we can use our custom classes to simulate monitors in C++/Win32 programs.

Modern Multithreading: Implementing, Testing, and Debugging Multithreaded Java and C++/Pthreads/Win32 Programs, By Richard H. Carver and Kuo-Chung Tai
Copyright © 2006 John Wiley & Sons, Inc.

4.1 DEFINITION OF MONITORS

A monitor encapsulates shared data, all the operations on the data, and any synchronization required for accessing the data. A monitor has separate constructs for mutual exclusion and condition synchronization. In fact, mutual exclusion is provided automatically by the monitor's implementation, freeing the programmer from the burden of implementing critical sections. We will use an object-oriented definition of a monitor in which a monitor is a synchronization object that is an instance of a special *monitor* class. A monitor class defines private variables and a set of public and private access methods. The variables of a monitor represent shared data. Threads communicate by calling monitor methods that access the shared variables. The need to synchronize access to shared variables distinguishes monitor classes from regular classes.

4.1.1 Mutual Exclusion

At most one thread is allowed to execute inside a monitor at any time. However, it is not the programmer's responsibility to provide mutual exclusion for the methods in a monitor. Mutual exclusion is provided by the monitor's implementation, using one of the techniques discussed in previous chapters. If a thread calls a monitor method but another thread is already executing inside the monitor, the calling thread must wait outside the monitor. A monitor has an entry queue to hold the calling threads that are waiting to enter the monitor (see Fig. 4.2).

4.1.2 Condition Variables and SC Signaling

Condition synchronization is achieved using condition variables and operations *wait()* and *signal()*. A condition variable denotes a queue of threads that are waiting for a specific condition to become true. (The condition is not explicitly specified as part of the condition variable.) A condition variable *cv* is declared as

condition Variable cv;

Operation *cv.wait()* is analogous to a *P* operation in that it is used to block a thread. Operation *cv.signal()* unblocks a thread and is analogous to a *V* operation. But as we will see below, operations *wait()* and *signal()* do more than just block and unblock threads.

A monitor has one entry queue plus one queue associated with each condition variable. For example, Listing 4.1 shows the structure of monitor class *boundedBuffer*. Class *boundedBuffer* inherits from class *monitor*. It has five data members, condition variables named *notFull* and *notEmpty*, and monitor methods *deposit()* and *withdraw()*. Figure 4.2 is a graphical view of class *boundedBuffer*, which shows its entry queue and the queues associated with condition variables *notFull* and *notEmpty*.

```
class boundedBuffer extends monitor {
    public void deposit(...) { ... }
    public int withdraw (...) { ... }
    public boundedBuffer( ) { ... }

    private int fullSlots = 0;        // # of full slots in the buffer
    private int capacity = 0;         // capacity of the buffer
    private int [] buffer = null;     // circular buffer of ints
    // in is index for next deposit, out is index for next withdrawal
    private int in = 0, out = 0;
    // producer waits on notFull when the buffer is full
    private conditionVariable notFull;
    // consumer waits on notEmpty when the buffer is empty
    private conditionVariable notEmpty;
}
```

Listing 4.1   Monitor class *boundedBuffer*.

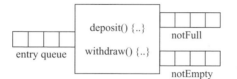

Figure 4.2   Graphical view of monitor class *boundedBuffer*.

A thread that is executing inside a monitor method blocks itself on condition variable *cv* by executing

cv.wait();

Executing a *wait()* operation releases mutual exclusion (to allow another thread to enter the monitor) and blocks the thread on the rear of the queue for *cv*. The threads blocked on a condition variable are considered to be outside the monitor. If a thread that is blocked on a condition variable is never awakened by another thread, a deadlock occurs.

A thread blocked on condition variable *cv* is awakened by the execution of

cv.signal();

If there are no threads blocked on *cv*, the *signal()* operation has no effect; otherwise, the *signal()* operation awakens the thread at the front of the queue for *cv*. What happens next depends on exactly how the *signal()* operation is defined. There are several different types of signaling disciplines. For now, we assume that the *signal-and-continue* (SC) discipline is used. This is the discipline used by Java's built-in monitor construct. Other types of signals are described in Section 4.4.

After a thread executes an SC signal to awaken a waiting thread, the signaling thread continues executing in the monitor and the awakened thread is moved to the entry queue. That is, the awakened thread does not reenter the monitor immediately; rather, it joins the entry queue and waits for its turn to enter. When SC signals are used, signaled threads have the same priority as threads trying to enter the monitor via public method calls.

Let A denote the set of threads that have been awakened by *signal()* operations and are waiting to reenter the monitor, S denote the set of signaling threads, and C denote the set of threads that have called a monitor method but have not yet entered the monitor. (The threads in sets A and C wait in the entry queue.) Then in an SC monitor, the relative priority associated with these three sets of threads is $S > C = A$.

Operation *cv.signalAll()* wakes up all the threads that are blocked on condition variable *cv*. Operations *empty()* and *length()* return information about the queue associated with a condition variable. The execution of

cv.empty()

returns *true* if the queue for *cv* is empty, and *false* otherwise. Executing

cv.length()

returns the current length of the queue for *cv*.

Listing 4.3 shows a complete *boundedBuffer* monitor. This solution uses condition variables *notEmpty* and *notFull*. Operations *deposit()* and *withdraw()* check the state of the buffer, perform their buffer operations, and signal each other at the end. As shown, the *signal()* statements at the ends of the methods are always executed. Alternatively, since *signal()* operations may involve context switches and thus may be relatively expensive, they can be guarded with if-statements so that they are only executed when it is possible that another thread is waiting.

Assume that the buffer is empty and that the thread at the front of the entry queue is Consumer$_1$ (C$_1$). The queues for condition variables *notFull* and *notEmpty* are also assumed to be empty (Fig. 4.4a). When Consumer$_1$ enters method *withdraw()*, it executes the statement

```
while (fullSlots == 0)
notEmpty.wait();
```

Since the buffer is empty, Consumer$_1$ blocks itself by executing a *wait()* operation on condition variable *notEmpty* (Fig. 4.4b).

Producer$_1$ (P$_1$) then enters the monitor. Since the buffer is not full, Producer$_1$ deposits an item and executes *notEmpty.signal()*. This signal operation awakens Consumer$_1$ and moves Consumer$_1$ to the rear of the entry queue behind

```
class boundedBuffer extends monitor {
    private int fullSlots = 0;        // number of full slots in the buffer
    private int capacity = 0;          // capacity of the buffer
    private int[] buffer = null;       // circular buffer of ints
    private int in = 0, out = 0;
    private conditionVariable notFull = new conditionVariable();
    private conditionVariable notEmpty = new conditionVariable();

    public boundedBuffer(int bufferCapacity ) {
        capacity = bufferCapacity;buffer = new int[bufferCapacity];}
        public void deposit(int value) {
        while (fullSlots == capacity)
            notFull.wait();
        buffer[in] = value;
        in = (in + 1) % capacity; ++fullSlots;
        notEmpty.signal(); //alternatively:if (fullSlots == 1) notEmpty.signal();
    }
    public int withdraw() {
        int value;
        while (fullSlots == 0)
            notEmpty.wait();
        value = buffer[out];
        out = (out + 1) % capacity; --fullSlots;
        notFull.signal(); //alternatively:if (fullSlots == capacity–1) notFull.signal();
        return value;
    }
}
...
boundedBuffer bb;
bb.deposit(...);                       // executed by Producers
bb.withdraw(...);                      // executed by Consumers
```

Listing 4.3   Monitor class *boundedBuffer*.

Consumer$_2$ (C$_2$) (Fig. 4.4c). After its *signal()* operation, Producer$_1$ can continue executing in the monitor, but since there are no more statements to execute, Producer$_1$ exits the monitor. Consumer$_2$ now barges ahead of Consumer$_1$ and consumes an item. Consumer$_2$ executes *notFull.signal()*, but there are no Producers waiting, so the signal has no effect. When Consumer$_2$ exits the monitor, Consumer$_1$ is allowed to reenter, but the loop condition (*fullSlots == 0*) is true again:

```
while (fullSlots == 0)
    notEmpty.wait();
```

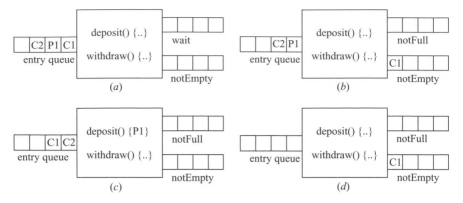

Figure 4.4 Bounded buffer monitor.

Thus, Consumer$_1$ is blocked once more on condition variable *notEmpty* (Fig. 4.4*d*). Even though Consumer$_1$ entered the monitor first, it is Consumer$_2$ that consumes the first item.

This example illustrates why the *wait()* operations in an SC monitor are usually found inside `while`-loops: A thread waiting on a condition variable cannot assume that the condition it is waiting for will be true when it reenters the monitor.

4.2 MONITOR-BASED SOLUTIONS TO CONCURRENT PROGRAMMING PROBLEMS

We now show several monitor-based solutions to classical concurrent programming problems. These solutions assume that condition variable queues are first-come-first-serve (FCFS).

4.2.1 Simulating Counting Semaphores

Solution 1 Listing 4.5 shows an SC monitor with methods *P()* and *V()* that simulates a counting semaphore. In this implementation, a waiting thread may get stuck forever in the `while`-loop in method *P()*. To see this, assume that the value of *permits* is 0 when thread T1 calls *P()*. Since the loop condition (*permits == 0*) is true, T1 will block itself by executing a *wait* operation. Now assume that some other thread executes *V()* and signals T1. Thread T1 will join the entry queue behind any threads that have called *P()* and are waiting to enter the monitor for the first time. These other threads can enter the monitor and decrement *permits* before T1 has a chance to reenter the monitor and examine its loop condition. If the value of *permits* is 0 when T1 eventually evaluates its loop condition, T1 will block itself again by issuing another *wait* operation.

```
class countingSemaphore1 extends monitor {
    private int permits; // The value of permits is never negative.
    private conditionVariable permitAvailable = new conditionVariable();
    public countingSemaphore1(int initialPermits) { permits = initialPermits;}
    public void P() {
        while (permits == 0)
            permitAvailable.wait();
        --permits;
}
public void V() {
    ++permits;
    permitAvailable.signal();
}
}
// Threads call methods P() and V():
countingSemaphore1 s;
s.P();
s.V();
```

Listing 4.5   Class *countingSemaphore1*.

Solution 2   The SC monitor in Listing 4.6 is based on Implementation 2 in Listing 3.3. Unlike solution 1, this solution does not suffer from a starvation problem. Threads that call *P()* cannot barge ahead of signaled threads and "steal" their permits. Consider the scenario that we described in Solution 1. If thread T1 calls *P()* when the value of *permits* is 0, T1 will decrement *permits* to -1 and block itself by executing a *wait* operation. When some other thread executes *V()*, it will increment *permits* to 0 and signal T1. Threads ahead of T1 in the entry queue can enter the monitor and decrement *permits* before T1 is allowed to reenter the monitor. However, these threads will block themselves on the *wait* operation in *P()*, since *permits* will have a negative value. Thread T1 will eventually be allowed to reenter the monitor, and since there are no statements to execute after the *wait* operation, T1 will complete its *P()* operation. Thus, in this solution, a waiting thread that is signaled is guaranteed to get a permit.

4.2.2   Simulating Binary Semaphores

The SC monitor in Listing 4.7 is based on Implementation 3 in Listing 3.4. Threads in *P()* wait on condition variable *allowP*, while threads in *V()* wait on condition variable *allowV*. Waiting threads may get stuck forever in the while-loops in methods *P()* and *V()*.

4.2.3   Dining Philosophers

Solution 1   The SC monitor in Listing 4.8 is similar to Solution 4 (using semaphores) in Section 3.5.3. A philosopher picks up two chopsticks only if

```
class countingSemaphore2 extends monitor {
    private int permits;  // The value of permits may be negative.
    private conditionVariable permitAvailable = new conditionVariable();
    public countingSemaphore2(int initialPermits) { permits = initialPermits;}
    public void P() {
        --permits;
        if (permits < 0)
            permitAvailable.wait();
    }
    public void V() {
        ++permits;
        permitAvailable.signal();
    }
}
```

Listing 4.6   Class *countingSemaphore2*.

```
class binarySemaphore extends monitor {
    private int permits;
    private conditionVariable allowP = new conditionVariable();
    private conditionVariable allowV = new conditionVariable();
    public binarySemaphore(int initialPermits) { permits = initialPermits;}
    public void P() {
        while (permits == 0)
            allowP.wait();
        permits = 0;
        allowV.signal();
    }
    public void V() {
        while (permits == 1)
            allowV.wait();
        permits = 1;
        allowP.signal();
    }
}
```

Listing 4.7   Class *binarySemaphore*.

both of them are available. Each philosopher has three possible states: thinking, hungry, and eating. A hungry philosopher can eat if her two neighbors are not eating. A philosopher blocks herself on a condition variable if she is hungry but unable to eat. After eating, a philosopher will unblock a hungry neighbor who is able to eat. This solution is deadlock-free but not starvation-free, since a philosopher can starve if one of its neighbors is always eating (Exercise 4.25). However, the chance of a philosopher starving may be so highly unlikely that perhaps it can be safely ignored [Turski 1991].

```
class diningPhilosopher1 extends monitor {
    final int n = ...;              // number of philosophers
    final int thinking = 0; final int hungry = 1; final int eating = 2;
    int state[] = new int[n];       // state[i] indicates the state of Philosopher i
    // philosopher i blocks herself on self[i] when she is hungry but unable to eat
    conditionVariable[] self = new conditionVariable[n];
    diningPhilosopher1() {
    for (int i = 0; i < n; i++) state[i] = thinking;
    for (int j = 0; j < n; j++) self[j] = new conditionVariable( );
    }
    public void pickUp(int i) {
        state[i] = hungry;
        test(i);               // change state to eating if Philosopher i is able to eat
        if (state[i] != eating)
        self[i].wait();
    }
    public void putDown(int i) {
        state[i] = thinking;
        test((n+i-1) % n);         // check the left neighbor
        test((i+1) % n);           // check the right neighbor
    }
    private void test(int k) {
    // if Philosopher k is hungry and can eat, change her state and signal her queue.
        if (( state[k] == hungry) && (state[(k+n-1) % n] != eating ) &&
                (state[(k+1) % n] != eating )) {
            state[k] = eating;
            self[k].signal(); // no effect if Philosopher k is not waiting on self[k]
        }
    }
}

Philosopher i executes:
while (true) {
    /* thinking */
    dp1.pickUp(i);
    /* eating */
    dp1.putDown(i)
}
```

Listing 4.8 Class *diningPhilosopher1*.

Solution 2   Solution 1 can be revised to prevent starvation. In Listing 4.9, each philosopher has an additional state called *starving*. A hungry philosopher is not allowed to eat if she has a starving neighbor, even if both chopsticks are available. Also, two neighboring philosophers are not allowed to be starving at the same

```
class diningPhilosopher2 extends monitor {
    final int n = ...;                    // number of philosophers
    final int thinking = 0; final int hungry = 1;
    final int starving = 2; final int eating = 3;
    int state[] = new int[n];       // state[i] indicates the state of Philosopher i
    // philosopher i blocks herself on self[i] when she is hungry, but unable to eat
    conditionVariable[] self = new conditionVariable[n];
    diningPhilosopher2() {
        for (int i = 0; i < n; i++) state[i] = thinking;
        for (int j = 0; j < n; j++) self[j] = new conditionVariable( );
    }
    public void pickUp(int i) {
        state[i] = hungry;
        test(i);
        if (state[i] != eating)
            self[i].wait();
    }
    public void putDown(int i) {
        state[i] = thinking;
        test((n+i-1) % n);
        test((i+1) % n);
    }
    private void test(int k) {
    // Determine whether the state of Philosopher k should be changed to
    // eating or starving. A hungry philosopher is not allowed to eat if she has a
    // neighbor who's starving or eating.
        if (( state[k] == hungry || state[k] == starving ) &&
            (state[(k+n-1) % n] != eating && state[(k+n-1) % n] != starving ) &&
            (state[(k+1) % n] != eating && state[(k+1) % n] !=starving)) {
                state[k] = eating;
                self[k].signal();   // no effect if Phil. k is not waiting on self[k],
        }                            // which is the case if test() was called from pickUp().
        // a hungry philosopher enters the ``starving'' state if she cannot eat and her
        // neighbors are not starving
        else if ((state[k] == hungry) && (state[(k+n-1) % n] != starving ) &&
                (state[(k+1) % n] != starving )) {
            state[k] = starving;
        }
    }
}
```

Listing 4.9   Class *diningPhilosopher2* .

time. Thus, a hungry philosopher enters the starving state if she cannot eat and her two neighbors are not starving. This solution avoids starvation. If there are five philosophers, no more than four philosophers can eat before a given hungry philosopher is allowed to eat. However, some philosophers may not be allowed to eat even when both chopsticks are available. Compared to Solution 1, this solution limits the maximum time that a philosopher can be hungry, but it can also increase the average time that philosophers are hungry [Robbins 2001].

4.2.4 Readers and Writers

Listing 4.10 is an SC monitor implementation of strategy R>W.1, which allows concurrent reading and gives readers a higher priority than writers (see Section 3.5.4). Reader and writer threads have the following form:

r_gt_w_1 rw;

Reader Threads	Writer Threads
rw.startRead();	rw.startWrite();
/* read shared data */	/* write to shared data */
rw.endRead();	rw.endWrite();

Writers are forced to wait in method *startWrite()* if any writers are writing or any readers are reading or waiting. In method *endWrite()*, all the waiting readers are signaled since readers have priority. However, one or more writers may enter method *startWrite()* before the signaled readers reenter the monitor. Variable *signaledReaders* is used to prevent these barging writers from writing when the signaled readers are waiting in the entry queue and no more readers are waiting in *readerQ*. Notice above that the shared data is read outside the monitor. This is necessary in order to allow concurrent reading.

4.3   MONITORS IN JAVA

As we mentioned in Chapter 3, Java's `wait`, `notify`, and `notifyAll` operations, combined with `synchronized` methods and user-defined classes, enables the construction of objects that have some of the characteristics of monitors. There are some notable differences, however, between Java's monitor-like objects and the monitors that we have been describing.

First, adding `synchronized` to the methods of a Java class automatically provides mutual exclusion for threads accessing the data members of an instance of this class. However, if some or all of the methods are inadvertently not `synchronized`, a data race may result. This enables the very types of bugs that monitors were designed to eliminate. Other languages, such as Concurrent Pascal [Brinch Hansen 1975], provide full support for monitors and make it possible for the compiler to prevent any data races from being written into the program.

```
class r_gt_w_1 extends monitor {
    int readerCount = 0;            // number of active readers
    boolean writing = false;        // true if a writer is writing
    conditionVariable readerQ = new conditionVariable();
    conditionVariable writerQ = new conditionVariable();
    int signaledReaders = 0;        // number of readers signaled in endWrite
    public void startRead() {
        if (writing) {              // readers must wait if a writer is writing
            readerQ.wait();
            --signaledReaders;      // another signaled reader has started reading
        }
        ++readerCount;
    }
    public void endRead() {
        --readerCount;
        if (readerCount == 0 && signaledReaders==0)
            // signal writer if no more readers are reading and the signaledReaders
            //   have read
            writerQ.signal();
    }
    public void startWrite() {
    // the writer waits if another writer is writing, or a reader is reading or waiting,
    // or the writer is barging
        while (readerCount > 0 || writing || !readerQ.empty() || signaledReaders>0)
            writerQ.wait();
        writing = true;
    }
    public void endWrite() {
        writing = false;
        if (!readerQ.empty()) {     // priority is given to waiting readers
            signaledReaders = readerQ.length();
            readerQ.signalAll();
        }
        else writerQ.signal();
    }
}
```

Listing 4.10 Class *r_gt_w_1* allows concurrent reading and gives readers a higher priority than writers.

The second major difference is that there are no explicit condition variables in Java. When a thread executes a `wait` operation, it can be viewed as waiting on a single, implicit condition variable associated with the object. Having only one condition variable available can make Java monitors hard to write.

Operations `wait`, `notify`, and `notifyAll` use SC signaling on the implicit condition variable:

- A thread must hold an object's lock before it can execute a `wait`, `notify`, or `notifyAll` operation. Thus, these operations must appear in a `synchronized` method or `synchronized` block (see below); otherwise, an *IllegalMonitorStateException* is thrown.
- Every Java object has a lock associated with it. Methods `wait`, `notify`, and `notifyAll` are inherited from class *Object*, which is the base class for all Java objects.
- When a thread executes `wait`, it releases the object's lock and waits in the *wait set* that is associated with the object. A `notify` operation awakens a single waiting thread in the wait set. A `notifyAll` operation awakens all the waiting threads. Operations `notify` and `notifyAll` are not guaranteed to wake up the thread that has been waiting the longest.
- A waiting thread T may be removed from the wait set due to any one of the following actions: a `notify` or `notifyAll` operation; an interrupt action being performed on T; a timeout for a timed wait [e.g., wait(1000) allows T to stop waiting after 1 second]; or a *spurious wakeup*, which removes T without explicit Java instructions to do so.
- A notified thread must reacquire the object's lock before it can begin executing in the method. Furthermore, notified threads that are trying to reacquire an object's lock compete with any threads that have called a method of the object and are trying to acquire the lock for the first time. The order in which these notified and calling threads obtain the lock is unpredictable.
- If a waiting thread T is interrupted at the same time that a notification occurs, the result depends on which version of Java is being used.
- In versions before J2SE 5.0 [JSR-133 2004], the notification may be "lost." For example, suppose that thread T and several other threads are in the wait set and thread T is notified and then interrupted before it reacquires the monitor lock. Then the `wait` operation that was executed by T throws *InterruptedException* and the notification gets lost since none of the other waiting threads is allowed to proceed. Thus, it is recommended that the catch block for *InterruptedException* execute an additional `notify` or `notifyAll` to make up for any lost notifications [Hartley 1999]. Alternatively, the programmer should use `notifyAll` instead of `notify` to wake up all waiting threads even when just one thread can logically proceed.
- J2SE 5.0 removes the possibility of lost notifications by specifying that if the interrupt of T occurs before T is notified, T's interrupt status is set to false, `wait` throws *InterruptedException*, and some other waiting thread (if any exist at the time of the notification) receives the notification. If the notification occurs first, T eventually returns normally from the wait with its interrupt status set to true.

Note that a thread can determine its interrupt status by invoking the static method *Thread.isInterrupted()*, and it can observe and clear its interrupt status by invoking the static method *Thread.interrupted()*.

4.3.1 Better *countingSemaphore*

Lea [1999] showed how to revise the *countingSemaphore* class in Listing 3.15 to handle interrupts and spurious wakeups. Class *countingSemaphore* in Listing 4.11 assumes that J2SE 5.0 interrupt semantics are used, which prevents notifications from being lost when a waiting thread is interrupted right before it is notified. Variable *notifyCount* counts the number of notifications that are made in method *V()*. The `if`-statement in method *V()* ensures that only as many notifications are done as there are waiting threads. A thread that awakens from a `wait` operation in *P()* executes `wait` again if *notifyCount* is zero since a spurious wakeup must have occurred (i.e., a notification must have been issued outside of *V()*.)

Assume that two threads are blocked on the `wait` operation in method *P()* and the value of *permits* is 0. Now suppose that three *V()* operations are performed and all three *V()* operations are completed before either of the two notified threads can reacquire the lock. Then the value of *permits* is 3 and the value of *waitCount* is still 2. A thread that then calls *P()* and barges ahead of the notified threads is not required to wait and does not execute `wait` since the condition (*permits* $<=$ *waitCount*) in the `if`-statement in method *P()* is false.

Finally, assume that two threads are blocked on the `wait` operation in method *P()* when two *V()* operations are executed. Then *notifyCount* and *permits* both become 2. But suppose that the two threads notified are interrupted so that *waitCount* becomes 0 (due to the interrupted threads decrementing *waitCount* in their `finally` blocks). If three threads now call method *P()*, two of the threads will be allowed to complete their *P()* operations, and before they complete *P()*, they will each decrement *notifyCount* since both will find that the condition (*notifyCount* $>$ *waitCount*) is true. Now *permits, notifyCount*, and *waitCount* are all 0. If another thread calls *P()*, it will be blocked by the `wait` operation in *P()*, and if it is awakened by a spurious wakeup, it will execute `wait` again since *notifyCount* is zero.

In Section 3.6.3 we described the *Semaphore* class in the J2SE 5.0 package *java.util.concurrent*. As we mentioned, class *Semaphore* provides methods *acquire()* and *release()* instead of *P()* and *V()*, respectively. The implementation of *acquire()* handles interrupts as follows. If a thread calling *acquire()* has its interrupted status set on entry to *acquire()*, or is interrupted while waiting for a permit, `InterruptedException` is thrown and the calling thread's interrupted status is cleared. Any permits that were to be assigned to this thread are, instead, assigned to other threads trying to acquire permits. Class *Semaphore* also provides method *acquireUninterruptibly()*. If a thread calling *acquireUninterruptibly()* is interrupted while waiting for a permit, it will continue to wait until it receives a permit. When the thread does return from this method, its interrupt status will be set.

```
public final class countingSemaphore {
    private int permits = 0; int waitCount = 0; int notifyCount=0;
    public countingSemaphore(int initialPermits) {
        if (initialPermits>0) permits = initialPermits;
    }
    synchronized public void P() throws InterruptedException {
        if (permits <= waitCount) {
            waitCount++;                    // one more thread is waiting
            try {
                do { wait(); }              // spurious wakeups do not increment
                while (notifyCount == 0); // notifyCount
            }
            finally { waitCount--; }    // one waiting thread notified or interrupted
            notifyCount--;              // one notification has been consumed
        }
        else {
            if (notifyCount > waitCount) // if some notified threads were
                notifyCount--;           // interrupted, adjust notifyCount
        }
        permits--;
    }

    synchronized public void V() {
        permits++;
        if (waitCount > notifyCount) { // if there are waiting threads yet to be
            notifyCount++;             // notified, notify one thread
            notify();
        }
    }
}
```

Listing 4.11 Java class *countingSemaphore*, which handles interrupts and spurious wakeups.

4.3.2 `notify` vs. `notifyAll`

A Java monitor has available to it only a single (implicit) condition variable. Since two or more threads waiting on the same implicit condition variable may be waiting for different conditions to become true, notify operations must be handled carefully. Listing 4.12 shows Java class *binarySemaphore*. Threads that are blocked in *P()* or *V()* are waiting in the single queue associated with the implicit condition variable. Any execution of `notifyAll` awakens all the waiting threads, even though one entire group of threads, either those waiting in *P()* or those waiting in *V()*, cannot possibly continue. (A notification that is issued in method *P()* is intended for a thread waiting in method *V()*, and vice versa.) All the

```
public final class binarySemaphore extends semaphore {
    public binarySemaphore(int initialPermits) {
        super(initialPermits);
        if (initialPermits != 0 && initialPermits != 1) throw new
IllegalArgumentException("initial value of binarySemaphore must be 0 or 1");
    }
    synchronized public void P() {
        while (permits == 0) // assume that no interrupts are possible
            try { wait(); } catch (InterruptedException ex) { }
        permits = 0;
        notifyAll();
    }
    synchronized public void V() {
        while (permits == 1) // assume that no interrupts are possible
            try { wait(); } catch (InterruptedException ex) { }
        permits = 1;
        notifyAll();
    }
}
```

Listing 4.12   Java class *binarySemaphore*.

threads signaled must reacquire the monitor lock one by one and then determine if their loop condition is true or false. The first thread, if any, to find that its loop condition is false exits the loop and completes its operation. The other threads may all end up blocking themselves again. This type of *semi-busy-waiting* can become a performance bottleneck [Anderson et al. 1989].

If `notify` were used instead of `notifyAll`, the single thread that was awakened might be a member of the wrong group. For example, a thread in method *P()* might notify another thread waiting in *P()* instead of a thread waiting in *V()*. The thread notified would execute another `wait` operation and the `notify` operation would be lost, potentially causing a deadlock.

Use `notifyAll` instead of `notify` unless the following requirements are met:

1. All the waiting threads are waiting on conditions that are signaled by the same notifications. This means that if one condition is signaled by a notification, the other conditions are also signaled by this notification. Usually, when this requirement is met, all the waiting threads are waiting on the exact same condition.
2. Each notification is intended to enable exactly one thread to continue. (In this case, it would be useless to wake up more than one thread.)

An example of a class that satisfies these requirements is the class *countingSemaphore* in Listing 3.15. All threads waiting in *P()* are waiting for the same condition ($permits \geq 0$), which is signaled by the `notify` operation in *V()*.

```
final class boundedBuffer {
    private int fullSlots=0; private int capacity = 0;
    private int[] buffer = null; private int in = 0, out = 0;
    public boundedBuffer(int bufferCapacity) {
        capacity = bufferCapacity; buffer = new int[capacity];
    }
    public synchronized void deposit (int value) {
        while (fullSlots == capacity) // assume that no interrupts are possible
            try { wait(); } catch (InterruptedException ex) { }
        buffer[in] = value;
        in = (in + 1) % capacity;
        if (fullSlots++ == 0)      // note the use of post-increment.
            notifyAll(); // it is possible that Consumers are waiting for ''not empty''
    }
    public synchronized int withdraw () {
        int value = 0;
        while (fullSlots == 0)        // assume that no interrupts are possible
            try { wait(); } catch (InterruptedException ex) { }
        value = buffer[out];
        out = (out + 1) % capacity;
        if (fullSlots-- == capacity)   // note the use of post-decrement.
            notifyAll(); // it is possible that Producers are waiting for ''not full''
        return value;
    }
}
```

Listing 4.13   Java monitor *boundedBuffer*.

Also, a `notify` operation enables one waiting thread to continue. Even though both of these requirements might be satisfied in a given class, they may not be satisfied in subclasses of this class, so using `notifyAll` may be safer. The potential for subclassing must be considered when deciding whether to use `notify` or `notifyAll`. (We used the `final` keyword for classes *binarySemaphore* and *countingSemaphore* to prevent any subclassing from them.)

Listing 4.13 shows a Java monitor *boundedBuffer*, which solves the bounded buffer problem. Monitor *boundedBuffer* uses `notifyAll` operations since *Producers* and *Consumers* wait on the same implicit condition variable and they wait for different conditions that are signaled by different notifications. *Producers* wait for the condition "not full" to be signaled by the notification in *withdraw()*, and *Consumers* wait for the condition "not empty" to be signaled by the notification in *deposit()*. The `notifyAll` operation is issued only if it is actually possible for threads to be waiting. Compare this with the real monitor solution in Listing 4.3, which uses two condition variables in order to separate the threads waiting in *P()* from the threads waiting in *V()*.

4.3.3   Simulating Multiple Condition Variables

It is possible to use simple Java objects to achieve an effect that is similar to the use of multiple condition variables. Listing 4.14 shows a new version of class *binarySemaphore* that uses objects *allowP* and *allowV* in the same way that condition variables are used. Threads waiting in methods *P()* and *V()* wait on objects *allowP* and *allowV*, respectively. Notice that methods *P()* and *V()* are not `synchronized` since it is objects *allowP* and *allowV* that must be `synchronized` in order to perform `wait` and `notify` operations on them. (Adding `synchronized` to methods *P()* and *V()* would synchronize the *binarySemaphore2* object, not objects *allowP* and *allowV*.)

   The use of a `synchronized` block,

```
synchronized (allowP) {
   /* block of code */
}
```

creates a block of code that is synchronized on object *allowP*. A thread must acquire *allowP's* lock before it can enter the block. The lock is released when the thread exits the block.

   Note that a `synchronized` method,

```
public synchronized void F() {
   /* body of F */
}
```

is equivalent to a method whose body consists of a single `synchronized` block:

```
public void F() {
   synchronized(this) {
      /* body of F */
   }
}
```

If methods *P()* or *V()* in Listing 4.14 were also synchronized, a thread that blocked itself on *allowP* or *allowV* would do so while holding the lock for the *binarySemaphore2*. This would result in a deadlock since no other thread would be able to execute inside *P()* or *V()*. Variables *pPermits* and *vPermits* are used to determine whether threads should block themselves on *allowP* and *allowV*, respectively.

4.4   MONITORS IN PTHREADS

Pthreads does not provide a monitor construct, but it provides condition variables, which enables the construction of monitor-like objects.

```
public final class binarySemaphore2 {
    int vPermits = 0;
    int pPermits = 0;
    Object allowP = null;              // queue of threads waiting in P()
    Object allowV = null;              // queue of threads waiting in V()
    public binarySemaphore2(int initialPermits) {
        if (initialPermits != 0 && initialPermits != 1) throw new
         IllegalArgumentException("initial binary semaphore value must be 0 or 1");
        pPermits = initialPermits;     // 1 or 0
        vPermits = 1 − pPermits;       // 0 or 1
        allowP = new Object();
        allowV = new Object();
    }
    public void P() {
        synchronized (allowP) {
            --pPermits;
            if (pPermits < 0) // assume that no interrupts are possible
                try { allowP.wait(); } catch (InterruptedException e) { }
        }
        synchronized (allowV) {
            ++vPermits;
            if (vPermits <=0)
                allowV.notify();       // signal thread waiting in V()
        }
    }

    public void V() {
        synchronized (allowV) {
            --vPermits;
            if (vPermits < 0) // assume that no interrupts are possible
                try { allowV.wait(); } catch (InterruptedException e) { }
        }
        synchronized (allowP) {
            ++pPermits;
            if(pPermits <= 0)
                allowP.notify();       // signal thread waiting in P()
        }
    }
}
```

Listing 4.14   Java class *binarySemaphore2*.

4.4.1 Pthreads Condition Variables

The operations that can be performed on a Pthreads condition variable are *pthread_cond_wait(), pthread_cond_signal(),* and *pthread_cond_broadcast().* The *signal* and *broadcast* operations are similar to Java's `notify` and `notifyAll` operations, respectively. Also like Java, *wait* operations are expected to be executed inside a critical section. Thus, a condition variable is associated with a *mutex* and this *mutex* is specified when a *wait* operation is performed.

A condition variable is initialized by calling *pthread_cond_init().*

- When a thread waits on a condition variable it must have the associated *mutex* locked. This means that a *wait* operation on a condition variable must be preceded by a lock operation on the *mutex* associated with the condition variable.

- Each condition variable must be associated at any given time with only one mutex. On the other hand, a mutex may have any number of condition variables associated with it.

- A *wait* operation unlocks the associated *mutex* automatically if the calling thread is blocked and tries to lock the associated *mutex* when the blocked thread is awakened by a *signal* or *broadcast* operation. The awakened thread competes with other threads for the *mutex*.

- A *signal* operation wakes up a single thread, while a *broadcast* operation wakes up all waiting threads.

- A thread can *signal* or *broadcast* a condition variable without holding the lock for the associated *mutex*. (This is different from Java since a Java *notify* or *notifyAll* operation must be performed in a `synchronized` method or block.) A thread that executes a *signal* or *broadcast* continues to execute. If the thread holds the lock for the associated *mutex* when it performs a *signal* or *broadcast*, it should eventually release the lock.

Listing 4.15 shows a C++/Pthreads monitor class named *boundedBuffer* that solves the bounded buffer problem. Producers wait on condition variable *notFull* and Consumers wait on condition variable *notEmpty*. The use of two explicit condition variables makes this Pthreads version similar to the solution in Listing 4.3. Note that the *wait* operations appear in loops since Pthreads uses the SC signaling discipline. Also, it is recommended that loops always be used because of the possibility of *spurious wakeups* (i.e., threads can be awakened without any *signal* or *broadcast* operations being performed).

4.4.2 Condition Variables in J2SE 5.0

Package *java.util.concurrent.locks* in Java release J2SE 5.0 contains a lock class called *ReentrantLock* (see Section 3.6.4) and a condition variable class called *Condition*. A *ReentrantLock* replaces the use of a `synchronized` method, and operations *await* and *signal* on a *Condition* replace the use of methods *wait* and

```cpp
#include <iostream>
#include <pthread.h>
#include "thread.h"

class boundedBuffer {
private:
    int fullSlots;                  // # of full slots in the buffer
    int capacity;
    int* buffer;
    int in, out;
    pthread_cond_t notFull;         // Producers wait on notFull
    pthread_cond_t notEmpty;        // Consumers wait on notEmpty
    pthread_mutex_t mutex;          // exclusion for deposit() and withdraw()
public:
    boundedBuffer(int capacity_) : capacity(capacity_), fullSlots(0), in(0),
        out(0), buffer(new int[capacity_]) {
            pthread_cond_init(&notFull,NULL);
            pthread_cond_init(&notEmpty,NULL);
            pthread_mutex_init(&mutex,NULL);
    }
    ~boundedBuffer() {
      delete [] buffer;
      pthread_cond_destroy(&notFull); pthread_cond_destroy(&notEmpty);
      pthread_mutex_destroy(&mutex);
    }
    void deposit(int value) {
       pthread_mutex_lock(&mutex);
       while (fullSlots == capacity)
           pthread_cond_wait(&notFull,&mutex);
       buffer[in] = value;
       in = (in + 1) % capacity;
       ++fullSlots;
       pthread_mutex_unlock(&mutex);
       pthread_cond_signal(&notEmpty);
    }
    int withdraw() {
       pthread_mutex_lock(&mutex);
       int value;
       while (fullSlots == 0)
           pthread_cond_wait(&notEmpty,&mutex);
       value = buffer[out];
       out = (out + 1) % capacity;
       --fullSlots;
       pthread_mutex_unlock(&mutex);
```

Listing 4.15   C++/Pthreads class *boundedBuffer*.

```
            pthread_cond_signal(&notFull);
            return value;
    }
};

class Producer : public Thread {
private:
    boundedBuffer& b;
    int num;
public:
    Producer (boundedBuffer* b_, int num_) : b(*b_), num(num_) { }
    virtual void* run () {
        std::cout << "Producer Running" << std::endl;
        for(int i = 0; i < 3; i++) {
            b.deposit(i);
            std::cout << "Producer # "  << num << " deposited " << i << std::endl;
        }
        return NULL;
    }
};

class Consumer : public Thread {
private:
    boundedBuffer& b;
    int num;
public:
    Consumer (boundedBuffer* b_, int num_) : b(*b_), num(num_) { }
    virtual void* run () {
        std::cout << "Consumer Running" << std::endl;
        int value = 0;
        for(int i = 0; i < 3; i++) {
            value = b.withdraw();
            std::cout << "Consumer # " << num << " withdrew " <<
              value << std::endl;
        }
        return NULL;
    }
};

int main ( ) {
    boundedBuffer* b1 = new boundedBuffer(3);
    Producer p1(b1, 1); Consumer c1(b1, 1);
    p1.start(); c1.start();
    p1.join(); c1.join();
    delete b1;
    return 0;
}
```

Listing 4.15   (*continued*)

notify. A *Condition* object is bound to its associated *ReentrantLock* object. Method *newCondition()* is used to obtain a *Condition* object from a *ReentrantLock*:

ReentrantLock mutex = new ReentrantLock();
Condition notFull = mutex.newCondition(); // *notFull* and *notEmpty* are both
                                          // bound to *mutex*
Condition notEmpty = mutex.newCondition();

Conditions provide operations *await, signal*, and *signallAll*, including those with timeouts. Listing 4.16 shows a Java version of class *boundedBuffer* using *Condition* objects. The `try-finally` clause ensures that *mutex* is unlocked no matter how the `try` block is executed. Furthermore, if an interrupt occurs before a *signal*, the *await* method must, after reacquiring the lock, throw `InterruptedException`. [If the interrupted thread is signaled, some other thread (if any exist at the time of the *signal*) receives the signal.] But if the interrupt occurs after a *signal*, the *await* method must return without throwing an exception, but with the current thread's interrupt status set. (See the discussion of interrupts in Section 4.3.)

4.5 SIGNALING DISCIPLINES

All the monitors that we have seen so far use the *signal-and-continue* (SC) discipline. Below we describe three other signaling disciplines. Monitors that use these new disciplines are often simpler than their SC counterparts. Later, we show how to implement all four signaling disciplines in Java and C++ so that we can choose which discipline to use in our programs.

4.5.1 Signal-and-Urgent-Wait

Signal-and-urgent-wait (SU) was defined by Hoare [Hoare 1974]. Below we describe the behavior of the `wait` and `signal` operations for an SU monitor.
    When a thread executes *cv.signal()*:

- If there are no threads waiting on condition variable *cv*, this operation has no effect.
- Otherwise, the thread executing `signal` (which is called the *signaler thread*) awakens one thread waiting on *cv* and blocks itself in a queue, called the *reentry queue*. Threads blocked in the reentry queue are considered to be outside the monitor. The thread signaled reenters the monitor immediately.

When a thread executes *cv.wait()*:

- If the reentry queue is not empty, the thread awakens one signaler thread from the reentry queue and then blocks itself on the queue for *cv*.
- Otherwise, the thread releases mutual exclusion (to allow a new thread to enter the monitor) and then blocks itself on the queue for *cv*.

```
import java.util.concurrent.locks.*;
final class boundedBuffer {
    private int fullSlots=0; private int capacity = 0; private int in = 0, out = 0;
    private int[] buffer = null;
    private ReentrantLock mutex;
    private Condition notFull;
    private Condition notEmpty;

    public boundedBuffer(int bufferCapacity) {
        capacity = bufferCapacity; buffer = new int[capacity];
        mutex = new ReentrantLock();
        // notFull and notEmpty are both attached to mutex
        notFull = mutex.newCondition(); notEmpty = mutex.newCondition();
    }
    public void deposit (int value) throws InterruptedException {
        mutex.lock();
        try {
            while (fullSlots == capacity)
                notFull.await();
            buffer[in] = value;
            in = (in + 1) % capacity;
            notEmpty.signal();
        } finally {mutex.unlock();}
    }
    public synchronized int withdraw () throws InterruptedException {
        mutex.lock();
        try {
            int value = 0;
            while (fullSlots == 0)
                notEmpty.await();
            value = buffer[out];
            out = (out + 1) % capacity;
            notFull.signal();
            return value;
        } finally {mutex.unlock();}
    }
}
```

Listing 4.16   Java class *boundedBuffer* using *Condition* objects.

When a thread completes and exits a monitor method:

- If the reentry queue is not empty, it awakens one signaler thread from the reentry queue.
- Otherwise, it releases mutual exclusion to allow a new thread to enter the monitor.

In an SU monitor, the threads waiting to enter a monitor have three levels of priority (from highest to lowest):

- The awakened thread (A), which is the thread awakened by a `signal` operation
- Signaler threads (S), which are the threads waiting in the reentry queue
- Calling threads (C), which are the threads that have called a monitor method and are waiting in the entry queue

A thread waiting in the entry queue is allowed to enter a monitor only when no other threads are inside the monitor and there is no signaled thread and no signaler threads. In an SU monitor, the relative priority associated with the three sets of threads is A > S > C. We will illustrate an SU monitor by considering again the *boundedBuffer* monitor in Listing 4.3. This time we assume that SU signals are used instead of SC signals. Assume that the buffer is empty and that the thread at the front of the entry queue is Consumer$_1$. The queues for condition variables *notFull* and *notEmpty* are also assumed to be empty (Fig. 4.17a).

When Consumer$_1$ enters method *withdraw()*, it executes the statement

```
while (fullSlots == 0)
    notEmpty.wait();
```

Since the buffer is empty, Consumer$_1$ is blocked by the *wait()* operation on condition variable *notEmpty* (Fig. 4.17b). Producer$_1$ then enters the monitor. Since the

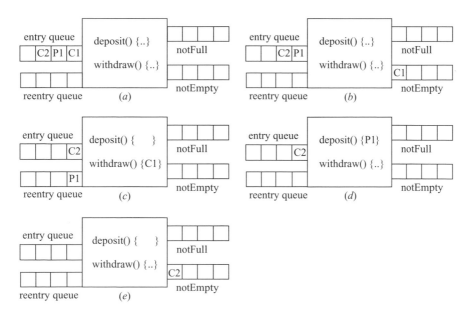

Figure 4.17   SU monitor *boundedBuffer*.

buffer is not full, Producer₁ deposits its item and executes *notEmpty.signal()*. This signal awakens Consumer₁ and moves Producer₁ to the reentry queue (Fig. 4.17*c*).

Consumer₁ can now consume an item. When Consumer₁ executes *notFull.signal()*, there are no Producers waiting, so none are signaled and Consumer₁ does not move to the reentry queue. When Consumer₁ exits the monitor, Producer₁ is allowed to reenter the monitor since the reentry queue has priority over the entry queue (Fig. 4.17*d*). Producer₁ has no more statements to execute, so Producer₁ exits the monitor. Since the reentry queue is empty, Consumer₂ is now allowed to enter the monitor. Consumer₂ finds that the buffer is empty and blocks itself on condition variable *notEmpty* (Fig. 4.17*e*).

Unlike the scenario that occurred when SC signals were used, Consumer₂ was not allowed to barge ahead of Consumer₁ and consume the first item. When Consumer₁ was signaled by Producer₁, instead of moving to the rear of the entry queue, Consumer₁ reentered the monitor and consumed the item deposited by Producer₁. Since signaled threads have priority over new threads, a thread waiting on a condition variable in an SU monitor can assume that the condition it is waiting for will be true when it reenters the monitor. In the *boundedBuffer* monitor, this means that we can safely replace the `while`-loops with `if`-statements and avoid the unnecessary reevaluation of the loop condition after a *wait()* operation returns.

As another example, Listing 4.18 shows an SU monitor implementation of strategy R>W.1. This implementation is simpler than the SC monitor in Section 4.2.4 since there is no threat of barging. When a writer signals waiting readers, these waiting readers are guaranteed to reenter the monitor before any new writers are allowed to enter *startWrite()*. Notice how waiting readers are signaled in *endWrite()* and *startRead()*. The first waiting reader is signaled in *endWrite()*. The awakened reader continues executing in *startRead()* and signals the second waiting reader, which signals the third waiting reader, and so on. This *cascaded wakeup* continues until all waiting readers have been signaled. (The last reader to be signaled issues a final signal that has no affect.)

4.5.2 Signal-and-Exit

Brinch Hansen [1975] defined a signaling discipline called *signal-and-exit* (SE) that is a special case of signal-and-urgent-wait (SU) [Andrews 1991]. When a thread executes an SE *signal* operation it does not enter the reentry queue; rather, it exits the monitor immediately. Thus, an SE *signal* statement is either the last statement of a method or is followed immediately by a return statement. As with SU signals, the thread awakened by a `signal` operation is always the next thread to enter the monitor. In an SE monitor, since there are no signaling threads that want to remain in or reenter the monitor, the relative priority associated with the sets of awakened (A) and calling (C) threads is A > C.

When a *signal* statement appears in a monitor method, it is very often the last statement of the method, regardless of the type of *signal*. Notice that this was the

```
class r_gt_w_1SU extends monitorSU {
    int readerCount = 0;          // number of active readers
    boolean writing = false;      // true if a writer is writing
    conditionVariable readerQ = new conditionVariable();
    conditionVariable writerQ = new conditionVariable();

    public void startRead() {
        if (writing)              // readers must wait if a writer is writing
            readerQ.wait();
        ++readerCount;
        readerQ.signal();         // continue cascaded wakeup of readers
    }
    public void endRead() {
        --readerCount;
        if (readerCount == 0)
            writerQ.signal();     // signal writer if there are no more readers reading
    }
    public void startWrite() {
    // writers wait if a writer is writing, or a reader is reading or waiting, or the
    // writer is barging
        while (readerCount > 0 || writing || !readerQ.empty())
            writerQ.wait();
        writing = true;
    }
    public void endWrite() {
        writing = false;
        if (!readerQ.empty()) {   // priority is given to waiting readers
            readerQ.signal();     // start cascaded wakeup of readers
        }
        else
            writerQ.signal();
    }
}
```

Listing 4.18 Class *r_gt_w_1SU* allows concurrent reading and gives readers a higher priority than writers.

case for all the SC monitor examples in Section 4.2 and for the SU monitor in Listing 4.18. Using SE semantics for these special SU *signal* operations avoids the extra cost of having a thread exit a monitor and join the reentry queue, and then later reenter the monitor only to exit the monitor again immediately. In the Java and C++ monitor classes that we present in the next section, we have provided a signal-and-exit operation that allows SE *signals* to be used at the end of SU monitor methods.

TABLE 4.1 Signaling Disciplines

Relative Priority	Name
S > A = C	Signal-and-continue [Lampson and Redell 1980]
A > S > C	Signal-and-urgent-wait [Hoare 1974]
A > C	Signal-and-exit [Brinch Hansen 1975]
S > A > C	Urgent-signal-and-continue [Howard 1976]

4.5.3 Urgent-Signal-and-Continue

In the *urgent-signal-and-continue* (USC) discipline, a thread that executes a *signal* operation continues to execute just as it would for an SC signal. But unlike SC signals, a thread awakened by a *signal* operation has priority over threads waiting in the entry queue. That is, a thread waiting in the entry queue is allowed to enter a monitor only when no other threads are inside the monitor and no signaled threads are waiting to reenter. When *signal* operations appear only at the end of monitor methods, which is usually the case, this discipline is the same as the SE discipline, which is a special case of the SU discipline. The USC discipline was originally called *signal-and-continue* [Howard 1976], but signal-and-continue is now the name commonly used for Java's semantics. (Java's semantics was originally called *wait-and-notify* [Lampson and Redell 1980].) In a USC monitor, the relative priority associated with the three sets of threads is S > A > C.

Table 4.1 lists the signaling disciplines and shows the relative priorities associated with the three sets of threads. Another signaling discipline is described in Exercise 4.17.

4.5.4 Comparing SU and SC Signals

If a thread executes an SU *signal* to notify another thread that a certain condition is true, this condition remains true when the signaled thread reenters the monitor. However, this does not hold for an SC *signal*. A *signal* operation in an SC monitor is only a "hint" to the signaled thread that it may be able to proceed [Lampson and Redell 1980]. Other threads may enter the monitor and make the condition false before the signaled thread reenters the monitor. This situation, called *barging*, may cause subtle errors in SC monitors and often makes SU monitors easier to program [Dahl 2000].

Listing 4.19 shows a monitor that uses the SU signaling discipline to simulate a counting semaphore correctly. If we assume that condition variable queues are FCFS, threads will exit *P()* in the same order that they enter *P()*. We now show that monitor *countingSemaphore3* is incorrect if SC signals are used. Assume that thread T1 is blocked on condition variable *permitAvailable* in method *P()*; thread T3 is waiting in the entry queue; and thread T2 has just executed ++*permits* in method *V()*, making the value of *permits* 1. The following scenario can occur:

- T2 executes *permitAvailable.signal()* and awakens T1, which blocks itself in the entry queue behind T3.

```
class countingSemaphore3 extends monitor {
    private int permits;    // The value of permits is never negative.
    private conditionVariable permitAvailable = new conditionVariable();
    public countingSemaphore3(int initialPermits) { permits = initialPermits;}
    public void P() {
       if (permits == 0)
           permitAvailable.wait();
       --permits;
    }
    public void V() {
       ++permits;
       permitAvailable.signal(); // SU signal
    }
}
```

Listing 4.19   Class *countingSemaphore3*.

- T2 exits the monitor, which allows T3 to enter, decrement *permits* from 1 to 0, and exit the monitor.
- T1 resumes execution, executes the statement *permits*, and exits the monitor. The value of *permits* is -1.

This scenario shows that monitor *countingSemaphore3* with SC signals is incorrect since a single *V()* operation has allowed the completion of two *P()* operations. The reason for this error is that when T1 resumes execution, the condition (*permits* > 0) is not true, but T1 completes method *P()* anyway. This error is fixed by replacing the if-statement in method *P()*,

```
if (permits == 0)
   permitAvailable.wait();
```

with the while-loop

```
while (permits == 0)
   permitAvailable.wait();
```

Now if condition (*permits* $== 0$) is not true when the *wait()* operation returns, the signaled thread will wait again. The resulting monitor is the same as *countingSemaphore1* in Listing 4.4, but as we mentioned, it does not implement a FCFS semaphore.

Using a while-loop instead of an if-statement in an SC monitor requires an extra evaluation of condition (*permits* $== 0$) after a *wait()*. On the other hand, the execution of an SU monitor requires additional context switches for managing the signaler threads in the Reentry queue. Using signal-and-exit semantics for a signal operation that appears at the end of an SU method avoids the costs of the extra condition evaluation and the extra context switches. Thus, we use signal-and-exit wherever possible.

4.6 USING SEMAPHORES TO IMPLEMENT MONITORS

Monitors can be implemented in the kernel [Andrews 2000]. In this section we show how to use semaphores to implement monitors with SC, SU, or SE signaling [Hoare 1974]. The implementation of USC signaling is left as an exercise. Semaphores provide mutual exclusion for threads inside the monitor and are used to implement *wait()* and *signal()* operations on condition variables.

If a language or API provides semaphores but not monitors, which is the case for Win32 and Pthreads, monitors can be simulated using this semaphore implementation. In Sections 4.7 and 4.8 we present Java and C++ monitor classes that use semaphores to simulate monitors. Then we extend these classes to support cyclical testing and debugging techniques for monitor-based programs. Even though Java provides built-in support for monitors, our custom Java monitor classes are still helpful since it is not easy to test and debug built-in Java monitors. Also, we can choose which type of monitor—SC, SU, SE, or USC—to use in our Java programs.

4.6.1 SC Signaling

The body of each public monitor method is implemented as

```
public returnType F(...) {
    mutex.P();
    /* body of F */
    mutex.V();
}
```

Semaphore *mutex* is initialized to 1. The calls to *mutex.P()* and *mutex.V()* ensure that monitor methods are executed with mutual exclusion.

Java class *conditionVariable* in Listing 4.20 implements condition variables with SC signals. Since it is not legal to overload `final` method *wait()* in Java, methods named *waitC()* and *signalC()* are used instead of *wait()* and *signal()*. A *signalCall()* operation, which behaves the same as Java's `notifyAll`, is also implemented, along with operations *empty()* and *length()*.

Each *conditionVariable* is implemented using a semaphore named *threadQueue*, which is initialized to 0. When a thread executes *waitC()*, it releases mutual exclusion and blocks itself using *threadQueue.P()*. Since *signalC()* operations must determine whether any threads are waiting on the condition variable, an integer variable named *numWaitingThreads* is used to count the waiting threads. The value of *numWaitingThreads* is incremented in *waitC()* and decremented in *signalC()* and *signalCall()*. The *signalC()* operation executes *threadQueue.V()* to

```
final class conditionVariable {
    private countingSemaphore threadQueue = new countingSemaphore(0);
    private int numWaitingThreads = 0;
    public void waitC() {
        numWaitingThreads++;          // one more thread is waiting in the queue
        threadQueue.VP(mutex);        // release exclusion and wait in threadQueue
        mutex.P();                    // wait to reenter the monitor
    }
    public void signalC() {
        if (numWaitingThreads > 0) {  // if any threads are waiting
            numWaitingThreads--;      //    wake up one thread in the queue
            threadQueue.V();
        }
    }
    public void signalCall() {
        while (numWaitingThreads > 0) {  // if any threads are waiting
            --numWaitingThreads;         //    wake up all the threads in the queue
            threadQueue.V();             //    one by one
        }
    }
    // returns true if the queue is empty
    public boolean empty() { return (numWaitingThreads == 0); }
    // returns the length of the queue
    public int length() { return numWaitingThreads; }
}
```

Listing 4.20 Java class *conditionVariable*.

signal one waiting thread. Operation *signalCall()* uses a `while`-loop to signal all the waiting threads one by one.

Notice that the implementation of method *waitC()* uses a *VP()* operation. Operation *threadQueue.VP(mutex)* prevents deadlocks that otherwise could occur if the *mutex.V()* and *threadQueue.P()* operations were issued separately (see Exercises 4.10 and 4.22). The *VP()* operation also guarantees that threads executing *waitC()* are blocked on semaphore *threadQueue* in the same order that they entered the monitor. Without *VP()*, context switches between the *V()* and *P()* operations would create a source of nondeterminism in the implementation of the monitor. We will see shortly how the *VP()* operation simplifies tracing and replay for monitor-based programs. (A monitor implementation that does not use *VP()* operations is considered in Exercise 4.23.)

4.6.2 SU Signaling

Java class *conditionVariable* in Listing 4.21 implements condition variables with SU signals. Threads that execute a *signalC()* operation must wait in the reentry

```
final class conditionVariable {
    private countingSemaphore threadQueue = new countingSemaphore(0);
    private int numWaitingThreads = 0;
    public void signalC() {
        if (numWaitingThreads > 0) {
            ++reentryCount;
            reentry.VP(threadQueue); // release exclusion and join reentry queue
            --reentryCount;
        }
    }
    public void waitC() {
        numWaitingThreads++;
        if (reentryCount > 0) threadQueue.VP(reentry); // the reentry queue has
        else threadQueue.VP(mutex);                    //  priority over entry queue
        --numWaitingThreads;
    }
    public boolean empty() { return (numWaitingThreads == 0); }
    public int length() { return numWaitingThreads; }
}
```

Listing 4.21   Java class *conditionVariable* for SU monitors.

queue. Therefore, each SU monitor has a semaphore named *reentry* (initialized to 0), on which signaling threads block themselves. If *signalC()* is executed when threads are waiting on the condition variable, *threadQueue.V()* is executed to signal a waiting thread, and *reentry.P()* is executed to block the signaler in the reentry queue. These *V()* and *P()* operations are executed together as *reentry.VP(threadQueue)*. As we mentioned above, this removes a possible source of deadlock and nondeterminism in the implementation of the monitor.

When a thread executes *waitC()*, the thread must determine whether any signaler threads are waiting in the *reentry* queue, since signaler threads in the reentry queue have priority over calling threads in the entry queue. If signalers are waiting, the thread releases a signaler by executing *reentry.V()*; otherwise, the thread releases mutual exclusion by executing *mutex.V()*. Integer *reentryCount* is used to count the number of threads waiting in *reentry*. Method *signalC()* increments and decrements *reentryCount* as threads enter and exit the *reentry* queue. Method *waitC()* uses the value of *reentryCount* to determine which *V()* operation to execute.

Threads exiting the monitor also use *reentryCount* to give signaler threads priority over new threads. The body of each public monitor method is implemented as

```
public returnType F(...) {
    mutex.P();
    /* body of F */
```

```
    if (reentryCount >0)
        reentry.V();        // allow a signaler thread to reenter the monitor
        else mutex.V();     // allow a calling thread to enter the monitor
}
```

4.7 MONITOR TOOLBOX FOR JAVA

A *monitor toolbox* is a program unit that is used to simulate the monitor construct [Boddy 1983]. The Java monitor toolboxes we use are class *monitorSC* for SC monitors and class *monitorSU* for SU monitors. Classes *monitorSC* and *monitorSU* implement operations *enterMonitor* and *exitMonitor* and contain a member class named *conditionVariable* that implements *waitC* and *signalC* operations on condition variables.

A regular Java class can be made into a monitor class by doing the following:

1. Extend class *monitorSC* or *monitorSU*.
2. Use operations *enterMonitor()* and *exitMonitor()* at the start and end of each public method.
3. Declare as many *conditionVariables* as needed.
4. Use operations *waitC(), signalC(), signalCall(), length()*, and *empty()*, on the *conditionVariables*.

Listing 4.22 shows part of a Java *boundedBuffer* class that illustrates the use of class *monitorSC*.

```
final class boundedBuffer extends monitorSC {
    ...
    private conditionVariable notFull = new conditionVariable();
    private conditionVariable notEmpty = new conditionVariable();
    ...
    public void deposit(int value) {
        enterMonitor();
        while (fullSlots == capacity)
            notFull.waitC();
        buffer[in] = value;
            in = (in + 1) % capacity;
        ++fullSlots;
        notEmpty.signalC();
        exitMonitor();
    }
    ...
}
```

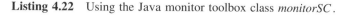

Listing 4.22   Using the Java monitor toolbox class *monitorSC*.

Simulated monitors are not as easy to use or as efficient as real monitors, but they have some advantages:

- A monitor toolbox can be used to simulate monitors in languages that do not support monitors directly. For example, as we show below, a monitor toolbox allows monitors to be used in C++/Win32/Pthreads programs.
- Different versions of the toolbox can be created for different types of signals. Java's built-in monitors use SC signaling. An SU toolbox can be used to allow SU signaling in Java.
- The toolbox can be extended to support testing and debugging.

The last advantage is an important one. If a language provides monitors but does not provide any mechanism for coping with nondeterminism during testing and debugging, it may be better to use simulated monitors to avoid time-consuming testing and debugging problems.

4.7.1 Toolbox for SC Signaling in Java

Listing 4.23 shows a monitor toolbox that uses semaphores to simulate monitors with SC signaling. Class *conditionVariable* is nested inside class *monitor*, which gives class *conditionVariable* access to member object *mutex* in the *monitorSC* class.

4.7.2 Toolbox for SU Signaling in Java

Listing 4.24 shows a Java monitor toolbox with SU signaling. The SU toolbox provides method *signalC_and_exitMonitor()*, which can be used when a signal operation is the last statement in a method (other than a `return` statement). When this method is called, the signaler does not wait in the *reentry* queue. For example, method *deposit()* using *signalC_and_exitMonitor()* becomes

```
public void deposit(int value) {
    enterMonitor();
    if (fullSlots == capacity)
        notFull.waitC();
    buffer[in] = value;
    in = (in + 1) % capacity;
    ++fullSlots;
    notEmpty.signalC_and_exitMonitor();
}
```

```
public class monitorSC { // monitor toolbox with SC signaling
    private binarySemaphore mutex = new binarySemaphore(1);
    protected final class conditionVariable {
        private countingSemaphore threadQueue = new countingSemaphore(0);
        private int numWaitingThreads = 0;
        public void signalC() {
            if (numWaitingThreads > 0) {
                numWaitingThreads--;
                threadQueue.V();
            }
        }
        public void signalCall() {
            while (numWaitingThreads > 0) {
                --numWaitingThreads;
                threadQueue.V();
            }
        }
        public void waitC() {
            numWaitingThreads++; threadQueue.VP(mutex); mutex.P();
        }
        public boolean empty() { return (numWaitingThreads == 0); }
        public int length() { return numWaitingThreads; }
    }
    protected void enterMonitor() { mutex.P(); }
    protected void exitMonitor() { mutex.V(); }
}
```

Listing 4.23   Java monitor toolbox *monitorSC* with SC signaling.

4.8   MONITOR TOOLBOX FOR WIN32/C++/PTHREADS

The C++ version of the monitor toolbox is very similar to the Java version. Listing 4.25 shows how to use the C++ *monitorSC* toolbox class to define a monitor for the bounded buffer problem. The major difference between using the Java and C++ toolboxes is in the creation of *conditionVariable* objects. The *conditionVariable* constructor receives a pointer to the monitor object that owns the variable. The *conditionVariable* uses this pointer to access the *mutex* object of the monitor.

```
boundedBuffer(int bufferCapacity_) : fullSlots(0), capacity(bufferCapacity),
    in(0), out(0),
    // each condition variable receives a pointer to this monitor, which is the
    // monitor that owns it
    notFull(this), notEmpty(this), buffer( new int[capacity]) {}
```

```
public class monitorSU { // monitor toolbox with SU signaling
    private binarySemaphore mutex = new binarySemaphore(1);
    private binarySemaphore reentry = new binarySemaphore(0);
    private int reentryCount = 0;
    proteced final class conditionVariable {
        private countingSemaphore threadQueue = new countingSemaphore(0);
        private int numWaitingThreads = 0;
        public void signalC() {
            if (numWaitingThreads > 0) {
                ++reentryCount;
                reentry.VP(threadQueue);
                --reentryCount;
            }
        }
        public void signalC_and_exitMonitor() { // does not execute reentry.P()
            if (numWaitingThreads > 0) threadQueue.V();
            else if (reentryCount > 0) reentry.V();
            else mutex.V();
        }
        public void waitC() {
            numWaitingThreads++;
            if (reentryCount > 0) threadQueue.VP(reentry);
            else threadQueue.VP(mutex);
            --numWaitingThreads;
        }
        public boolean empty() { return (numWaitingThreads == 0); }
        public int length() { return numWaitingThreads; }
    }
    public void enterMonitor() { mutex.P(); }
    public void exitMonitor() {
        if (reentryCount > 0) reentry.V();
        else mutex.V();
    }
}
```

Listing 4.24 Java monitor toolbox *monitorSU* with SU signaling.

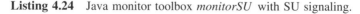

Monitor methods are written just as they are in Java:

```
void boundedBuffer::deposit(int value) {
    enterMonitor();
    while (fullSlots == capacity)
        notFull.waitC();
    buffer[in] = value;
```

```
class boundedBuffer : private monitorSC {  // Note the use of private inheritance–
private:         // methods of monitorSC cannot be called outside of boundedbuffer.
    int fullSlots;          // # of full slots in the buffer
    int capacity;           // # of slots in the buffer
    int* buffer;
    int in, out;
    conditionVariable notFull;
    conditionVariable notEmpty;
public:
    boundedBuffer(int bufferCapacity);
    ~boundedBuffer();
    void deposit(int value, int ID);
    int withdraw(int ID);
};
```

Listing 4.25   Using the C++ *monitorSC* toolbox class.

```
    in = (in + 1) % capacity;
    ++fullSlots;
    notEmpty.signalC();
    exitMonitor();
}
```

4.8.1   Toolbox for SC Signaling in C++/Win32/Pthreads

Listing 4.26 shows a C++/Win32/Pthreads monitor toolbox with SC signaling. Class *conditionVariable* is a friend of class *monitorSC*. This gives *conditionVariables* access to private member *mutex* of class *monitor*. Class *conditionVariable* could be nested inside class *monitorSC*, as we did in the Java toolbox, but that would not give class *conditionVariable* direct access to member object *mutex* in class *monitorSC*. C++ and Java rules for nested classes are different. (This may change in a future version of C++.)

4.8.2   Toolbox for SU Signaling in C++/Win32/Pthreads

Listing 4.27 shows a C++/Win32/Pthreads monitor toolbox with SU signaling.

4.9   NESTED MONITOR CALLS

A thread T executing in a method of monitor *M1* may call a method in another monitor *M2*. This is called a *nested monitor call*. If thread T releases mutual exclusion in *M1* when it makes the nested call to *M2*, it is said to be an *open call*. If mutual exclusion is not released, it is a *closed call*. Closed calls do not

```cpp
class monitorSC { // monitor toolbox with SC signaling
protected:
    monitorSC() : mutex(1) { }
    void enterMonitor() { mutex.P(); }
    void exitMonitor() { mutex.V(); }
private:
    binarySemaphore mutex;
    friend class conditionVariable;   // conditionVariable needs access to mutex
};
class conditionVariable {
private:
    binarySemaphore threadQueue;
    int numWaitingThreads;
    monitorSC& m;     // reference to the monitor that owns this conditionVariable
public:
    conditionVariable(monitorSC* mon) :
threadQueue(0),numWaitingThreads(0),m(*mon) { }
    void signalC();
    void signalCall();
    void waitC();
    bool empty() { return (numWaitingThreads == 0); }
    int length() { return numWaitingThreads; }
};

void conditionVariable::signalC() {
    if (numWaitingThreads > 0) {
        --numWaitingThreads;
        threadQueue.V();
    }
}
void conditionVariable::signalCall() {
    while (numWaitingThreads > 0) {
        --numWaitingThreads;
        threadQueue.V();
    }
}
void conditionVariable::waitC(int ID) {
    numWaitingThreads++;
    threadQueue.VP(&(m.mutex));
    m.mutex.P();
}
```

Listing 4.26   C++ monitor toolbox for SC signaling.

```
class monitorSU { // monitor toolbox with SU signaling
protected:
    monitorSU() : reentryCount(0), mutex(1), reentry(0) { }
    void enterMonitor() { mutex.P(); }
    void exitMonitor(){
        if (reentryCount > 0) reentry.V();
        else mutex.V();
    }
private:
    binarySemaphore mutex; binarySemaphore reentry;
    int reentryCount; friend class conditionVariable;
};
class conditionVariable {
private:
    binarySemaphore threadQueue;
    int numWaitingThreads;
    monitorSU& m;
public:
    conditionVariable(monitorSU* mon) : threadQueue(0), numWaitingThreads(0),
        m(*mon) { }
    void signalC();
    void signalC_and_exitMonitor();
    void waitC();
    bool empty() { return (numWaitingThreads == 0); }
    int length() { return numWaitingThreads; }
};
void conditionVariable::signalC() {
    if (numWaitingThreads > 0) {
        ++(m.reentryCount);
        m.reentry.VP(&threadQueue);
        --(m.reentryCount);
    }
}
void conditionVariable::signalC_and_exitMonitor() {
    if (numWaitingThreads > 0) threadQueue.V();
    else if (m.reentryCount > 0) m.reentry.V();
    else m.mutex.V();
}
void conditionVariable::waitC() {
    numWaitingThreads++;
    if (m.reentryCount > 0) threadQueue.VP(&(m.reentry));
    else threadQueue.VP(&(m.mutex));
    --numWaitingThreads;
}
```

Listing 4.27 C++ monitor toolbox for SU signaling.

require any extra effort to implement, since they do not affect the monitor in which the call is made. Closed calls, however, are prone to create deadlocks. Consider the following monitor classes:

```
class First extends monitorSU {      class Second extends monitorSU {
    Second M2;
    public void A1() {                   public void A2() {
        ...                                  ...
        M2.A2();                             wait();        // Thread A is blocked
        ...                                  ...
    }                                    }
    public void B1() {                   public void B2() {
        ...                                  ...
        M2.B2();                             ...
                                             // wake up Thread A
        ...                                  signal-and-exit();
    }                                    }
}
```

Suppose that we create an instance of the first monitor:

First M1;

and that this instance is used by two threads:

Thread A	Thread B
M1.A1();	M1.B1();

Assume that Thread *A* enters method *A1()* of monitor *M1* first and makes a closed monitor call to *M2.A2()*. Assume that Thread *A* is then blocked on the *wait* statement in method *A2()*. Thread *B* intends to signal Thread *A* by calling method *M1.B1*, which issues a nested call to *M2.B2()*, where the signal is performed. But this is impossible since Thread *A* retains mutual exclusion for monitor *M1* while Thread *A* is blocked on the wait statement in monitor *M2*. Thus, Thread *B* is unable to enter *M1* and a deadlock occurs.

Open monitor calls are implemented by having the calling thread release mutual exclusion when the call is made and reacquire mutual exclusion when the call returns. The monitor toolboxes described in Section 4.8 make this easy to do. For example, method *A1()* above becomes

```
public void A1() {
    enterMonitor();   // acquire mutual exclusion
    ...
    exitMonitor();    // release mutual exclusion
```

```
    M2.A2();
    enterMonitor();   // reacquire mutual exclusion
    ...
    exitMonitor();     // release mutual exclusion
}
```

This gives equal priority to the threads returning from a nested call and the threads trying to enter the monitor for the first time, since both groups of threads call *enterMonitor()*. Alternatively, the monitor toolboxes can be modified to give returning threads higher priority so that they will reenter the monitor first (see Exercise 4.3).

Open calls can create a problem if shared variables in monitor $M1$ are used as arguments and passed by reference on nested calls to $M2$. This allows shared variables of $M1$ to be accessed concurrently by a thread in $M1$ and a thread in $M2$, violating the requirement for mutual exclusion.

4.10 TRACING AND REPLAY FOR MONITORS

In this section we present techniques for tracing, replaying, and testing monitor-based programs. We first define a simple M-sequence of a monitor-based program. Then we show how to trace and replay simple M-sequences during debugging and how to modify the SC and SU monitor toolboxes to support our tracing and replay techniques. After that, we define a complete M-sequence and present a technique for using complete M-sequences to test monitor-based programs. Finally, we show how to apply reachability testing to monitor-based programs.

4.10.1 Simple M-Sequences

In Sections 4.6 and 4.7 we described monitor toolboxes for SC and SU monitors. Let M be a monitor that is implemented using one of these implementations. An execution of a program that uses M can be viewed as a sequence of *P()* and *V()* operations on the semaphores in the implementation of M. (Recall that each monitor is implemented using one semaphore for mutual exclusion and one semaphore for each of the condition variables in the monitor. SU monitors also use a semaphore to implement the reentry queue.) Hence, a simple SYN-sequence for M is the collection of simple PV-sequences for the semaphores in the implementation of M.

We can replay an execution of a program that uses M by applying the replay method that was presented in Chapter 3 for replaying PV-sequences of semaphore-based programs. However, special properties of the monitor toolboxes allow us to simplify this replay method. These monitor toolboxes use semaphores with FCFS notifications and *VP()* operations, both of which place extra constraints on the behavior of threads once they (re)enter a monitor:

- The execution of threads inside an SU monitor is determined completely by the order in which the threads enter the monitor via monitor calls and the values of the parameters on these calls.

- The execution of threads inside an SC monitor is determined completely by the order in which the threads enter the monitor via monitor calls, the values of the parameters on these calls, and the order in which signaled threads reenter the monitor.

Thus, the only nondeterminism that is present in these SU and SC monitors is the order in which threads (re)enter the monitor. We refer to this as *entry-based execution*: The execution of threads in a monitor having entry-based execution is determined completely by the order in which the threads (re)enter the monitor and the values of the parameters on the calls to the monitor.

This observation about entry-based execution leads to the following definition of a simple SYN-sequence for a monitor-based program. Let CP be a concurrent program that uses monitors. The synchronization objects in CP are its monitors. The synchronization events in a simple SYN-sequence of CP depend on the type of monitors being used:

1. *SC monitors*: A simple SYN-sequence for an SC monitor is a sequence of events of the following types:
   - Entry into the monitor by a calling thread
   - Reentry into the monitor by a signaled thread
2. *SU monitors*: A simple SYN-sequence for an SU monitor is a sequence of events of the following type:
   - Entry into the monitor by a calling thread

Simple SYN-sequences of monitors are called *simple M-sequences*. An event in a simple M-sequence is denoted by the identifier (ID) of the thread that executed the event. The simple M-sequence of a program CP is a collection of simple M-sequences for the monitors in CP. We can replay an execution of CP by replaying the simple M-sequence for each monitor.

To illustrate these definitions, consider the SC bounded buffer monitor in Listing 4.3. A possible simple M-sequence of *boundedBuffer* for a single *Producer* thread (with ID 1) and a single *Consumer* thread (with ID 2) is

$$(2, 1, 2, 1, 1, 2, 2).$$

This sequence is generated when the *Consumer* enters the monitor first and executes *notEmpty.wait()*. The *Producer* then enters the monitor, deposits an item, and signals the *Consumer*. The *Consumer* then reenters the monitor and consumes an item. Thus, this sequence begins with 2, 1, 2 since the *Consumer* generates one event when it enters the monitor (the first 2) and one event when it reenters the monitor (the second 2). If the same scenario were to occur when *boundedBuffer* was an SU monitor, the simple M-sequence of *boundedBuffer* would be

$$(2, 1, 1, 1, 2, 2).$$

In this sequence, the *Consumer* does not generate an event when it reenters the monitor, since *boundedBuffer* is an SU monitor. Thus, the sequence begins with 2, 1 and is followed by a second entry event for the *Producer* (the second 1) and not a reentry event for the *Consumer*.

We are making several important assumptions in our definition of simple M-sequences:

1. All shared variables are accessed inside a monitor, and monitor (re)entry is the only source of nondeterminism in the program.

2. Semaphores with FCFS notifications are used in the implementation of condition variables. If notifications wake up waiting threads in an unpredictable order, nondeterminism is introduced in the implementation of the monitor.

3. *VP()* operations are used in the semaphore implementation of a monitor. Without *VP()* or some other mechanism (see Exercise 4.23), context switches can occur between *V()* and *P()* operations, which introduces nondeterminism in the implementation of the monitor.

Assumptions 2 and 3 are necessary for entry-based execution. If assumption 1 does not hold, replaying the simple M-sequences of an execution may not replay the execution.

4.10.2   Tracing and Replaying Simple M-Sequences

We now show how to modify the monitor toolboxes so that they can trace and replay simple M-sequences. In the SU toolbox, semaphore *mutex* controls entry into the monitor. During execution, the identifier of a thread that completes a *mutex.P()* operation is recorded and saved to a trace file. Toolbox method *enterMonitor()* is easily modified (see below) to send monitor entry events to a *control* monitor that records and saves them.

Tracing for SC monitors is almost as easy. In the SC toolbox, semaphore *mutex* controls entry into the monitor for threads calling the monitor, and reentry into the monitor for signaled threads. As with SU monitors, the identifier of the thread that completes a *mutex.P()* operation is recorded and saved to a trace file. This requires modifications to methods *enterMonitor()* in class *monitor* and method *waitC()* in class *conditionVariable*.

To replay a simple M-sequence, we use the same basic technique that we used with semaphores. Before each *mutex.P()* operation, a thread calls *control.requestEntryPermit(ID)* to request permission to enter the monitor. After completing *mutex.P()*, the thread calls *control.releaseEntryPermit()* to allow the next thread in the simple M-sequence to enter the monitor. Method *enterMonitor()* in the SU and SC toolboxes becomes

```
public final void enterMonitor() {
    if (replayMode)
        control.requestEntryPermit(ID);
```

```
        mutex.P();

        if (replayMode)
            control.releaseEntryPermit();
        else if (traceMode)
            control.traceMonitorEntry(ID);
}
```

Method *waitC( )* in the SC toolbox becomes

```
public void waitC() {
    numWaitingThreads++;
    threadQueue.VP(mutex);

        if (replayMode)
            control.requestEntryPermit(ID);

    mutex.P();

        if (replayMode)
            control.releaseEntryPermit();
        else if (traceMode)
            control.traceMonitorReEntry(ID);
}
```

Java monitor class *monitorTracingAndReplay* in Listing 4.28 is very similar to the control object in Listing 3.32 that was used for replaying simple PV-sequences. Threads that try to enter the monitor out of turn are delayed in method *requestEntryPermit( )* on a separate *conditionVariable* in the *threads* array. A thread uses its *ID* to determine which *conditionVariable* in the *threads* array to wait on.

Method *releaseEntryPermit( )* increments *index* to allow the next (re)entry operation in the *simpleMSequence* to occur. Suppose that thread T is expected to execute the next (re)entry operation. Since thread T may already have been delayed by a *waitC( )* operation when T called method *requestEntryPermit( )*, method *releaseEntryPermit( )* performs a *signalC_and_exitMonitor( )* operation. If thread T is blocked on the *waitC( )* operation in *requestEntryPermit( )*, it will be awakened by this signal. Otherwise, when thread T eventually calls *requestEntryPermit( )*, it will not call *waitC( )* (since T's ID will match the next ID in the *simpleMSequence*), and thus thread T will not be blocked.

4.10.3   Other Approaches to Program Replay

Another approach to replaying an execution of a multithreaded Java program is to trace and replay the scheduling events of the operating system. A thread schedule

```
class monitorTracingAndReplay extends monitorSU {
    monitorTracingAndReplay () {
    /* input sequence of Integer IDs into vector simpleMSequence
        and initialize the threads array */
    }
    public requestEntryPermit(int ID) {
        enterMonitor();
        if (ID != ((Integer)simpleMSequence.elementAt(index)).intValue())
        threads[ID].waitC();          // thread with identifier ID is delayed on
        exitMonitor();                // condition variable threads[ID]
    }
    public releaseEntryPermit() {
        enterMonitor();
        if (index < simpleMSequence.size()-1) {
            ++index;
            // if the next thread in the simpleMSequence was delayed in
            // requestEntryPermit(), wake it up.
            threads[((Integer)simpleMSequence.elementAt(index)).intValue()].
                signalC_and_exitMonitor();
            return;
        }
        exitMonitor();
    }
    // record integer ID of entering thread in trace file
    public void traceMonitorEntry(int ID) { ... }
    // record integer ID of reentering thread in trace file
    public void traceMonitorReEntry(int ID) { ... }
    // simple M-sequence traced during a previous execution.
    private vector simpleMSequence;
    // out of order threads are delayed on condition variables.
    private conditionVariable[] threads;
    // index of the next event in simpleMSequence to be replayed.
    private int index = 1;
}
```

Listing 4.28 Java monitor *monitorTracingAndReplay* for tracing and replaying simple M-sequences.

is a sequence of time slices, where a time slice is the interval of time between two context switches. A thread schedule of an execution can be replayed by forcing context switches to occur at the exact same points during the execution. Since detailed scheduling information is not always available from the operating system, a logical thread schedule can be used instead. A logical thread schedule of an execution is a record of the number of critical operations that the threads executed during their time slices. Critical operations are read and write operations on shared variables, entering and exiting `synchronized` methods and blocks, and `wait` and `notify` operations. A logical thread schedule can be replayed my modifying the Java Virtual Machine (JVM) to count critical operations. For example, assume that Thread1 executes 50 critical operations during its time quantum. This can be represented by recording an event such as (1, 20, 69) to represent the fact that Thread1 executed the (50) operations numbered 20 through 69. (A similar representation was also discussed in Section 2.5.2.) Using this scheme, a time slice consisting of thousands of critical operations can be encoded very efficiently by a single event. The DejaVu system [Choi and Srinivasan 1998] uses logical thread schedules to replay multithreaded Java programs. Java applications can be traced and replayed in DejaVu without any modifications to the source code.

4.11 TESTING MONITOR-BASED PROGRAMS

In this section we present a technique for testing monitor-based programs. A *complete M-sequence* can be used during (regression) testing to determine whether a particular behavior is allowed by a program. We also show how to modify the SC and SU monitor toolboxes to support this testing technique.

4.11.1 M-Sequences

Simple M-sequences help us carry out an important part of a typical debugging session. Debugging begins after a program is executed and a failure is observed. The simple M-sequence of the execution is replayed, perhaps several times, to locate the fault that caused the failure. When the fault is located, the program is modified and replay stops. However, this is not the end of the process. The modification must be tested to make sure that the fault has been corrected and that no new faults were introduced by the modification. This is commonly known as *regression testing*.

For a concurrent program, regression testing requires that we determine whether or not a particular SYN-sequence is feasible. (A feasible SYN-sequence is a sequence that can be exercised by the program.) The SYN-sequence may represent an illegal (or *invalid*) behavior that was observed when the program failed. For example, a sequence of three consecutive deposits into a bounded buffer with only two slots is an invalid sequence. In this case, we hope that the modification has corrected the program by making this invalid SYN-sequence infeasible. If, on the other hand, a SYN-sequence represents a legal (or *valid*) behavior that was exhibited previously, this valid sequence should remain feasible after the modifications.

Determining the feasibility of a SYN-sequence is a problem that is subtly different from the replay problem. Replaying a SYN-sequence involves repeating a sequence that is known to be feasible since, presumably, the sequence was just exercised and the program has not been modified. The feasibility of a sequence is not in question during replay.

During regression testing, we want to know whether or not a program that is executed with a given input can exercise a particular sequence and produce a particular output. To answer this question for a program that uses monitors, we need more information than is contained in a simple M-sequence. Consider a program that contains an SU monitor for a two-slot bounded buffer. Assume that an execution of the program with a single *Producer* (with ID 1) and a single *Consumer* (with ID 2) exercises the following simple M-sequence:

(1, 1, 1, 2, 2).

During replay, we can assume that the *Producer* will be the first thread to enter the monitor, and it will enter the monitor by calling the same method as it did in the original execution. But which method did it call? The name of the method does not appear in a simple M-sequence. Granted, the bounded buffer program is very simple, and we might insist that the *Producer* is calling method *deposit()*. However, in general, when we test a program we don't know for sure if the threads in the program are calling the correct methods in the correct order. Hence, during testing, we must check the names of the monitor methods.

Suppose now that we specify the name of the method and the thread ID for each entry event in the test sequence:

((1,deposit), (1,deposit), (1,deposit), (2,withdraw), (2,withdraw)).

Furthermore, suppose that we check that the method name and ID for each entry event in the sequence matches the actual method name and ID for each entry event that occurs during execution. This sequence shows the *Producer* entering the monitor three consecutive times without any intervening withdraw. If the third item was deposited into a full buffer, the first item was lost. But if the *Producer* executed *notFull.wait()*, a third deposit was not made until after a withdrawal, and a failure was avoided. We simply cannot, from the information in this sequence, determine what happened. Even after checking the output, we may still be unsure about what happened. If the items deposited were C, A, and C, the items withdrawn are also C, A, and C, even if the first item is overwritten by the third item.

To characterize the execution of a monitor-based program more completely, we consider the following types of monitor events:

1. The entry of a monitor method and, for SC monitors, the reentry of a monitor method
2. The exit of a monitor method
3. The start of execution of a *wait* operation
4. The start of execution of a *signal*, or *signalAndExit*, or *signalAll* operation

Notice that this list does not include events that mark the end of execution of a *wait* or *signal* operation, or the resumption of a monitor method after a *wait* or an SU *signal* operation. We omit these events since their occurrence can be inferred by the occurrence of events of types 1 through 4. However, it may still be desirable to trace these events to aid in understanding executions.

A sequence of events of types 1 through 4 is called a *complete M-sequence*. In the remainder of the book, the term *M-sequence* always refers to a complete M-sequence. We will continue to use the term *simple M-sequence* to refer to the simpler format that is used for replay. The format of an M-sequence for a monitor is

(($Type_1$,$Thread_1$,$Method_1$,$ConditionVariable_1$), ($Type_2$,$Thread_2$,$Method_2$, $ConditionVariable_2$), ...)

where ($Type_i$, $Thread_i$, $Method_i$, $ConditionVariable_1$) denotes the ith, i > 0, event in the M-sequence. The fields in an event are:

- *Type*: the type of this event
- *Thread*: the ID of the thread executing this event
- *Method*: the monitor method of this event, qualified with the monitor name if there are multiple monitors
- *ConditionVariable*: the name of the condition variable if this event is a *wait, signal, signalAndExit,* or *signalAll* event; and "NA" otherwise.

The M-sequence of a program CP is a collection of M-sequences for the monitors in CP. As an example, a possible M-sequence of the SC bounded buffer monitor in Listing 4.3 is

((enter,	consumer,	withdraw,	NA	),
(wait,	consumer,	withdraw,	notEmpty	),
(enter,	producer,	deposit,	NA	),
(signal,	producer,	deposit,	notEmpty	),
(exit,	producer,	deposit,	NA	),
(reenter,	consumer,	withdraw,	NA	),
(signal,	consumer,	withdraw,	notFull	),
(exit,	consumer,	withdraw,	NA	)).

To make this sequence more readable, we've used the names of the producer and consumer threads in place of their IDs.

Another way to make an M-sequence clearer is to allow user-level events to appear in the sequence. These events label the (atomic) communication actions that occur inside the monitor. A call to method *exerciseEvent("event")* generates a communication event labeled "event" and records it in the M-sequence. For example, in the following SC bounded buffer monitor, we have inserted calls to *exerciseEvent()* to generate communication events labeled "deposit" and "withdraw":

```
public void deposit(int value) {
    enterMonitor();
    while (fullSlots == capacity)
        notFull.waitC();
    buffer[in] = value;
    exerciseEvent("deposit");              // generate a "deposit" event
    in = (in + 1) % capacity; ++fullSlots;
    notEmpty.signalC();
    exitMonitor();
}
public int withdraw() {
    enterMonitor();
    int value;
    while (fullSlots == 0)
        notEmpty.waitC();
    value = buffer[out];
    exerciseEvent("withdraw");   // generate a "withdraw" event
    out = (out + 1) % capacity; --fullSlots;
    notFull.signalC();
    exitMonitor();
    return value;
}
```

The M-sequence shown above with communication events "deposit" and "withdraw" added is

```
((enter,   consumer, withdraw, NA        ),
(wait,     consumer, withdraw, notEmpty ),
(enter,    producer, deposit,  NA        ),
(comm,     producer, deposit,  NA        ), // comm. event
(signal,   producer, deposit,  notEmpty ),
(exit,     producer, deposit,  NA        ),
(reenter,  consumer, withdraw, NA        ),
(comm,     consumer, withdraw, NA        ), // comm. event
(signal,   consumer, withdraw, notFull  ),
(exit,     consumer, withdraw, NA        ().
```

For each communication event, we record its label and the ID of the thread that executed the event.

A sequence of communication events is useful for understanding *what* happened, that is, the communication that occurred among the threads, without any details about *how* the threads were synchronized to achieve that communication:

```
(comm,  producer, deposit,  NA    ),
(comm,  consumer, withdraw, NA    ).
```

It is easy to imagine several different monitors that are equivalent in the sense that they allow the same set of communication sequences, even if some of the monitors are SC monitors and some are SU monitors.

If all shared variables are accessed inside monitors, the result of an execution of a monitor-based program can be determined by the program, the input, and the M-sequence of this execution. Notice that this same statement holds when we substitute "simple M-sequence" for "M-sequence," which is why we can use simple M-sequences for replay. (Again, we are assuming that monitor entry is the only source of nondeterminism in the program.)

M-sequences contain more information than a simple M-sequence because they are used to solve a different problem. When we modify a program to correct a fault, we want an answer to the following question: If we execute the program with the same the input that detected the fault, can the same path be exercised and the same output be produced? An M-sequence partially identifies the path exercised by a program and helps us answer this question.

Consider the following monitor method:

```
public void F() {
    enterMonitor();
    if (...) {
        condition.waitC();
    }

    if (...) {
        /* true-part*/
    }
    else {
        /* false-part */
    }

    condition.signalC();
    exitMonitor();
}
```

An M-sequence for an execution of a program containing method $F()$ indicates the order in which threads entered $F()$ and whether or not the *wait()* operation in $F()$ was executed. (The *signal()* operation is always executed.) This tells us a lot about the path through $F()$ that each thread executed. However, an M-sequence, by itself, does not indicate whether the threads executed the true or the false part of the second if-statement in $F()$. A path consists of more than just an M-sequence.

Whenever we determine the feasibility of an M-sequence, we will also check the output that is produced during the execution. The output of an execution involving method $F()$ is likely to indicate whether the true or the false part was executed. Thus, the M-sequence and the output of an execution, together, describe the execution very well.

Despite the fact that M-sequences offer only a partial characterization of the path of an execution, they still tell us a lot about what happened. We can often examine an M-sequence and determine whether there is a fault in the program without looking at the output or any additional information that was recorded about the execution. In fact, some executions can produce outputs that mask faults. So even though an execution produces correct outputs, an examination of the M-sequence may show that a fault is present.

This discussion raises the question of how to define a path of a concurrent program. Many path-based testing techniques have been developed for sequential programs. In a sequential program, where there is a single thread of control, a path is simply the sequence of statements exercised during an execution. But in a concurrent program, each thread executes its own sequence of statements. Furthermore, even if the threads in a program execute the same sequence of statements during two different executions, it is possible that these two executions produce different results. Thus, the sequence of statements executed by each thread does not provide sufficient information to characterize the path that was executed. (You may already have guessed that the SYN-sequence of an execution provides the missing information about the path.) This issue is resolved in Chapter 7.

4.11.2 Determining the Feasibility of an M-Sequence

The feasibility of an M-sequence is determined using the same technique that was used for replay. Before a thread can perform a monitor operation, it requests permission from a control module. The control module is responsible for reading an M-sequence and forcing the execution to proceed according to this sequence. If the M-sequence is determined to be infeasible, the control module displays a message and terminates the program.

Modifying Monitor Operations   Each monitor operation is modified by adding one or more calls to the controller. Below we describe the modifications made to the SC monitor operations. The modifications for the SU monitor operations are very similar.

Method *enterMonitor()* contains calls to *control.requestMPermit()* and *control.releaseMPermit()* to control entry into the monitor during *testMode*. The call to *control.trace(...)* is made during *traceMode* to record the necessary information about each monitor entry.

```
public final void enterMonitor(String methodName) {
    if (testMode)
        control.requestMPermit(ENTRY,threadID,methodName,"NA");

    mutex.P();

    if (testMode)
        control.releaseMPermit();
    else if (traceMode)
        control.trace(ENTRY,threadID,methodName,"NA");
}
```

The arguments for the call to *control.requestMPermit()* are

(ENTRY, ID, methodName, "NA"),

which correspond to the type of event (ENTRY), the identifier (ID) of the entering thread, the method name, and the name of the associated *conditionVariable*. Since the name of a *conditionVariable* is not applicable on monitor entries, "NA" is used.

For the method name to be available inside the toolbox, it must be passed by the user as an argument to *enterMonitor()*:

```
public void deposit(char value) {
    enterMonitor("deposit");
    ...
}
```

The *methodName* passed to *enterMonitor()* is saved locally in the monitor so that it can be used by any *waitC(), signalC(), signalCall(),* or *exitMonitor()* operations that appear in the same monitor method.

Method *waitC()* in the SC toolbox has a call to *control.requestMPermit()* with event type WAIT. This call occurs before the *VP()* operation that implements the wait. There is also a call to *control.requestMPermit()* with event type REENTRY. This call appears immediately before the *mutex.P()* operation that guards reentry. The value of *methodName* is the name that was saved in *enterMonitor()*, and the value of *conditionName* is the name of the *conditionVariable*.

```
public void waitC() {
    if (testMode)
        control.requestMPermit(WAIT,threadID,methodName,conditionName);
    else if (traceMode)
        control.trace(WAIT,threadID,methodName,conditionName);
```

```
        numWaitingThreads++;
        threadQueue.VP(mutex);

    if (testMode)
        control.requestMPermit(REENTRY,threadID,methodName,"NA");

    mutex.P();

    if (testMode)
        control.releaseMPermit();
    else if (traceMode)
        control.trace(REENTRY,threadID,methodName,"NA");
    }
```

A *conditionVariable's* name is generated automatically when the *conditionVariable* is constructed. This internal name is generated using the same technique that is used to generate thread names (see Section 1.7.2). Alternatively, a more descriptive name can be specified when the *conditionVariable* is constructed, but each name must be unique:

```
    notFull = new conditionVariable("notFull");
```

The call to *releaseMPermit( )* after the *mutex.P( )* operation notifies the controller that reentry has occurred and that the next monitor event can be permitted.

There is no call *to releaseMPermit( )* after a WAIT event since such a call is not necessary. The same thing is true for events of types SIGNAL and EXIT (see below). This is because *wait, signal,* and *exit* operations all occur within critical sections. Thus, once permission is received to perform one of these operations, the operation is guaranteed to occur before the next operation in the sequence (for the same monitor). This guarantee is based on the fact that mutual exclusion is not released until after the `wait`, `signal` or `exit` operation is performed, so no other operation can possibly barge ahead.

For ENTRY and REENTRY events, the controller must confirm that the current ENTRY or REENTRY event has occurred before it allows the next event to occur. To see why, assume that thread T1 is required to enter the monitor before thread T2. T1 will receive permission to enter the monitor first; however, a context switch may occur after T1 receives permission but before T1 enters the monitor. Now T2 can receive permission to enter the monitor and barge ahead of T1. To prevent this from happening, the controller will wait for T1 to enter the monitor and call *releaseMPermit( )* before the controller will give T2 permission to enter. Thread T2 may try to enter the monitor before T1 exits, but T2 will not be able to enter until T1 releases mutual exclusion by executing *exitMonitor( )* or *waitC( )*.

Threads executing *signalC()* or *exitMonitor()* in an SC monitor must request permission before executing a SIGNAL or EXIT event:

```
public void signalC() {
    if (testMode)
        control.requestMPermit(SIGNAL,threadID,methodName,conditionName);
    else if (traceMode)
        control.trace(SIGNAL,threadID,methodName,conditionName);
    if (numWaitingThreads > 0) {
        numWaitingThreads--;
        threadQueue.V();
    }
}

public void exitMonitor() {
    if (testMode)
        control.requestMPermit(EXIT,threadID,methodName,"NA");
    else if (traceMode)
        control.trace(EXIT,threadID,methodName,"NA");
    mutex.V();
}
```

If a monitor contains calls to *exerciseEvent()*, threads executing *exerciseEvent()* must request permission before executing a communication (COMM) event:

```
public void exerciseEvent(String eventLabel) {
    if (testMode)
        control.requestMPermit(COMM,threadID,eventlabel,"NA");
    else if (traceMode)
        control.trace(COMM,threadID,eventLabel,"NA");
}
```

Controller   The function of the controller is very similar to that of the controller used for replay. It attempts to force a deterministic execution of the program according to the M-sequence that it inputs. The M-sequence is feasible if and only if the M-sequence is exercised completely. We would like the controller to display a message if it finds that an M-sequence definitely cannot be exercised. However, the problem of determining whether a concurrent program terminates for a given input and SYN-sequence is, in general, undecidable. (This problem can be reduced to the halting problem [Hamburger and Richards 2002], which is undecidable.)

A practical way to deal with this undecidable problem is to specify a maximum time interval that is allowed between two consecutive events. In other words, this timeout value represents the maximum amount of time that the controller is willing to wait for the next event to occur. If a timeout occurs, the sequence is assumed to be infeasible. It is always possible that some larger timeout value would give the next event enough time to occur and allow the sequence to complete. However, the timeout value can be made large enough so that a timeout always indicates that a real problem exits: Either the event cannot occur, or possibly it can occur but something else is wrong and is holding up the event.

The controller is implemented in two parts. The first part is the control monitor shown in Listing 4.29. The control monitor inputs an M-sequence and then forces the execution to proceed according to the order of events in the M-sequence. The event in *Msequence[index]* is the next event to be exercised. Threads call *requestMPermit()* to request permission to perform a monitor operation. If a requesting thread with identifier ID attempts to perform its operation out of sequence, the thread is delayed on condition variable *threads[ID]*. When the ID of the requesting thread matches the ID for the next event, the controller verifies that the requested event's type and method name match the expected values for the next event. For WAIT and SIGNAL events, the condition name is also checked. If a mismatch is detected, a diagnostic is issued and the program is terminated.

For ENTRY and REENTRY events, the controller waits for a call to *releaseM-Permit()* before incrementing *index* to allow the next event to be issued. For WAIT, SIGNAL, COMM and EXIT events, no *releaseMPermit()* calls will be made, so *index* is incremented when permission is granted in *requestMPermit()*. At any point in the sequence, if an expected request does not arrive within the timeout interval, a diagnostic is issued and the program is terminated. This time-out function of the controller is handled by a *watchdog thread* that monitors the value of *index* to make sure that progress is being made. If the value of *index* does not change within the timeout interval, the M-sequence is assumed to be infeasible.

```
final class watchDog extends Thread {
    public void run() {
        while (index < MSequence.size()) {
            int saveIndex = index;
            try { Thread.sleep(2000); } // 2-second timeout interval
            catch (InterruptedException e) { }
            if (saveIndex == index) {
                /* issue diagnostic and exit program */
            }
        }
    }
}
```

Splitting the controller into a monitor and a watchdog thread is one way to implement the dual functions of the controller, which are ordering monitor events and handling timeouts. In Chapter 5 we show how both functions can be handled by a single thread.

```
public void requestMPermit(eventType op, int ID, String methodName,
    String conditionName) {
    //get the next event in the M-sequence
    monitorEvent nextEvent = (monitorEvent) MSequence.elementAt(index);
    // compare the ID of the requesting thread with the ID of the thread
    // for the next event
    if(ID != nextEvent.getThreadID()) {
        // the nextEvent does not involve the requesting thread
        threads[ID].waitC(); // thread ID must wait for its turn
        //get nextEvent again since it may have changed during the wait
        nextEvent = (monitorEvent)MSequence.elementAt(index);
    }
    // verify that the requested event has the expected type
    if (!(op.equals(nextEvent.getEventType()))) { /* issue msg and terminate */ }
    // verify the requested event has the expected method name (for COMM events
    // this is the event label)
    if (!(methodName.equals(nextEvent.getMethodName()))) {
        /* issue diagnostic and terminate */ }
    if (op.equals(WAIT) || op.equals(SIGNAL)) {
        // the event is a WAIT or SIGNAL so check the condition name
        if (!(conditionName.equals(nextEvent.getConditionName()))) {
            /*issue diagnostic and terminate */ }
        ++index;
        if (index < MSequence.size()) // signal thread waiting for next event
            threads[((monitorEvent)MSequence.elementAt(index)).getThreadID()].
                signalC();
    }
    else if (op.equals(EXIT) || op.equals(COMM)) {
        // event is EXIT or COMM so signal any thread waiting for the next event
        ++index;
        if (index < MSequence.size())
            threads[((monitorEvent)MSequence.elementAt(index)).getThreadID()].
                signalC();
    }
}

public void releaseMPermit() {
// This method is called when the current event is of type ENTRY or REENTRY.
// It will signal the thread waiting for the next event. Events of type WAIT,
// SIGNAL, or EXIT do not issue a call to releaseMPermit(). Thus, the thread
// waiting for the next event is signaled in requestMPermit() when the ENTRY or
// REENTRY event occurs.
    ++index;
    if (index < MSequence.size())
        threads[((monitorEvent)MSequence.elementAt(index)).getThreadID()].
            signalC();
}
```

Listing 4.29   Control monitor for checking feasibility.

4.11.3   Determining the Feasibility of a Communication-Sequence

A *Communication-sequence* is a sequence of communication events. A set of Communication-sequences can be generated to test a monitor without knowing the details about the synchronization events in the monitor. The details that are abstracted away include calls to methods *waitC()* and *signalC()* and the names of the condition variables and monitor methods.

The feasibility of a Communication-sequence is determined just like that of an M-sequence, except that only the thread IDs and event labels of communication-events are checked. Monitor (re)entry events do not appear in a Communication-sequence and thus they need not be checked, but they must be controlled. The rule for controlling monitor (re)entry is as follows: If Thread$_i$ is expected to execute the next communication-event (inside the monitor), only Thread$_i$ is permitted to (re)enter the monitor.

Threads that wish to (re)enter a monitor must request permission from the controller first. The controller grants permission for Thread$_i$ to enter the monitor only if Thread$_i$ is the thread expected to execute the next communication event in the sequence. In other words, the order in which threads execute communication events must match the order in which they (re)enter the monitor. If this is not possible, the Communication-sequence is not feasible. Monitor events of types EXIT and SIGNAL do not require any permission from the controller, so no calls to the controller are made in methods *exitMonitor()* and *signalC()*. Threads in method *waitC()* of an SC monitor must call the controller before they reenter the monitor. Section 4.10.5 shows an example of how to use Communication-sequences to test a program.

4.11.4   Reachability Testing for Monitors

In Section 3.8.5 we described reachability testing and showed how to use reachability testing to test programs that use semaphores and locks. Reachability testing can also be used to derive and exercise automatically every (partially ordered) M-sequence of a monitor-based program. Reachability testing identifies race conditions in an execution trace and uses the race conditions to generate race variants. Recall from Chapter 3 that a race variant represents an alternative execution behavior that definitely could have happened, but didn't, due to the way that race conditions were arbitrarily resolved during execution. Replaying a race variant ensures that different behavior is observed during the next execution.

Figure 4.30a shows an execution trace of a bounded buffer program with two producers (P1 and P2), two consumers (C1 and C2), and an SC monitor M. A solid arrow from a producer or consumer thread to monitor M indicates that the thread called and entered monitor M. In this execution, the producer and consumer threads enter the monitor in the order (C1, P1, C1, P2, C2). Note that the second entry by C1 occurs when C1 reenters the monitor after being signaled by P1.

Informally, there is a race between two monitor calls in an execution trace if the entries for these calls could occur in a different order during another execution. In Fig. 4.30a we have identified the racing threads, called the *race*

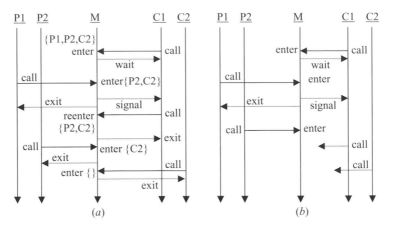

Figure 4.30 Execution trace and a race variant.

set, for each entry event. For example, the race set for C1's reentry event is shown beside the reentry event as {P2, C2}. This indicates that P2 or C2 could have entered the monitor instead of C1. Note that the monitor calls made by P2 and C2 were concurrent with C1's call to reenter the monitor. This is how the racing monitor calls were identified. Mechanisms for identifying concurrent events are presented in Chapter 6.

A race variant is created by changing the calling thread for a monitor (re)entry event. The new calling thread must be a member of the race set for the (re)entry event. Figure 4.30*b* shows one of the eight race variants for the trace in Fig. 4.30*a*. In this variant, P2 enters the monitor before C1 reenters the monitor. The dotted arrows for C1 and C2 indicate that the variant contains the monitor calls made by C1 and C2, but not their entries. When this race variant is replayed, the two producers will both deposit their items before either consumer withdraws one. The order in which the two consumers will (re)enter the monitor and withdraw their items after the variant is replayed is nondeterministic. The complete trace of whichever sequence occurs can be analyzed to derive more variants, which can be replayed to generate more traces, and so on. This iterative process ensures that producers and consumers will enter the monitor in all possible orders so that all possible M-sequences are exercised during reachability testing.

We have implemented reachability testing for the *monitorSC* and *monitorSU* toolbox classes. Details about reachability testing for monitors are given in Chapter 7. Here we present the results of applying reachability testing to several monitor programs. The three Java programs and the results are shown in Table 4.2. This table has the same format as that of Table 3.2. Program BB is the bounded-buffer program in Listing 4.3. Program DP2 is the second solution to the dining philosophers program in Listing 4.8. Program RW is the readers and writers program in Listing 4.9. For the sake of comparison, we have shown

TABLE 4.2 Reachability Testing Results for the Example Programs in Section 4.2

Program	Config.	No. Seqs.
BB-MonitorSU	3P + 3C + 2S	720
BB-MonitorSC	3P + 3C + 2S	12096
RW-MonitorSU	3R + 2W	13320
RW-MonitorSC	3R + 2W	70020
DP2-MonitorSU	3	30
DP2-MonitorSU	4	624
DP2-MonitorSU	5	19330

the results for two versions of BB and RW, one version using class *monitorSU* and one version using class *monitorSC*.

The results in Table 4.2 indicate that the choice of signaling discipline has a large effect on the number of M-sequences generated during reachability testing. SC monitors generate more M-sequences than SU monitors since SC monitors have races between signaled threads that are trying to reenter the monitor and calling threads that are trying to enter the monitor for the first time. SU monitors avoid these races by giving signaled threads priority over calling threads. These results help to quantify the difference between SU and SC monitors.

As we discussed in Section 3.10.5 regarding Table 3.2, the number of sequences exercised during reachability testing can be reduced by considering the symmetry of the threads in the programs. For the bounded-buffer program, reachability testing considers all the possible orders in which a group of producers can perform their deposit operations or a group of consumers can perform their withdraws. For example, the order in which Producer threads enter the monitor may be (Producer$_1$, Producer$_2$, Producer$_3$), or (Producer$_2$, Producer$_1$, Producer$_3$), or (Producer$_3$, Producer$_2$, Producer$_1$), and so on. If you use the symmetry of the threads, the number of sequences exercised for the two bounded buffer programs drops from 720 and 12096 to 20 and 60, respectively.

4.11.5 Putting It All Together

Next we demonstrate how to use the monitor toolbox classes to trace, test, and replay Java and C++/Win32/Pthreads monitor-based programs.

Using Java Toolboxes Java program *Buffer* is shown in Listing 4.31. This program creates two pairs of *Producer* and *Consumer* threads and two SC *boundedBuffer* monitors, one for each *Producer–Consumer* pair. The *Producer* and *Consumer* classes extend class *TDThread* instead of class *Thread*. This ensures that each thread receives a unique ID. We chose to supply names for the threads, monitors, and condition variables to make the traces more readable. These names can also be used in any test sequences that we generate by hand.

```java
public final class Buffer {
    public static void main (String args[]) {
        boundedBuffer b1 = new boundedBuffer(3,1);
        boundedBuffer b2 = new boundedBuffer(3,2);
        Producer p1 = new Producer (b1, 1); Consumer c1 = new Consumer (b1, 1);
        Producer p2 = new Producer (b2, 2); Consumer c2 = new Consumer (b2, 2);
        p1.start(); c1.start(); p2.start(); c2.start();
    }
}
final class Producer extends TDThread {
    private boundedBuffer b;   private int num;
    Producer (boundedBuffer b, int num) {super(''Producer''+num); this.b = b;
        this.num = num; }
    public void run () {
        for (int i = 0; i < 3; i++) {
            b.deposit(i);
            System.out.println ("Producer # "+ num + "deposited "+ i);
        }
    }
}
final class Consumer extends TDThread {
    private boundedBuffer b;
    private int num;
    Consumer (boundedBuffer b, int num) {
        super(''Consumer''+num);this.b = b; this.num = num;}
    public void run () {
        int value = 0;
        for (int i = 0; i < 3; i++) {
            value = b.withdraw();
            System.out.println ("Consumer # "+ num + "withdrew "+ value);
        }
    }
}

final class boundedBuffer extends monitorSC { // SC monitor
    private int fullSlots = 0; // # of full slots in the buffer
    private int capacity = 0;
    private int[] buffer = null; private int in = 0, out = 0;
    private conditionVariable notFull; private conditionVariable notEmpty;

    public boundedBuffer(int bufferCapacity, int num) {
        super("Buffer"+num);
        capacity = bufferCapacity;
```

Listing 4.31   Bounded buffer using the Java monitor toolbox.

```
      buffer = new int[capacity];
      notFull = new conditionVariable("notFull"+num);
      notEmpty = new conditionVariable("notEmpty"+num);
   }

   public void deposit(int value) {
      // the method name "deposit" is required for feasibility checking
      enterMonitor("deposit");
      while (fullSlots == capacity)
         notFull.waitC();
      buffer[in] = value;
      // generate communication event "deposit" for the Producer
      exerciseEvent("deposit");
      in = (in + 1) % capacity;
      ++fullSlots;
      notEmpty.signalC();
      exitMonitor();
   }

   public int withdraw() {
      // the method name "withdraw" is required for feasibility checking
      enterMonitor("withdraw");
      int value;
      while (fullSlots == 0)
         notEmpty.waitC();
      value = buffer[out];
      // generate communication event "withdraw" for the Consumer
      exerciseEvent("withdraw");
      out = (out + 1) % capacity;
      --fullSlots;
      notFull.signalC();
      exitMonitor();
      return value;
   }
}
```

Listing 4.31   (*continued*)

When *Buffer* is executed, a property named *mode* specifies the function (tracing, replay, or testing) to be performed. An execution of *Buffer* is traced using the command

  java −Dmode=trace Buffer

This creates three files. File monitor-replay.txt contains the simple M-sequence of the execution; file monitor-test.txt contains the M-sequence of the execution; and file monitor-comm.txt contains the Communication-sequence of the execution. One control module is used to trace both monitors, so the simple M-sequence that is recorded is a totally ordered sequence containing events from both monitors. The same is true for the M-sequence and Communication-sequence that are recorded. Random delays can be executed during trace mode by setting property *randomDelay* to the value *on*.

    java −Dmode=trace −DrandomDelay=on Buffer

When *on* is specified, random delays are executed before each (re)entry of a monitor. To turn random delays off, use *off*; this is also the default value. The value of property *randomDelay* is ignored during replay and test modes. The deadlock detection method described in Section 3.8.4 has also been implemented in the monitor toolbox classes. To turn deadlock detection on during tracing or reachability testing, specify −DdeadlockDetection=on. To turn deadlock detection off, set property *deadlockDetection* to *off*; this is also the default value.

If separate sequences are desired for each monitor, the *controllers* property can be used to create one controller per monitor. Valid values for this property are *single*, which is the default value, and *multiple*. For example,

    java −Dmode=trace −DrandomDelay=on −Dcontrollers=multiple Buffer

creates multiple controllers, resulting in a separate simple M-sequence, complete M-sequence, and Communication-sequence for each monitor.

The simple M-sequence in file monitor-replay.txt is replayed using

    java −Dmode=replay Buffer

As in Chapter 3, reachability testing is performed on *Buffer* by setting the *mode* property to *rt* and executing a driver process named *RTDriver*:

    java −Dmode=rt −DdeadlockDetection=0n RTDriver Buffer

The feasibility of the M-sequence in file monitor-test.txt is determined using

    java −Dmode=test Buffer

The feasibility of the Communication-sequence in file monitor-comm.txt is determined using

    java −Dmode=commTest Buffer

The value used for property *controllers* during replay and testing must match the value that was used during tracing. If the mode is not specified, the default value for the mode property turns tracing, replay, and testing off. Specifying "−Dmode=none" has the same effect.

The M-sequence recorded during a program's execution can be used to replay the execution. If the program is not modified after the M-sequence is recorded, the M-sequence remains feasible, and checking the feasibility of this feasible M-sequence (using –Dmode=test) amounts to replaying the execution. This means that we never actually have to use replay mode, since test mode can be used for replay, albeit with more overhead.

In trace mode, with random delays *on*, it is likely that nondeterministic testing will exercise several different M-sequences of the *boundedBuffer* monitor. This monitor is expected to have a capacity of 3. Even if we never see a trace with four consecutive *deposit* operations during nondeterministic testing, it is possible that *boundedBuffer* contains a fault that allows a *deposit* into a full buffer. Similarly, it is possible that a *withdrawal* is allowed from an empty buffer. To test these cases, we can specify two Communication-sequences and check their feasibility. A sequence that checks for an invalid *withdrawal* is

(comm, consumer,**withdraw**, NA)   // withdraw from an empty buffer

The following invalid sequence contains four consecutive *deposits*:

(comm, producer, **deposit**, NA),
(comm, producer, **deposit**, NA),
(comm, producer, **deposit**, NA),
(comm, producer, **deposit**, NA). // deposit into a full buffer

If either of these Communication-sequences is feasible, a fault is detected in *boundedBuffer*. Alternatively, we can use reachability testing to check the feasibility of these sequences indirectly. That is, if neither of these sequences is exercised during reachability testing, they are infeasible.

Selecting sequences and checking their feasibility is part of a general testing technique called *deterministic testing*. In general, valid sequences are expected to be feasible and invalid sequences are expected to be infeasible. In Chapter 5 we describe deterministic testing and compare it to nondeterministic testing. In Chapter 7 the sets of valid and feasible sequences are used to provide a general definition of correctness for concurrent programs.

Using C++/Win32/Pthreads Toolboxes   C++ program *Buffer* is shown in Listing 4.32. The mode of execution is specified using the environment variable MODE. The possible values for MODE are TRACE, REPLAY, TEST, RT (for *R*eachability *T*esting), COMMTEST (to determine the feasibility of a Communication-sequence), and NONE. For example, an execution of *Buffer* is traced in Windows by executing the command

set MODE=TRACE   // Unix: setenv MODE TRACE

and then executing program *Buffer*. In trace mode, random delays are controlled by variable RANDOMDELAY, just as we did for semaphores in Chapter 3:

set RANDOMDELAY=ON   // Unix: setenv RANDOMDELAY ON

```cpp
class boundedBuffer : private monitorSC {  // An SC bounded-buffer monitor
private:
    int fullSlots;                              // # of full slots in the buffer
    int capacity; int* buffer; int in, out;
    conditionVariable notFull; conditionVariable notEmpty;
public:
    boundedBuffer(int capacity_, std::string ID)
        : monitorSC("boundedBuffer"+ ID), fullSlots(0),
        capacity(capacity_), in(0), out(0), notFull(this,"notFull"+ID),
        notEmpty(this,"notEmpty"+ID) {
          buffer = new int[capacity];
    }
    ~boundedBuffer() {delete [] buffer;}
    void deposit(int value) {
        enterMonitor("deposit");
        while (fullSlots == capacity)
            notFull.waitC();
        buffer[in] = value;
        in = (in + 1) % capacity;
        ++fullSlots;
        notEmpty.signalC();
        exitMonitor();
    }

    int withdraw() {
        enterMonitor("withdraw");
        int value;
        while (fullSlots == 0)
            notEmpty.waitC();
        value = buffer[out];
        out = (out + 1) % capacity;
        --fullSlots;
        notFull.signalC();
        exitMonitor();
        return value;
    }
};

class Producer : public TDThread {
private:
    boundedBuffer& b;   std::string num;
public:
    Producer (boundedBuffer* b_, std::string num_) :
```

Listing 4.32   Bounded buffer using the C++/Win32/Pthreads monitor toolbox.

```
TDThread("Producer"+num_), b(*b_), num(num_) { }
    void* run () {
        std::cout << "Producer Running" << std::endl;
        for (int i = 0; i < 3; i++) {
            b.deposit(i);
            std::cout << "Producer # " << num << " deposited " << i << std::endl;
        }
        return 0;
    }
};

class Consumer : public TDThread {
private:
    boundedBuffer& b;    std::string num;
public:
    Consumer (boundedBuffer* b_, std::string num_)
      : TDThread("Consumer"+num_), b(*b_), num(num_) { }
    void* run () {
        std::cout << "Consumer Running" << std::endl;
        int value = 0;
        for (int i = 0; i < 3; i++) {
            value = b.withdraw();
            std::cout << "Consumer # " << num << " withdrew "
                << value << std::endl;
        }
        return 0;
    }
};

int main ( ) {
    boundedBuffer* b1 = new boundedBuffer(3,"1");
    boundedBuffer* b2 = new boundedBuffer(3,"2");
    std::auto_ptr<Producer> p1(new Producer (b1, "1"));
    std::auto_ptr<Consumer> c1(new Consumer (b1, "1"));
    std::auto_ptr<Producer> p2(new Producer (b2, "2"));
    std::auto_ptr<Consumer> c2(new Consumer (b2, "2"));
    p1->start(); c1->start(); p2->start(); c2->start();
    p1->join(); c1->join(); p2->join(); c2->join();
    delete b1; delete b2;
    return 0;
}
```

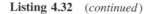

Listing 4.32   (*continued*)

Similarly, deadlock detection is controlled by variable DEADLOCKDETEC-TION:

    set DEADLOCKDETECTION=ON
       // Unix: setenv DEADLOCKDETECTION ON

An execution in TRACE mode creates trace files that contain the simple M-sequence, the M-sequence, and the Communication-sequence of the execution. (The files names are the same as those created by the Java trace mode.) The value of environment variable CONTROLLERS determines how many sequence files are created:

    set CONTROLLERS=SINGLE   // one simple M-sequence and M-sequence
                                           // per program
                                           // Unix: setenv CONTROLLERS SINGLE

    set CONTROLLERS=MULTIPLE // one simple M-sequence and M-sequence
                                             // per monitor
                                         // Unix: setenv CONTROLLERS MULTIPLE

The default value for CONTROLLERS is SINGLE.

As in Chapter 3, reachability testing is performed on *Buffer* by setting the MODE to RT and customizing the driver process in file *RTDriver*.cpp, which is part of the synchronization library. Directions for customizing the driver process are in the file.

Some development environments have powerful debuggers that make it possible to stop threads, examine the call stacks and variables of threads, suspend and resume threads, and more. Working with these debuggers may be frustrating, however, since stopping one thread may not stop the others, depending on the debugger. These debuggers are easier to use with a monitor toolbox. In replay mode you can set a breakpoint inside the control monitor at the point where a thread receives permission to execute the next event:

```
if (ID != nextEvent.getThreadID()) {
    // nextEvent does not involve the requesting thread
    threads[ID].waitC();   // wait for permission
    //get nextEvent again since it may have changed during the wait
    nextEvent = (monitorEvent)MSequence.elementAt(index);
}
// set breakpoint here; a thread has received permission to execute the next event.
```

With this breakpoint in place, it is possible to step through the execution and replay monitor events one at a time. Additional breakpoints can be set in the *run()* methods of the threads to watch what each thread does between events, without disturbing the replay. The Win32 *OutputDebugString()* function can be used to send text messages to the debugger while the program is running. (In the Visual C++ environment, these messages appear in the tabbed window labeled "Debug.") Of course, this entire process would be improved if tracing, testing, and replay were implemented as native functions of the development environment. In that case, the monitor toolbox classes can serve as portable, high-level designs for these implementations.

FURTHER READING

Per Brinch Hansen [2002] has written a personal account of how the monitor concept was invented. Hoare's [1974] monitor paper presented the SU monitor construct and showed how to implement monitors using semaphores. The concept of a monitor toolbox is from Boddy [1983]. Brinch Hansen's [1978] paper on reproducible testing of monitors is the earliest paper we know of on testing and replaying concurrent programs. Brinch Hansen [1973] also wrote an earlier paper on reproducible testing for operating systems. The monitor replay techniques presented in this chapter are from [Carver 1985; Carver and Tai 1991].

Greg Andrews [1991] shows how to prove the correctness of a monitor. Magee and Kramer's book [1999] shows how to use labeled transition systems (LTS) to model monitor-based programs. They also show how to verify mechanically that a model satisfies specified correctness properties. Steven Robbins [2001] has developed a simulator for monitor solutions to the dining philosopher problem. This simulator can be used to explore how these solutions might behave in practice.

REFERENCES

Anderson, T. E., E. D. Lazowska, and Henry M. Levy (1989). The performance implications of thread management alternatives for shared-memory multiprocessors. *IEEE Transactions on Computers*, Vol. 38. No. 12, pp. 1631–1644.

Andrews, Gregory, R. (1991). *Concurrent Programming: Principles and Practice*. Redwood City, CA: Benjamin-Cummings.

Andrews, Gregory, R. (2000). *Foundations of Multithreaded, Parallel, and Distributed Programming*. Reading, MA: Addison-Wesley.

Boddy, D. E. (1983). Implementing data abstractions and monitors in UCSD Pascal. *SIGPLAN Notices*, Vol. 18, No. 5 (May), pp. 15–24.

Brinch Hansen, P. (1973). Testing a multiprogramming system. *Software: Practice and Experience*, Vol. 3, No. 2 (February), pp. 145–150.

Brinch Hansen, P. (1975). The programming language concurrent Pascal. *IEEE Transactions on Software Engineering*, Vol. 1, No. 2 (February), pp. 199–207.

Brinch Hansen, P. (1978). Reproducible testing of monitors. *Software: Practice and Experience*, Vol. 8, No. 6, pp. 721–729.

Brinch Hansen, P. (2002). *The Origin of Concurrent Programming: From Semaphores to Remote Procedure Calls*. New York: Springer-Verlag.

Butenhof, David R. (1997). *Programming with POSIX Threads*. Reading, MA: Addison-Wesley.

Carver, R. H. (1985). Reproducible testing of concurrent programs based on shared variables. Master's thesis, Computer Science Department, North Carolina State University, Raleigh, NC, 1985.

Carver, R. H., and K. C. Tai (1986). Reproducible testing of concurrent programs based on shared variables. *Proc. 6th International Conference on Distributed Computing Systems*, pp. 428–433.

Carver R. H., and K. C. Tai (1991). Replay and testing for concurrent programs. *IEEE Software*, Vol. 8. No. 2, pp. 66–74.

Choi, J., and H. Srinivasan (1998). Deterministic replay of Java multithreaded applications. *Proc. ACM Sigmetrics Symposium on Parallel and Distributed Tools*, pp. 48–59.

Dahl, Ole-Johan (2000). A note on monitor versions. In Jim Davies, A. W. Roscoe, and Jim Woodcock (Eds.), *Millennial Perspectives in Computer Science: Proceedings of the 1999 Oxford–Microsoft Symposium in Honour of Sir Tony Hoare*. Upper Saddle River, NJ: Prentice Hall.

Dahl, Ole-Johan, B. Myhrhaug, and K. Nygaard (1970). *The SIMULA 67 Common Base Language*. Technical Report, Publication S-22. Oslo, Norway: Norwegian Computing Center.

Hamburger, Henry, and Dana Richards (2002). *Logic and Language Models for Computer Science*. Upper Saddle River, NJ: Prentice Hall.

Hartley, Steven J. (1999). Alfonse, wait here for my signal! *Proc. SIGCSE'99*, pp. 58–62.

Hoare, C. A. R. (1974). Monitors: an operating system structure concept. *Communication of the ACM*, Vol. 17, No. 10 (October), pp. 549–557.

Howard, John H. (1976). Proving monitors, *Communications of the ACM*, Vol. 19, No. 5 (May), pp. 273–279.

JSR-133 (2004). Java memory model and thread specification. http://www.jcp.org/aboutJava/communityprocess/review/jsr133/.

Lampson, Butler W., and David D. Redell (1980). Experience with processes and monitors in Mesa. *Communications of the ACM*, Vol. 23, No. 2 (February), pp. 105–117.

Lea, Doug (1999) Personal communication from Doug Lea to Steven J. Hartley in Hartley [1999].

Magee, Jeff, and Jeff Kramer (1999). *Concurrency: State Models and Java Programs*. New York: Wiley.

Parnas, D. L. (1972). On the criteria to be used in decomposing systems into modules. *Communications of the ACM*, Vol. 15, No. 12 (December), pp. 1053–1058.

Robbins, Steven (2001). Starving philosophers: experimentation with monitor synchronization. *Proc. 32nd SIGCSE Technical Symposium on Computer Science Education*, pp. 317–321.

Turski, W. M. (1991). On starvation and some related issues. *Information Processing Letters*, Vol. 37, pp. 171–174.

EXERCISES

4.1. Modify monitor *r_gt_w_1SC* in Listing 4.10 so that it uses the cascaded wakeup technique of Listing 4.18 to wake up waiting readers.

4.2. Write an SU monitor that implements the strategy R<W.2. This strategy gives writers a higher priority than readers, except that when a writer arrives, if it is a lead writer (i.e., no writer is writing or waiting), it waits until all readers that arrived earlier have finished.

4.3. In Section 4.9, threads execute *exitMonitor()* before making a nested monitor call and *enterMonitor()* when the call returns. This gives returning threads the same priority as new threads that are trying to enter the monitor for the first time. Consider using the reentry queue to give returning threads higher priority than new threads. Returning threads call method *reenterMonitor()*:

    exitMonitor();
    /* nested monitor call;*/
    reenterMonitor();

(a) Assume that methods *exitMonitor()* and *reenterMonitor()* are implemented as follows:

    exitMonitor(): if (reentryCount >0) reentry.V(); else mutex.V();
    reenterMonitor():reentry.P();

Describe the problem with this implementation.

(b) Assume that methods *exitMonitor()* and *reenterMonitor()* are implemented as follows:

    exitMonitor(): if (reentryCount >0) reentry.V(); else mutex.V();
    reenterMonitor():reentryCount ++ reentry.P();reentryCount --;

Describe the problem with this implementation.

(c) Show how to implement method *reenterMonitor()* correctly, and show any modifications that need to be made to the other methods in class *monitorSU*.

4.4. The following implementation of methods *waitC()* and *signalC()* for an SC monitor is incorrect:

    public void waitC() {
        ++numWaitingThreads;
        threadQueue.VP(mutex);
        mutex.P();

```
        --numWaitingThreads;
    }
    public void signalC() {
        if (numWaitingThreads > 0)
            threadQueue.V();
        // continue in the monitor; perhaps send more signals
    }
```

Why is this implementation incorrect? Consider what can happen if two successive *signal* operations are performed on a condition variable on which one thread is waiting.

4.5. Section 4.7 shows toolboxes for SC and SU monitors in Java. These toolboxes use a *binarySemaphore* named *mutex*:

   (a) In the SC toolbox, can *mutex* be a *mutexLock* instead of a *binarySemaphore*? Explain your answer.

   (b) In the SC toolbox, can *mutex* be a *mutexLock* instead of a *binarySemaphore*? Explain your answer.

   If you answer "no," be sure to describe a scenario that causes a problem (e.g., "Thread1 enters the monitor and does a wait, Thread2 enters the monitor ...").

4.6. When semaphore programs are being replayed, we assume that all semaphores are FCFS (threads are awakened by V operations in the same order that they were blocked in P operations). This assumption is necessary to make P and V operations deterministic. The monitor toolboxes in Section 4.5 use *binarySemaphores*. A solution for replaying simple M-sequences is presented in Section 4.7. Is this solution guaranteed to work if the semaphores in the toolboxes are not FCFS? Specifically:

   (a) If semaphore *mutex* in the SC toolbox is not FCFS, is the solution guaranteed to work?

   (b) If semaphore *mutex* in the SU toolbox is not FCFS, is the solution guaranteed to work?

   (c) If semaphore *reentry* in the SU toolbox is not FCFS, is the solution guaranteed to work?

   Explain your answers.

4.7. *The sleeping barber problem.* A barbershop consists of a waiting room with n chairs, and the barber room containing the barber chair. If there are no customers to be served, the barber goes to sleep. If a customer enters the barbershop and all the chairs are occupied, the customer leaves the shop. If the barber is busy, but chairs are available, the customer sits in one of the free chairs. If the barber is asleep, the customer wakes up the barber. Here is a semaphore solution to the problem.

```
binarySemaphore mutex(1);
countingSemaphore customer(0), done(0), chair(0);
int waiting = 0; // count of waiting customers
barber() {
    while (true) {
        customer.P();           // wait for or get the next customer
        mutex.P();
        --waiting;              // one fewer waiting customer
        chair.V();              // show customer to chair
        mutex.V();
        sleep(...);             // cut hair
        done.V();               // tell the customer that the haircut is done
    }
}
customer() {
    while (true) {
        mutex.P();
        if (waiting < numChairs) {
            ++waiting;
            customer.V();       // wake up the barber if he's asleep
            mutex.V();
            chair.P();          // wait for the barber to show you to a chair
            done.P();           // wait until the barber says that you're done
        }
        else mutex.();
    }
}
```

The barber waits on semaphore *customer* for the next customer. When a customer is available, the barber decrements the count of waiting customers and signals the semaphore *chair*, allowing the next customer into the barber chair for a haircut. A customer who needs a haircut accesses the count of *waiting* customers and increments the count if there is a free chair in the waiting room. After entering the waiting room, a customer signals the semaphore *customer*, which wakes up the barber, and then waits on semaphore *chair* for a chair. The barber releases the customer with the *done* semaphore.

(a) Write an SU monitor that solves the sleeping barber problem.

(b) In method *barber()* of the semaphore solution, *customer.V()* occurs before *mutex.V()*. Is the program correct if *customer.V()* occurs immediately after *mutex.V()*? Explain.

(c) Does *numChairs* include the barber chair? Explain.

4.8. Develop monitor solutions to the *unisex bathroom problem*. Your monitor should have four methods: *enterMen( ), exitMen( ), enterWomen( ), exitWomen( )*, and it should use the SU signaling discipline.

   (a) Develop a monitor solution that allows any number of men or any number of women (but not both) in the bathroom at the same time. Your solution should ensure the required exclusion and avoid deadlock, but it need not be fair (i.e., some people may never get to use the bathroom).

   (b) Develop a monitor solution that ensures fairness:

   - All men and women eventually get to use the bathroom.
   - When the last man in the bathroom exits, all women who are currently waiting are allowed to enter the bathroom.
   - When the last woman in the bathroom exits, all men who are currently waiting are allowed to enter the bathroom.
   - If men are in the bathroom, another man cannot enter the bathroom if women are waiting.
   - If women are in the bathroom, another women cannot enter the bathroom if men are waiting.

4.9. Develop an SU monitor solution to the following strategy for the readers and writers problem: Many readers or one writer with writers having a higher priority, except that at the end of writing, waiting readers have a higher priority than waiting writers. (That is, readers that are waiting when the write ends are allowed to read, but not the readers that arrive afterward.) Use methods *startRead( ), endRead( ), startWrite( )*, and *endWrite( )* like the solution in Section 4.2.4. Note that this strategy does not create starving readers or writers. A waiting writer does not starve since the number of readers allowed to proceed at the end of each writing is finite. A waiting reader does not starve since it will be allowed to proceed when the next write ends.

4.10. Suppose that monitor *threadOrderer* below uses an SC toolbox that is implemented without *VP( )* operations.

   (a) Describe how monitor *threadOrderer* orders the operations by the three threads.

   (b) SC toolbox "monitorNoVP" is like the SC toolbox presented in Section 4.7 except that it uses separate *V( )* and *P( )* operations in place of a *VP( )* operation. Does this cause any problems in monitor *threadOrderer*? If so, show a scenario that illustrates the problem.

```
import java.util.*;
public final class Order {
    public static void main (String args[]) {
        threadOrderer c = new threadOrderer();
        orderedThread t0 = new orderedThread (c,0);
```

```
                orderedThread t1 = new orderedThread (c,1);
                orderedThread t2 = new orderedThread (c,2);
                t0.start(); t1.start(); t2.start();
            }
        }
        final class orderedThread extends Thread {
        // a simple thread that calls operations beginOp and endOp of a monitor.
            private int num; // ID of thread.
            threadOrderer c; // monitor to call
            orderedThread (threadOrderer c, int num) {this.c = c; this.num = num; }
            public void run () {
                try {
                    for (int i=0; i<10; i++) {
                        Thread.sleep((long)(Math.random()*1000));
                        c.beginOp(num);
                        System.out.println(num+ "Did op");
                        c.endOp();
                    }
                } catch (InterruptedException e) {}
            }
        }
        final class threadOrderer extends monitorSCNoVP {
            private int next=0;
            private int wakeCount=0; // number of waiting threads that have been
                                     // awakened
            private int waitCount=0;   // number of waiting threads
            private int[] sequence;
            private conditionVariable myTurn = new conditionVariable();
            public threadOrderer() {
                sequence = new int[3]; // three threads in the program
                sequence[0] = 2; sequence[1] = 1; sequence[2] = 0;
            }
        public void beginOp(int ID) {
            enterMonitor();
            if (ID != sequence[next]) {
                ++waitCount;
                System.out.println(ID + "waiting");
                myTurn.waitC();                // first waitC()
                while (ID != sequence[next]) {
                    ++wakeCount;
                    if (wakeCount < waitCount) {
                        myTurn.signalC(); // wake up next thread
                        myTurn.waitC();        // second waitC()
                    }
                    else
```

```
                myTurn.waitC();        // third waitC(). All threads have had a
                  turn
           }
          -- waitCount;
      }
      exitMonitor();
  }
  public void endOp() {
      enterMonitor();
      next = (next+1) %3;
      System.out.println("waitCount is " + waitCount);
      if (waitCount>0) {
         wakeCount=0;
         myTurn.signalC();                 // wake up first thread
      }
      exitMonitor();
  }
}
```

4.11. Below is an implementation of the strategy R<W.2 using SC monitors. This strategy allows concurrent reading and generally gives writers a higher priority than readers. Readers have priority in the following situation: when a writer requests to write, if it is a lead writer (i.e., no other writer is writing or waiting), it waits until all readers that arrived earlier have finished reading.

(a) Is this implementation correct? If not, give a scenario that demonstrates any errors that you found. Methods *startRead()* and *startWrite()* contain if-statements that determine whether a *waitC()* operation is executed.

(b) If these if-statements are changed to while-loops, is the implementation correct? If not, give a scenario that demonstrates any errors that you found.

(c) If you believe that the implementations in parts (a) and (b) are incorrect, show how to modify the implementation below to correct it.

```
public final class r_lt_w_2 extends monitorSC {
    int readerCount = 0;          // number of active readers
    boolean writing = false;
    int waitForReaders = 0;       // if waitForReaders > 0, lead writer waits
                                  // for readers that arrived earlier
    conditionVariable readerQ = new conditionVariable();
    conditionVariable writerQ = new conditionVariable();
    public void startRead() {
```

```
                enterMonitor();
                if (writing || !(writerQ.empty()) || waitForReaders > 0)
                    readerQ.waitC();
                ++readerCount;
                if (waitForReaders>0)
                    waitForReaders--;
                exitMonitor();
            }
            public void endRead() {
                enterMonitor();
                --readerCount;
                if (readerCount==0)
                    writerQ.signalC();
                exitMonitor();
            }
            public void startWrite() {
                enterMonitor();
                if (readerCount > 0 || writing || waitForReaders > 0)
                    writerQ.waitC();
                writing = true;
                exitMonitor();
            }
            public void endWrite() {
                enterMonitor();
                writing = false;
                if (!(writerQ.empty()))
                    writerQ.signalC();
                else {
                    waitForReaders = readerQ.length();
                    for (int i = 1; i <= waitForReaders; i++)
                        readerQ.signalC();
                }
                exitMonitor();
            }
        }
```

4.12. Write a correct SC monitor implementation of strategy R<W.2. Your monitor should have methods *request(int ID, boolean isReadRequest)*, *startRead(int ID), endRead(), startWrite(int ID)*, and *endWrite()*. Reader and writer threads pass their IDs on calls to *request(ID,isReadRequest)*, *startRead(ID)*, and *startWrite(ID)*. Method *request()* saves read requests in a queue for reader requests and write requests in a queue for writer requests. The request queues are used in methods *startRead()* and *startWrite()* to force reader and writer threads to read and write in the correct order. For

example, method *startWrite(int ID)* might contain an `if`-statement such as
the following:

if (writing ||	// writer writing
readerCount>0 ||	// reader(s) reading
earlierReadersHavePriority ||	// readers temporarily
	// have priority
ID != ((request)writeRequests.getFirst()).ID	// ID not first in the
	// write request queue
)	
waitingWriters[ID].waitC();	// wait on the condition
	// variable used by thread ID

4.13. Section 3.5.4.2 showed a semaphore implementation of strategy R>W.2.
This strategy allows concurrent reading and generally gives readers a
higher priority than writers. Writers have priority in the following case:
When a reader requests to read, if it is a "lead reader" (i.e., no other
reader is reading or waiting), it waits until all writers that arrived earlier have finished writing. Below is an SU monitor implementation of this
strategy.

(a) Is this monitor solution equivalent to the semaphore-based solution in
Section 3.5? Explain.

(b) If they are not equivalent, show how to modify the monitor solution
to make it equivalent to the semaphore solution.

```
int readers = 0; /* number of readers */
boolean writing = false;
conditionVariable writers_readers_que;
conditionVariable readers_que;
public void startRead() {
    if (writing)
        if (readers == 0)
            writers_readers_que.wait();
        else readers_que.wait();
    readers++;
}
public void endRead() {
    --readers;
    if (readers == 0) writers_readers_que.signal();
}
public void startWrite() {
    if (writing || readers > 0) writers_readers_que.wait();
    writing = true;
}
```

```
public void endWrite() {
    writing = false; writers_readers_que.signal();
}
```

4.14. Write a monitor implementation of an Event object that is similar to the
Event object in Win32. Event objects have operations *block()* and *set()*.
A call to *block()* always blocks the caller. A call to *set()* awakens every
thread that has called *block()* since the last time *set()* was called.

   (a) Write implementations of operations *block()* and *set()* for an SU monitor. Declare and initialize any variables and condition variables that
   you use.

   (b) Write implementations of operations *block()* and *set()* for an SC monitor. Declare and initialize any variables and condition variables that
   you use.

4.15. Show how to modify classes *monitorSC* and *conditionVariable* to produce a monitor with urgent-signal-and-continue (USC) semantics (see Section 4.5.3) such that signaled threads have priority over new threads. In
class *monitorSC* in Section 4.7.1, waiting threads that are signaled wait in
the *mutex* queue with new threads:

```
public void waitC() {
    numWaitingThreads++;
    threadQueue.VP(mutex);
    mutex.P(); // enter the mutex queue with new threads.
}
```

In your new implementation, waiting threads will not join the *mutex* queue
when they are signaled. If threads have been signaled but have not yet
reentered the monitor, they should be allowed to reenter before new threads
can enter. Threads that execute *signalC()* are allowed to continue. Check
your implementation to make sure that you allow only one thread in the
monitor at a time.

4.16. In an SU monitor, the reentry queue is used to keep signaling threads, and
each condition variable has a queue to keep waiting threads. Consider the
two queuing strategies FIFO (first-in-first-out) and LIFO (last-in-first-out).

   (a) Compare the effects of using these strategies for the reentry queue in
   terms of fairness and correctness.

   (b) Compare the effects of using these strategies for the condition queues
   in terms of fairness and correctness.

4.17. Show how to modify the SC monitor toolbox to create a signal-and-wait
(SW) [Howard 1976; Andrews 2000] monitor toolbox. In an SW monitor, a
thread calling *signalC()* joins the rear of the entry queue and the awakened

thread enters the monitor immediately. The resulting relative priorities are
A(wakened) > S(ignaling) = C(alling).

4.18. Section 4.5.1 shows an SU monitor solution for strategy R>W.1 of
the readers and writers problem. Below is a revised version of method
startRead.

```
public void startRead {
    if (writing)
    readerQ.wait();
    readerQ.signal();
    ++readerCount;
}
```

(a) Assume that the monitor is still of type SU; does the revised solution
still implement strategy R>W.1?

(b) Assume that the monitor is of type SW (see Exercise 4.17); does the
revised solution still implement strategy R>W.1?

(c) Assume that the monitor is of type SC; does the revised solution implement strategy R>W.1?

Justify your answers.

4.19. The *bear and the honeybees* (see Exercise 3.13). The bear calls method
sleep() to wait for a full honey pot, then method *eat()* to eat the honey.
The bees call method *fillPot()*.

(a) Write implementations of monitor methods *eat()*, *sleep()*, and
fillPot() as members of an SU monitor using operations *wait()*, *signal()*,
and *signalAndExit()*.

(b) Write implementations of monitor methods *eat()*, *sleep()*, and
fillPot() as members of an SC monitor using operations *wait()*, *signal()*,
and *signalAll()*.

4.20. In Exercise 3.11 you were asked to write a semaphore implementation of
method *waitB()* in class *Barrier*. Here you are asked to write a monitor
implementation. Threads call B.*waitB()* to wait at *Barrier* B:

```
class Barrier extends monitor {
    public Barrier(int n) {this.n = n;}
    private conditionVariable go; // a condition variable for waiting threads
    public void waitB() { .. }
}
```

Assume that *conditionVariables* are FCFS.

(a) Write an SU monitor implementation of method *waitB()*.

(b) Write an SC monitor implementation of method *waitB()*. (Be careful to make sure that new threads will be delayed if there are old threads that have been signaled but have not yet had a chance to leave the barrier.)

4.21. In Listing 4.11, assume that there are many threads blocked in methods *P()* and *V()*. Suppose that a thread executes the `notifyAll` operation in method *V()*. One notified thread that was waiting in *P()* may find that the condition it is waiting for is true. Are all the other notified threads (that were waiting in *P()* or *V()*) guaranteed to find that the condition they are waiting for is false?

4.22. Suppose that monitor *alternateThreads* below uses either an SC toolbox (Listing 4.23) or a USC toolbox (see Exercise 4.15) that is implemented without *VP()* operations. (That is, toolboxes *monitorSCNoVP* and *monitorUSCNoVP* use separate *V()* and *P()* operations in place of a *VP()* operation.) Method *alternate()* forces two threads to alternate execution with one another. Each time a thread calls *alternate()* it signals condition *other* (unblocking the other thread) and then blocks itself. The thread remains blocked until the other thread calls *alternate()*. Suppose that these toolboxes use strong FCFS semaphores (and no *VP()* operations, as mentioned above). Is monitor *alternateThreads* correct? If not, show a scenario that illustrates the problem.

```
final class alternateThreads extends monitorSCNoVP
/*or extends monitorUSCNoVP*/ {
    conditionVariable other = new conditionVariable();
    public final void alternate() {
        other.signalC();
        other.waitC();
    }
}
```

4.23. The SC toolbox in Listing 4.23 uses operation *VP()*. Show how to achieve the same effect without using *VP()*. That is, without using *VP()*, make sure that threads are signaled in the same order that they execute *waitC()*. To help you design a solution, you may want to examine the FCFS implementations of classes *countingSemaphore* and *binarySemaphore*.

4.24. Below is an SC monitor implementation of strategy R>W.1, which allows concurrent reading and gives readers a higher priority than writers. Variable *stopBarging* is used to prevent barging writers from writing when the signaled reader is waiting in the entry queue and no more readers are waiting in the *readerQ* Is this solution correct? If two readers are waiting when a writer executes *endWrite()*, are both readers guaranteed to read before another writer can write?

```
class r_gt_w_1 extends monitor {
    int readerCount = 0;           // number of active readers
    boolean writing = false;       // true if a writer is writing
    boolean stopBarging = true;    // set to true to stop writers from barging
                                   // ahead of readers
    conditionVariable readerQ = new conditionVariable();
    conditionVariable writerQ = new conditionVariable();
    public void startRead() {
        if (writing)               // readers must wait if a writer is writing
            readerQ.wait();
        ++readerCount;
        stopBarging = false;       // writers will still be delayed since
                                   // readerCount > 0 is now true
        readerQ.signal();          // awaken the next waiting reader
    }
    public void endRead() {
        --readerCount;
        if (readerCount == 0)      // a writer is signaled if there are no
                                   // more readers reading
            writerQ.signal();
    }
    public void startWrite() {
    // writers wait if a writer is writing, or a reader is reading or waiting,
    // or the writer is barging
        while (readerCount > 0 || writing || !readerQ.empty() || stopBarging)
            writerQ.wait();
        writing = true;
    }
    public void endWrite() {
        writing = false;
        if (!readerQ.empty()) {    // priority is given to waiting readers
            readerQ.signal();
            stopBarging = true;    // if writers barge ahead of the
                                   // signaled reader, they will be delayed
        }
        else
            writerQ.signal();
    }
}
```

4.25. For the solutions to the dining philosophers problem in Section 4.2.3:

    (a) Give a scenario for Solution 1 that illustrates how a philosopher can starve.

    (b) Show how this scenario is avoided in Solution 2.

4.26. In Exercise 3.18 you were asked to give a scenario that demonstrates how class *countingSemaphore* in Section 3.6.1 may fail if threads blocked on the *wait* operation in method $P()$ can be interrupted or if spurious wakeups can occur. Describe how this scenario is prevented by the *countingSemaphore* class in Listing 4.11.

4.27. Solve the problem in Exercise 4.12 using either Java or Pthreads condition variables.

4.28. Implement the SC monitor toolbox for Win32 from Section 4.8.1 using Win32 Semaphores and Events. Use Semaphores for mutual exclusion. Threads that block in *waitC()* should block on a Win32 Event. You can use operation *SignalObjectAndWait()* (see Section 3.7.5) in place of *VP()*.

5

MESSAGE PASSING

In Chapters 3 and 4, threads used shared variables to communicate and they used semaphores, locks, and monitors to synchronize. Threads can also communicate and synchronize by sending and receiving messages across channels. A channel is an abstraction of a communication path between threads. If shared memory is available, channels can be implemented as objects that are shared by threads. Without shared memory, channels can be implemented using kernel routines that transport messages across a communication network.

Chapter 6 deals with message passing for distributed programs, in which messages are passed between processes that run on separate nodes in a network. The focus of this chapter is message passing between threads that run in the same process. Programming problems will be solved by sending and receiving messages across channels instcad of reading and writing shared variables protected by semaphores and monitors. This offers us a new style for solving familiar problems. First, we describe basic message passing using send and receive commands. Then we will see how to use a higher-level mechanism called *rendezvous*. Finally, we show how to test and debug message-passing programs.

5.1 CHANNEL OBJECTS

Threads running in the same program (or process) can access channel objects in shared memory. If the programming language does not provide built-in channel objects, a *channel* class can be defined at the user level. In the program

Modern Multithreading: Implementing, Testing, and Debugging Multithreaded Java and C++/Pthreads/Win32 Programs, By Richard H. Carver and Kuo-Chung Tai
Copyright © 2006 John Wiley & Sons, Inc.

below, Thread1 and Thread2 use methods *send()* and *receive()* to send and receive messages through two *channel* objects. Thread1 sends requests through the *requestChannel*, and Thread2 responds through the *replyChannel*:

```
channel requestChannel = new channel();
channel replyChannel = new channel();
```

Thread1	Thread2
requestChannel.send(request); $\Rightarrow$ request = requestChannel.receive();	
reply = replyChannel.receive(); $\Leftarrow$ replyChannel.send(reply);	

A thread that calls *send()* or *receive()* may be blocked. Thus, send and receive operations are used both for communication and synchronization. Several types of send and receive operations can be defined:

- *Blocking send*: The sender is blocked until the message is received (by a *receive()* operation).
- *Buffer-blocking send*: Messages are queued in a bounded message buffer, and the sender is blocked only if the buffer is full.
- *Nonblocking send*: Messages are queued in an unbounded message buffer, and the sender is never blocked.
- *Blocking receive*: The receiver is blocked until a message is available.
- *Nonblocking receive*: The receiver is never blocked. A receive command returns an indication of whether or not a message was received.

Asynchronous message passing occurs when blocking receive operations are used with either nonblocking or buffer-blocking send operations. *Synchronous message passing* is the term used when the send and receive operations are both blocking. When synchronous message passing is used, either the sender or the receiver thread will be blocked, whichever one executes its operation first. Even if the receiver is waiting for a message to arrive, the sender may be blocked since the sender has to wait for an acknowledgment that the message was received. Thus, there are more delays associated with synchronous message passing.

Synchronous message passing can be simulated using asynchronous message passing. For instance, if a blocking send command is not available, the sender can issue a buffer-blocking send followed immediately by a blocking receive. This also works in cases where the message sent to a receiver represents a request for the receiver to perform some service. The receiver can examine the request, perform the service at the appropriate time, and then send a reply to the waiting sender.

5.1.1   Channel Objects in Java

Threads in the same Java Virtual Machine (JVM) can communicate and synchronize by passing messages through user-defined channels that are implemented as shared objects. We have written Java classes that implement several different types of channels. Interface *channel* specifies the form of *send()* and *receive()* operations supported by *channel* objects.

```
public abstract class channel {
     public abstract void send(Object m);     // send a message object
     public abstract void send();               // send with no message object
                                                // acts as a signal to the receiver
     public abstract Object receive();          // receive an object
}
```

There are three types of channels, which differ in the number of sender and receiver threads that are allowed to access a channel object:

- *Mailbox*: Many senders and many receivers may access a mailbox object.
- *Port*: Many senders but only one receiver may access a port object.
- *Link*: Only one sender and one receiver may access a link object.

Each of the three types of channels has a synchronous version and an asynchronous version. A synchronous *mailbox* class is shown in Listing 5.1. Operations *send()* and *receive()* are implemented using a member variable named *message* and two binary semaphores. A sending thread copies its message into the channel's *message* object and issues *sent.V()* to signal that the message is available. The sending thread then executes *received.P()* to wait until the message is received. The receiving thread executes *sent.P()* to wait for a message from the sender. When the sender signals that a message is available, the receiver makes a copy of the *message* object and executes *received.V()* to signal the sender that the message has been received.

For convenience, *mailbox* provides a *send()* operation with no message parameter, which sends a null message. A *send()* operation with no message acts as a signal to the receiver that some event has occurred. (In other words, the signal *is* the message.) Such a send is analogous to a *V()* operation on a semaphore, which allows one thread to signal another but does not exchange any data between the threads.

The *send()* methods for classes *port* and *mailbox* are the same. The *receive()* methods for classes *port* and *link* are also the same. Only one thread can ever execute a *receive* operation on a *port* or *link* object. In Listing 5.2 we have modified the *receive* method of Listing 5.1 to check for multiple receivers. An exception is thrown if multiple receivers are detected. Since a *link* can have only one sender, a similar check is performed in the *send()* method of class *link*.

An asynchronous *mailbox* class is shown in Listing 5.3. The implementation of the buffer-blocking *send()* operation is based on the bounded-buffer solution in Section 3.5.2. The *send()* will block if the message buffer is full. The messages that a thread sends to a particular mailbox are guaranteed to be received in the order they are sent. If Thread1 executes a *send()* operation on a particular mailbox

```
public class mailbox extends channel {
    private Object message = null;
    private final Object sending = new Object();
    private final Object receiving = new Object();
    private final binarySemaphore sent = new binarySemaphore(0);
    private final binarySemaphore received = new binarySemaphore(0);
    public final void send(Object sentMsg) {
        if (sentMsg == null) {throw new
            NullPointerException("Null message passed to send()");
        }
        synchronized (sending) {
        message = sentMsg;
        sent.V();                          // signal that the message is available
        received.P();                      // wait until the message is received
        }
    }
    public final void send() {
        synchronized (sending) {
            message = new Object();        // send a null message
            sent.V();                      // signal that message is available
            received.P();                  // wait until the message is received
        }
    }
    public final Object receive() {
        Object receivedMessage = null;
        synchronized (receiving) {
            sent.P();                      // wait for message to be sent
            receivedMessage = message;
            received.V();                  // signal the sender that the message has
        }                                  //   been received
        return receivedMessage;
    }
}
```

Listing 5.1   Synchronous *mailbox* class.

before Thread2 executes a *send()* operation on the same mailbox, Thread1's message will be received from that mailbox before Thread2's message.

The asynchronous *link* and *port* classes are very similar to the *mailbox* class. In the asynchronous *link* class, methods *send()* and *receive()* must check for multiple senders and receivers. In the asynchronous *port* class, method *receive* must check for multiple receivers. Since *links* have a single sender, there is no need for semaphore *senderMutex* in method *send*. Similarly, there is no need for semaphore *receiverMutex* in the *receive()* methods of classes *link* and *port*.

```
public final Object receive() {
   synchronized(receiving) {
          if (receiver == null) // save the first thread to call receive
              receiver = Thread.currentThread();
          // if currentThread() is not first thread to call receive, throw an exception
          if (Thread.currentThread() != receiver) throw new
                 InvalidLinkUsage("Attempted to use link with multiple receivers");
          Object receivedMessage = null;
          sent.P();                          // wait for the message to be sent
          receivedMessage = message;
          received.V();                      // signal the sender that the message has
          return receivedMessage;            // been received
   }
}
```

Listing 5.2   Synchronous *receive* method for the *link* and *port* classes.


```
public final class asynchMailbox extends channel {
     private final int capacity = 100;
     private Object messages[] = new Object[capacity];      // message buffer
     private countingSemaphore messageAvailable = new countingSemaphore(0);
     private countingSemaphore slotAvailable = new
         countingSemaphore(capacity);
     private binarySemaphore senderMutex = new binarySemaphore(1);
     private binarySemaphore receiverMutex = new binarySemaphore(1);
     private int in = 0, out = 0;

     public final void send(Object sentMessage) {
         if (sentMessage == null) {
             throw new NullPointerException("null message passed to send()");
         }
         slotAvailable.P();
         senderMutex.P();
         messages[in] = sentMessage;
         in = (in + 1) % capacity;
         senderMutex.V();
         messageAvailable.V();
     }

     public final void send() {
     /* same as send(Object sentMessage) above except that the line
         ''messages[in] = sentMessage;'' becomes ''messages[in] = new Object();'' */
     }
```

Listing 5.3   Asynchronous *asynchMailbox* class.

```
    public final Object receive() {
        messageAvailable.P();
        receiverMutex.P();
        Object receivedMessage = messages[out];
        out = (out + 1) % capacity;
        receiverMutex.V();
        slotAvailable.V();
        return receivedMessage;
    }
}
```

Listing 5.3 (*continued*)

Listing 5.4 shows how to use the *link* class. *Producer* and *Consumer* threads exchange messages with a *Buffer* thread using links *deposit* and *withdraw*. The *Buffer* thread implements a one-slot bounded buffer. The *Producer* builds a *Message* object and sends it to the *Buffer* over the *deposit* link. The *Buffer* then sends the *Message* to the *Consumer* over the *withdraw* link.

5.1.2   Channel Objects in C++/Win32

Listing 5.5 shows a C++ version of the synchronous *mailbox* class. Methods *send()* and *receive()* operate on objects of type *message_ptr* <T>. A *message_ptr* <T> object is a *smart pointer*. Smart pointers mimic simple pointers by providing pointer operations such as dereferencing (using operator *) and indirection (using operator ->). Smart pointers also manage memory and ownership for their pointed-to objects. We use smart pointers to help manage message objects that are passed between threads.

A *message_ptr*<T> object contains a pointer to a message object of type T. The *message_ptr* <T> class template uses reference counting to manage message objects. Ownership and memory management are handled by maintaining a count of the *message_ptr* objects that point to the same message. Copying a *message_ptr* object adds one to the count. The message is deleted when the count becomes zero. Sending and receiving *message_ptr* <T> objects simulates message passing in Java. Messages are essentially shared by the sending and receiving threads, and messages are deleted automatically when they are no longer being referenced. As in Java, virtually any type T of message object can be used.

A message that contains an integer can be defined as follows:

```
class Message {
public:
    int contents;
    Message(int contents_) : contents(contents_){ }
    Message(const Message& m) : contents(m.contents) { }
    Message* clone() const {return new Message(*this);}
};
```

```
public final class boundedBuffer {
    public static void main (String args[]) {
        link deposit = new link();
        link withdraw = new link();
        Producer producer = new Producer(deposit);
        Consumer consumer = new Consumer(withdraw);
        Buffer buffer = new Buffer(deposit,withdraw);
        // buffer will be terminated when producer and consumer are finished
        buffer.setDaemon(true); buffer.start();
        producer.start();
        consumer.start();
    }
}
final class Message {
    public int number;
    Message(int number ) {this.number = number;}
}
final class Producer extends Thread {
    private link deposit;
    public Producer (link deposit) { this.deposit = deposit; }
    public void run () {
        for (int i = 0; i<3; i++) {
            System.out.println("Produced " + i);
            deposit.send(new Message(i));
        }
    }
}

final class Consumer extends Thread {
    private link withdraw;
    public Consumer (link withdraw) { this.withdraw = withdraw; }
    public void run () {
        for (int i = 0; i<3; i++) {
        Message m = (Message) withdraw.receive(); // message from Buffer
        System.out.println("Consumed " + m.number);
        }
    }
}

final class Buffer extends Thread {
    private link deposit, withdraw;
    public Buffer (link deposit, link withdraw) { this.deposit = deposit;
        this.withdraw = withdraw; }
```

Listing 5.4   Java bounded buffer using channels.

```
        public void run () {
          while (true) {
            Message m = ((Message) deposit.receive()); // message from Producer
            withdraw.send(m); // send message to Consumer
          }
        }
    }
```

Listing 5.4 (*continued*)

```
template <class T>
class mailbox {
public:
    mailbox() : sent(0), received(0), msg(0) { }
    void send(message_ptr<T> sentMsg) {
        if (sentMsg.get() == NULL) {
            throw new NullMessageException("Null message passed to send()");
        }
        mutexSending.lock();
        msg = sentMsg;
        sent.V();
        received.P();
        mutexSending.unlock();
    }
    message_ptr<T> receive() {
        mutexReceiving.lock();
        sent.P();
        message_ptr<T> receivedMessage = msg;
        received.V();
        mutexReceiving.unlock();
        return receivedMessage;
    }
    void send() {
        mutexSending.lock();
        sent.V();
        received.P();
        mutexSending.unlock();
    }
private:
    message_ptr<T> msg;
    mutexLock mutexSending;
    mutexLock mutexReceiving;
    win32Semaphore sent; // or use a POSIXSemaphore
    win32Semaphore received;
};
```

Listing 5.5 C++ synchronous *mailbox* class.

A message object can be sent over channel *deposit* using

mailbox<Message> deposit;   // create a mailbox for message
                                                  // objects
message_ptr<Message> m(new Message(i));   // create a message object *m*
deposit.send(m);   // send message *m*

Message objects are received using

message_ptr<Message> m = deposit.receive();
std::cout << "Received:" << m->contents << std::endl;

Notice that nothing prevents the sending thread from accessing a message after it has been received. This may interfere with the receiving thread, since the receiver is expecting mutually exclusive access to the message. If the sender needs to access a message after it is sent, or just to be completely safe, the sender should send a copy of the message:

Message m1(1);
message_ptr<Message> m2(m1.clone());   // send a copy of *m1* to ensure mutual
                                        // exclusion
deposit.send(m2);

Java threads that use the Java *channel* classes should also consider sending cloned messages to prevent the sending and receiving threads from referencing the same message objects.

Other ownership schemes can be implemented with help from class templates such as *auto_ptr* or other smart pointer classes. The use of such classes depends on the level of support that the compiler provides for C++ templates, which varies from compiler to compiler. The *link* and *port* classes can easily be produced from C++ class *mailbox<T>* and the Java *link* and *port* counterparts. Listing 5.6 shows a C++/Win32/Pthreads version of the Java bounded buffer program in Listing 5.4.

5.2 RENDEZVOUS

The following message-passing paradigm is common in a client–server environment:

Client$_i$		Server
		loop {
request.send(clientRequest);	$\Rightarrow$	clientRequest = request.receive();
		/* process *clientRequest* and compute *result* */
result = reply$_i$.receive();	$\Leftarrow$	reply$_i$.send(result);
		}

```cpp
class Message {
public:
    int contents;
    Message(int contents_) : contents(contents_){}
    Message(const Message& m) : contents(m.contents) {}
    Message* clone() const {return new Message(*this);}
};
class Producer : public Thread {
private:
    mailbox<Message>& deposit;
public:
    Producer (mailbox<Message>& deposit_) : deposit(deposit_) {}
    virtual void* run () {
        for (int i=0; i<3; i++) {
            message_ptr<Message> m(new Message(i));
            std::cout << "Producing " << i << std::endl;
            deposit.send(m);
        }
        return 0;
    }
};
class Consumer : public Thread {
private:
    mailbox<Message>& withdraw;
public:
    Consumer (mailbox<Message>& withdraw_) : withdraw(withdraw_) {}
    virtual void* run () {
        for (int i=0; i<3; i++) {
            message_ptr<Message> m = withdraw.receive();
            std::cout << "Consumed " << m->contents << std::endl;
        }
        return 0;
    }
};
class Buffer : public Thread {
private:
    mailbox<Message>& deposit; mailbox<Message>& withdraw;
public:
    Buffer (mailbox<Message>& deposit_, mailbox<Message>& withdraw_)
      : deposit(deposit_), withdraw(withdraw_) {}
    virtual void* run () {
      for (int i=0; i<3; i++) {
          message_ptr<Message> m = deposit.receive(); withdraw.send(m);
```

Listing 5.6   C++ bounded buffer using channels.

```
        }
        return 0;
    }
};
int main () {
    mailbox<Message> deposit; mailbox<Message> withdraw;
    std::auto_ptr<Producer> producer(new Producer(deposit));
    std::auto_ptr<Consumer> consumer(new Consumer(withdraw));
    std::auto_ptr<Buffer> buffer(new Buffer(deposit,withdraw));
    producer->start(); consumer->start(); buffer->start();
    producer->join(); consumer->join(); buffer->join();
    return 0;
}
```

Listing 5.6   (*continued*)

Implementing this paradigm with basic message passing requires one channel
that the server can use to receive client requests and one channel for each
client's reply. That is, each client uses a separate channel to receive a reply
from the server.

This paradigm can be implemented instead as follows:

Client	Server
	entry E;
	loop {
	E.accept(clientRequest, result) {
E.call(clientRequest,result); ⇔	/* process Client's request and compute *result* */
	} // end accept()
	} // end loop

The server uses a new type of channel called an *entry*. Clients issue requests by
making entry calls to the server. In the client, the pair of send and receive statements

```
    request.send(clientRequest);
    result = reply.receive();
```

is combined into the single entry call statement

```
    E.call(clientRequest, result);
```

This call on entry E is very similar to a procedure call with arguments *clientRequest* and *result*. Object *clientRequest* holds the message being sent to the
server. When the call returns, object *result* will hold the server's reply.

In the server, the code that handles the client's request is in the form of an `accept` statement for entry E:

```
E.accept(clientRequest,result) {
    /* process the clientRequest and compute result*/
    result = ...;
}
```

Only one thread can `accept` the entry calls made to a given entry. When a server thread executes an `accept` statement for entry E:

- If no entry call for entry E has arrived, the server waits.
- If one or more entry calls for E have arrived, the server accepts one call and executes the body of the `accept` statement. When the execution of the `accept` statement is complete, the entry call returns to the client with the server's reply, and the client and server continue execution.

This interaction is referred to as a *rendezvous*. Rendezvous are a form of synchronous communication. A client making an entry call is blocked until the call is accepted and a reply is returned. Executing an `accept` statement blocks the server until an entry call arrives.

Java does not have built-in support for entries and rendezvous. Listing 5.7 shows a Java class named *entry* that simulates a rendezvous [Magee and Kramer 1999]. Class *entry* uses the *link* and *port* channels of Section 5.1. A client issues an entry call to entry E as follows:

```
reply = E.call(clientRequest);
```

Method *call( )* is implemented using a *send( )* operation on a port named *request-Channel*. The *send( )* operation sends the *clientRequest*, along with a *link* named *replyChannel*, to the server. A new *replyChannel* is created on each execution of *call( )*, so that each client sends its own *replyChannel* to the server. The *call( )* operation ends with *replyChannel.receive( )*, allowing the client to wait for the server's reply.

The server accepts entry calls from its client and issues a reply:

```
request = E.accept();        // accept client's call to entry E
...
E.reply(response);           // reply to the client
```

The *accept( )* method in class *Entry* is implemented using a *receive( )* operation on the *requestChannel* (see Fig. 5.8). Method *accept( )* receives the *clientRequest* and the *replyChannel* that was sent with it. Method *accept( )* then saves the *reply-Channel* and returns the *clientRequest* to the server thread. The *reply( )* method sends the server's response back to the client using *replyChannel.send( )*. As

```
class entry {
    private port requestChannel = new port();
    private callMsg cm;
    public Object call(Object request) throws InterruptedException {
        link replyChannel = new link();
        requestChannel.send(new callMsg(request,replyChannel));
        return replyChannel.receive();
    }
    public Object call() throws InterruptedException {
        link replyChannel = new link();
        requestChannel.send(new callMsg(replyChannel));
        return replyChannel.receive();
    }
    public Object accept() throws InterruptedException {
    // check the for multiple callers is not shown
        cm = (callMsg) requestChannel.receive();
        return cm.request;
    }
    public void reply(Object response) throws InterruptedException {
        cm.replyChannel.send(response);
    }
    public void reply() throws InterruptedException { cm.replyChannel.send(); }
    public Object acceptAndReply() throws InterruptedException {
    // the check for multiple callers is not shown
        cm = (callMsg) requestChannel.receive();
        cm.replyChannel.send(new Object()); // send empty reply back to client
        return cm.request;
    }
    private class callMsg {
        Object request;
        link replyChannel;
        callMsg(Object m, link c) {request=m; replyChannel=c;}
        callMsg(link c) {request = new Object(); replyChannel=c;}
    }
}
```

Listing 5.7   Java class *entry*.

we mentioned above, the client waits for the server's response by executing
r*eplyChannel.receive()* in method *call()*.

If the server does not need to compute a reply for the client, the server can
execute method *acceptAndReply()*. This method accepts the client's request and
sends an empty reply back to the client so that the client is not delayed. The
client simply ignores the reply. Listing 5.9 shows a client and server program
using Java *entries* and rendezvous.

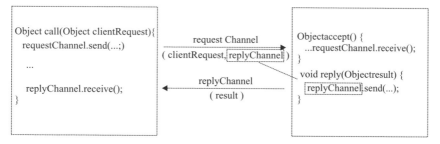

Figure 5.8 Entries are implemented using a port named *requestChannel* and a link named *replyChannel*. The *call()* operation sends the *clientRequest* along with a *reply-Channel* that the server can use for its reply. The *call()* and *accept()* operations are both blocking.

```
public final class clientServer {
    public static void main (String args[]) {
        entry E = new entry();
        Client c1 = new Client(E, 2);    // send value 2 to the server using entry E
        Client c2 = new Client(E, 4);    // send value 4 to the server using entry E
        Server s = new Server(E);
        s.setDaemon(true);
        s.start();
        c1.start(); c2.start();
    }
}
final class Message {
        public int number;
        Message(int number) { this.number = number; }
}
final class Client extends Thread {
    private entry E;
    int number;
    public Client (entry E, int number) { this.E = E; this.number = number;   }
    public void run () {
        try {
            // send number and wait for reply
            int i = ((Integer)E.call(new Message(number))).intValue();
            System.out.println (number + "x " + number + " = " + i);
            // (e.g., 2 × 2 = 4)
        }
        catch(InterruptedException e) { }
    }
}
final class Server extends Thread {
    private entry E;
```

Listing 5.9 Client and server using Java *entries* and rendezvous.

```
public Server (entry E) { this.E = E; }
public void run () {
    Message m;
    int number;
    while (true) {
        try {
            m = ((Message) E.accept());              // accept number from client
            number = m.number;
            E.reply(new Integer(number*number)); // reply to client
        }
        catch(InterruptedException e) { }
    }
}
}
```

Listing 5.9 (*continued*)

5.3 SELECTIVE WAIT

Assume that server thread *boundedBuffer* has entries *deposit* and *withdraw*. Two possible implementations of the *run()* method of thread *boundedBuffer* follow.

Implementation 1	Implementation 2
```while (true) { if (buffer is not full) { item = deposit.acceptAndReply(); ... } if (buffer is not empty) { withdraw.accept(); ... withdraw.reply(item); } }```	```while (true) { if (buffer is not empty) { withdraw.accept(); ... withdraw.reply(item); } if (buffer is not full) { item = deposit.acceptAndReply(); ... } }```

Both implementations create unnecessary delays for threads calling entries *deposit* and *withdraw*:

- In Implementation 1, while *boundedBuffer* is blocked waiting to accept an entry call to *deposit*, it is possible that a call to *withdraw* has arrived and is waiting to be accepted.
- In Implementation 2, while *boundedBuffer* is blocked waiting to accept an entry call to *withdraw*, it is possible that a call to *deposit* has arrived and is waiting to be accepted.

This problem is solved by allowing a thread to wait for a set of entries instead of a single entry. When one or more of the entries becomes acceptable, one of them is selected for execution. This idea is captured by the following `select` statement:

```
select:
    when (the buffer is not full) => accept a call to entry deposit and deposit
        the item;
or
    when (the buffer is not empty) => accept a call to entry withdraw and return
        an item;
end select;
```

When one of the entries is acceptable and the other is not, the acceptable entry is selected for execution. When both entries are acceptable, one of them is selected for execution.

The Ada language provides a `select` statement just like the one above. A `select` statement can optionally contain either a `delay` or an `else` alternative. These alternatives limit the amount of time that a select statement will wait for an acceptable entry:

- A `delay` `t` alternative is selected if no entry can be accepted within `t` seconds.
- An `else` alternative is executed immediately if no entries are acceptable.

Ada's selective wait statement can be simulated in Java. Magee and Kramer [1999] showed how to simulate a selective wait containing multiple *accept()* alternatives. Below we describe how to use a class named *selectiveWait* that allows a selection over *accept(), delay*, and *else* alternatives.

First, create a *selectiveWait* object:

selectiveWait select = new selectiveWait();

Then add one or more *selectableEntry* objects to the *selectiveWait*:

selectableEntry deposit = new selectableEntry();
selectableEntry withdraw = new selectableEntry();
select.add(deposit);
select.add(withdraw);

The *selectableEntry* objects are *entry* objects that have been extended so they can be used as alternatives in a *selectiveWait*. A *selectiveWait* can also contain one *delayAlternative*:

selectiveWait.delayAlternative delayA = select.new delayAlternative(500);
// delay for half a second

or one *elseAlternative* (but not both):

selectiveWait.elseAlternative elseA = select.new elseAlternative();

The timeout value for a *delayAlternative* is specified as an argument to the constructor. A *delay* or *else* alternative is added to a selective wait in the same way as a *selectableEntry*:

select.add(delayA);

Each *selectableEntry* and *delayAlternative* is associated with a condition, called a *guard*, which determines whether the alternative is allowed to be selected. The guard for each *selectableEntry* and *delayAlternative* must be evaluated before a selection takes place. Method *guard()* is called with a *boolean* expression that sets the guard to *true* or *false*:

```
deposit.guard (fullSlots<capacity);    // guard is set to the boolean value of
                                       // (fullSlots<capacity)
withdraw.guard(fullSlots>0);           // guard is set to the boolean value of
                                       // (fullSlots>0)
delayA.guard(true);                    // guard is always set to true
```

Method *choose()* selects one of the alternatives with a true guard:

```
switch (select.choose()) {
    case 1:     deposit.acceptAndReply();    /* alternative 1 */
                ...
                break;
    case 2:     withdraw.accept();           /* alternative 2 */
                ...
                withdraw.reply(value);
                break;
    case 3:     delayA.accept();             /* alternative 3 */
                break;
}
```

Method *choose()* returns the alternative number of the alternative selected. Alternative numbers are based on the order in which the alternatives are added to the selective wait. In the example above, the *selectableEntry* object *deposit* was added first; thus, its alternative number is 1. The alternative number for *withdraw* is 2 and the number for *delayA* is 3. A switch statement uses the alternative number to execute the appropriate alternative.

When the *selectiveWait* contains no *delay* or *else* alternatives:

- *choose()* will select an open *accept()* alternative (i.e., one with a true guard) that has a waiting entry call.

- If several *accept()* alternatives are open and have waiting entry calls, the one whose entry call arrived first is selected.
- if one or more *accept()* alternatives are open but none have a waiting entry call, *choose()* blocks until an entry call arrives for one of the open *accept()* alternatives.

When the *selectiveWait* has an *else* or *delay* alternative:

- An *else* alternative is executed if all the *accept()* alternatives are closed or all the open *accept()* alternatives have no waiting entry calls.
- An open *delay* alternative is selected when its expiration time is reached if no open *accept()* alternatives can be selected prior to the expiration time.

When all of the guards of the accept alternatives are false and there is no delay alternative with a true guard and no else alternative, method *choose()* throws a *SelectException* indicating that a deadlock has been detected.

Listing 5.10 shows a *boundedBuffer* server class that uses a selective wait. The *delayAlternative* simply displays a message when it is accepted. Note that the guards of all the alternatives are evaluated each iteration of the while-loop. Changes made to variables *fullSlots* and *emptySlots* in the alternatives of the switch statement may change the values of the guards for entries *deposit* and *withdraw*. This requires each guard to be reevaluated before the next selection occurs.

If a *boundedBuffer* thread is marked as a Java daemon thread before it is started, it will stop automatically when its clients have stopped. A C++ version of class *boundedBuffer* would look very similar to the Java version, without the daemon threads. Instead, we can use a *delayAlternative* to detect when the clients have stopped.

```
case 3:    delayA.accept();    // terminate the boundedBuffer thread when it
                               // becomes inactive for some period
return;
```

The *delayAternative* will stop the *boundedBuffer* thread after a period of inactivity.

5.4 MESSAGE-BASED SOLUTIONS TO CONCURRENT PROGRAMMING PROBLEMS

Below we show solutions to three classical synchronization problems. All three solutions use message passing with selective waits.

5.4.1 Readers and Writers

Listing 5.11 shows a solution to the readers and writers problem for strategy R>W.1 (many readers or one writer, with readers having a higher priority). Class

```
final class boundedBuffer extends Thread {
    private selectableEntry deposit, withdraw;
    private int fullSlots=0; private int capacity = 0;
    private Object[] buffer = null; private int in = 0, out = 0;
    public boundedBuffer(selectableEntry deposit, selectableEntry withdraw,
        int capacity) {
            this.deposit = deposit; this.withdraw = withdraw; this.capacity = capacity;
            buffer = new Object[capacity];
    }

    public void run() {
      try {
          selectiveWait select = new selectiveWait();
          selectiveWait.delayAlternative delayA =
              select.new delayAlternative(500);
          select.add(deposit);              // alternative 1
          select.add(withdraw);             // alternative 2
          select.add(delayA);               // alternative 3
          while(true) {
              withdraw.guard(fullSlots>0);
              deposit.guard (fullSlots<capacity);
              delayA.guard(true);
              switch (select.choose()) {
                  case 1:     Object o = deposit.acceptAndReply();
                              buffer[in] = o;
                              in = (in + 1) % capacity; ++fullSlots;
                              break;
                  case 2:     withdraw.accept();
                              Object value = buffer[out];
                              withdraw.reply(value);
                              out = (out + 1) % capacity; --fullSlots;
                              break;
                  case 3:     delayA.accept();
                              System.out.println("delay selected");
                              break;
              }
          }
      } catch (InterruptedException e) { }
        catch (SelectException e) {System.out.println("deadlock detected");
          System.exit(1); }
    }
}
```

Listing 5.10   Java bounded buffer using a *selectiveWait*.

```
final class Controller extends Thread {
//Strategy R>W.1 : Many readers or one writer; readers have a higher priority
    private selectablePort startRead = new selectablePort ();
    private selectablePort endRead = new selectablePort ();
    private selectablePort startWrite = new selectablePort ();
    private selectablePort endWrite = new selectablePort ();
    private boolean writerPresent = false;
    private int readerCount = 0;
    private int sharedValue = 0;

    public int read() {
        try {startRead.send();} catch(Exception e) { }
        int value = sharedValue;
        try {endRead.send();} catch(Exception e) { }
        return value;
    }

    public void write(int value) {
        try {startWrite.send();} catch(Exception e) { }
        sharedValue = value;
        try {endWrite.send();} catch(Exception e) { }
    }

    public void run() {
        try {
            selectiveWait select = new selectiveWait();
            select.add(startRead);              // alternative 1
            select.add(endRead);               // alternative 2
            select.add(startWrite);            // alternative 3
            select.add(endWrite);             // alternative 4
            while(true) {
                startRead.guard(!writerPresent);
                endRead.guard(true);
                startWrite.guard(!writerPresent && readerCount == 0 &&
                    startRead.count() == 0);
                endWrite.guard(true);
                switch (select.choose()) {
                    case 1:    startRead.receive();
                               ++readerCount;
                               break;
                    case 2:    endRead.receive();
                               --readerCount;
                               break;
```

Listing 5.11   Readers and writers using a *selectiveWait*.

```
        case 3:     startWrite.receive();
                    writerPresent = true;
                    break;
        case 4:     endWrite.receive();
                    writerPresent = false;
                    break;
        }
      }
    } catch (InterruptedException e) { }
  }
}
```

Listing 5.11   (*continued*)

Controller uses a *selectiveWait* with *selectablePort* objects *startRead, endRead, startWrite*, and *endWrite*. A *selectablePort* object is a synchronous port that can be used in selective waits. The guard for *startRead* is (*!writerPresent*), which ensures that no writers are writing when a reader is allowed to start reading. The guard for *startWrite* is (*!writerPresent && readerCount == 0 && startRead. count() == 0*). This allows a writer to start writing only if no other writer is writing, no readers are reading, and no reader is waiting for its call to *startRead* to be accepted. The call to *startRead.count()* returns the number of *startRead.send()* operations that are waiting to be received.

Notice that the *selectablePorts* are private members of *Controller* and thus cannot be accessed directly by reader and writer threads. Instead, readers and writers call public methods *read()* and *write()*, respectively. These public methods just pass their calls on to the private entries, ensuring that the entries are called in the correct order (i.e., *startRead* is called before *endRead*, and *startWrite* is called before *endWrite*).

5.4.2   Resource Allocation

Listing 5.12 shows a solution to the resource allocation problem. A *resource-Server* manages three resources. A client calls entry *acquire* to get a resource and entry *release* to return the resource when it is finished. Vector *resources* contains the IDs of the available resources. The integer *available* is used to count the number of resources available. A resource can be acquired if the guard (*available* > 0) is true. A resource's ID is given to the client that *acquires* the resource. The client gives the resource ID back when it *releases* the resource. Notice that both `case` alternatives contain statements that occur after the server replies to the client. Replying early completes the rendezvous with the client and allows the client to proceed as soon as possible.

Listing 5.13 shows an SU monitor solution for this same resource alloca-tion problem. Monitor *resourceMonitor* and thread *resourceServer* demonstrate a mapping between monitors and server threads. Thread *resourceServer* is an

```
final class resourceServer extends Thread {
    private selectableEntry acquire;
    private selectableEntry release;
    private final int numResources = 3;
    private int available = numResources;
    Vector resources = new Vector(numResources);

    public resourceServer(selectableEntry acquire, selectableEntry release) {
        this.acquire = acquire;
        this.release = release;
        resources.addElement(new Integer(1));
        resources.addElement(new Integer(2));
        resources.addElement(new Integer(3));
    }

    public void run() {
        int unitID;
        try {
            selectiveWait select = new selectiveWait();
            select.add(acquire);              // alternative 1
            select.add(release);              // alternative 2
            while(true) {
                acquire.guard(available > 0);
                release.guard(true);
                switch (select.choose()) {
                    case 1:   acquire.accept();
                              unitID = ((Integer)
                              resources.firstElement()).intValue();
                              acquire.reply(new Integer(unitID));
                              --available;
                              resources.removeElementAt(0);
                              break;
                    case 2:   unitID = ((Integer)
                              release.acceptAndReply()).intValue();
                              ++available;
                              resources.addElement(new Integer(unitID));
                              break;
                }
            }
        } catch (InterruptedException e) { }
    }
}
```

Listing 5.12   Resource allocation using a *selectiveWait*.

```
final class resourceMonitor extends monitorSU {
    private conditionVariable freeResource = new conditionVariable();
    private int available = 3;
    Vector resources = new Vector(3);
    public resourceMonitor() {
        resources.addElement(new Integer(1));
        resources.addElement(new Integer(2));
        resources.addElement(new Integer(3));
    }
    public int acquire() {
        int unitID;
        enterMonitor();
        if (available == 0)
            freeResource.waitC();
        else
            --available;
        unitID = ((Integer)resources.firstElement()).intValue();
        resources.removeElementAt(0);
        exitMonitor();
        return unitID;
    }
    public void release(int unitID) {
        enterMonitor();
        resources.addElement(new Integer(unitID));
        if (freeResource.empty()) {
            ++available;
            exitMonitor();
        }
        else
            freeResource.signalC_and_exitMonitor();
    }
}
```

Listing 5.13   Resource allocation using a monitor.

active object that executes concurrently with the threads that call it. The *resource-Monitor* is a passive object, not a thread, which does not execute until it is called. A monitor cannot prevent a thread from entering one of its methods (although the monitor can force threads to enter one at a time). However, once a thread enters the monitor, the thread may be forced to wait on a condition variable until a condition becomes true. Condition synchronization in a server thread works in the opposite way. A server thread will prevent an entry call from being accepted until the condition for accepting the call becomes true.

The conversion between a monitor and a server thread is usually simple (except for cases where the server contains a timeout alternative). It has been shown

```
final class countingSemaphore extends Thread {
    private selectablePort V, P;
    private int permits;
    public countingSemaphore(int initialPermits) {permits = initialPermits;}
    public void P() { P.send();}
    public void V() {V.send();}
    public void run() {
        try {
            selectiveWait select = new selectiveWait();
            select.add(P);                    // alternative1
            select.add(V);                    // alternative 2
            while(true) {
                P.guard(permits>0);
                V.guard(true);
                switch (select.choose()) {
                    case 1: P.receive();
                            --permits;
                            break;
                    case 2: V.receive();
                            ++permits;
                            break;
                }
            }
        } catch (InterruptedException e) {}
    }
}
```

Listing 5.14   Using a *selectiveWait* to simulate a counting semaphore.

elsewhere that communication using shared variables and communication using message passing are equivalent (i.e., they have the same expressive power). Thus, a program that uses shared variables with semaphores or monitors can be transformed into an equivalent program that uses message passing, and vice versa.

5.4.3   Simulating Counting Semaphores

Listing 5.14 shows an implementation of a *countingSemaphore* that uses a *selectiveWait* with *selectablePorts* named *P* and *V*. Clients call public methods *P()* and *V()*, which pass the calls on to the (private) ports. A *P()* operation can be performed only if the guard (*permits* > 0) is true.

5.5   TRACING, TESTING, AND REPLAY FOR MESSAGE-PASSING PROGRAMS

In this section we define SYN-sequences for channel-based programs and present solutions to the replay and feasibility problems. We show how to modify the *channel* classes so that they can be used to trace, replay, and check the feasibility of SYN-sequences. We will also describe how to perform reachability testing for programs that use the *channel* classes.

5.5.1 SR-Sequences

We begin by defining an object-based SYN-sequence of a message-passing program, which means that there is one SYN-sequence for each synchronization object in the program. A thread-based SYN-sequence, which has one SYN-sequence for each thread, is defined after that.

Object-Based SR-Sequences   Let CP be a concurrent program that uses *channels*. Assume for now that CP has no selective wait statements. The synchronization objects in CP are its channels, and the synchronization events in CP are executions of *send()* and *receive()* operations on these channels. A SYN-sequence for a channel is a sequence of send and receive events (or *SR-events*) of the following types:

- *SRsynchronization*: a synchronization between send and receive operations on a synchronous channel
- *asynchronousSendArrival*: an arrival of an asynchronous send operation whose message is eventually received
- *asynchronousReceive*: a receive operation that eventually receives a message on an asynchronous channel
- *unacceptedSend*: a synchronous send operation whose message is never received
- *unacceptedAsynchSend*: an asynchronous send operation whose message is never received
- *unacceptedReceive*: a receive on an asynchronous or synchronous channel that never receives a message
- *sendException*: a send operation on an asynchronous or synchronous channel that causes an exception to be thrown
- *receiveException*: a receive operation on an asynchronous or synchronous channel that causes an exception to be thrown
- *startEntry*: the start of a rendezvous on an entry
- *endEntry*: the end of a rendezvous on an entry

Notice that for asynchronous messages, there are *arrival* events but no *send* events. This is because it is the order in which messages arrive that determines the result of an execution, not the order in which messages are sent. As we will see later, send events are needed for reachability testing, where they are used to identify the race conditions that occur during an execution.

An object-based SR-event for channel C is denoted by

$$(S, R, N_S, N_R, eventType)$$

where

- S is the sending thread of a send operation or the calling thread of an entry call.
- R is the receiving thread of a receive operation or the accepting thread of an entry call.
- N_S is the sender's order number, which gives the relative order of this event among all of the sending/calling thread's events.
- N_R is the receiver's order number, which gives the relative order of this event among all of the receiving/accepting thread's events.
- eventType is one of the send−receive event types, which are listed above.

The order number of an event executed by thread T gives the relative order of this event among all the events exercised by T. For example, an event T with order number 2 is the second event exercised by T. For *asynchronousSendArrival, unacceptedSend*, and *sendException* events, R and N_R are not applicable (NA) since no receiving thread is involved with these events. Similarly, for *unacceptedReceive* and *receiveException* events, S and N_S are not applicable since there is no sending thread. The order number of an *asynchronousSendArrival* event is for the send operation of the thread that generated it.

The program in Listing 5.15 shows why order numbers are needed in SR-events. Assume that order numbers are not specified. Then the only feasible SR-sequence for channel *C1* (without order numbers) contains the single event ·

(Thread1, Thread2, SRsynchronization).

The only feasible SR-sequence for *C2* also contains a single event:

(Thread1, Thread3, SRsynchronization).

Suppose now that we create a new program by reversing the order of the send operations in *Thread1*:

Thread1	Thread2	Thread3
C2.*send()*;	C1.receive();	C2.receive();
C1.*send()*;		

mailbox C1, C2; // synchronous mailboxes

Thread1	Thread2	Thread3
C1.send();	C1.receive();	C2.receive();
C2.send();		

Listing 5.15 Demonstrating the need for order numbers.

Then the feasible SR-sequences (without order numbers) for channels *C1* and *C2* in the new program are the same as in the original program, even though the two programs are different in an obvious and important way.

Adding order numbers to the SR-events distinguishes between these two different programs. The SR-sequence for *C1* in the first program becomes

(Thread1, Thread2, 1, 1, SRsynchronization).   // first event of Thread1 and
                                                    // first event of Thread2

and the SR-sequence for *C1* in the second program becomes

(Thread1, Thread2, 2, 1, SRsynchronization).   // second event of Thread1 and
                                                    // first event of Thread2

When order numbers are specified, an SR-sequence of *C1* that is feasible for the first program will be infeasible for the second, and vice versa.

Given the format above for an object-based SR-event, an SR-sequence of channel C is denoted as

$$C: ((S_1, R_1, N_{S1}, N_{R1}, eventType_1), (S_2, R_2, N_{S2}, N_{R2}, eventType_2), ...)$$

where $(S_i, R_i, N_{Si}, N_{Ri}, eventType_i)$ denotes the ith, $i > 0$, SR-event in the SR-sequence of C. An object-based SR-sequence of a program contains an SR-sequence for each channel in the program.

Thread-Based SR-Sequences   We now define two formats for thread-based SR-sequences. Each thread in the program has its own SR-sequence. There are two possible formats for the SR-events in a thread-based SR-sequence.

Format 1   A thread-based SR-event for thread T is denoted by

(C, N_C, eventType)

where

- C is the channel name.
- N_C is the channel order number.
- eventType is the type of the event.

The channel order number N_C gives the relative order of this event among all the events involving channel C. The list of event types is the same as that above for object-based events, except that we remove type *SRsynchronization* and add separate event types for synchronous send and receive operations:

- *Send*: a synchronous send operation executed by thread T where the message is eventually accepted

- *Receive*: a synchronous receive operation executed by thread T that eventually receives a message

We could also have used separate synchronous-send and synchronous-receive events for the events in object-based sequences, but combining them into a single send-receive synchronization event makes object-based sequences easier to read.

The second format for thread-based SR-sequences is used for programs that have selective wait statements. Format 2 below has the same amount of information as Format 1, but the two formats are best suited for different tasks: Format 2 better matches the solution that we have developed for determining feasibility and replaying SR-sequences, while Format 1 is a better format for visualizing the trace of an execution. The trace tool that we will describe later outputs thread-based SR-sequences in both formats.

In Format 2, each channel has one thread that is considered to be the "owner" of the channel. For a *link, port,* or *entry* (or actually, their *selectable* versions), the owner is the thread that executes *receive()* operations on the channel. For these types of channels, there is only one thread that can be the receiver. A *mailbox* can have multiple receiving threads, so one of the receivers must be chosen arbitrarily to be the owner.

If a thread T contains a selective wait, the selective wait will choose among one or more channels, all of which we require to be owned by thread T. To simplify things, we add another restriction on selective waits, which is that the channels of a selective wait in T must be *links, ports,* or *entries* that are owned by T. This means that *mailboxes* cannot be used in selective waits. Since thread T is associated with all the channel events generated by its selective waits, it is convenient to record these events in the SR-sequence for thread T.

Format 2   A thread-based SR-event for thread T, where T is the owner of the channel associated with the event, is denoted by

(S, N$_S$, C, eventType)

where

- S is the sending thread (T is always the receiver).
- N$_S$ is the sender's order number.
- C is the channel name.
- eventType is the type of the event.

The list of thread-based SR-event types is the same as that above for object-based events, except that we add an *elseDelay* event type for selective wait statements:

- *elseDelay*: selection of an else or delay alternative.

An *SRsynchronization* event representing a synchronization between send and receive operations on a synchronous channel appears in the SR-sequence for the owning thread (i.e., the receiving thread). There is no corresponding send event in the sequence for the sending thread. In Format 2, no order number is required for channel C since the SR-sequence of the owning thread T contains all the events for channel C, and thus the order numbers for events on C are given implicitly (i.e., the ith event for C implicitly has order number i).

As we mentioned above, we are grouping the events involving channels owned by thread T into one sequence: the SR-sequence of T. This gives Format 2 its thread-based flavor. On the other hand, Format 2 is derived from the format used for object-based events. Format 2 is slightly simpler than the object-based SR-event format since the receiving thread is always the owning thread, and thus the receiving thread does not need to be specified in Format 2. Also, the order number of the owning thread is given implicitly by the order of events in the sequence.

Given the two formats for thread-based SR-events, we can now define thread-based SR-sequences for threads and programs. For Format 1, an SR-sequence of thread T is denoted as

$T: ((C_1, V_{C1}, \text{eventType}_1), (C_2, V_{C2}, \text{eventType}_2), \ldots).$

For Format 2, an SR-sequence of thread T is denoted as

$T: ((S_1, N_{S1}, C_1, \text{eventType}_1), (S_2, N_{S2}, C_2, \text{eventType}_2), \ldots).$

A thread-based SR-sequence of a program contains a thread-based SR-sequence for each thread in the program.

We can easily translate a thread-based SR-sequence into an object-based SR-sequence, and vice versa. Consider again the simple program in Listing 5.15. The object-based SR-sequence of this program is

C_1: (Thread1, Thread2, 1, 1, SRsynchronization)
C_2: (Thread1, Thread3, 2, 1, SRsynchronization).

The corresponding thread-based SR-sequence using Format 1 is

Thread$_1$: (C1, 1, send), (C2, 1, send)
Thread$_2$: (C1, 1, receive)
Thread$_3$: (C2, 1, receive).

The thread-based SR-sequence using Format 2 is

Thread1:   // send events do not appear in
                                                           // SR-sequence of the sender
Thread2: (Thread1, 1, C1, SRsynchronization)   // 1 is Thread1's order number
                                                           // for its first *send* operation

Thread3: (Thread1, 2, C2, SRsynchronization).   // 2 is Thread1's order number
                                                  // for its second *send* operation

Thread1's sequence is empty under Format 2, since Thread1 only executes send events, and these send events appear as *SRsynchronization* events in Thread2 and Thread3.

No information is lost in this translation. Order numbers for threads are specified explicitly in the object-based sequences but are implicit in the ordering of events in the SR-sequence for each thread. Similarly, order numbers for channels appear explicitly in thread-based SR-sequences using Format 1 but are implicit in the object-based SR-sequence for each channel.

Totally Ordered SR-Sequences   The object- and thread-based SR-sequences defined above are all partially ordered; there is a separate sequence for each channel or thread in the program. We can also create totally ordered SR-sequences. That is, there is only one SR-sequence for the program and this sequence includes events for all the channels and threads.

An SR-event in a totally ordered SR-sequence is denoted by

(S, R, C, eventType)

where

- S is the sending thread of a send operation or the calling thread of an entry call.
- R is the receiving thread of a receive operation or the accepting thread of an entry call.
- C is the channel name.
- eventType is one of the types listed above for Format 2.

A totally ordered SR-sequence contains no order numbers for channels or threads, since this information is specified implicitly by the ordering of events in the sequence. A totally ordered SR-sequence of program CP is denoted as

$((S_1, R_1, C_1, eventType_1), (S_1, R_2, C_2, eventType_2), ...).$

For example, a totally ordered SR-sequence for the program in Listing 5.15 is

$((Thread_1, Thread_2, C_1, SRsynchronization), (Thread_1, Thread_3, C_2, SRsynchronization)).$

A programmer must choose between the various formats for SR-sequences: total order vs. partial order and object-based vs. thread-based. A totally ordered SR-sequence can be translated into a partially ordered sequence, and vice versa.

Similarly, we have already seen that object- and thread-based SR-sequences can easily be translated into one another.

A totally ordered sequence is usually easier to understand than is a partially ordered one. If a program is running on a single CPU, a single controller can easily record a totally ordered sequence. However, using a single controller creates a bottleneck during execution. Since threads and channels are user-level objects in the program, they can be instrumented to collect either thread- or object-based sequences.

In a distributed program, which involves multiple machines, a channel is typically not a user-level object, so object-based sequences may be difficult to collect. If multiple controllers (e.g., one controller per machine) are used to collect partially ordered SR-sequences, a bottleneck is avoided, but the trace files will be created on separate machines across the network. This makes it less convenient to view the trace files and to create a totally ordered sequence from the files. If a single controller is used to collect a totally ordered SR-sequence from a distributed program, certain event-ordering issues must be addressed so that the SR-sequence is captured accurately (see Section 6.3).

5.5.2   Simple SR-Sequences

Object-based simple SR-sequences can be used for replaying channel-based programs. The format of a simple send−receive event depends on the type of channel being used:

- *Mailbox.* A simple send−receive event for *mailbox* M is denoted by (S, R), where S is the ID of the sending thread and R is the ID of receiving thread for mailbox M.
- *Port or Entry.* A simple send−receive event for *port* P or *entry* E is denoted by (S), where S is the ID of the sending thread for *port* P or the calling thread for *entry* E. The receiving thread is not recorded since the receiving thread for a *port* or *entry* is always the same thread, which is the owner of the *port* or *entry*.
- *Link.* A simple send−receive event for a *link* requires no information about the sender and receiver. This is because the sender and receiver are always the same thread. If program CP uses only *links* for communication and no selective wait statements, there is no nondeterminism that needs to be controlled during replay. (This assumes that message passing is the only possible source of nondeterminism in CP.)

To simplify the recording and replaying of simple SR-sequences, we use the common format (S, R) for all channel types, where S is the ID of the sending thread and R is the ID of the receiving thread for the *link, port, entry*, or *mailbox*. Using a common format simplifies the design of the replay tool, and even though information about the sender and receiver threads is not always required for replay, it is useful for other things, such as understanding and visualizing the trace.

A simple object-based SR-sequence of channel C is denoted as

$C: ((S_1, R_1), (S_2, R_2) \ldots).$

An object-based simple SR-sequence of a program contains a simple SR-sequence for each channel in the program.

A thread-based simple SR-event has two possible formats, corresponding to Formats 1 and 2 defined above.

Format 1   A simple SR-event is denoted as (N_C), where N_C is the order number of channel C, which is the *mailbox, port, entry*, or *link* that is involved in this event. A simple SR-sequence of a thread T using Format 1 is denoted as

$T: ((N_{C1}), (N_{C2}), \ldots)$

Format 2   A simple SR-event is denoted as (S), where S is the sending thread for this event. A simple SR-sequence of a thread T using Format 2 is denoted as

$T: ((S_1), (S_2), \ldots)$

A totally ordered simple SR-sequence of program CP is denoted as

$((S_1, R_1) (S_2, R_2), \ldots)$

where

- S is the sending thread of a send operation or the calling thread of an entry call.
- R is the receiving thread of a receive operation or the accepting thread of an entry call.

For the program in Listing 5.15, the object-based simple SR-sequence of this program is

C1: (Thread1, Thread2)
C2: (Thread2, Thread3)

The thread-based simple SR-sequence using Format 1 is

Thread1: (1), (1)
Thread2: (1)
Thread3: (1)

Let Thread2 be the owner of channel *C1* and Thread3 be the owner of channel *C2*; the thread-based simple SR-sequence using Format 2 is

Thread2: (Thread1)
Thread3: (Thread1).

The thread-based totally ordered simple SR-sequence is

(Thread1, Thread2), (Thread1, Thread3).

5.5.3 Determining the Feasibility of an SR-Sequence

The feasibility of an SR-sequence is determined using the same general technique that was used to determine the feasibility of an M-sequence for monitors. Before a thread can perform a send or receive operation, it must request permission from a control module. The controller is responsible for reading an SR-sequence and forcing the execution to proceed according to this sequence. We will show how to implement the controller using a single thread. This controller thread uses channels and a selective wait statement to perform both functions of the control module: ordering events and handling timeouts.

The *send()* and *receive()* methods in the *channel* classes are modified by adding one or more calls to the controller. Listing 5.16 shows a sketch of Java class *link* with the modifications highlighted. In trace mode, methods *send()* and *receive()* notify the controller of any exceptions that occur. Operation *receive()* notifies the controller when a message is received, which causes an *SRsynchronization* event to be recorded. The arguments on the calls refer to the fields of an SR-event, which were defined in Section 5.5.2. The fields were sender (S), receiver (R), order number of the sender (N_S), order number of the receiver (N_R), channel name (C), order number of the channel (N_C), and the various event types. In test mode, methods *send()* and *receive()* issue a call to the controller to request permission to exercise send and receive events. The call to *control.msgReceived()* notifies the controller that the event has occurred, so that permission can be given for the next event.

The controller uses channels to communicate with the threads. For example, there is an array of *selectableEntrys* that are used by threads requesting the *sendPermit*:

```
private selectableEntry requestSendPermit[];
requestSendPermit = new selectableEntry[numberOfThreads+1];
for (int i=0; i<(numberOfThreads+1);i++)
    requestSendPermit[i] = new selectableEntry();
```

When a thread makes a method call to *control.requestSendPermit()*, the call is forwarded as an entry call over the channel associated with that thread. The implementation of method *requestSendPermit(...)* is shown below. The ID of the

```
public class link extends channel {
    ...
    public final void send(Object sentMsg) {
        if(mode == TEST)
            control.requestSendPermit(S,NS,C);
        synchronized(sending) {
            // save first thread to call send
            if (sender == null) sender = Thread.currentThread();
            if (Thread.currentThread() != sender) {
                if (mode == TRACE)
                    control.traceMsg(S, NS, C, VC, sendException);
                if (mode == TEST) {
                    control.requestSendExceptionPermit(S, NS, C);
                    control.msgReceived();
                }
                throw new InvalidLinkUsage
                    ("Attempted to use link with multiple senders");
            }
            if (sentMsg == null) {
                if (mode == TRACE)
                    control.traceMsg(S, NS, C, VC, sendException);
                if (mode == TEST) {
                    control.requestSendExceptionPermit(S, NS, C);
                    control.msgReceived();
                }
                throw new NullPointerException("Null message passed to send()");
            }
            message = sentMsg;
            sent.V();
            received.P();
        }
    }
    public final Object receive() {
        Object receivedMessage = null;
        if (mode == TEST) control.requestReceivePermit(R,NR,C);
        synchronized (receiving) {
            // save first thread to call receive
            if (receiver == null) receiver = Thread.currentThread();
            f (Thread.currentThread() != receiver) {
                if (mode == TRACE)
                control.traceMsg(R,NR,C,VC,receiveException);
```

Listing 5.16 Class *link* modified for tracing and feasibility.

```
            if (mode == TEST) {
                control.requestReceiveExceptionPermit(R, N_R, C);
                control.msgReceived();
            }
            throw new InvalidLinkUsage
                ("Attempted to use link with multiple receivers");
        }
        sent.P();
        receivedMessage = message;
        if (mode == TRACE) control.traceMsg
            (S, R, N_S, N_R, C, VC, SR_SYNCHRONIZATION);
        else if (mode == TEST) control.msgReceived();
        received.V();
        return receivedMessage;
    }
  }
}
```

Listing 5.16   (*continued*)

sending thread, in this case *S*, is used to select the proper channel for requesting the *sendPermit*:

```
public void requestSendPermit(int S, int N_S, String C) {
// sender (S), order number of sender (N_S), channel name (C)
    try {
        requestPermitMessage m = new requestPermitMessage(S, N_S, C);
        requestSendPermit[S].call(m); // S is the ID of the calling thread
    } catch(InterruptedException e) {...}
}
```

A sketch of the controller thread's *run()* method is shown in Listing 5.17. The controller inputs an SR-sequence and then issues permits based on the order of events in the SR-sequence. The controller uses a selective wait statement with a delay alternative to control the execution of events. The selective wait statement contains alternatives for each of the five types of permits—*sendPermit, receivePermit, sendExceptionPermit, receiveExceptionPermit, and elseDelayPermit*—and a delay alternative named *timeout*. For each permit, there is an array of *selectableEntrys* (see above), one entry per thread. As explained above, a thread requests permission by using its thread ID to index the array and call the proper channel (e.g., *requestSendPermit[ID].call(...)*).

If the next event in the SR-sequence indicates that thread T is expected to request a certain permit, the guard of the selective wait alternative corresponding to T's channel is set to true and the other thread's guards are set to false. The controller will wait for T to issue an entry call to the appropriate channel. If no

```
// Method run() for the controller thread:
while (the next SR-event is available) {
    nextEvent = SR-sequence[index]; // get the next event in the SR-sequence
    // Let T be the ID of the thread executing the next rendezvous event;
    if (T is expected to request the sendPermit) requestSendPermit[T].guard(true);
    else if (T is expected to request the receivePermit)
        requestReceivePermit[T].guard(true);
    else if (T is expected to request the sendExceptionPermit)
        requestSendExceptionPermit[T].guard(true)
    else if (T is expected to request the receiveExceptionPermit)
        requestReceiveExceptionPermit[T].guard(true)
    else if (T is expected to request a permit for a selective wait event)
        requestSelectPermit[T].guard(true);
    else if (T is expected to request the elseDelayPermit)
        requestElseDelayPermit[T].guard(true);
    Set all other guards to false;
    choice = select.choose();
    if (choice <= (numberOfThreads+1)) {
        requestedEvent =
            (requestPermitMessage)requestSendPermit[choice-1].accept();
        /* if (the channel name and order numbers of requestedEvent do not match
            those of nextEvent) issue diagnostic and terminate */
        requestSendPermit[choice-1].reply();
        if (nextEvent.getEventType().equals(UNACCEPTED_SYNCH_SEND))
            index++;
    } else if (choice <= 2*(numberOfThreads+1)) {
        requestedEvent = (requestPermitMessage)
        requestReceivePermit[choice-(numberOfThreads+1)-1].accept();
        /* if (the channel name and order numbers of requestedEvent do not match
            those of nextEvent) issue diagnostic and terminate; */
        requestReceivePermit[choice-(numberOfThreads+1)-1].reply();
        if (nextEvent.getEventType().equals(UNACCEPTED_RECEIVE))
            index++;
    } else if (choice <= 3*(numberOfThreads+1)) {
        requestSelectPermit[choice-(2*(numberOfThreads+1))-1].accept();
        boolean oneArrival = true; int caller = nextEvent.getOtherThread();
        if (caller != -1) oneArrival = true; else oneArrival = false;
        requestSelectPermit[choice-(2*(numberOfThreads+1))-1].
            reply(new Boolean(oneArrival));
    } else if (choice <= 4*(numberOfThreads+1)) {
        requestedEvent = (requestPermitMessage)
        requestElseDelayPermit[choice-(3*(numberOfThreads+1))-1].accept();
```

Listing 5.17   Method *run()* for the controller thread.

```
        /* if (order number of requestedEvent doesn't match that of nextEvent)
            issue diagnostic and terminate; */
        requestElseDelayPermit[choice-(3*(numberOfThreads+1))-1].reply();
    } else if (choice <= 5*(numberOfThreads+1)) {
        requestedEvent = (requestPermitMessage)
        requestSendExceptionPermit[choice-(4*(numberOfThreads+1))-1].accept();
        /* if (the channel name and order numbers of requestedEvent do not match
            those of nextEvent) issue diagnostic and terminate; */
        requestSendExceptionPermit[choice-(4*(numberOfThreads+1))-1].reply();
    } else if (choice <= 6*(numberOfThreads+1)) {
        requestedEvent = (requestPermitMessage)
        requestReceiveExceptionPermit[choice-(5*(numberOfThreads+1))
            -1].accept();
        /* if (the channel name and order numbers of requestedEvent do not match
            those of nextEvent) issue diagnostic and terminate; */
        requestReceiveExceptionPermit[choice-(5*(numberOfThreads+1))
            -1].reply();
    } else if (choice == (6*(numberOfThreads+1))+1){
        msgReceived.acceptAndReply(); ++index; // go on to next event
    } else { timeout.accept(); /* issue a diagnostic and terminate */ }
}
```

Listing 5.17   (*continued*)

call arrives before the timeout in the delay alternative expires, the sequence is assumed to be infeasible.

The selective wait alternative also contains alternatives for entry *requestSelectPermit*. These entries are used to control the execution of any selective wait statements in the program. Let W be a selective wait in Thread j. The *choose()* method for class *selectiveWait* is instrumented as follows:

```
public synchronized int choose(){
    if (mode == TEST) {
        boolean oneArrival = control.requestSelectPermit(((TDThread)Thread.
            currentThread()).getID());
        if (oneArrival) { // wait for entry call to arrive before making choice
            currentArrivals = number of entry calls that have arrived for the
                channels in the selective wait
            if (currentArrivals < 1)
                wait(); // wait until an entry call arrives
        }
    }
    /* rest of choose() */
}
```

The purpose of the code at the start of *choose()* is to guarantee that when a choice is made:

1. If an *accept()* or *receive()* alternative in W is expected to be selected (according to the SR-sequence), this alternative is the only one having a call to accept.
2. If a *delay* or *else* alternative in W is expected to be selected, no call is available for acceptance.

The call to *requestSelectPermit(j)* is accepted by the controller when, according to the given SR-sequence, the next SR-event has Thread j as the accepting or receiving thread. When the controller accepts this call, it determines whether an entry call is required to arrive before the execution of W:

- If an entry is to be accepted by Thread j, an arrival is needed.
- If an *else* or *delay* alternative is to be selected by Thread j, no arrivals are needed.

The call to *requestSelectPermit()* returns a boolean value *oneArrival* to indicate whether an arrival is needed. In addition, if an arrival is needed, the controller will give permission to the corresponding caller to make its entry call.

The rest of the code in *choose()* does the following. When an arrival is needed, Thread j computes the current number of entry call arrivals for the channels in *selectiveWait* W; a nonzero value indicates that a call has arrived. If an entry call arrival is needed (i.e., *oneArrival* is true, but no call has arrived), Thread j executes *wait()* to block itself until the call arrives. After the call arrives, W is executed and the expected *SRsynchronization* occurs. If no arrival is needed (i.e., *oneArrival* is false), W is executed immediately, and either a *delay* or *else* alternative is selected.

The *accept()* method for *else* and *delay* alternatives traces an *elseDelay* event in trace mode and requests the *elseDelayPermit* in test mode:

```
void accept() {
    if (mode == TRACE)
        control.traceMsg(R, N_R, elseDelay)        // notify controller that an
                                                    // else/delay event has occurred
    else if (mode == TEST) {
        control.requestElseDelayPermit(R, N_R);     // request permission to
                                                    // execute else/delay event
        control.msgReceived();                      // notify controller that else/
                                                    // delay was accepted
    }
}
```

We mention again that the code shown above at the beginning of *choose()* is executed at the beginning of a selective wait, before any *accept()* statement is executed. If the next event in the SR-sequence is expected to be an *elseDelay* event, the code in *choose()* ensures that no entry call has arrived when the choice is made, so that an else/delay can be selected.

In all cases, if the thread expected to request permission does not do so before the timeout, or the thread receives permission but executes an event with an unexpected attribute (i.e., unexpected channel name, unexpected order number, etc.), the controller issues a message that the SR-sequence is infeasible.

5.5.4 Deterministic Testing

A collection of tracing, replay, and feasibility tools enables us to test our programs using a strategy called *deterministic testing*. Deterministic testing of a concurrent program CP involves the following steps:

1. Select a set of tests, each of the form (X, S), where X and S are an input and a complete SYN-sequence of CP, respectively.
2. For each test (X, S) selected, force a deterministic execution of CP with input X according to S. This forced execution determines whether S is feasible for CP with input X. (Since S is a complete SYN-sequence of CP, the result of such an execution is deterministic.)
3. Compare the expected and actual results (including the output, feasibility of S, and termination condition) of the forced execution. If the expected and actual results are different, a fault is detected. The replay tool can be used to locate the fault.

Note that for deterministic testing, a test for CP is not just an input of CP. A test consists of an input and a SYN-sequence and is referred to as an *IN-SYN test*. Deterministic testing is similar to the concept of *forcing a path* mentioned in [Taylor et al. 1992].

The selection of IN-SYN tests for CP can be done in different ways:

- Select inputs and then select a set of SYN-sequences for each input.
- Select SYN-sequences and then select a set of inputs for each SYN-sequence.
- Select inputs and SYN-sequences separately and then combine them.
- Select pairs of inputs and SYN-sequences together.

To use an IN-SYN test (X, S) for deterministic testing of CP, we need to specify the expected output, the expected feasibility of SYN-sequence S (feasible or infeasible), and the expected termination condition (normal or abnormal). Different symbols may be used for different types of abnormal termination, such as divide-by-zero, deadlock, and so on. Also, different threads in CP may have different termination conditions.

A combination of nondeterministic and deterministic testing is used during reachability testing, which was described in Chapters 3 and 4. Assume that every execution of CP with input X terminates and the number of distinct feasible SYN-sequences of CP with input X is finite. Reachability testing is a systematic way of exercising all possible SYN-sequences of CP with input X. By doing so, reachability testing can determine the correctness of CP with input X.

5.5.5 Reachability Testing for Message-Passing Programs

Reachability testing can be used to derive and exercise automatically every partially ordered SR-sequence of a message-passing program. Reachability testing identifies race conditions in an execution trace and uses the race conditions to generate race variants. Recall from Chapters 3 and 4 that a race variant represents an alternative execution behavior that could have happened, but didn't, due to the way that race conditions were resolved arbitrarily during execution. Replaying a race variant ensures that a different behavior is observed during the next execution.

Figure 5.18*a* shows an execution trace for three threads that use asynchronous ports for message passing. Thread1 and Thread3 each send a single message to Thread2. In this trace, Thread2 receives the message from Thread1 first. Figure 5-18*b* shows a race variant of this trace. In this variant, Thread2 receives the message from Thread3 first. The dotted arrow indicates that Thread1's message is sent but not received in the variant. Note that the race variant in Fig. 5.18*b* contains only one receive event for Thread2. We cannot include a second receive event for Thread2 since we cannot be sure that Thread2 will execute another receive statement after the variant is replayed. To see this, suppose that Thread2 executes the following statements:

```
x = p2.receive();
if(x)
  p2.receive();
```

In the execution trace in Fig. 5.18*a*, Thread2 executes both receive events. Thus, we can say with certainty that the value *x* received from Thread2 caused the condition in Thread2's if-statement to be evaluated to *true*. In the race variant in Fig. 5.18*b*, we have changed the sending thread for Thread2's first receive to Thread3. The value Thread2 receives from Thread3 may or may not cause the condition in Thread2's if-statement to be evaluated to *true*. Since we generate variants without examining the source code of the program, we can no longer be

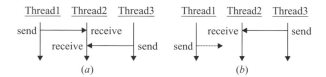

Figure 5.18   Execution trace and a race variant.

sure what will happen after Thread$_2$'s first receive. Thus, to be safe, we remove from the variant all events that happen after the changed receive event.

Another point about race analysis is that the variants of a trace depend on the type of synchronization that is provided by the channels. For asynchronous ports, there are several possible synchronization schemes. Figure 5.19a shows a program that uses asynchronous ports. An execution trace of this program is given in Fig. 5.19b. Assume that the ports used in the program of Fig. 5.19a are the asynchronous ports implemented in Section 5.1. Note that Thread1's send to Thread3 definitely happens before Thread2's send to Thread3 since Thread1 and Thread2 synchronize in between sending their messages to Thread3. Based on this "happened before" relation, the port implementation used in this chapter guarantees that Thread3 will receive the message sent by Thread1 before it receives the message sent by Thread2. In general, if a message m_1 is sent to thread T before another message m_2 is sent to T, message m_1 is received by T before m_2 is received. This type of synchronization is called *causal synchronization*. If causal synchronization is used, no race variants can be generated for the trace in Fig. 5.19b. Formal definitions of the "happens before" relation and causality are given in Chapter 6.

Causal synchronization is not always guaranteed. *FIFO synchronization* is commonly used in distributed programs, which send messages across a communications network. FIFO synchronization guarantees that messages sent from one thread to another thread are received in the order in which they are sent. Figure 5.19c shows a variant of the trace in Fig. 5.19b. This variant assumes that FIFO synchronization is used, which allows Thread3 to receive messages from Thread1 and Thread2 in the reverse order that they were sent. (FIFO synchronization guarantees that Thread3 receives Thread1's messages in the order that Thread1 sends them, and that Thread3 receives Thread2's messages in the order that Thread2 sends them, but the first message Thread3 receives can be from Thread1 or from Thread2.)

Distributed programming is discussed in Chapter 6. To prepare for Chapter 6, we have implemented a special asynchronous channel port with FIFO synchronization and support for reachability testing. These FIFO ports make it possible

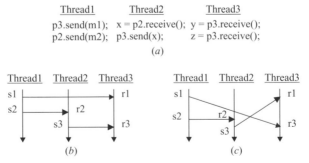

Figure 5.19   Execution trace and a variant for asynchronous ports with FIFO synchronization.

TABLE 5.1 Reachability Testing Results for Message-Passing Programs

Program	Config.	No. Seqs.
BB-Select	3P + 3C + 2S	144
RW-Select	3R + 2W	768

to write programs that behave like distributed programs but run on a single computer and so are easier to write and easier to debug. Writing such a program is a good first step toward writing a real distributed program.

Table 5.1 shows the results of applying reachability testing to programs that use message passing with selective waits. This table has the same format as that of Tables 3.2 and Table 4.2. Program BB is the bounded buffer program in Listing 5.10. Program RW is the readers and writers program in Listing 5.11. Notice that these programs, which use selective waits, generate far fewer sequences than the corresponding bounded buffer and reader and writer programs in Chapters 3 and 4 that used semaphores and monitors. We say more about this in Chapter 7.

5.5.6 Putting It All Together

Next, we demonstrate how to use the channel classes to trace, test, and replay Java and C++/Win32/Pthreads message-passing programs.

Using Java Channel Classes To test and debug executions of channel-based Java programs, use the property *mode* to specify the function (tracing, replay, feasibility, or reachability testing) to be performed. An execution of program *Buffer* in Listing 5.20 is traced by setting the mode to *trace*:

  −Dmode=trace

and then specifying whether the tracing strategy should be object- or thread-based:

  −Dstrategy=object // collect object-based SR-sequences
  −Dstrategy=thread // collect thread-based SR-sequences

and whether there should be a single Controller or multiple Controllers:

  −Dcontrollers=single // single Controller thread
  −Dcontrollers=multiple // multiple Controller threads

Using a single Controller results in a totally ordered (object- or thread-based) SR-sequence. If multiple Controllers are used, the SR-sequence collected will be partially ordered (one per thread or object). If the program contains a *selectiveWait*, the tracing strategy must be thread-based and mailboxes cannot be used in the *selectiveWait*. When a thread-based strategy is used, the owner of each *link, port, mailbox*, or *entry* P must be indicated by calling P.setOwner(T), where thread T is the owner of port P. An example of this is shown in the *main()* method in Listing 5.20.

The command

> java −Dmode=trace −Dstrategy=thread −Dcontrollers=single Buffer

creates several trace files for *Buffer*. The file channel-replay.txt contains a totally ordered simple SR-sequence of the execution, and the file channel-test.txt contains a totally ordered complete SR-sequence. The command

> java −Dmode=trace −Dstrategy=thread −Dcontrollers=multiple Buffer

creates files that contain a separate simple SR-sequence and complete SR-sequence for each of the *Producer, Consumer*, and *boundedBuffer* threads.

Random delays are executed during trace mode by setting *−DrandomDelay = on*. When *on* is specified, random delays are executed before each *send()* and *receive()*. To turn random delays off, use *off*; this is also the default value. The value of property *randomDelay* is ignored during replay and test modes. The deadlock detection method described in Section 3.8.4 has also been implemented in the channel classes. To turn deadlock detection on during tracing, specify *−DdeadlockDetection = on*. To turn deadlock detection off, use *off*; this is also the default value.

A simple SR-sequence is replayed by specifying *replay* mode and using the same values for the *strategy* and *controllers* that were used during tracing:

> java −Dmode=replay −Dstrategy=thread −Dcontrollers=single Buffer

As in Chapters 3 and 4, reachability testing is performed on *Buffer* by setting the *mode* property to *rt* and executing a driver process named *RTDriver* with "Buffer" as the command-line argument:

> java −Dmode=rt RTDriver Buffer

The feasibility of an SR-sequence is determined in *test* mode:

> java −Dmode=test −Dstrategy=thread −Dcontrollers=single Buffer

If the mode is not specified, the default value for the *mode* property will turn tracing, replay, and testing off.

The default value for the strategy property is *object* and the default value for the *controllers* property is *single*.

Using the C++ Channel Classes   To test and debug executions of channel-based C++/Win32/Pthreads programs, use environment variable MODE to specify the function (tracing, replay, feasibility, or reachability testing) to be performed. In Windows, an execution of a C++ version of program *Buffer* in Listing 5.20 is traced by executing the command

```
set MODE=TRACE        // Unix: setenv MODE TRACE
```

and then specifying whether the tracing strategy should be object- or thread-based:

```
set STRATEGY=OBJECT    // collect object-based SR-sequences;
// Unix: setenv STRATEGY OBJECT
set STRATEGY=THREAD    // collect thread-based SR-sequences;
// Unix: setenv STRATEGY THREAD
```

and whether there should be a single Controller or multiple Controllers:

```
set CONTROLLERS=SINGLE      // single Controller thread;
// Unix: setenv CONTROLLERS SINGLE
set CONTROLLERS=MULTIPLE // multiple Controller threads;
// Unix: setenv CONTROLLERS MULTIPLE
```

Using a single Controller results in a totally ordered (object- or thread-based) SR-sequence. If multiple Controllers are used, the collected SR-sequence will be partially ordered (one per thread or object). If the program contains a *selective-Wait*, the tracing strategy must be thread-based. When a thread-based strategy is used, the owner of each link, port, or entry P must be indicated by calling P.setOwner(T), where thread T is the owner of port P. An example of this is shown in the *main( )* method in Listing 5.20.

Tracing an execution with a THREAD strategy and a SINGLE controller creates several trace files for *Buffer*. The file channel-replay.txt contains a totally ordered simple SR-sequence of the execution, and the file channel-test.txt contains a totally ordered complete SR-sequence. Using MULTIPLE controllers creates files that contain a separate simple SR-sequence and complete SR-sequence for each of the *Producer, Consumer*, and *boundedBuffer* threads.

Random delays can be executed during trace mode using "set RANDOMDE-LAY=ON." When ON is specified, random delays are executed before each *send( )* and *receive( )*. To turn random delays off, use OFF; this is also the default value. The value of variable RANDOMDELAY is ignored during replay and test modes. The deadlock detection method described in Section 3.8.4 has also been implemented in the channel classes. To turn deadlock detection on during tracing or reachability testing, execute "set DEADLOCKDETECTION=ON." To turn deadlock detection off, use OFF; this is also the default value. A simple SR-sequence is replayed by executing "set MODE=REPLAY" and using the same values for the STRATEGY and the CONTROLLERS variables that were used during tracing.

As in Chapter 3, reachability testing is performed on *Buffer* by setting the MODE to RT and customizing the driver process in file *RTDriver*.cpp. This

```
publicfinal class Buffer {
    public static void main (String args[]) {
        selectableEntry deposit = new selectableEntry();
        selectableEntry withdraw = new selectableEntry();
        boundedBuffer b = new boundedBuffer(deposit,withdraw,3);
        Producer pl = new Producer (deposit, 1);
        Consumer cl = new Consumer (withdraw, 1);
        deposit.setOwner(b); withdraw.setOwner(b);
        b.setDaemon(true);
        b.start(); cl.start(); pl.start();
        try{cl.join(); pl.join();}
        catch (InterruptedException e) {System.exit(1);}
    }
}
final class Producer extends TDThread {
    private selectableEntry deposit;
    private int num;
    Producer (selectableEntry deposit, int num) {
        this.deposit = deposit;this.num = num;}
    public void run () {
        System.out.println ("Producer Running");
        for (int i = 0; i < 3; i++) {
            try {
                System.out.println ("Producer calling deposit.");
                deposit.call(new Integer(i));
            }
            catch(InterruptedException e) {}
            System.out.println ("Producer # " + num + "deposited " + i);
        }
    }
}
final class Consumer extends TDThread {
    private selectableEntry withdraw;
    private int num;
    Consumer (selectableEntry withdraw, int num) {
        this.withdraw = withdraw; this.num = num;}
    public void run () {
        Object value = null;
        System.out.println ("Consumer running");
        for (int i = 0; i < 3; i++) {
            try {
                System.out.println ("Consumer calling withdraw.");
                value = withdraw.call();
            }
            catch (InterruptedException e) {}
            System.out.println ("Consumer # " + num + "withdrew " +
```

Listing 5.20 Bounded buffer using *entries* and a *selectiveWait*.

```
                    ((Integer)value).intValue()); // + value);
            }
        }
    }
final class boundedBuffer extends TDThread {
    private selectableEntry deposit, withdraw;
    private int fullSlots=0; private int capacity = 0;
    private Object[] buffer = null; private int in = 0, out = 0;
    public boundedBuffer(selectableEntry deposit, selectableEntry withdraw,
            int capacity) {
        this.deposit = deposit; this.withdraw = withdraw;
        this.capacity = capacity;
        buffer = new Object[capacity];
    }
    public void run() {
        System.out.println ("Buffer running");
        try {
            selectiveWait select = new selectiveWait();
            select.add(deposit);            // alternative 1
            select.add(withdraw);           // alternative 2
            while(true) {
                withdraw.guard(fullSlots>0);
                deposit.guard (fullSlots<capacity);
                int choice = select.choose();
                switch (choice) {
                    case 1:    Object o = deposit.accept();
                               buffer[in] = o;
                               deposit.reply();
                               in = (in + 1) % capacity;
                               ++fullSlots;
                               break;
                    case 2:    withdraw.accept();
                               Object value = buffer[out];
                               withdraw.reply(value);
                               out = (out + 1) % capacity;
                               --fullSlots;
                               break;
                }
            }
        } catch (InterruptedException e) {}
          catch (SelectException e) {
            System.out.println("deadlock detected");System.exit(1);
          }
    }
}
```

Listing 5.20 (*continued*)

file is part of the synchronization library. Directions for customizing the driver process are in the file. The feasibility of an SR-sequence is determined in TEST mode: set MODE TEST. If the mode is not specified, the default value for the MODE variable will turn tracing, replay, and testing off. The default value for the STRATEGY variable is OBJECT and the default value for the CONTROLLERS variable is SINGLE.

FURTHER READING

The *entry* and *selectiveWait* classes were developed by Magee and Kramer [1999]. More message-passing classes may be found in Hartley's book [Hartley 1998]. Entries, rendezvous, and selective wait statements are part of the Ada language [*Ada Language Reference Manual* 1983]. The testing and debugging techniques presented in Section 5.5 were originally developed for concurrent Ada programs [Tai 1985a,b; Tai et al. 1991].

REFERENCES

Ada Language Reference Manual (1983). ANSI/MIL-STD-1815A-1983. New York: American National Standards Institute.

Hartley, Steven J. (1998). *Concurrent Programming: The Java Programming Language*. New York: Oxford University Press.

Magee, Jeff, and Jeff Kramer (1999). *Concurrency: State Models and Java Programs*. New York: Wiley.

Tai, K. C. (1985a). Reproducible testing of concurrent Ada programs. *Proc. Softfair II*, pp. 114–120.

Tai, K. C. (1985b). On testing concurrent programs. *Proc. COMPSAC'85*, pp. 310–317.

Tai, K. C., R. H. Carver, and E. Obaid (1991). Debugging concurrent Ada programs by deterministic execution. *IEEE Transactions on Software Engineering*, Vol. 17, No. 1 (January), pp. 45–63.

Taylor, R. N., D. L. Levine, and C. D. Kelly (1992). Structural testing of concurrent programs. *IEEE Transactions on Software Engineering*, Vol. 18, No. 3 (March), pp. 206–215.

EXERCISES

5.1. In Exercise 4.14 we asked you to write a monitor implementation of a Win32 Event object. *Event* objects have operations *block()* and *set()*. A call to *block* always blocks the caller. A call to *set()* awakens every thread that has called *block()* since the last time *set()* was called. Here you are asked to write implementations of operations *block()* and *set()* using *selectablePorts* and a selective wait statement. Declare and initialize any variables that you use.

5.2. In Exercise 3.11 you were asked to write a semaphore implementation of operation *waitB()* in class *Barrier*. Here you are asked to write an implementation using *send()* and *receive()* operations and a selective wait statement. Threads call B.*waitB()* to wait at *Barrier* B:

```
class Barrier extends Thread {
    public Barrier(int n) {this.n = n;}
    public void waitB() {arrive.send(); block.send(); }
    public void run() { /* receive calls to ports arrive and block */ }
    private selectablePort arrive = new selectablePort();
    private selectablePort block = new selectablePort();
}
```

Inside method *waitB()*, a call to *arrive.send()* signals a thread's arrival at the barrier. The call to *block.send()* blocks the threads until all *n* threads have arrived at the barrier. Assume that the message queues for ports are FCFS. Implement method *run()* using a selective wait statement.

5.3. In Exercise 4.8 you were asked to write a monitor implementation of the unisex bathroom problem. Here you are asked to write an implementation using *send()* and *receive()* operations on *selectablePorts*.

(a) Implement the strategy in Exercise 4.8, part (a).

(b) Implement the strategy in Exercise 4.8, part (b).

Your implementation should complete the *run()* method below. Provide expressions for the guards, and implement the body for each of the four cases. Remember that a call to *E.count()* returns the number of messages that are waiting to be received for port *E*.

```
public void run() {
    try {
        selectiveWait select = new selectiveWait();
        select.add(menEnter);            // alternative 1
        select.add(menExit);             // alternative 2
        select.add(womenEnter);          // alternative 3
        select.add(womenExit);           // alternative 4
        while(true) {
            menEnter.guard(/* TBD */);
            menExit.guard(/* TBD */);
            womenEnter.guard(/* TBD */);
            womenExit.guard(/* TBD */);
            int choice = select.choose();
            switch (choice) {
                case 1:    menEnter.receive(); /* ...; TBD; ...; */ break;
                case 2:    menExit.receive(); /* ...; TBD; ...;*/ break;
                case 3:    womenEnter.receive(); /* ...; TBD; ...; */ break;
```

```
                    case 4:    womenExit.receive(); /* ...; TBD; ...; */ break;
                }
            }
        } catch (InterruptedException e) { }
    }
```

5.4. *The bear and the honeybees* (see Exercise 3.13). Solve this problem using *selectablePorts* and a selective wait statement. The bear calls port *eat* to eat the honey. The bees call port *fillPot*. Your implementation should complete the *run()* method below. Provide expressions for the guards, and implement the body for both cases.

```
    public void run() {
        try {
            selectiveWait select = new selectiveWait();
            select.add(eat);        // alternative 1
            select.add(fillPot);    // alternative 2
            while(true) {
                eat.guard(/* TBD */);
                fillPot.guard(/* TBD */);
                int choice = select.choose();
                switch (choice) {
                    case 1:  eat.receive(); /* ...; TBD; ...; */ break;
                    case 2:  fillPot.receive(); /* ...; TBD; ...;*/ break;
                }
            }
        } catch (InterruptedException e) { }
    }
```

5.5. This exercise compares `if-else` statements and selective wait statements.

(a) Consider the following `if-else` statement:

```
        if (condition) // this can be any condition (e.g., A > 0)
            E1.receive();
        else
            E2.receive();
```

Show how to simulate this `if-else` statement by using a *selectiveWait*. If you cannot write an exact simulation, explain why.

(b) Consider the following `if-else` statement:

```
        if (condition)     // this can be any condition (e.g., A > 0)
            E1.receive();
```

Show how to simulate this `if`-statement by using a *selectiveWait*. If you cannot write an exact simulation, explain why.

5.6. An else alternative of a selective wait is selected if (1) there are no other open alternatives (i.e., no alternatives with a true guard), or (2) at least one open alternative exists, but no messages are waiting for the open alternatives. Assume that the other alternatives are accept alternatives for ports E1, E2, ..., En. Is (2) equivalent to the following condition? If not, try to correct this condition:

(!E1.guard() || E1.Count()==0) && (!E2.guard() || E2.Count()==0) && ...
&& (!En.guard() || En.Count()==0)

5.7. An implementation of readers and writers strategy R>W.1 is given below. Modify this implementation of R>W.1 to implement the following three strategies:

(a) R<W.1: Many readers or one writer, with writers having a higher priority.

(b) R<W.2: Same as R<W.1, except that when a writer requests to write, if no writer is writing or waiting, it waits until all readers that issued earlier requests have finished reading.

(c) R<W.3: Same as R<W.1 except that at the end of writing, waiting readers have a higher priority than waiting writers (see Exercise 4.9).

Strategies R<W.1 and R<W.2 differ as follows. Assume that when writer W1 arrives, reader R1 is reading and another reader, R2, has requested to read but has not started reading. R<W.1 lets W1 start before R2, while R<W.2 lets W1 start after R2. For R<W.1 and R<W.2, readers starve if before a writer finishes writing, the next writer requests to write.

In strategy R<W.3, at the end of a writing, waiting readers have higher priority than waiting writers. Note that waiting readers are readers that have already requested to read and are waiting when the write completes, not readers who request to read after the write completes. This strategy does not create starving readers or writers. A waiting writer does not starve since the number of readers allowed to proceed at the end of each write is finite. A waiting reader does not starve since it will be allowed to proceed before the writers that request to write after this reader.

The R>W.1 implementation contains a *timestamp* that you can use in strategies R<W.2 and R<W.3 to order the requests (i.e., determine whether a request was issued earlier or later than another request).

```
import java.util.*;
final class requestMessage {
    public requestMessage(int ID, boolean isRead) {this.ID = ID;
        this.isRead = isRead;}
    public int ID;                    // ID of reader (0,1,2) or writer (0,1)
```

```
      public boolean isRead;           // true if requesting to read
      int timeStamp;                   // value of clock when request is made
}
public final class readersAndWriters {
   public static void main (String args[]) {
      Controller c = new Controller();
      Reader r0 = new Reader (c,0);        Reader r1 = new Reader (c,1);
      Reader r2 = new Reader (c,2);
      Writer w0 = new Writer (c,0);        Writer w1 = new Writer (c,1);
      c.setDaemon(true); c.start();
      w0.start();     w1.start();     r0.start();     r1.start();     r2.start();
      try{r0.join(); r1.join(); r2.join(); w0.join(); w1.join();}
      catch (InterruptedException e) {System.exit(1);}
   }
}
final class Reader extends Thread {
   private int num;private Controller c;
   Reader (Controller c, int num) { this.c = c;this.num = num;}
   public void run () {
      try {
         // random returns value between 0 and 1 using time of day as seed
         Thread.sleep((long)(Math.random()*1000)); // sleep 0...1 second
      } catch (InterruptedException e) {}
      int value = c.read(num);
   }
}
final classWriter extends Thread {
   private int num; private Controller c;
   Writer (Controller c, int num) {this.c = c; this.num = num; }
   public void run () {
      try {
         // random returns value between 0 and 1 using time of day as seed
         Thread.sleep((long)(Math.random()*1000)); //sleep 0...1 second
      } catch (InterruptedException e) {}
      c.write(num);
   }
}
final class Controller extends Thread {
// Strategy R>W.1 : Many readers or one writer, with readers having a
// higher priority
   final int numReaders = 3; final int numWriters = 2;
   private selectableEntry request = new selectableEntry();
   // reader i calls entry startRead[i]
   private selectableEntry[] startRead = new selectableEntry[numReaders];
   private selectableEntry endRead = new selectableEntry();
```

```
// writer i calls entry startWrite[i]
private selectableEntry[] startWrite = new selectableEntry[numWriters];
private selectableEntry endWrite = new selectableEntry();
private boolean writerPresent = false;
private int readerCount = 0; private int sharedValue = 0;
private ArrayList readersQueue = new ArrayList(); // queue of reader IDs
private ArrayList writersQueue = new ArrayList(); // queue of writer IDs
private int clock = 1;
public Controller() {
for (int i = 0; i<numReaders; i++) startRead[i] = new selectableEntry();
for (int i = 0; i<numWriters; i++) startWrite[i] = new selectableEntry();
}
public int read(int ID) {
    requestMessage req = new requestMessage(ID,true);
    try {request.call(req);} catch(InterruptedException e) {}
    try {startRead[ID].call();} catch(InterruptedException e) {}
    int value = ID;
    System.out.println ("Reader #" + ID + "Read " + value);
    try {endRead.call();} catch(InterruptedException e) {}
    return value;
}
public void write(int ID) {
    requestMessage req = new requestMessage(ID,false);
    try {request.call(req);} catch(InterruptedException e) {}
    try {startWrite[ID].call();} catch(InterruptedException e) {}
    sharedValue = ID;
    System.out.println ("Writer #" + ID + "Wrote " + ID);
    try {endWrite.call();} catch(InterruptedException e) {}
}
publicvoid run() {
    try {
        selectiveWait select = new selectiveWait();
        select.add(request);        // alternative 1
        select.add(startRead[0]);   // alternative 2
        select.add(startRead[1]);   // alternative 3
        select.add(startRead[2]);   // alternative 4
        select.add(endRead);        // alternative 5
        select.add(startWrite[0]);  // alternative 6
        select.add(startWrite[1]);  // alternative 7
        select.add(endWrite);       // alternative 8
        while(true) {
            request.guard(true);
            // startRead if no writers writing and this reader is at head of the
            // readersQueue
            startRead[0].guard(!writerPresent && readersQueue.size() >
```

```
            0 && ((requestMessage)readersQueue.get(0)).ID==0);
        startRead[1].guard(!writerPresent && readersQueue.size() >
            0 && ((requestMessage)readersQueue.get(0)).ID==1);
        startRead[2].guard(!writerPresent && readersQueue.size() >
            0 && ((requestMessage)readersQueue.get(0)).ID==2);
        endRead.guard(true);
        // startWrite if no readers reading or requesting and this
        // writer is at head of the writersQueue
        startWrite[0].guard(!writerPresent && readerCount == 0 &&
            readersQueue.size() == 0
                && writersQueue.size() > 0 && ((requestMessage)
                    writersQueue.get(0)).ID==0);
        startWrite[1].guard(!writerPresent && readerCount == 0 &&
            readersQueue.size() == 0
                && writersQueue.size() > 0 && ((requestMessage)
                    writersQueue.get(0)).ID==1);
        endWrite.guard(true);
        int choice = select.choose();
        switch (choice) {
            case 1:  requestMessage req = (requestMessage)request.
                        acceptAndReply();
                    // Note: timeStamps are not used in R>W.1
                    req.timeStamp = clock++; // save arrival time
                    if (req.isRead ) // true when it's a read request
                        readersQueue.add(req);
                    else writersQueue.add(req);
                    break;
            case 2:  startRead[0].acceptAndReply(); ++readerCount;
                        readersQueue.remove(0); break;
            case 3:  startRead[1].acceptAndReply(); ++readerCount;
                        readersQueue.remove(0); break;
            case 4:  startRead[2].acceptAndReply(); ++readerCount;
                        readersQueue.remove(0); break;
            case 5:  endRead.acceptAndReply(); --readerCount; break;
            case 6:  startWrite[0].acceptAndReply(); writerPresent = true;
                        writersQueue.remove(0); break;
            case 7:  startWrite[1].acceptAndReply(); writerPresent = true;
                        writersQueue.remove(0); break;
            case 8:  endWrite.acceptAndReply(); writerPresent = false;
                        break;
        }
    }
} catch (InterruptedException e) {}
    }
}
```

5.8. In Section 5.5.2 we say that if program CP uses only *links* for communication and no selective wait statements, there is no nondeterminism that needs to be controlled during replay. But the implementation of class *link* uses $P()$ and $V()$ operations on semaphores. Chapter 3 describes a replay method for semaphores. Why is it that the $P()$ and $V()$ operations in the *link* class do not need to be controlled during replay?

6

MESSAGE PASSING IN DISTRIBUTED PROGRAMS

A *distributed program* is a collection of concurrent processes that run on a network of computers. Typically, each process is a multithreaded program that executes on a single computer. A process (or program) on one computer communicates with processes on other computers by passing messages across the network. The threads in a single process all execute on the same computer, so they can use message passing and/or shared variables to communicate.

In this chapter we examine low- and high-level mechanisms for message passing in distributed programs. Since Java provides a class library for network programming, we focus on Java. We also design our own Java message-passing classes and use them to develop distributed solutions to several classical synchronization problems. Entire books have been written about distributed programming, so this chapter is only a small introduction to a large topic. However, we hope to shed some new light on ways to trace, test, and replay distributed programs.

6.1 TCP SOCKETS

The channel objects in Chapter 5 were regular program objects shared by the threads in a single program. In this chapter we are working with a collection of programs that run on different machines. Since a program on one machine cannot directly reference objects in programs on other machines, channels can

Modern Multithreading: Implementing, Testing, and Debugging Multithreaded Java and C++/Pthreads/Win32 Programs, By Richard H. Carver and Kuo-Chung Tai
Copyright © 2006 John Wiley & Sons, Inc.

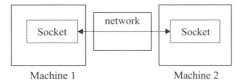

Figure 6.1 Sockets are the endpoints of channels across a network.

no longer be implemented as regular program objects. Instead, channels will be formed across a communications network, with help from the operating system.

When two threads want to exchange messages over a channel, each thread creates an endpoint object that represents its end of the network channel. The operating system manages the hardware and software that is used to transport messages between the endpoints (i.e., "across the channel"). These endpoint objects are called *sockets* (Fig. 6.1):

- The client thread's socket specifies a local I/O port to be used for sending messages (or the I/O port can be chosen by the operating system). The client's socket also specifies the address of the destination machine and the port number that is expected to be bound to the server thread's socket.
- The server's socket specifies a local I/O port for receiving messages. Messages can be received from any client that knows both the server's machine address and the port number bound to the server's socket.
- The client issues a request to the server to form a connection between the two sockets. Once the server accepts the connection request, messages can be passed in either direction across the channel.

6.1.1 Channel Reliability

Messages that travel across a network may be lost or corrupted, or they may arrive out of order. Some applications may be able to tolerate this. For example, if the data being sent across the network represents music, losing a message may create only a slight distortion in the sound. This might sound better to the listener than a pause in the music while lost messages are resent.

An application can choose how reliably its messages are transmitted by selecting a transport protocol:

- Transmission Control Protocol (TCP) ensures the reliable transmission of messages. TCP guarantees that messages are not lost or corrupted and that messages are delivered in the correct order. However, this adds some overhead to message transport.
- User Data Protocol (UDP) is a fast but unreliable method for transporting messages. Messages sent using UDP will not be corrupted, but they may be lost or duplicated, and they may arrive in an order different from the order

in which they were sent. If this is not acceptable, the application must take
care of error handling itself, or use TCP instead.

Both TCP and UDP utilize the Internet Protocol (IP) to carry packets of data.
The IP standard defines the packet format, which includes formats for specifying
source and destination addresses and I/O ports.

6.1.2 TCP Sockets in Java

The java.net class library provides classes *Socket* and *ServerSocket* for TCP-
based message passing.

Class Socket   We will use a simple client and server example to illustrate the
use of TCP sockets in Java. A client's first step is to create a TCP socket and
try to connect to the server:

```
InetAddress host;                          // server's machine address
int serverPort = 2020;                     // port number bound to
                                           // server's socket
Socket socket;                             // client's socket
try {host = InetAddress.getByName("www.cs.gmu.edu"); }
catch (UnknownHostException) { ... }
try {socket = new Socket(host,serverPort); }   // create a socket and
                                           // request a connection to host
catch (IOException e) { ... }
```

The client assumes that the server is listening for TCP connection requests on
port *serverPort*. The *Socket* constructor throws an *IOException* if it cannot make
a connection.

When the client's request is accepted, the client creates an input stream to
receive data from its socket and an output stream to send data to the socket
at the server's end of the channel. To the programmer, sending and receiving
messages using TCP sockets looks just like reading and writing data from files:

```
PrintWriter toServer = new PrintWriter(socket.getOutputStream(),true);
BufferedReader fromServer = new BufferedReader(new inputStreamReader
   (socket.getInputStream()));
toServer.println("Hello");                 // send a message to the
                                           // server
String line = fromServer.readLine();       // receive the server's reply
System.out.println ("Client received: "+ line + " from Server");
toServer.close(); fromServer.close(); socket.close();
```

A read operation on the *InputStream* associated with a *Socket* normally blocks.
It is possible to set a timeout so that a read operation will not block for more

than a specified number of milliseconds. To set a 1-second timeout, call the *setSoTimeout( )* method:

```
socket.setSoTimeout(1000);        // set a 1-second timeout
```

When the timeout expires, a *java.net.SocketTimeoutException* is raised and the *Socket* is still valid.

Class ServerSocket   The server begins by creating a *ServerSocket*:

```
int serverPort = 2020;
ServerSocket listen;
try { listen = new ServerSocket(serverPort); }
catch (IOException e) { ... }
```

The server then calls the *accept( )* method of the *ServerSocket* in order to *listen* for connection requests from clients. Method *accept( )* waits until a client requests a connection; then it returns a *Socket* that connects the client to the server. The server then gets input and output streams from the *Socket* and uses them to communicate with the client. When the interaction ends, the client, server, or both, close the connection, and the server waits for a connection request from another client.

```
try {
    listen = new ServerSocket(serverPort);
    while (true) {
        Socket socket = listen.accept();         // wait for a connection request
                                                  // from a client
        toClient = new PrintWriter(socket.getOutputStream(),true);
        fromClient = new BufferedReader(new InputStreamReader(socket.
            getInputStream()));
        String line = fromClient.readLine();      // receive a message from the client
        System.out.println("Server received "+ line);
        toClient.println("Good-bye");             // send a reply to the client
    }
}
catch (IOException e) { ... }
finally { if (listen != null) try { listen.close();} catch (IOException e)
    { e.printStackTrace(); }}
```

If the client–server interaction is not short, the server can create a separate thread to handle the client's requests. Here we construct a *clientHandler* Thread to handle the socket returned by method *accept( )*:

```
Socket socket = listen.accept();
clientHandler c = new clientHandler(socket); // class clientHandler extends Thread
c.start();
```

The *run()* method of class *clientHandler* uses input and output streams obtained from the *Socket* to communicate with the client, exactly as shown above.

Listing 6.2 shows a client and server program using TCP sockets. *Message* objects are serialized and passed between the client and the server. If the client sends a *Message* containing the integer n, the server replies with a message containing n^2. For example, if the client program is executed using "java Client 2," the client will send the value 2 to the server, receive the value 4 from the server, and display the message "$2 \times 2 = 4$."

```
import java.net.*;
import java.io.*;
public final class Client {
    public static void main (String args[]) {
        int serverPort = 2020; Socket socket = null;
        ObjectOutputStream toServer = null; ObjectInputStream fromServer=null;
        try {
            if (args.length != 1) {
                System.out.println("need 1 argument"); System.exit(1);
            }
            int number = Integer.parseInt(args[0]);
            // client and server run on the same machine, known as the Local Host
            InetAddress serverHost = InetAddress.getLocalHost();
            socket = new Socket(serverHost,serverPort);
            // send a value to the server
            toServer = new ObjectOutputStream(new BufferedOutputStream
                    (socket.getOutputStream()));
            Message msgToSend = new Message(number);
            toServer.writeObject(msgToSend); toServer.flush();
            // This will block until the corresponding ObjectOutputStream in the
            // server has written an object and flushed the header.
            fromServer = new ObjectInputStream(new
            BufferedInputStream(socket.getInputStream()));
            Message msgFromReply = (Message) fromServer.readObject();
            System.out.println (number + "x "+ number + "= "+
                    msgFromReply.number);
        }
        catch (IOException e) { e.printStackTrace(); System.exit(1); }
        catch (ClassNotFoundException e) {e.printStackTrace(); System.exit(1); }
        finally { if (socket != null) try { socket.close();} catch (IOException e) {
            e.printStackTrace(); }}
    }
}
public final class Server {
```

Listing 6.2   Client and server using TCP sockets.

```
public static void main (String args[]) {
    int serverPort = 2020; ServerSocket listen=null;
    ObjectOutputStream toClient; ObjectInputStream fromClient;
    try {
        listen = new ServerSocket(serverPort);
        while (true) {
        Socket socket = listen.accept();
        toClient = new ObjectOutputStream(new BufferedOutputStream
        (socket.getOutputStream()));
        // This will block until the corresponding ObjectOutputStream in the
        // client has written an object and flushed the header.
        fromClient = new ObjectInputStream(new BufferedInputStream
        (socket.getInputStream()));
        Message msgRequest = (Message) fromClient.readObject();
        // compute a reply and send it back to the client
        int number = msgRequest.number;
        toClient.writeObject(new Message(number*number));
        toClient.flush();
        }
    }
    catch (IOException e) {e.printStackTrace(); System.exit(1); }
    catch (ClassNotFoundException e) {e.printStackTrace(); System.exit(1); }
    finally { if (listen != null) try { listen.close();} catch (IOException e) {
        e.printStackTrace(); }}
    }
}
public final class Message implements Serializable {
    public int number;
    Message(int number) {this.number = number; }
}
```

Listing 6.2 *(continued)*

6.2 JAVA TCP CHANNEL CLASSES

We have created three pairs of channel classes for TCP-based communication. These classes provide asynchronous and synchronous message passing and can be used with the selective wait statement presented in Chapter 5. There are many possible ways to design a set of channel classes. Our main objective was to create some easy-to-use classes that hid the complexity of using TCP and enabled us to illustrate how deterministic testing and debugging techniques can be used in a distributed environment. We also tried to be consistent with the channel classes in Chapter 5 so that much of what we covered there would carry over to this chapter. As such, our classes are not built on a client–server paradigm. Instead, they are based on the notion of a mailbox that holds messages deposited by senders and

withdrawn by receivers. Channel classes for client–server interactions are left as
an exercise (Exercise 6.9).

6.2.1   Classes *TCPSender* and *TCPMailbox*

The first pair of channel classes consists of classes *TCPSender* and *TCPMailbox*.
Classes *TCPSender* and *TCPMailbox* provide asynchronous message passing
using a buffer-blocking *send()* method and a blocking *receive()* method, respectively. Listing 6.3 illustrates the use of these classes in a distributed solution
to the bounded-buffer problem. Program *Producer* creates a *TCPSender* object
named *deposit* for sending items to program *Buffer*. Program *Buffer* creates a
TCPMailbox object named *deposit* for receiving items from the *Producer*, and a
TCPSender object named *withdraw* for sending items to the *Consumer*. Program
Buffer acts as a one-slot bounded buffer, receiving items from the *Producer* and
forwarding them to the *Consumer*. Program *Consumer* has a *TCPMailbox* object
named *withdraw* to receive the messages sent by *Buffer*.

```
import java.net.*;
import java.io.*;
public final class Producer {
    public static void main (String args[]) {
        final int bufferPort = 2020; String bufferHost = null;
        try {
            bufferHost = InetAddress.getLocalHost().getHostName();
            TCPSender deposit = new TCPSender(bufferHost,bufferPort);
            deposit.connect();
            for (int i=0; i<3; i++) {
                System.out.println("Producing"+ i);
                messageParts msg = new messageParts(new Message(i));
                deposit.send(msg);
            }
            deposit.close();
        }
        catch (UnknownHostException e) {e.printStackTrace();}
        catch (TCPChannelException e) {e.printStackTrace();}
    }
}
public final class Buffer {
    public static void main (String args[]) {
        final int bufferPort = 2020; final int consumerPort = 2022;
        try {
            String consumerHost = InetAddress.getLocalHost().getHostName();
            TCPMailbox deposit = new TCPMailbox(bufferPort,"deposit");
            TCPSender withdraw = new TCPSender(consumerHost,consumerPort);
```

Listing 6.3   Distributed bounded buffer using *TCPSender* and *TCPMailbox*.

```
                withdraw.connect();
                for (int i=0; i<3; i++) {
                    messageParts m = (messageParts) deposit.receive();
                    withdraw.send(m);
                }
                withdraw.close(); deposit.close();
            }
            catch (UnknownHostException e) {e.printStackTrace();}
            catch (TCPChannelException e) {e.printStackTrace();}
        }
    }
    public final class Consumer {
        public static void main (String args[]) {
            final int consumerPort = 2022;
            try {
                TCPMailbox withdraw = new TCPMailbox(consumerPort,"withdraw");
                for (int i=0; i<3; i++) {
                    messageParts m = (messageParts) withdraw.receive();
                    Message msg = (Message) m.obj;
                    System.out.println("Consumed "+ msg.number);
                }
                withdraw.close();
            }
            catch (TCPChannelException e) {e.printStackTrace();}
        }
    }
    public final class messageParts implements Serializable {
        public Object obj;         // message to be sent
        public String host;        // host address of the sender
        public int port;           // port where sender will wait for a reply, if any
        messageParts(Object obj, String host, int port) {
            this.obj = obj; this.host = host; this.port = port;
        }
        // no return address
        messageParts(Object obj) {this.obj = obj; this.host = ""; this.port = 0;}
    }
```

Listing 6.3   (*continued*)

Method *connect()* must be called before a *TCPSender* can be used to send messages. A call to *connect()* opens a TCP connection using the host and port number specified when the *TCPSender* object is constructed. When there are no more messages to send, method *close()* is called and the TCP connection is closed. Methods *send()* and *receive()* both operate on *messageParts* objects. A *messageParts* object packages the message to be sent with the return address of the sender. (The return address is optional.) The return address information includes the sender's host address and a port number that the sender will use to wait for a reply. A thread that calls *receive( )* receives a *messageParts* object. The return address in this object can be saved and used later to reply to the sender. If no return address is needed, a *messageParts* object can be constructed without a return address.

Listing 6.4 shows classes *TCPSender* and *TCPMailbox*. Class *TCPSender* provides method *send( )*, which simply encapsulates the code for sending messages using TCP. A *TCPSender* object is used to send messages to a particular *TCPMailbox*. The host address and port number of the destination *TCPMailbox* are specified when the *TCPSender* object is constructed. Method *connect( )* is used to connect the *TCPSender* to the *TCPMailbox*. Once the connection is made, each call to *send( )* uses the same connection. The connection is closed with a call to method *close( )*.

A single *TCPMailbox* object may receive connection requests from any number of *TCPSenders*. A *TCPMailbox* objects begins listening for connection requests when the *TCPMailbox* object is constructed. If multiple *TCPSenders* connect to the same *TCPMailbox*, the connections are handled concurrently. When method *close( )* is called on a *TCPMailbox* object, it stops listening for new connection requests. (This is not to be confused with a call to method *close( )* on a *TCPSender* object, which closes the *TCPSender* object's connection with its *TCPMailbox*.)

Method *receive( )* of class *TCPMailbox* returns a *messageParts* object. The *messageParts* object returned by *receive( )* is withdrawn from a *messageBuffer* called *buffer*. A *messageBuffer* is simply a bounded buffer of *messagePart* objects implemented as an SU monitor (see Listing 6.4). The interesting thing about *TCPMailbox* is the way in which *messagePart* objects are deposited into *buffer*. A *TCPMailbox* object is an *active object*—during construction it automatically starts an internal thread to receive messages:

```
public class TCPMailbox implements Runnable {
  ...
  public TCPMailbox( int port, String channelName ) throws
    TCPChannelException {
    this.port = port;
    this.channelName = channelName;
    try {listen = new ServerSocket( port ); }
    catch (IOException e) { e.printStackTrace(); throw new
      TCPChannelException(e.getMessage());}
    buffer = new messageBuffer(100);
    Thread internal = new Thread(this);
    internal.start(); // internal thread executes method run()
  }
  ...
}
```

```java
import java.net.*;
import java.io.*;
import java.util.*;
public class TCPSender {
    String destinationHostname = null;    // destination host of this channel
    int destinationPort;                  // destination port of this channel
    Socket socket = null;
    ObjectOutputStream to = null;
    Object lock = new Object();
    public TCPSender(String destinationHostname, int destinationPort ) {
        this.destinationHostname = destinationHostname;
        this.destinationPort = destinationPort;
    }
    public void connect() throws TCPChannelException {
        try {
            socket = new Socket( destinationHostname, destinationPort );
            to = new ObjectOutputStream(socket.getOutputStream());
        } catch (Exception e) { e.printStackTrace(); throw new
            TCPChannelException(e.getMessage());}
    }

    public void send( messageParts message) throws TCPChannelException{
        try {synchronized (lock) {to.writeObject(message); to.flush();}}
        catch (NullPointerException e) {
            e.printStackTrace();
            throw new TCPChannelException
                    ("null stream - call connect() before sending messages");
        }
        catch (Exception e) { e.printStackTrace(); throw new
            TCPChannelException (e.getMessage());}
    }
    public void send( ) throws TCPChannelException{
        send(new messageParts(new nullObject())); }
    public void close() throws TCPChannelException {
        try {
            if (to != null) to.close(); if (socket != null) socket.close();
        } catch (Exception e) { e.printStackTrace(); throw new
            TCPChannelException(e.getMessage());}
    }
}
public class TCPMailbox implements Runnable {
    private ServerSocket listen = null;
    private messageBuffer buffer = null;
    Socket socket = null;
    int port;
```

Listing 6.4   Classes *TCPSender* and *TCPMailbox*.

```
String channelName = "";
ObjectInputStream from = null;
private boolean closed = false;
Object lock = new Object();
public TCPMailbox( int port) throws TCPChannelException {this(port,"");}
public TCPMailbox( int port, String channelName ) throws
        TCPChannelException {
    this.port = port;
    this.channelName = channelName;
    try {listen = new ServerSocket( port ); }
    catch (IOException e) { e.printStackTrace(); throw new
        TCPChannelException(e.getMessage());}
    buffer = new messageBuffer(100);
    Thread internal = new Thread(this);
    internal.start();   // internal thread executes method run()
}
public messageParts receive( ) throws TCPChannelException {
    try {
        synchronized(lock) {
            messageParts msg = buffer.withdraw();
            return msg;
        } // end synchronized lock
    } catch (Exception e) {e.printStackTrace(); throw new
        TCPChannelException(e.getMessage());}
}
public synchronized void close() throws TCPChannelException {
    try {if (listen != null) {closed = true;listen.close();}}
    catch (Exception e) {e.printStackTrace(); throw new
        TCPChannelException(e.getMessage());}
}

public void run() {
    try {
        while (true) {
            // listen for connection requests from senders
            Socket socket = listen.accept();
            (new connectionHandler(socket)).start();
        }
    }
    catch (SocketException e) { if (!closed) e.printStackTrace(); }
    catch (Exception e) {e.printStackTrace();}
    finally {
        try { if (listen != null) listen.close(); }
        catch (IOException e2) { e2.printStackTrace(); }
    }
}
```

Listing 6.4   (*continued*)

```
class connectionHandler extends Thread { //handle client connections
    private ObjectInputStream from;
    private Socket socket;
    connectionHandler(Socket socket) throws IOException {
        this.socket = socket;
        from = new ObjectInputStream(socket.getInputStream());
    }

    public void run() {
        try { // run
            messageParts closeMessage = null;
            while (true) { // read objects until get EOF
                messageParts msg = null;
                try {
                    msg = (messageParts) from.readObject(); // read message
                    buffer.deposit(msg);
                }
                catch (EOFException e) {break; } // end catch
            } // end while true
            // issue passive close (after active close by sender)
            from.close(); socket.close();
        } // end try run
        catch (SocketException e) { if (!closed) e.printStackTrace(); }
        catch (Exception e) {e.printStackTrace();}
        finally {
            try { if (from != null) from.close(); }
            catch (IOException e2) { e2.printStackTrace(); }
            try { if (socket != null) socket.close(); }
            catch (IOException e3) { e3.printStackTrace(); }
        }
    } // run
} // connectionHandler
}

class messageBuffer extends monitor { // SU monitor
    private int fullSlots = 0;            // # of full slots in the buffer
    private int capacity = 0;
    private conditionVariable notFull = new conditionVariable();
    private conditionVariable notEmpty = new conditionVariable();
    private LinkedList buffer;
    public messageBuffer( int capacity ) {
        this.capacity = capacity;
        buffer = new LinkedList();
```

Listing 6.4   (*continued*)

```
    }
    public void deposit( messageParts msg ) {
        enterMonitor();
        if (fullSlots == capacity)
            notFull.waitC();
        buffer.addLast(msg);
        ++fullSlots;
        notEmpty.signalC_and_exitMonitor();
    }
    public messageParts withdraw() {
        enterMonitor();
        if (fullSlots == 0)
            notEmpty.waitC();
        messageParts msg = (messageParts) buffer.getFirst();
        buffer.removeFirst();
        --fullSlots;
        notFull.signalC_and_exitMonitor();
        return(msg);
    }
}
```

Listing 6.4 (*continued*)

The *run()* method of *TCPMailbox* accepts connection requests from *TCPSender* objects and starts a *connectionHandler* thread to handle the connection:

```
public void run() {
    while (true) {
        Socket socket = listen.accept(); // listen for connection requests from
                                         // senders
        (new connectionHandler(socket)).start();
    }
}
```

The *connectionHandler* thread obtains an input stream from the *socket*:

```
connectionHandler (Socket socket) throws IOException {
    this.socket = socket;
    from = new ObjectInputStream(socket.getInputStream());
}
```

and then uses the input stream to receive *messageParts* objects. The *messagePart* objects are deposited into the *messageBuffer*:

```
while (true) { // read objects until get EOF
    messageParts msg = null;
    try {
        msg = (messageParts) from.readObject();   // receive messageParts object
        buffer.deposit(msg);                       // deposit messageParts object
                                                   // into Buffer

    }
    catch (EOFException e) { break;}
}
```

If *buffer* becomes full, method *deposit()* will block. This will prevent any more *messagePart* objects from being received until a *messagePart* object is withdrawn using method *receive()*.

There are two basic ways to use *TCPSender* and *TCPMailbox* objects. A single *TCPMailbox* object *R* can be used to receive messages from multiple senders. Each sender constructs a *TCPSender* object *S* with *R*'s host and port address, and executes the following operations each time it sends a message to *R*:

S.connect(); S.send(message); S.close();

TCPMailbox object *R* will receive all the messages that the sender sends to it.

This connect–send–close scheme can cause a problem if many messages are sent to the same *TCPMailbox* object. Each execution of connect–send–close requires a new connection to be opened and closed. Operation *connect()* relies on the operating system to choose a local port for each new connection. After the message is sent and the connection is closed, the socket enters a TIME_WAIT state on the sender's machine. This means that a new socket connection with the same port numbers (local and remote) and the same host addresses (local and remote) will be unavailable on the sender's machine for a specified period of time, which is usually 4 minutes.

Without this 4-minute wait, an "old" message that was sent over socket *A* but that failed to arrive before socket *A* was closed, could eventually arrive and be mistaken as a "new" message sent on a different socket *B*, where *B* was constructed after A with the same port number and host address as *A*. The TIME_WAIT state gives time for old messages to wash out of the network.

Of course, the operating system can choose a different local port number for each *connect()* operation, but the number of these "ephemeral" ports is limited and is different for different operating systems. (Each system has its own default number of ephemeral ports, which can usually be increased [Gleason 2001].) Thus, it is possible to exhaust the supply of ephemeral ports if thousands of messages are sent within 4 minutes.

The preferred way to use a *TCPSender* object S is to issue an *S.close()* operation only after all the messages have been sent. Using this scheme, an *S.connect()* operation appears at the beginning of the program and an *S.close()* operation appears at the end (refer back to Listing 6.3). All the messages sent over S will use a single connection, so the number of ephemeral ports is less of an issue. If multiple *TCPSender* objects connect to the same *TCPMailbox*, the *TCPMailbox* will handle the connections concurrently.

6.2.2   Classes *TCPSynchronousSender* and *TCPSynchronousMailbox*

As we mentioned, *TCPSender and TCPMailbox* implement asynchronous channels. Synchronous channels can be created by forcing method *send()* to wait for an acknowledgment that the sent message has been received by the destination thread. The *receive()* method sends an acknowledgment when the message is withdrawn from the *messageBuffer*, indicating that the destination thread has received the message.

Classes *TCPSynchronousSender* and *TCPSynchronousMailbox* incorporate these changes. Methods *connect()*, *send()*, and *receive()* are shown in Listing 6.5, along with a portion of the *connectionHandler* thread. Method *connect()* in *TCPSynchronousSender* connects to the associated *TCPMailbox* and obtains an output stream for sending a message and an input stream for receiving an acknowledgment. Method *send()* sends the message and then waits for an acknowledgment. The message is received by a *connectionHandler* thread in the *TCPMailbox*. The *connectionHandler* deposits the message, along with the *ObjectOutputStream* to be used for sending the acknowledgment, into the message *buffer*. Method *receive()* in *TCPSynchronousMailbox* withdraws a message and its associated *ObjectOutputStream* from *buffer* and uses the *ObjectOutputStream* to send a *nullObject* as an acknowledgment.

```
public void connect() throws TCPChannelException {
// from class TCPSynchronousSender
    try {
        socket = new Socket( destinationHostname, destinationPort );
        to = new ObjectOutputStream(socket.getOutputStream());
        from = new ObjectInputStream(socket.getInputStream());
    } catch (Exception e) { e.printStackTrace(); throw new
        TCPChannelException(e.getMessage());}
}
public void send( messageParts message) throws TCPChannelException {
// from class TCPSynchronousSender
    try {
        synchronized(lock) {
        to.writeObject(message); to.flush();
        nullObject msg = (nullObject) from.readObject();
        }
    }
```

Listing 6.5   Methods *connect()*, *send()*, and *receive()* in classes *TCPSynchronousSender* and *TCPSynchronousMailbox*.

```
        catch (NullPointerException e) {
            e.printStackTrace();
            throw new TCPChannelException
                        ("null stream - call connect() before sending messages");
        }
        catch (Exception e) { e.printStackTrace(); throw new
            TCPChannelException(e.getMessage());}
    }
class connectionHandler extends Thread {
// from class TCPSynchronousMailbox
    ...
    // for receiving message objects from the sender
    from = new ObjectInputStream(socket.getInputStream());
    // for sending acknowledgements to the sender
    to = new ObjectOutputStream(socket.getOutputStream());
    ...
    public void run() {
        ...
        msg = (messageParts) from.readObject(); // read message from sender
        // stream to is used to send acknowledgment back to sender
        msg.to = to;
        buffer.deposit(msg); // msg will be withdrawn in receive() by receiving
        ...             // thread and msg.to will be used to send an acknowledgment
    }
}
public messageParts receive( ) throws TCPChannelException {
// from class TCPSynchronousMailbox
    try {
        synchronized(lock) {
            messageParts msg = buffer.withdraw();
            // stream to is still connected to the sending thread
            ObjectOutputStream to = msg.to;
            // receiver is not given access to the acknowledgment stream
            msg.to = null;
            to.writeObject(new nullObject()); // send null object as ack.
        } // end synchronized lock
    } catch (Exception e) {
        e.printStackTrace();
        throw new TCPChannelException(e.getMessage());
    }
}
```

Listing 6.5   *(continued)*

6.2.3   Class *TCPSelectableSynchronousMailbox*

Our final TCP-based class is *TCPSelectableSynchronousMailbox*. As its name implies, this class enables synchronous TCP mailbox objects to be used in selective wait statements. A *TCPSelectableSynchronousMailbox* object is used just like a *selectableEntry* or *selectablePort* object in Chapter 5. Listing 6.6 shows bounded buffer program *Buffer*, which uses a *selectiveWait* object and *TCPSelectableSynchronousMailbox* objects *deposit* and *withdraw*. Distributed *Producer* and *Consumer* processes can use *TCPSynchronousSender* objects in the usual way to send messages to *Buffer*. Recall that a *messageParts* object contains an optional return address, which the *Buffer* uses to send a withdrawn item back to the *Consumer*.

Notice that *Buffer* selects *deposit* and *withdraw* alternatives in an infinite loop. One way to terminate this loop is to add a *delay* alternative to the selective wait, which would give *Buffer* a chance to timeout and terminate after a period of inactivity. In general, detecting the point at which a distributed computation has terminated is not trivial since no process has complete knowledge of the global state of the computation, and neither global time nor common memory exists in a distributed system. Alternatives to global time are described in the next section. Distributed algorithms for termination detection are presented in [Brzezinski et al.

```
public final class Buffer {
   public static void main (String args[]) {
        final int depositPort = 2020;
        final int withdrawPort = 2021;
        final int withdrawReplyPort = 2022;
        int fullSlots=0;
        int capacity = 2;
        Object[] buffer = new Object[capacity];
        int in = 0, out = 0;
        try {
            TCPSelectableSynchronousMailbox deposit = new
               TCPSelectableSynchronousMailbox(depositPort);
            TCPSelectableSynchronousMailbox withdraw = new
            TCPSelectableSynchronousMailbox (withdrawPort);
            String consumerHost = InetAddress.getLocalHost().getHostName();
            TCPSender withdrawReply = new
            TCPSender(consumerHost,withdrawReplyPort);
            selectiveWait select = new selectiveWait();
            select.add(deposit);           // alternative 1
            select.add(withdraw);          // alternative 2
            while(true) {
                withdraw.guard(fullSlots>0);
```

Listing 6.6   Using a *selectiveWait* statement in a distributed program.

```
            deposit.guard (fullSlots<capacity);
            switch (select.choose()) {
                case 1:    Object o = deposit.receive(); // item from Producer
                           buffer[in] = o;
                           in = (in + 1) %capacity; ++fullSlots;
                           break;
                case 2:    messageParts withdrawRequest = withdraw.receive();
                           messageParts m = (messageParts) buffer[out];
                           try {// send an item back to the Consumer
                               withdrawReply.send(m);
                           } catch (TCPChannelException e)
                               {e.printStackTrace();}
                           out = (out + 1) %capacity; --fullSlots;
                           break;
                }
            }
        }
        catch (InterruptedException e) {e.printStackTrace();System.exit(1);}
        catch (TCPChannelException e) {e.printStackTrace();System.exit(1);}
        catch (UnknownHostException e) {e.printStackTrace();}
    }
}
```

Listing 6.6   (*continued*)

1993]. These algorithms could be incorporated into the channel classes presented in this chapter and in Chapter 5, along with a "terminate" alternative for selective wits that would be chosen when termination is detected.

6.3   TIMESTAMPS AND EVENT ORDERING

In a distributed environment, it is difficult to determine the execution order of events. This problem occurs in many contexts. For example, distributed processes that need access to a shared resource must send each other requests to obtain exclusive access to the resource. Processes can access the shared resource in the order of their requests, but the request order is not easy to determine. This is the *distributed mutual exclusion problem.*

Event ordering is also a critical problem during testing and debugging. When synchronization events occur during an execution, trace messages can be sent to a special controller process so that the events can be recorded for replay. But care must be taken to ensure that the event order observed by the controller process is consistent with the event order that actually occurred. Similarly, reachability testing depends on accurate event ordering to identify concurrent events and generate race variants. Since event ordering is a prerequisite for solving many distributed programming problems, we'll look first at mechanisms for ordering events and then we examine several distributed solutions to classical synchronization problems.

6.3.1 Event-Ordering Problems

Fidge [1996] pointed out several problems that can occur when the controller relies on the arrival order of trace messages to order events. A convenient way to visualize these problems is to view an execution of a distributed program as a space-time diagram. In a space-time diagram, each thread is represented as a directed line, with time moving from top to bottom. The events of a thread are shown along its time line according to their order of occurrence, with earlier events at the top and later events at the bottom. Message passing is depicted by an arrow connecting send events with their corresponding receive events. An asynchronous message that is passed from send event s to receive event r is represented using a single-headed arrow $s \rightarrow r$. A double-headed arrow $s \leftrightarrow r$ represents synchronous message passing between s and r.

Consider the following program, which uses asynchronous communication:

Thread1	Thread2	Thread3
(a) send A to Thread2;	(b) receive X;	(d) send B to Thread2;
	(c) receive Y;	

The possible executions of this program are represented by diagrams D1 and D2 in Fig. 6.7. In diagram D1, the messages are $a \rightarrow b$ and $d \rightarrow c$, whereas in D2, the messages are $a \rightarrow c$ and $d \rightarrow b$.

Assume that the threads in diagram D1 send asynchronous trace messages to the controller whenever they execute a message passing event. Figure 6.8 illustrates two *observability problems* that can occur when the controller relies on the arrival order of the trace messages to determine the order of events:

- *Incorrect orderings.* The controller observes event b occur before event a, which is not what happened.

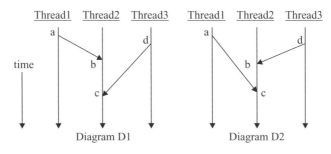

Figure 6.7 Diagrams D1 and D2.

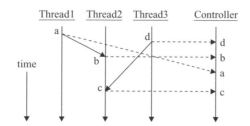

Figure 6.8   Observability Problems for Diagram D1

TABLE 6.1   Effectiveness of Timestamping Mechanisms

Observability Problems	Arrival Order	Local Real-Time Clocks	Global Real-Time Clock	Totally Ordered Logical Clocks	Partially Ordered Logical Clocks
			Timestamp Mechanisms		
Incorrect orderings	×	×			
Arbitrary orderings	×	×	×	×	

Source: Fidge [1996].
[a] An × indicates that a problem exists.

- *Arbitrary orderings.* The controller observes event *d* occur before event *b*. Since *d* and *b* are concurrent events they can occur in either order, and the order the controller will observe is nondeterministic. However, the controller cannot distinguish nondeterministic orderings from orderings that are enforced by the program. During debugging, a programmer may see that *d* precedes *b* and mistakenly conclude that *d must* precede *b*. Similarly, the programmer may feel the need to create a test case where the order of events *d* and *b* is reversed, even though this change in ordering is not significant.

To overcome these observability problems, extra information, in the form of a timestamp, must be attached to the trace messages. The controller can use the timestamps to order events accurately. Table 6.1 shows five timestamp mechanisms (including arrival order) and their ability to overcome observability problems. An × indicates that a timestamp mechanism has a particular observability problem.

Four of these timestamping mechanisms involve the use of clock values. The first two clock schemes use real-time clocks.

6.3.2   Local Real-Time Clocks

This simple scheme uses the real-time clock available on each processor as the source of the timestamp. Since the real-time clocks on different processors are

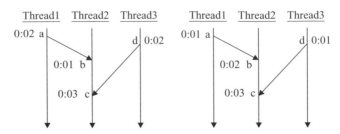

Figure 6.9   Timestamps using unsynchronized local real-time clocks.

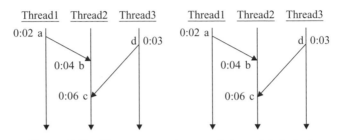

Figure 6.10   Timestamps using a real-time global clock.

not synchronized, incorrect orderings may be seen, and concurrent events are arbitrarily ordered. Figure 6.9 shows two ways in which the events in diagram D1 of Fig. 6.7 can be timestamped. On the left, the clock of Thread1's processor is ahead of the clock of Thread2's processor, so event b appears erroneously to occur before event a. The ordering of events d and b is arbitrary and depends on the relative speeds of the threads and the amount by which the processor's real-time clocks differ.

6.3.3   Global Real-Time Clocks

If the local real-time clocks are synchronized, there is a global reference for real time. This avoids incorrect orderings, but as shown in Fig. 6.10, arbitrary orderings are still imposed on concurrent events d and b. Also, sufficiently accurate clock synchronization is difficult and sometimes impossible to achieve.

6.3.4   Causality

The remaining two schemes use logical clocks instead of real-time clocks. Logical clock schemes rely on the semantics of program operations to determine whether one event occurred before another event. For example, if events A and B are local events in the same thread and A is executed before B, then A's logical timestamp will indicate that A happened before B. Similarly, if S is an asynchronous send event in one thread and R is the corresponding receive event in another thread,

S's logical timestamp will indicate that S occurred before R. (More accurately, S occurred before the *completion* of R, since the send operation S might have occurred long after the receive operation R started waiting for a message to arrive.) It is the execution of program operations that governs the passage of logical time, not the ticking of a real-time clock.

If we consider a *send* operation and its corresponding *receive* operation to have a cause-and-effect relationship, ordering the *send* before the *receive* places the cause before the effect. It is important that any event ordering is consistent with the cause-and-effect relationships between the events. Thus, if event C can potentially cause or influence another event E, we will say that C occurs before E in causal order.

The causality or *happened-before relation* "$\Rightarrow$" for an execution of a message-passing program is defined as follows [Lamport 1978]:

(C1) If events e and f are events in the same thread and e occurs before f, then $e \Rightarrow f$.

(C2) If there is a message $e \rightarrow f$ (i.e., e is a nonblocking send and f is the corresponding receive), then $e \Rightarrow f$.

(C3) If there is a message $e \leftrightarrow f$ or $f \leftrightarrow e$ (i.e., one of e or f is a blocking send and the other is the corresponding blocking receive), for event g such that $e \Rightarrow g$, we have $f \Rightarrow g$, and for event h such that $h \Rightarrow f$, we have $h \Rightarrow e$.

(C4) If $e \Rightarrow f$ and $f \Rightarrow g$, then $e \Rightarrow g$. (Thus, "$\Rightarrow$" is transitive.)

It is easy to examine a space-time diagram visually and determine the causal relations. For two events e and f in a space-time diagram, $e \Rightarrow f$ if and only if there is no message $e \leftrightarrow f$ or $f \leftrightarrow e$ and there exists a path from e to f that follows the vertical lines and arrows in the diagram. (A double-headed arrow allows a path to cross in either direction.)

For events e and f of an execution, if neither $e \Rightarrow f$ nor $f \Rightarrow e$, then e and f are said to be *concurrent*, denoted as $e||f$. This also means that if there is a message $e \leftrightarrow f$ or $f \leftrightarrow e$, then e and f are concurrent events. Since $e||f$ and $f||e$ are equivalent, the "$||$" relation is symmetric. However, the "$||$" relation is not transitive. In diagram D1, $a \rightarrow b$, $b \rightarrow c$, $d \rightarrow c$, $a \rightarrow c$, $a||d$, and $d||b$, but a and b are not concurrent events. In diagram D2, $a \rightarrow c$, $b \rightarrow c$, $d \rightarrow c$, $d \rightarrow c$, $b||a$, and $a||d$, but b and d are not concurrent events.

Since two concurrent events are not ordered (i.e., they can happen in either order), the causality relation only partially orders the events in an execution trace, but a partial order is still useful: Given a program, an input, and a partially ordered execution trace of synchronization events that is based on the causality relationship, there is only one possible result. Thus, a partially ordered trace of synchronization events that is based on the causality relation is sufficient for tracing and replaying an execution. SYN-sequence definitions for distributed programs are given in Section 6.5.

We will consider two or more executions that have the same input and the same partially ordered synchronization sequence to be equivalent executions. Furthermore, the relative order of events in an execution will be determined using a partial order, not a total order, of the execution's events. By doing so, if we say that event a happens before event b during an execution E with a given input, a happens before b in all other executions that have the same input and the same partially ordered synchronization sequence as E.

6.3.5 Integer Timestamps

Our objective is to determine the causality relationships of the events in an execution. We will do this by using logical clocks. Logical clocks serve as a substitute for real-time clocks with respect to the causality relation. Each event receives a logical timestamp, and these timestamps are used to order the events. Consider a message-passing program that uses asynchronous communication and contains threads $Thread_1$, $Thread_2$, ..., and $Thread_n$. $Thread_i$, $1 \leq i \leq n$, contains a logical clock C_i, which is simply an integer variable initialized to 0. During execution, logical time flows as follows:

(IT1) $Thread_i$ increments C_i by one immediately before each event it executes.

(IT2) When $Thread_i$ sends a message, it also sends the value of C_i as the timestamp for the send event.

(IT3) When $Thread_i$ receives a message with ts as its timestamp, if $ts \geq C_i$, then $Thread_i$ sets C_i to $ts + 1$ and assigns $ts + 1$ as the timestamp for the receive event. Hence, $C_i = max(C_i, ts + 1)$.

Denote the integer timestamp recorded for event e as IT(e), and let s and t be two events of an execution. If $s \Rightarrow t$, then IT(s) will definitely be less than IT(t). That is, the integer timestamps will never indicate that an event occurred before any other events that might have caused it. However, the converse is not true. The fact that IT(s) is less than IT(t) does not imply that $s \Rightarrow t$. If s and t are concurrent, their timestamps will be consistent with one of their two possible causal orderings. Thus, we cannot determine whether or not $s \Rightarrow t$ by using the integer timestamps recorded for s and t.

Diagram D3 in Fig. 6.11 represents an execution of three threads that use asynchronous communication. The messages in this diagram are $a \rightarrow o$, $c \rightarrow r$, $q \rightarrow x$, $w \rightarrow p$, and $z \rightarrow d$. Diagram D3 also shows the integer timestamp for each event. Notice that the integer timestamp for event v is less than the integer timestamp for event b, but $v \Rightarrow b$ does not hold. (There is no path from v to b in diagram D3.)

Although integer timestamps cannot tell us the causality relationships that hold between the events, we can use integer timestamps to produce one or more total orders that preserve the causal order. For example, in Section 6.4.1 we show how to use integer timestamps to order the requests made when distributed processes want to enter their critical sections. The strategy for producing a total

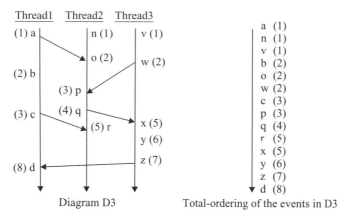

Figure 6.11   Diagram D3 and a total-ordering for D3.

ordering is the following: Order the events in ascending order of their integer timestamps. For the events that have the same integer timestamp, break the tie in some consistent way.

One method for tie breaking is to order events with the same integer timestamps in increasing order of their thread identifiers. The total ordering that results from applying this method to the events in diagram D3 is also shown in Fig. 6.11. Referring back to Table 6.1, integer timestamps solve only one of the observability problems, since incorrect orderings are avoided but independent events are ordered arbitrarily. Thus, integer timestamps have the same advantages as global real-time clocks, while being easier to implement.

6.3.6   Vector Timestamps

Integer timestamps produce a total ordering of events that is consistent with the causality relationship. Because of this, integer timestamps can be used to order events in distributed algorithms that require an ordering. However, integer timestamps cannot be used to determine that two events are *not* causally related. To do this, each thread must maintain a vector of logical clock values instead of a single logical clock. A vector timestamp consists of n clock values, where n is the number of threads involved in an execution.

Consider a message-passing program that uses asynchronous and/or synchronous communication and contains $Thread_1$, $Thread_2$, ..., and $Thread_n$. Each thread maintains a vector clock, which is a vector of integer clock values. The vector clock for $Thread_i$, $1 \leq i \leq n$, is denoted as VC_i, where $VC_i[j]$, $1 \leq j \leq n$, refers to the jth element of vector clock VC_i. The value $VC_i[i]$ is similar to the logical clock C_i used for computing integer timestamps. The value $VC_i[j]$, where $j \neq i$, denotes the best estimate $Thread_i$ is able to make about $Thread_j$'s current logical clock value $VCj[j]$, that is, the number of events in $Thread_j$ that $Thread_i$ "knows about" through direct communication with $Thread_j$

or through communication with other threads that have communicated with
Thread$_j$ and Thread$_i$.

Mattern [1989] described how to assign vector timestamps for events involving asynchronous communication (i.e., nonblocking sends and blocking receives). Fidge [1991] described how to assign timestamps for events involving asynchronous or synchronous communication or a mix of both. At the beginning of an execution, VC$_i$, $1 \leq i \leq n$, is initialized to a vector of zeros. During execution, vector time is maintained as follows:

(VT1) Thread$_i$ increments VC$_i$[i] by one before each event of Thread$_i$.

(VT2) When Thread$_i$ executes a nonblocking send, it sends the value of its vector clock VC$_i$ as the timestamp for the send operation.

(VT3) When Thread$_i$ receives a message with timestamp VT$_m$ from a non-blocking send of another thread, Thread$_i$ sets VC$_i$ to the maximum of VC$_i$ and VT$_m$ and assigns VC$_i$ as the timestamp for the receive event. Hence, VC$_i$ = max (VC$_i$, VT$_m$), that is, for (k = 1; k <= n; k++) VC$_i$[k] = max(VC$_i$[k], VT$_m$[k]).

(VT4) When one of Thread$_i$ or Thread$_j$ executes a blocking send that is received by the other, Thread$_i$ and Thread$_j$ exchange their vector clock values, set their vector clocks to the maximum of the two vector clock values, and assign their new vector clocks (which now have the same value) as the timestamps for the send and receive events. Hence, Thread$_i$ performs the following operations:

- Thread$_i$ sends VC$_i$ to Thread$_j$ and receives VC$_j$ from Thread$_j$.
- Thread$_i$ sets VC$_i$ = max (VC$_i$, VC$_j$).
- Thread$_i$ assigns VC$_i$ as the timestamp for the send or receive event that Thread$_i$ performed.

Thread$_j$ performs similar operations.

Diagram D4 in Fig. 6.12 shows two asynchronous messages $a \rightarrow d$ and $b \rightarrow c$ from Thread 1 to Thread 2. These two messages are not received in the order they are sent. The vector timestamps for the events in D4 are also shown. Diagram D5 in Fig. 6.13 is the same as diagram D3 in Fig. 6.11, except that the vector timestamps for the events are shown.

Denote the vector timestamp recorded for event e as VT(e). For a given execution, let e$_i$ be an event in Thread$_i$ and e$_j$ an event in (possibly the same thread)

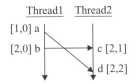

Figure 6.12   Diagram D4.

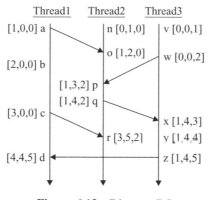

Figure 6.13   Diagram D5.

Thread$_j$. Threads are permitted to use asynchronous or synchronous communication, or a mix of both. As mentioned earlier, $e_i \Rightarrow e_j$ if and only if there exists a path from e_i to e_j in the space-time diagram of the execution and there is no message $e_i \leftrightarrow e_j$ or $e_j \leftrightarrow e_i$. Thus:

(HB1) $e_i \Rightarrow e_j$ if and only if (for $1 \le k \le n$, $VT(e_i)[k] \le VT(e_j)[k]$) and

(VT(e_i) $\ne$ VT(e_j)).

Note that if there is a message $e_i \leftrightarrow e_j$ or $e_j \leftrightarrow e_i$, then $VT(e_i) = VT(e_j)$ and (HB1) cannot be true.

Actually, we only need to compare two pairs of values, as the following rule shows:

(HB2) $e_i \Rightarrow e_j$ if and only if ($VT(e_i)[i] \le VT(e_j)[i]$) and

($VT(e_i)[j] < VT(e_j)[j]$).

If there is a message $e_i \leftrightarrow e_j$ or $e_j \leftrightarrow e_i$, then $e_i \Rightarrow e_j$ is not true and ($VT(e_i)[j] < VT(e_j)[j]$) cannot be true (since the timestamps of e_i and e_j will be the same). This is also true if e_i and e_j are the same event. In Fig. 6.13, events v and p are in Thread3 and Thread2, respectively, where $VT(v) = [0, 0, 1]$ and $VT(p) = [1, 3, 2]$. Since ($VT(v)[3] \le VT(p)[3]$) and ($VT(v)[2] < VT(p)[2]$), we can conclude that $v \Rightarrow p$. For event w in Thread3 we have $VT(w) = [0, 0, 2]$. Since there is a message $w \leftrightarrow p$, the timestamps for w and p are the same, which means that $VT(v)[3] \le VT(w)[3]$ must be true and that $VT(v)[2] < VT(w)[2]$ cannot be true. Hence, $w \Rightarrow p$ is not true, as expected. In general, suppose that the value of $VT(e_i)[j]$ is x and the value of $VT(e_j)[j]$ is y. Then the only way for $VT(e_i)[j] < VT(e_j)[j]$ to be false is if Thread$_i$ knows (through communication with Thread$_j$ or with other threads that have communicated with Thread$_j$) that

$Thread_j$ already performed its xth event, which was either e_j or an event that happened after e_j (as $x \geq y$). In either case, $e_i \Rightarrow e_j$ can't be true (otherwise, we would have $e_i \Rightarrow e_j \Rightarrow e_i$, which is impossible).

If events e_i and e_j are in different threads and only asynchronous communication is used, the rule can be simplified further to

$$\text{(HB3)} \quad e_i \Rightarrow e_j \text{ if and only if } VT(e_i)[i] \leq VT(e_j)[i].$$

Diagram D6 in Fig. 6.14 represents an execution of three threads that use both asynchronous and synchronous communication. The asynchronous messages in this diagram are $a \rightarrow o, q \rightarrow x$, and $z \rightarrow d$. The synchronous messages in this diagram are $c \leftrightarrow r$ and $p \leftrightarrow w$. Diagram D6 shows the vector timestamps for the events.

Referring back to Table 6.1, vector timestamps solve both of the observability problems—incorrect orderings are avoided and independent events are not arbitrarily ordered. A controller process can use vector timestamps to ensure that the SYN-sequence it records is consistent with the causal ordering of events. A recording algorithm that implements causal ordering is as follows [Schwarz and Mattern 1994]:

(R1) The controller maintains a vector *observed*, initialized to all zeros.

(R2) On receiving a trace message m = (e,i) indicating that $Thread_i$ executed event *e* with vector timestamp VT(e), the recording of message *m* is delayed until it becomes recordable.

(R3) Message m = (e,i) is recordable iff (observed[i] = VT(e)[i] − 1) and observed[j] ≥ VT(e)[j] for all j ≠ i.

(R4) If message *m* = (e,i) is or becomes recordable, *m* is recorded and observed[i] = observed[i] + 1;

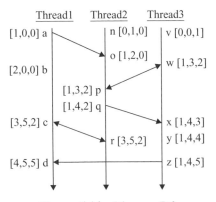

Figure 6.14   Diagram D6.

The vector *observed* counts, for each thread, the number of events that have been observed so far. Step (R3) ensures that all the events that Thread$_i$ executed before it executed e have already been observed, and that any events that other threads executed that could have influenced e (i.e., the first VT(e)[j] events of Thread$_j$, $j \neq i$) have already been observed, too. Other applications of vector timestamps are discussed in [Raynal 1988] and [Baldoni and Raynal 2002].

In previous chapters we did not use vector or integer timestamps during tracing and replay. SYN-events were collected by a control module, but timestamps are not used to order the events. Timestamps are not needed to trace events accurately since (1) we were able to build the tracing mechanism into the implementations of the various synchronization operations, and (2) we used synchronous, shared variable communication to notify the control module that an event had occurred. Thus, the totally ordered or partially ordered SYN-sequences that were recorded in previous chapters were guaranteed to be consistent with the causal ordering of events. It is also the case that vector timestamps can be computed for the events by analyzing the recorded SYN-sequences. (Actually, vector timestamps are generated for the message passing events in Chapter 5, and these timestamps are recorded in special trace files in case they are needed by the user, but the timestamps are not used for tracing and replay.)

6.3.7 Timestamps for Programs Using Messages and Shared Variables

Some programs use both message passing and shared variable communication. In such programs, vector timestamps must be assigned to send and receive events and also to events involving shared variables, such as read and write events or entering a monitor. Netzer and Miller [1993] showed how to generate timestamps for read and write events on shared variables. Bechini and Tai [1998] showed how to combine Fidge's scheme [1991] for send and receive events with Netzer's scheme for read and write events. The testing and debugging tools presented in Section 6.5 incorporate these schemes, so we describe them below.

First, we extend the causality relation by adding a fifth rule. For two read/write events e and f on a shared variable V, let $e \xrightarrow{V} f$ denote that event e occurs before f on V.

(C1–C4) Same as rules C1 to C4 above for send and receive events.

    (C5) For two different events e and f on shared variable V such that at least one of them is a write event, if $e \xrightarrow{V} f$, then $e \Rightarrow f$.

Rule (C5) does not affect the other rules.

Next, we show how to assign vector timestamps to read and write events using the rules of [Netzer and Miller 1993]. Timestamps for send and receive events are assigned as described earlier. For each shared variable V, we maintain two vector timestamps:

- *VT_LastWrite(V)*: contains the vector timestamp of the last write event on V, initially all zeros.
- *VT_Current(V)*: the current vector clock of V, initially all zeros.

When Thread$_i$ performs an event e:

> (VT1–VT4) If e is a send or receive event, the same as (VT1–VT4) in Section 6.3.6.
>
> > (VT5) If e is a write operation on shared variable V, Thread$_i$ performs the following operations after performing write operation e:
> >
> > (VT5.1) $VC_i = max(VC_i, VT\_Current(V))$.
> >
> > (VT5.2) $VT\_LastWrite(V) = VC_i$.
> >
> > (VT5.3) $VT\_Current(V) = VC_i$.
> >
> > (VT6) If e is a read operation on shared variable V, Thread$_i$ performs the following operations after performing read operation e:
> >
> > (VT6.1) $VC_i = max(VC_i, VT\_LastWrite(V))$.
> >
> > (VT6.2) $VT\_Current(V) = max(VC_i, VT\_Current(V))$.

For write event e in rule (VT5), VC_i is set to $max(VC_i, VT\_Current(V))$. For read event e in rule (VT6), VC_i is set to $max(VC_i, VT\_LastWrite(V))$. The reason for the difference is the following. A write event on V causally precedes all the read and write events on V that follow it. A read event on V is concurrent with other read events on V that happen after the most recent write event on V and happen before the next write event, provided that there are no causal relations between these read events due to messages or accesses to other shared variables. Figure 6.15 shows the vector timestamps for an execution involving synchronous and asynchronous message passing and read and write operations on a shared variable V. Values of VT_LastWrite(V) and VT_Current(V) are also shown.

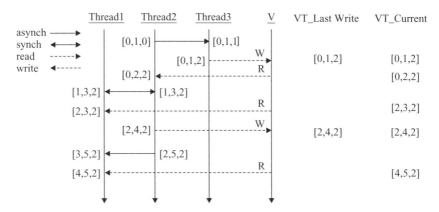

Figure 6.15 Timestamps for a program that uses message passing and shared variables.

6.4   MESSAGE-BASED SOLUTIONS TO DISTRIBUTED PROGRAMMING PROBLEMS

Below, we first show distributed solutions to two classical synchronization problems: the mutual exclusion problem and the readers and writers problem. Both problems involve events that must be totally ordered, such as requests to read or write, or requests to enter a critical section. Requests are ordered using integer timestamps as described in Section 6.3.5. We then show an implementation of the alternating bit protocol (ABP). The ABP is used to ensure the reliable transfer of data over faulty communication lines. Protocols similar to ABP are used by TCP.

6.4.1   Distributed Mutual Exclusion

Assume that two or more distributed processes need mutually exclusive access to some resource (e.g., a network printer). Here we show how to solve the mutual exclusion problem by using message passing. Ricart and Agrawala [1981] developed the following permission-based algorithm. When a process wishes to enter its critical section, it requests and waits for permission from all the other processes. When a process receives a request:

- If the process is not interested in entering its critical section, the process gives its permission by sending a reply as soon as it receives the request.
- If the process does want to enter its critical section, it may defer its reply, depending on the relative order of its request among the requests made by other processes.

Requests are ordered based on a sequence number that is associated with each request and a sequence number maintained locally by each process. Sequence numbers are essentially integer timestamps that are computed using logical clocks as described in Section 6.3. If a process receives a request having a sequence number that is the same as the local sequence number of the process, the tie is resolved in favor of the process with the lowest ID. Since requests can be totally ordered using sequence numbers and IDs, there is always just one process that can enter its critical section next. This assumes that each process will eventually respond to all the requests sent to it.

In program *distributedMutualExclusion* in Listing 6.16, thread *distributedProcess* is started with an ID assigned by the user. We assume that there are three *distributedMutualExclusion* programs running at the same time, so the *numberOfProcesses* is 3 and the IDs of the processes are 0, 1, and 2.

Each *distributedProcess* uses an array of three *TCPSender* objects for sending requests, and another array of three *TCPSender* objects for sending replies. (A process never sends messages to itself, so each process actually uses only two of the *TCPSender* elements in the array.) When a *TCPSender* object is constructed, it is associated with the host address and port number of a *TCPMailbox*

```
import java.io.*;
import java.net.*;
class distributedMutualExclusion {
    public static void main(String[] args) {
        if (args.length != 1) {
            System.out.println("need 1 argument: process ID (IDs start with 0)");
            System.exit(1);
        }
        int ID = Integer.parseInt(args[0]);
        new distributedProcess(ID).start();
    }
}
class distributedProcess extends TDThreadD {
    private int ID;                              // process ID
    private int number;        // the sequence number sent in request messages
    private int replyCount;                      // number of replies received so far
    final private int numberOfProcesses = 4;
    final private int basePort = 2020;
    String processHost = null;
    // requests sent to other processes
    private TCPSender[] sendRequests = new TCPSender[numberOfProcesses];
    private TCPSender[] sendReplies = new TCPSender[numberOfProcesses];
    private TCPMailbox receiveRequests = null;
    private TCPMailbox receiveReplies = null;
    private boolean[] deferred = null; // true means reply was deferred
    private Coordinator C; // monitor C coordinates distributedProcess and helper
    private Helper helper; // manages incoming requests for distributedProcess
    distributedProcess(int ID) {
        this.ID = ID;
        try {processHost = InetAddress.getLocalHost().getHostName(); }
        catch (UnknownHostException e) {e.printStackTrace();System.exit(1);}
        for (int i = 0; i < numberOfProcesses; i++) {
            sendRequests[i] = new TCPSender(processHost,basePort+(2*i));
            sendReplies[i] = new TCPSender(processHost,basePort+(2*i)+1);
        }
        receiveRequests = new TCPMailbox(basePort+(2*ID),"RequestsFor"+ID);
        receiveReplies = new TCPMailbox(basePort+(2*ID)+1,"RepliesFor"+ID);
        C = new Coordinator();
        deferred = new boolean[numberOfProcesses];
        for (int i=0; i<numberOfProcesses; i++) deferred[i] = false;
        helper = new Helper();
        helper.setDaemon(true); // start helper in run() method
    }
    class Helper extends TDThreadD {
    // manages requests from other distributed processes
```

Listing 6.16 Permission-based algorithm for distributed mutual exclusion.

```
public void run() { // handle requests from other distributedProcesses
   while (true) {
      messageParts msg = (messageParts) receiveRequests.receive();
      requestMessage m = (requestMessage) msg.obj;
      if (!(C.deferrMessage(m))) { // if no deferral, then send a reply
         messageParts reply = new messageParts(new Integer(ID),
            processHost,basePort+(2*ID));
         sendReplies[m.ID].send(reply);
      }
   }
}
}
class Coordinator extends monitorSC {
// Synchronizes the distributed process and its helper
   // requestingOrExecuting true if in or trying to enter CS
   private boolean requestingOrExecuting = false;
   private int highNumber; // highest sequence number seen so far
   public boolean deferrMessage(requestMessage m) {
      enterMonitor("decideAboutDeferral");
      highNumber = Math.max(highNumber,m.number);
      boolean deferMessage = requestingOrExecuting &&
         ((number < m.number) ||| (number == m.number && ID < m.ID));
      if (deferMessage)
         deferred[m.ID] = true; // remember that the reply was deferred
      exitMonitor();
      return deferMessage;
   }
   public int chooseNumberAndSetRequesting() {
   // choose sequence number and indicate process has entered or is
   // requesting to enter critical section
      enterMonitor("chooseNumberAndSetRequesting");
      requestingOrExecuting = true;
      number = highNumber + 1; // get the next sequence number
      exitMonitor();
      return number;
   }
   public void resetRequesting() {
      enterMonitor("resetRequesting");
      requestingOrExecuting = false;
      exitMonitor();
   }
}
public void run() {
   int count = 0;
   try {Thread.sleep(2000);} // give other processes time to start
```

Listing 6.16   (*continued*)

```
    catch (InterruptedException e) {e.printStackTrace();System.exit(1);}
    System.out.println("Process "+ ID + "starting");
    helper.start();
    for (int i = 0; i < numberOfProcesses; i++) {
    // connect to the mailboxes of the other processes
        if (i != ID) {
            sendRequests[i].connect(); sendReplies[i].connect();
        }
    }
    while (count++<3) {
        System.out.println(ID + "Before Critical Section"); System.out.flush();
        int number = C.chooseNumberAndSetRequesting();
        sendRequests();
        waitForReplies();
        System.out.println(ID + "Leaving Critical Section-"+count);
        System.out.flush();
        try {Thread.sleep(500);} catch (InterruptedException e) { }
        C.resetRequesting();
        replytoDeferredProcesses();
    }
    try {Thread.sleep(10000);} // let other processes finish
    catch (InterruptedException e) {e.printStackTrace();System.exit(1);}
    for (int i = 0; i < numberOfProcesses; i++)// close connections
        if (i != ID) {sendRequests[i].close(); sendReplies[i].close();}
}
public void sendRequests() {
    replyCount = 0;
    for (int i = 0; i < numberOfProcesses; i++) {
        if (i != ID) {
            messageParts msg = new messageParts(new
                requestMessage(number,ID));
            sendRequests[i].send(msg); // send sequence number and process ID
            System.out.println(ID + "sent request to Thread "+ i);
            try {Thread.sleep(1000);} catch (InterruptedException e) { }
        }
    }
}
public void replytoDeferredProcesses() {
    System.out.println("replying to deferred processes");
    for (int i=0; i < numberOfProcesses; i++)
        if (deferred[i]) {
            deferred[i] = false; // ID sent as a convenience for identifying sender
            messageParts msg = new messageParts(new Integer(ID));
            sendReplies[i].send(msg);
```

Listing 6.16   *(continued)*

```
        }
    }
    public void waitForReplies() { // wait for all the other processes to reply
        while (true) {
            messageParts m = (messageParts) receiveReplies.receive();
            // ID of replying thread is available but not needed
            int receivedID = ((Integer)m.obj).intValue();
            replyCount++;
            if (replyCount == numberOfProcesses-1)
                break; // all replies have been received
        }
    }
}
class requestMessage implements Serializable {
    public int ID;                          // process ID
    public int number;                      // sequence number
    public requestMessage(int number, int ID) {
        this.ID = ID; this.number = number;}
}
```

Listing 6.16   (*continued*)

object owned by one of the distributed processes. All messages sent through the *TCPSender* object are addressed to the associated *TCPMailbox*. This allows us to address messages once, when we construct the *TCPSender* objects, instead of specifying an address each time we send a message.

Each *distributedProcess* uses *TCPMailbox* objects named *receiveRequests* and *receiveReplies* to receive request and reply messages from the other processes. Connections between all the *TCPSender* and *TCPMailbox* objects are made by calling the *connect()* method of each *TCPSender* object at the start of the *run()* method for each *distributedProcess*.

We assume that all three *distributedMutualExclusion* programs run on the same computer. The port numbers used for *TCPMailbox* objects *receiveRequests* and *receiveReplies* are as follows: *distributedProcess0* uses 2020 and 2021 for its two *TCPMailbox* objects, *distributedProcess1* uses 2022 and 2023 for its two *TCPMailbox* objects, and *distributedProcess2* uses 2024 and 2025 for its two *TCPMailbox* objects. So, for example, when *distributedProcess0* sends requests to the other two processes, it sends them to ports 2022 and 2024. Requests from the other two processes to *distributedProcess0* are addressed to port 2020, while replies from the other two processes to *distributedProcess0* are addressed to 2021. Replies from *distributedProcess0* to *distributedProcess1* and *distributed-Process2* are addressed to ports 2023 and 2025, respectively. Thus, each port number P is associated with one *TCPMailbox* object, which is used by one of the *distributedProcesses* to receive messages. The other two *distributedProcesses* use *TCPSender* objects associated with P to send messages to the *TCPMailboxes* associated with P.

When a *distributedProcess* wants to enter its critical section in method *run( )*, it computes a sequence number and sets flag *requestingOrExecuting* to true. It then sends a request to each of the other processes and waits for each of the processes to reply.

Each *distributedProcess* has a *Helper* thread that handles requests received from the other processes [Hartley 1998]. If the *Helper* for *distributedProcess i* receives a *requestMessage* from *distributedProcess j*, the *Helper* replies immediately if the sequence number in *j*'s request is less than the sequence number stored at *i* or if d*istributedProcess i* is not trying to enter its critical section. The *Helper* defers the reply if *distributedProcess i* is in its critical section, or if *distributedProcess i* wants to enter its critical section and the *requestMessage* from *distributedProcess j* has a higher sequence number. If the sequence numbers are the same, the tie is broken by comparing process identifiers. (Each request message contains a sequence number and the identifier of the sending process.)

When a *distributedProcess* sends its request, it computes a sequence number by adding one to the highest sequence number it has received in requests from other processes. Class *Coordinator* is a monitor that synchronizes a *distributedProcess* thread and its *Helper* thread. A sample execution for this program is given in Section 6.5.4, where we show how to trace and replay its executions.

6.4.2   Distributed Readers and Writers

Here we show how to solve the distributed readers and writers problem by using message passing. The strategy we implement is R = W.2, which allows concurrent reading and gives readers and writers equal priority. Mutual exclusion is provided using the permission-based distributed mutual exclusion algorithm described earlier. When a process wants to perform its read or write operation, it sends a request to each of the other processes and waits for replies. A request consists of the same pair of values (sequence number and ID) used in the mutual exclusion algorithm, along with a flag that indicates the type of operation (read or write) being requested. When process *i* receives a request from process *j*, process *i* sends *j* an immediate reply if:

- Process *i* is not executing or requesting to execute its read or write operation.
- Process *i* is executing or requesting to execute a "compatible" operation. Two read operations are compatible, but two write operations, or a read and a write operation, are not compatible.
- Process *i* is also requesting to execute a noncompatible operation, but process *j*'s request has priority over process *i*'s request.

Program *distributedReadersAndWriters* is almost identical to program *distributedMutualExclusion* in Listing 6.16, so here we will only show the differences. First, each *distributedProcess* is either a reader or a writer. The user indicates the type of process and the process ID when the program is started:

java distributedReadersAndWriters 0 Reader   // Reader process with ID 0

The integer variable *readerOrWriter* is assigned the value READER or the value WRITER, depending on the command-line argument.

The second difference is in the *decideAboutDeferral()* method of the *Coordinator* monitor, which is shown in Listing 6.17. The flag *requestingOrExecuting* is true when a *distributedProcess* is requesting to execute or is executing its read or write operation. The *requestMessage m* contains the type of *operation* being requested and the sequence *number* and *ID* of the requesting process. If the receiving process is executing its operation or is requesting to execute its operation, method *compatible()* is used to determine whether or not the two operations are compatible.

We point out that if process i is executing read or write operation OP when it receives a request m from process j, the condition (*number* < *m.number*) in method *decideAboutDeferral()* must be true. This is because process j must have already received process i's request for operation OP, sent its permission to i, and updated its sequence number to be higher than the number in process i's request. In this case, if process j's operation is not compatible, it will definitely be deferred.

```
public void decideAboutDeferral(requestMessage m) {
    enterMonitor();
    highNumber = Math.max(highNumber,m.number);
    boolean deferMessage = requestingOrExecuting &&
        !compatible(m.operation) && ((number < m.number) ||
            (number == m.number && ID < m.ID));
    if (deferMessage) {
        deferred[m.ID] = true;
    }
    else {
        messageParts msg = new messageParts(new Integer(ID));
        sendReplies[m.ID].send(msg);
    }
    exitMonitor();
}

private boolean compatible(int requestedOperation) {
    if (readerOrWriter == READER && requestedOperation == READER)
        return true;       // only READER operations are compatible
    else // READER/WRITER and WRITER/WRITER operations incompatible
        return false;
}
```

Listing 6.17 Methods   *decideAboutDeferral()* and   *compatible()* in   program *distributedReadersAndWriters*.

6.4.3 Alternating Bit Protocol

The Alternating Bit Protocol (ABP) is designed to ensure the reliable transfer of data over an unreliable communication medium [Bartlet et al. 1969]. The name of the protocol refers to the method used—messages are sent tagged with the bits 1 and 0 alternately, and these bits are also sent as acknowledgments.

Listing 6.18 shows classes *ABPSender* and *ABPReceiver* and two client threads. Thread *client1* is a source of messages for an *ABPSender* thread called *sender*. The *sender* receives messages from *client1* and sends the messages to an *ABPReceiver* thread called *receiver*. The *receiver* thread passes each message it receives to thread *client2*, which displays the message. We assume that messages sent between an *ABPSender* and an *ABPReceiver* will not be corrupted, duplicated, or reordered, but they may be lost. The ABP will handle the detection and retransmission of lost messages.

An *ABPSender* S works as follows. After accepting a message from its client, S sends the message and sets a timer. To detect when the medium has lost a message, S also appends a 1-bit sequence number (initially 1) to each message it sends out. There are then three possibilities:

- S receives an acknowledgment from *ABPReceiver* R with the same sequence number. If this happens, the sequence number is incremented (modulo 2), and S is ready to accept the next message from its client.
- S receives an acknowledgment with the wrong sequence number. In this case S resends the message (with the original sequence number), sets a timer, and waits for another acknowledgment from R.
- S gets a timeout from the timer while waiting for an acknowledgment. In this case, S resends the message (with the original sequence number), sets a timer, and waits for an acknowledgment from R.

An *ABPReceiver* R receives a message and checks that the message has the expected sequence number (initially, 1). There are two possibilities:

- R receives a message with a sequence number that matches the sequence number that R expects. If this happens, R delivers the message to its client and sends an acknowledgment to S. The acknowledgment contains the same sequence number that R received. R then increments the expected sequence number (modulo 2) and waits for the next message.
- R receives a message but the sequence number does not match the sequence number that R expects. In this case, R sends S an acknowledgment that contains the sequence number that R received (i.e., the unexpected number) and then waits for S to resend the message.

Note that in both cases, the acknowledgment sent by R contains the sequence number that R received.

Communication between the sender and its client, and the receiver and its client, is through shared *link* channels. Class *link* was presented in Chapter 5.

```
public final class abp {
    public static void main(String args[]) {
        link nextMessage = new link();
        source client1 = new source(nextMessage);
        ABPSender sender = new ABPSender(nextMessage);
        link deliver = new link();
        destination client2 = new destination(deliver);
        ABPReceiver receiver = new ABPReceiver(deliver);
        client1.start(); client2.start(); sender.start(); receiver.start();
    }
}
final class source extends TDThreadD {
    private link nextMessage;
    public source(link nextMessage) {this.nextMessage = nextMessage;}
    public void run() {nextMessage.send("one"); nextMessage.send("two");
    nextMessage.send("three"); }
}
final class destination extends TDThreadD {
    private link deliver;
    public destination(link deliver) {this.deliver = deliver;}
    public void run() {
        String msg;
        msg = (String) deliver.receive();    System.out.println(msg);
        msg = (String) deliver.receive();    System.out.println(msg);
        msg = (String) deliver.receive();    System.out.println(msg);
    }
}
final class ABPSender extends TDThreadD {
    private link nextMessage;
    private TCPSender messageSender;
    private TCPUnreliableSelectableMailbox ackMailbox; // loses 50% of the acks
    private final int receiverPort = 2022; private final int senderPort = 2020;
    private String receiverHost = null; private int sequenceNumber = 1;
    public ABPSender(link nextMessage) {this.nextMessage = nextMessage;}
    public void run() {
        try {
            receiverHost = InetAddress.getLocalHost().getHostName();
            ackMailbox = new TCPUnreliableSelectableMailbox (senderPort);
            messageSender = new TCPSender(receiverHost,receiverPort);
            selectiveWait select = new selectiveWait();
            selectiveWait.delayAlternative delayA = select.new
                delayAlternative(3000);
            select.add(ackMailbox);          // alternative 1
```

Listing 6.18 Classes *ABPSender* and *ABPReceiver* and their clients.

```
          select.add(delayA);           // alternative 2
          ackMailbox.guard(true);
          delayA.guard(true);
          while (true) {
            // accept message from client 1
            String nextMsg = (String) nextMessage.receive();
            abpPacket packet = new abpPacket(nextMsg,sequenceNumber);
            messageParts msg = new messageParts(packet);
            boolean receivedAck = false;
            while (!receivedAck) {
                messageSender.send(msg); // (re)send message to receiver
                switch (select.choose()) {
                    case 1:   messageParts m = ackMailbox.receive();
                              // receive ack
                              int ackNumber = ((Integer)m.obj).intValue();
                              if (ackNumber == sequenceNumber) {
                                  receivedAck = true;
                              }
                              break;
                    case 2:   delayA.accept(); // timeout
                              break;
                }
            }
            sequenceNumber = (sequenceNumber+1)%2; // increment mod 2
          }
      }
      catch (InterruptedException e) {e.printStackTrace();}
      catch (UnknownHostException e) {e.printStackTrace();}
      catch (TCPChannelException e) {e.printStackTrace();}
    }
}
final class ABPReceiver extends TDThreadD {
    private link deliver;
    private TCPSender ackSender;
    private TCPUnreliableMailbox messageMailbox; // loses 50%of the messages
    private final int receiverPort = 2022;
    private final int senderPort = 2020;
    private String senderHost = null;
    private int expectedSequenceNumber = 1;
    public ABPReceiver(link deliver) {this.deliver = deliver;}
    public void run() {
        try {
            senderHost = InetAddress.getLocalHost().getHostName();
```

Listing 6.18   (*continued*)

```
                messageMailbox = new TCPUnreliableMailbox (receiverPort);
                ackSender = new TCPSender(senderHost,senderPort);
                while (true) {
                    // receive message from sender
                    messageParts msg = (messageParts) messageMailbox.receive();
                    abpPacket packet = (abpPacket) msg.obj;
                    if (packet.sequenceNumber == expectedSequenceNumber) {
                        deliver.send(packet.obj); // deliver message to client 2
                        msg = new messageParts(new
                            Integer(packet.sequenceNumber));
                        ackSender.send(msg); // send ack to sender
                        expectedSequenceNumber = (expectedSequenceNumber+1)%2;
                    }
                    else {
                        msg = new messageParts(new
                            Integer(packet.sequenceNumber));
                        ackSender.send(msg); // resend ack to sender
                    }
                }
            }
        catch (UnknownHostException e) {e.printStackTrace();}
        catch (TCPChannelException e) {e.printStackTrace();}
        }
    }
    class abpPacket implements Serializable{
        public abpPacket(Object obj,int sequenceNumber) {
            this.obj = obj;this.sequenceNumber = sequenceNumber;
        }
        public Object obj;               // message
        public int sequenceNumber;   // sequence number: 0 or 1
    }
```

Listing 6.18   (*continued*)

The sender and receiver threads communicate using *TCPSender* and *TCPMailbox* objects, and a selectable asynchronous mailbox called *TCPSelectableMailbox*. The *delayAlternative* in the *sender's* selective wait statement allows the *sender* to timeout while it is waiting to receive an acknowledgment from the *receiver*.
    To simulate the operation of ABP over an unreliable medium, we have modified classes *TCPMailbox* and *TCPSelectableMailbox* so that they randomly discard messages and acknowledgments sent between the *sender* and *receiver*. These unreliable mailbox classes are called *TCPUnreliableMailbox* and *TCPUnreliableSelectableMailbox*. Figure 6.19 shows one possible flow of messages through the ABP program. In this scenario, no message or acknowledgment is lost. In Figure 6.20, the *ABPSender's* message is lost. In this case, the *ABPSender*

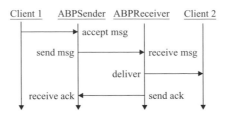

Figure 6.19   ABP scenario in which no messages or acknowledgements are lost.

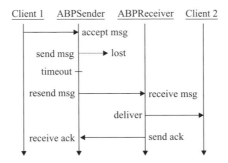

Figure 6.20   ABP scenario with no lost message or acknowledgement.

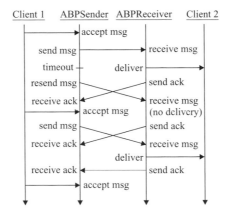

Figure 6.21   ABP scenario with a spurious timeout.

receives a timeout from its timer and resends the message. In Figure 6.21, the *ABPSender's* message is not lost, but the *ABPSender* still receives a timeout before it receives an acknowledgment. In this case, the *ABPReceiver* delivers and acknowledges the first message but only acknowledges the second. The *ABPSender* receives two acknowledgments, but it ignores the second one.

6.5   TESTING AND DEBUGGING DISTRIBUTED PROGRAMS

A tracing and replay technique for shared memory channels was presented in Chapter 5. That same technique can be applied here with certain modifications that are necessary in a distributed environment. We begin by defining SYN-sequences for distributed Java programs that use classes *TCPSender* and *TCPMailbox* for message passing. Afterward, we present solutions to the tracing, replay, and feasibility problems. We did not implement reachability testing for the *TCPSender* and *TCPMailbox* classes. The overhead of running in a distributed environment, including the cost of open and closing connections and detecting termination, would slow down reachability testing significantly. Still, it could be done since tracing, replay, and timestamping have already been implemented. On the other hand, it is easy to transform a program that uses the TCP classes into one that uses the channel classes in Chapter 5. This allows distributed algorithms to be tested in a friendlier environment.

Let DP be a distributed program. We assume that DP consists of multiple Java programs and that there are one or more Java programs running on each node in the system. Each Java program contains one or more threads. These threads use *TCPSender* and *TCPMailbox* objects to communicate with threads in other programs and possibly on other nodes. Threads in the same Java program can communicate and synchronize using shared variables and the channel, semaphore, or monitor objects presented in previous chapters. Shared variable communication and synchronization can be traced, tested, and replayed using the techniques described previously. Here, we focus on message passing between programs on different nodes.

6.5.1   Object-Based Sequences

The SYN-sequence definitions in this chapter are similar to the definitions presented in Chapter 5 for shared channel objects. We begin by defining an object-based SYN-sequence, which means that there is one SYN-sequence for each synchronization object in the program. The synchronization objects in a distributed Java program DP are its *TCPMailbox* objects. The threads in DP execute synchronization events of the following four types:

- *Connection.* A connection is created between a *TCPSender* object and its associated *TCPMailbox* object by calling *connect()* on the *TCPSender*. (The host address and port number of a *TCPMailbox* is associated with a *TCPSender* object when the *TCPSender* object is constructed.)
- *Arrival.* A message M is sent by a thread that calls operation *send(M)* on a *TCPSender* object. The arrival of message M at the corresponding *TCPMailbox* occurs some time after M it is sent. When message M arrives, it is queued in the message buffer of the *TCPMailbox* object.
- *Receive.* A message is received by a thread that calls operation *receive()* on a *TCPMailbox* object. A *receive()* operation withdraws and returns a message from the message buffer of the *TCPMailbox* object.

- *Close.* A connection between a *TCPSender* object and its associated *TCP-Mailbox* object is closed by calling *close()* on the *TCPSender* object.

We refer to these events as CARC (*ConectArrivalReceiveClose*) events.

Notice that there are *arrival* events but no *send* events. This is because it is the order in which messages arrive that determines the result of an execution, not the order in which messages are sent. This list of event types hides some of the complexity of TCP-level message passing. For instance, several TCP message passing events occur during the execution of operations *connect()* and *close()*. Both operations involve the exchange of multiple TCP messages as part of a *handshaking process* that occurs when a TCP connection is opened or closed. As another example, a *send()* operation may require a TCP packet to be sent and then resent multiple times before it arrives. Similarly, TCP acknowledgments are issued to the sender when a message arrives at its destination. None of these TCP-level message passing events appear in SYN-sequences of programs using *TCPSender* and *TCPMailbox* objects.

To illustrate the four types of CARC events, consider the distributed bounded buffer program in Listing 6.22. This is the program in Listing 6.3 with two minor modifications for tracing, testing, and replay: (1) The *Producer, Buffer*, and *Consumer* programs use *TCPSender* and *TCPMailbox* objects named "deposit" and "withdraw" to pass messages. The names are assigned when the objects are constructed. (2) Classes *Producer, Buffer*, and *Consumer* inherit from class *TDThreadD*, which is class *TDThread* modified for distributed programs.

Figure 6.23 shows a diagram of the three threads in Listing 6.22, their thread IDs, and the *TCPSender* and *TCPMailbox* objects they use to communicate with each other. Figure 6.24 shows part of a feasible sequence of *connect, arrival, receive*, and *close* events for this program.

An object-based CARC-event for a *TCPMailbox* M is denoted by

(threadID, orderNumber, eventType)

where

- *threadID* is the ID of the thread that executed this event. This means that this thread sent a message that arrived at mailbox M, or opened or closed a connection with M, or received a message from M.
- *orderNumber* is the order number of the thread that executed this event, which gives the relative order of this event among all of the thread's CARC-events.
- *eventType* is the type of this event, which is either *connection, arrival, receive*, or *close*.

Technically, there is no sending thread involved in a *receive()* operation. This is because a *receive()* operation only withdraws a message from the message buffer of a *TCPMailbox* object, as opposed to actually receiving a message over

```java
import java.net.*;
public final class Producer extends TDThreadD {
    public static void main (String args[]) {(new Producer()).start();}
    public void run() {
        final int bufferPort = 2020;
        String bufferHost = null;
        try {
            bufferHost = InetAddress.getLocalHost().getHostName();
            TCPSender deposit = new TCPSender(bufferHost,bufferPort,"deposit");
            // assign name "deposit"
            deposit.connect();
            for (int i=0; i<3; i++) {
                System.out.println("Producing"+ i);
                messageParts msg = new messageParts(new Message(i));
                deposit.send(msg);
            }
            deposit.close();
        }
        catch (UnknownHostException e) {e.printStackTrace();}
        catch (TCPChannelException e) {e.printStackTrace();}
    }
}
public final class Buffer extends TDThreadD {
    public static void main (String args[]) {(new Buffer()).start();}
    public void run() {
        final int bufferPort = 2020; final int consumerPort = 2022;
        try {
            String consumerHost = InetAddress.getLocalHost().getHostName();
            TCPMailbox deposit = new TCPMailbox(bufferPort,"deposit");
            TCPSender withdraw = new
                TCPSender(consumerHost,consumerPort,"withdraw");
            withdraw.connect();
            for (int i=0; i<3; i++) {
                messageParts m = (messageParts) deposit.receive();
                withdraw.send(m);
            }
            withdraw.close(); deposit.close();
        }
        catch (UnknownHostException e) {e.printStackTrace();}
        catch (TCPChannelException e) {e.printStackTrace();}
    }
}
```

Listing 6.22 Distributed bounded-buffer program in Listing 6.4 modified for tracing, testing, and replay.

```
public final class Consumer extends TDThreadD {
    public static void main (String args[]) { (new Consumer()).start();}
    public void run() {
        final int consumerPort = 2022;
        try {
            TCPMailbox withdraw = new TCPMailbox(consumerPort,"withdraw");
            // name is ''withdraw''
            for (int i=0; i<3; i++) {
                messageParts m = (messageParts) withdraw.receive();
                Message msg = (Message) m.obj;
                System.out.println("Consumed "+ msg.number);
            }
            withdraw.close();
        }
        catch (TCPChannelException e) {e.printStackTrace();}
    }
}
```

Listing 6.22   (*continued*)

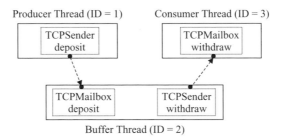

Figure 6.23   Threads and mailboxes in the distributed bounded buffer program.

the network. The message withdrawn by a *receive()* operation is one that arrived earlier. Thus, it was a previous *arrival* event that actually involved receiving the message from the sender and depositing the message into the message buffer. The order number of an *arrival* event is the order number of the send operation that generated it.

Even though the sending thread is not specified on a *receive()* operation, it is nevertheless helpful to include the sending thread's ID in the information recorded for *receive* events. This and other information, such as the vector timestamp generated for each event, is helpful for understanding and visualizing an execution. For this reason, our trace tool generates a separate trace file containing extra information about the execution.

Given the format above for an object-based CARC-event, a CARC-sequence of *TCPMailbox M* is denoted by

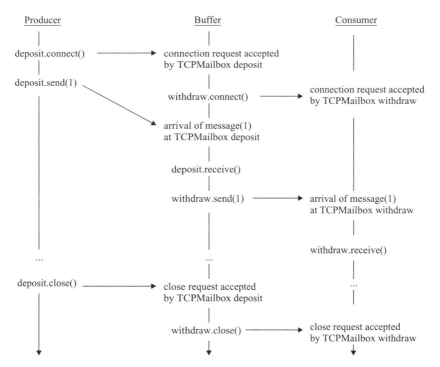

Figure 6.24 Sequence of *connect, arrival, receive*, and *close* events for the program in Listing 6.22.

M: (($threadID_1$, $orderNumber_1$, $eventType_1$), ($threadID_2$, $orderNumber_2$, $eventType_2$), ...)

where ($threadID_i$ $orderNumber_i$, $eventType_i$) denotes the ith, $i > 0$, CARC-event in the CARC-sequence of M. An object-based CARC-sequence of a program contains a CARC-sequence for each *TCPMailbox* in the program.

For a *TCPSynchronousMailbox* object M, there are *connection* and *close* events as defined above, and a third event type:

• SRsynchronization: a synchronization between a *send()* and *receive()* operation involving M.

No *arrival* events are recorded for a *TCPSynchronousMailbox* object since the order of arrivals is implied by the order of *SRsynchronization* events.

An object-based *connection, SRsynchronization*, or *close* event (CSC-event) for *TCPSynchronousMailbox* M is denoted by

(callingThreadID, calledThreadID, callerOrderNumber, calledOrderNumber, eventType)

where

- *callingThreadID* is the ID of the thread that opened or closed a connection with M, or the ID of the sending thread in an *SRsynchronization* at M.
- *calledThreadID* is the ID of the receiving thread in an *SRsynchronization* at M. There is no *calledThread* for *connection* or *close* events involving M.
- *callingOrderNumber* is the order number of the *callingThread*, which gives the relative order of this event among all the *callingThread's* events.
- *calledOrderNumber* is the order number of the *calledThread*, which gives the relative order of this event among all the *calledThread's* events. There is no *calledOrderNumber* for *connection* and *close* events involving M.
- *eventType* is the type of this event, which is either *connection, SRsynchronization*, or *close*.

We will use the value -1 for the *calledThread* and *calledOrderNumber* in *connection* and *close* events to indicate that the information about the called thread is not applicable.

Thread-Based Sequences   We now define two formats for thread-based CARC- and CSC-sequences.

Format 1   A thread-based CARC- or CSC-event for thread T is denoted by

(mailbox, mailboxOrderNumber, eventType)

where

- *mailbox* is the *TCPMailbox* name.
- *mailboxOrderNumber* is the order number of *mailbox*.
- *eventType* is the type of the event.

The order number of M gives the relative order of this event among all the events involving M. The list of event types is the same as that above for object-based events.

In Format 2, each *TCPMailbox* and *TCPSynchronousMailbox* has one receiving thread that is considered to be the "owner" of the mailbox. Since a mailbox can have multiple receiving threads, one of the receivers must be arbitrarily chosen to be the owner. If a thread T contains a selective wait, the selective wait will choose among one or more *TCPSelectableSynchronousMailboxes*, all of which we require to be owned by thread T. As in Chapter 5, we need to add a new event type for selective waits:

- *elseDelay*: selection of an *else* or *delay* alternative

Since thread T is associated with all of the mailbox and *elseDelay* events generated by its selective waits, it is convenient to record these events in the sequence for thread T.

Format 2   A thread-based CARC- or CSC-event for thread T, where T is the owner of the mailbox associated with the event, is denoted by

   (sendingThreadID, sendingThreadOrderNumber, mailbox, eventType)

where

- *sendingThreadID* is the ID of the sending thread (and T is always the receiver).
- *sendingThreadOrderNumber* is the sending thread's order number.
- *mailbox* is the name of the mailbox.
- *eventType* is the type of this event.

An *SRsynchronization* event representing a synchronization between send and receive operations on a synchronous mailbox appears in the CSC-sequence for the owning thread (i.e., the receiving thread). There is no corresponding send event in the sequence for the sending thread. In Format 2, no order number is required for mailbox M since the CARC- or CSC-sequence of M's owning thread T contains all of the events for mailbox M, and thus the order numbers for M are given implicitly (i.e., the ith event for M implicitly has order number i).

Given the two formats for thread-based CARC- and CSC-events, we can now define thread-based sequences for threads and for programs. For Format 1, a CARC- or CSC-sequence of thread T is denoted by

   T: ((mailbox$_1$, mailboxOrderNumber$_1$, eventType$_1$), (mailbox$_2$,
      mailboxOrderNumber$_2$, eventType$_2$), ...).

For Format 2, a CARC- or CSC-sequence of thread T is denoted by

   T: ((sendingThreadID$_1$, sendingThreadOrderNumber$_1$, mailbox$_1$, eventType$_1$),
      (sendingThreadID$_2$, sendingThreadOrderNumber$_2$, mailbox$_2$, eventType$_2$),
      ...).

A thread-based CARC- or CSC-sequence of a program contains a thread-based CARC- or CSC-sequence for each thread in the program.

Totally Ordered Sequences   When totally ordered sequences are used, there is only one sequence for the program, and this sequence contains all the events for all the mailboxes and threads. A CARC-event in a totally ordered sequence is denoted by

   (threadID, mailbox, eventType)

where

- *mailbox* is the name of the *mailbox*. Each mailbox is associated with a name that is generated when it is constructed. (We assume that the user supplies a name for each mailbox, or the name will be generated automatically as we have done for other objects.)
- *threadID* is the ID of the thread that executed this event. This means that this thread sent a message to the *mailbox*, or opened or closed a connection with the *mailbox*, or executed a *receive()* operation on the *mailbox*.
- *eventType* is the type of this event, which is either *connection, arrival, receive*, or *close*.

A CSC-event in a totally ordered sequence is denoted by

(callingThreadID, calledThreadID, mailbox, eventType)

which requires both the calling and the called thread to be specified for *SRsynchronization* events.

A totally ordered CARC- or CSC-sequence contains no order numbers for mailboxes or threads, since this information is specified implicitly by the ordering of events in the sequence. A totally ordered CARC-sequence of program DP is denoted as

DP: ((threadID$_1$, mailbox$_1$, eventType$_1$), (threadID$_1$, mailbox$_2$, eventType$_2$), ...)

A totally ordered CSC-sequence of program DP is denoted as

DP: ((callingThreadID$_1$, calledThreadID$_1$, mailbox$_1$, eventType$_1$),
      (callingThreadID$_2$, calledThreadID$_2$, mailbox$_2$, eventType$_2$), ...)

Node-Based Sequences   The tracing, replay, and testing tools described in the next section do not use any of the SYN-sequence formats that we have seen so far. To simplify the tracing and replay process, these tools use one sequence for each node in the system. There may be several programs running on a single node. A totally ordered CARC-sequence of node N is denoted by

N: (eventType$_1$, threadID$_1$, mailbox$_1$, orderNumber$_1$), (eventType$_2$, threadID$_2$, mailbox$_2$, orderNumber$_2$) . . .

where *threadID$_i$* is the ID of the thread that executed the ith event, *orderNumber$_i$* is the order number of the thread that executed the ith event, and *mailbox$_i$* is the name of the *TCPMailbox* involved in this event. Mailbox *mailbox$_i$* must be a mailbox created in a program on node N. This means that the only events in a CARC-sequence of node N are events that involve some *TCPMailbox* created on node N. If a thread running on node N is a calling thread for a *connection,* *arrival*, or *close* event, that event appears in the CARC-sequence of the receiving node, not the CARC-sequence of N. Since the sender's order number is recorded in *connection, arrival*, and *close* events, the total order of the sending thread's events can be determined by analyzing the CARC-sequence(s) for all the nodes.

A totally ordered CSC-sequence of node N is denoted by

N: ((eventType$_1$, callingThreadID$_1$, calledThreadID$_1$, callerOrderNumber$_1$,
     calledOrderNumber$_1$, mailbox$_1$),
     (eventType$_2$, callingThreadID$_2$, calledThreadID$_2$, callerOrderNumber$_2$,
     calledOrderNumber$_2$, mailbox$_2$), ...)

Again, *mailbox$_i$* must be a mailbox created in a program on node N.

A CARC- or CSC-sequence of a distributed program DP contains a CARC- or CSC-sequence for each node in the program. Figure 6.25 shows a feasible CARC-sequence of the distributed bounded buffer program in Listing 6.22. Since the *Producer, Buffer*, and *Consumer* programs are all executed on the same node, there is a single totally ordered sequence of CARC-events. If the three programs were executed on three separate nodes, the CARC-sequence for the *Producer's* node would be empty, since the *Producer* is always the sending thread for the events it is involved with.

A complete tracing and replay solution must consider how to handle any exceptions that are raised during an execution. But the exceptions that are raised by operations of the *TCPSender* and *TCPMailbox* classes may be raised due to physical network failures that are impossible to replay. One strategy is to simulate the exceptions during replay (i.e., throw an exception whenever the

(connection,2,withdraw,1)	// buffer connects to mailbox *withdraw*
(connection,1,deposit,1)	// producer connects to mailbox *deposit*
(arrival,1,deposit,2)	// producer's first message arrives at mailbox *deposit*
(receive,2,deposit,2)	// buffer receives producer's first message
(arrival,2,withdraw,3)	// buffer's first message arrives at mailbox *withdraw*
(receive,3,withdraw,1)	// consumer receives first message from *withdraw*
(arrival,1,deposit,3)	// producer's second msg arrives at mailbox *deposit*
(receive,2,deposit,4)	// buffer receives producer's second message
(arrival,1,deposit,4)	// producer's third message arrives at mailbox *deposit*
(arrival,2,withdraw,5)	// buffer's second message arrives at *withdraw*
(receive,2,deposit,6)	// buffer receives producer's third message
(close,1,deposit,5)	// producer closes connection with *deposit*
(arrival,2,withdraw,7)	// buffer's third message arrives at *withdraw*
(close,2,withdraw,8)	// buffer closes connection with *withdraw*
(receive,3 ,withdraw,2)	// consumer receives second message from *withdraw*
(receive,3,withdraw,3)	// consumer receives third message from *withdraw*

Figure 6.25 CARC-sequence of the distributed bounded-buffer program in Listing 6.19.

trace file shows that an exception is needed). To simplify tracing and replay, we use a different strategy, which is to trace exceptions but not replay them. Testing a program's response to exceptions is important, but it can often be done by simulating failures without running the entire system. If the response is simple, such as terminating the program, this may be sufficient. Some errors, such as assigning the same port number to multiple *TCPMailboxes*, are exasperating but can be debugged without any replay. We are more interested in uncovering logic errors that involve the coordinated behavior of several threads, such as the threads in the distributed mutual exclusion program. Using our scheme, we can replay an execution up to the point where an exception was generated, but we do not replay the exception itself. Our solution can be extended to simulate exceptions during testing and replay.

6.5.2   Simple Sequences

During deterministic testing, we check the feasibility of a (complete) CARC- or CSC-sequence. Simpler sequences can be used for replay. A simple CARC-event for a *TCPMailbox* is denoted as

(threadID)

where *threadID* is the ID of the thread that executed the CARC-event. A simple CARC-sequence of node N is denoted by

(threadID$_1$), (threadID$_2$), ...

where the *TCPMailbox* for each event is some mailbox created on node N. A simple CARC-sequence of a distributed program DP contains a simple CARC-sequence for each node in the program. Figure 6.26 shows the simple CARC-sequence corresponding to the complete CARC-sequence in Fig. 6.25.

For *TCPSynchronousMailboxes* and *TCPSelectableSynchronousMailboxes*, a simple CARC-event is denoted by

(callingThreadID, calledThreadID)

which identifies the IDs of the calling and called threads for the event. For *connect* and *close* events, there is no called thread. For *elseDelay* events, there is no calling thread. In these cases, we use −1 as the ID of the missing calling or called thread.

6.5.3   Tracing, Testing, and Replaying CARC-Sequences and CSC-Sequences

The general technique that we use for tracing, replaying, or determining the feasibility of a CARC-sequence is the same as the one used in Chapter 5. Before a thread can perform a *connect(), close(), send(),* or *receive()* operation, it must

(1)
(1)
(2)
(2)
(1)
(2)
(1)
(1)
(3)
(2)
(2)
(2)
(2)
(3)
(3)

Figure 6.26   Simple CARC-sequence of the distributed bounded-buffer program.

request permission from a control module. The control module is responsible for reading a complete or simple CARC- or CSC-sequence and forcing the execution to proceed according to this sequence.

Since we are tracing and replaying one sequence per node, we use one *Controller* per node. The *Controller* is a separate program that runs on the node along with the programs being tested and debugged. An alternative scheme would be to use a single *Controller* for the entire system. The global *Controller* would trace or replay a totally ordered sequence that contained all the events of all the nodes. In such a scheme, the *Controller* is a bottleneck, but it is convenient to have a single global trace of all the events when you are trying to understand an execution. Yet another alternative is to create a separate *Controller* for each mailbox or each thread, based on the object and thread-based CARC- and CSC-sequence definitions above. This creates a potentially large number of *Controllers*, and it also complicates tracing and replay due to the complexity of addressing all of the *Controllers* in a distributed environment.

Modifying Classes TCPSender and TCPMailbox   Methods *connect(), send(), close()*, and *receive()* in classes *TCPSender* and *TCPMailbox* are modified by adding one or more calls to the *Controller*. In replay and test mode, methods *connect(), send(),* and *close()* shown below issue a call to the *Controller* to request permission to exercise a *connection, arrival,* or *close* event, respectively. The arguments on the calls to *requestSRPermit()* refer to the thread ID, order number, and event type of the CARC- or CSC-event being executed. Method *requestSRPermit()* sends a request message to the *Controller* and waits for a reply indicating that permission has been received to execute the operation.

Methods *connect()*, *send()*, and *close()* do not trace any *connection, arrival*, or *close* events during trace mode. Instead, these events are traced by the destination *TCPMailbox*. To trace an event, the *TCPMailbox* needs the thread ID and order number of the calling thread. Since this information is not provided by the underlying Java implementation of TCP, it must be sent as part of each operation. Thus, method *connect()* sends this information immediately after the connection is opened; method *close()* sends this information immediately before the connection is closed; and method *send()* sends this information with each user message.

```
public void connect() throws TCPChannelException {
    try {
        if (mode == REPLAY)
            // wait for permission from Controller
            requestSRPermit(ID);
        else if (mode == TEST)
            // wait for permission from Controller
            requestSRPermit(ID,orderNumber,CONNECT);
        synchronized(lock) {
            // open a connection
            socket = new Socket( destinationHostname, destinationPort );
            to = new ObjectOutputStream(socket.getOutputStream());
            if (mode == TRACE || mode == REPLAY || mode == TEST) {
                // send caller's ID and order number
                messageParts message = new messageParts(new nullObject());
                message.caller = ID; message.orderNumber = orderNumber;
                to.writeObject(message); to.flush();
            }
        }
    } catch (...) {...}
}
public void close() throws TCPChannelException {
    try {
        if (mode == REPLAY)
            // wait for permission from Controller
            requestSRPermit(ID);
        else if (mode == TEST)
            // wait for permission from Controller
            requestSRPermit(ID,orderNumber,CLOSE);
        synchronized (lock) {
            if (mode == TRACE || mode == REPLAY || mode == TEST) {
                // send caller's ID and order number
                messageParts message = new messageParts(new nullObject());
                message.caller = ID; message.orderNumber = orderNumber;
                // this is a special control message
```

```
                    message.isCLOSE = true;
                    // not a user-level message
                    to.writeObject(message); to.flush();
                    }
                    if (to != null) to.close();              // close the connection
                    if (socket != null) socket.close();
             }
        } catch(...) {...}
   }

   public void send( messageParts message) throws TCPChannelException{
        try {
           if (mode == REPLAY)
                // wait for permission from Controller
                requestSRPermit (ID);
           else if (mode == TEST)
                // wait for permission from Controller
                requestSRPermit(ID,orderNumber,ARRIVAL);
           synchronized (lock) {
                message.caller = ID; message.orderNumber = orderNumber;
                to.writeObject(message); to.flush();   // send the message
           }
        } catch(...) {...}
   }
```

In replay and test mode, method *receive( )* issues a call to the *Controller* to request permission to exercise a receive event. Since the message buffer is FCFS, we are sure that messages are withdrawn in the order in which they are deposited. Thus, in replay and test mode, controlling the order in which messages arrive and the order in which *receive( )* operations are executed by receiving threads ensures that a *receive( )* operation withdraws the same message from the same sending thread that was recorded during tracing. What happens after a message is withdrawn from the message buffer depends on the execution mode. In trace mode, *receive( )* notifies the *Controller* that a receive event has occurred. In replay mode, *receive( )* calls *nextEvent( )* to notify the *Controller* that the receive event has occurred and that permission can be given for the next event in the sequence. In test mode, *receive( )* calls *acknowledgeEvent( )*, which sends information about the receive event to the *Controller*. The *Controller* checks whether the expected event has occurred and, if so, gives permission for the next event in the sequence. If an unexpected receive event occurs, the *Controller* issues a diagnostic message. If the *Controller* does not receive a request for the next event within a specified time period, the *Controller* assumes that the sequence is infeasible and issues a diagnostic message.

Note that the message *buffer* is a monitor object; thus, we are indirectly replaying the monitor operations in the implementation of the *TCPMailbox* object. More precisely, in method *receive()* we are replaying the order in which the receiving threads call operation *withdraw()*. The *deposit()* operations are performed by the internal threads of the *TCPMailbox* object and, as we show below, these *deposit()* operations are implicitly replayed when we replay *arrival* events.

```
public messageParts receive( ) throws TCPChannelException {
    try {
        if (mode == REPLAY)
            // wait for permission from Controller
            requestSRPermit(ID);
        else if (mode == TEST)
            // wait for permission from Controller
            requestSRPermit(ID,channelName,orderNumber,RECEIVE);
        synchronized(lock) {
            // withdraw a message
            messageParts msg = buffer.withdraw();
            if (traceOrReplay mode == TRACE)
                // trace the receive event
                traceEvent(ID,channelName,orderNumber,RECEIVE);
            else if (mode == REPLAY)
                // notify Controller that a receive event occurred
                nextEvent();
            else if ( mode == TEST)
                // verify event with Controller
                acknowledgeEvent(ID,channelName,orderNumber,RECEIVE);
            return msg;
        }
    } catch(...) {...}
}
```

The *run()* method of the *connectionHandler* thread in *TCPMailbox* traces all of the *connection, arrival,* and *close* events of the *TCPMailbox* object:

- Method *run()* reads the connection information sent when a thread executes method *connect()* and passes this information to the *Controller.*
- Message arrivals are traced in method *deposit()* of the message buffer.
- Method *run()* reads the information sent when a thread executes method *close()* and passes this information to the *Controller.*

In replay mode, method *nextEvent()* notifies the *Controller* that an event has occurred so that permission can be given for the next event in the sequence. In test mode, method *acknowledgeEvent()* sends information about the *connection, arrival*, or *close* event that just occurred to the *Controller*, which checks whether the event that occurred is the expected event.

```
class connectionHandler extends Thread {
    ...
    public void run() {
        try { // run
            if (mode == REPLAY)
                // notify Controller that the connection event occurred
                nextEvent();
            if (mode == TRACE || mode == REPLAY || mode == TEST) {
                // read the connection information sent by the client
                messageParts connectionInfo = ((messageParts) from.readObject());
                if (mode == TRACE)                    // trace the connection event
                    traceEvent(connectionInfo.caller,connectionInfo.
                        callerOrderNumber,channelName,CONNECT);
                else if (mode == TEST)
                    // verify the connection event with the Controller
                    acknowledgeEvent(connectionInfo.caller,connectionInfo.
                        callerOrderNumber,channelName,CONNECT);
            }
            messageParts closeMessage = null;
            while (true) { // read objects until EOF
                messageParts msg = null;
                try {
                    msg = (messageParts) from.readObject(); // read message
                    if (!msg.isClose)
                        // if it's a user message, deposit it in message buffer
                        buffer.deposit(msg);
                    else { // else it's a close message; EOFException will be
                        // raised when the actual close occurs
                        // save close message information
                        closeMessage = new messageParts(new nullObject());
                        closeMessage.caller = msg.caller;
                        closeMessage.orderNumber = msg.orderNumber;
                        closeMessage.senderChannelName = msg.
                            senderChannelName;
                        closeMessage.isClose = true;
                    }
                }
                catch (EOFException e) {   // raised when TCP connection is closed
                    if (mode == TRACE)          // trace close event
                        traceEvent(closeMessage.caller,
```

```
                              closeMessage.callerOrderNumber,channelName,
                                 CLOSE);
                       else if (mode == REPLAY)
                          // notify Controller that a close event occurred
                          nextEvent();
                       else if (mode == TEST)
                          // verify the close event with the Controller
                          acknowledgeEvent(closeMessage.caller,closeMessage.
                             callerOrderNumber,channelName,CLOSE);
                       break;
                       }
                   }
                   from.close();
                   socket.close();
               }
           catch (..) {...}
       }
}


// Method deposit() of the messageBuffer class
public void deposit( messageParts msg ) {
    enterMonitor();
    try { // trace arrival event
        if (traceOrReplay == propertyParameters.TRACE) { // trace close event
            String name = channelName;
            traceEvent(msg.caller,called,msg.callerOrderNumber,-1,name,
                ARRIVAL);
        }
        else if (traceOrReplay == propertyParameters.REPLAY) {
            nextEvent(); // notify Controller that an arrival event occurred
        }
        else if (traceOrReplay==propertyParameters.TEST) {
            String name = channelName;
            // verify the arrival event with the Controller
            acknowledgeEvent(msg.caller,-1,msg.callerOrderNumber, -1,
                name, ARRIVAL);
        }
    }
    catch (Exception e) {System.out.println("Trace/Replay Error.");
        e.printStackTrace(); System.exit(1)};
    if (fullSlots == capacity)
            notFull.waitC();
    buffer.addLast(msg);
    ++fullSlots;
```

```
        notEmpty.signalC_and_exitMonitor();
    }
```

Modifying Class TCPSynchronousMailbox   Tracing, testing, and replaying
CSC-sequences for *TCPSynchronousMailboxes* requires several minor changes.
Since there are no *arrival* events in CSC-sequences, no *arrival* events are traced
in the *run()* method of the *connectionHandler*. Instead, the *receive()* method
traces *SRsynchronization* events whenever a message is received.

The testing and replay code for *TCPSynchronousMailbox* is the same as the
code for *TCPMailbox* as shown above, except that *arrival* events are ignored.
The *Controller* module allows thread T to send a message when the next event
is an *SRsynchronization* with thread T as the sending thread. *Connection* and
close events are handled as shown above.

Controller Program   The design of the *Controller* program is almost identical
to the *Controller* in Chapter 5. The major difference is that the *Controller* uses
vector timestamps to ensure that the CARC- or CSC-sequence it records in trace
mode is consistent with the causal ordering of events. The recording algorithm
was given in Section 6.3.6.

To handle communications with the user programs the *Controller* use four
TCPSelectableMailboxes. These mailboxes receive trace events, requests for permission to execute events, acknowledgment events, and next message notifications. The ports used by these mailboxes are computed as offsets to a base port
(basePort + 0, basePort+1, etc.), where the base port is hard coded as port 4040.
The *Controller* maintains an open connection between itself and each of the other
nodes in the system. All the threads on a given node share that node's connection
with the *Controller* and use the connection to send messages to the *Controller*.
During replay and testing, each node uses a *TCPMailbox* to receive replies from
the *Controller*. All the threads on a node share this *TCPMailbox*. By sharing
connections, the number of connections between each node and the *Controller*
is limited to one connection for tracing, three connections for replay, and four
connections for checking feasibility.

6.5.4 Putting It All Together

To trace, test, and debug executions, use the *mode* property to specify the function
(tracing, testing, or replay) to be performed. An execution of the distributed
mutual exclusion (DME) program in Listing 6.16 is traced as follows. First,
execute the *Controller* program. The *Controller* will start and then immediately
wait for trace events to arrive. Next, start each of the four user programs. The
commands to run the *Controller* and the DME programs on a single node are
shown below. (Run each program in a separate window.)

```
java−Dmode=trace−DprocessName=Node1 Controller
java−Dmode=trace−DstartID=1−DprocessName=process0
    distributedMutualExclusion0
```

```
java–Dmode=trace–DstartID=5–DprocessName=process1
    distributedMutualExclusion1
java–Dmode=trace–DstartID=9–DprocessName=process2
    distributedMutualExclusion2
java–Dmode=trace–DstartID=13–DprocessName=process3
    distributedMutualExclusion3
```

The *processName* property specifies a unique name for each DME program. This name is used as a prefix for all the names and files generated for that program. The *startID* property specifies the starting value for the identifiers to be generated for the threads in this program. Each of the DME programs requires four thread IDs. One ID is required for the main thread and one for its helper. There is also one ID reserved for each of the two *TCPMailbox* objects. This ensures that space is allocated for four objects in the vector timestamps. Recall that the timestamps are used to ensure that the *Controller* process records a correct ordering of events during tracing. After 10 seconds of inactivity, the *Controller* will assume that the execution has stopped and terminate itself.

In *trace* mode, the *Controller* creates several trace files:

- Node1_channel-replay.txt contains a simple totally ordered CARC-sequence.
- Node1_channel-test.txt contains a totally ordered CARC-sequence.
- Node1_channel-trace.txt contains a trace of additional information, such as the value of the vector timestamp for each event.

Since each DME program uses a monitor to synchronize the communication between the *main* thread and its *helper* thread, trace files are also generated for the monitor events as explained in Chapter 4. The trace files generated for the monitor in the program named "process1" are:

- process1_monitor-replay.txt   //simple M-sequence of the monitor in
                                    //process1
- process1_monitor-test.txt   //M-sequence of the monitor in process1
- process1_monitorID.txt   //monitor IDs for process1
- process1_ThreadID.txt   //thread IDs for process 1

A similar set of four files is produced for the monitors in the other three programs.

A simple SR-sequence is replayed by running the *Controller* and each user program in *replay* mode:

```
java–Dmode=replay -DprocessName=Node1 Controller
java –Dmode=replay -DstartID=1–DprocessName=process0–DackPort=3030
    distributedMutualExclusion0
java–Dmode=replay -DstartID=5–DprocessName=process1–DackPort=3032
    distributedMutualExclusion1
java–Dmode=replay -DstartID=9–DprocessName=process2–DackPort=3034
```

distributedMutualExclusion2
java-Dmode=replay -DstartID=13-DprocessName=process3-DackPort=3036
distributedMutualExclusion3

The *processNames* and *startIDs* must be the same ones used during tracing. The *ackPort* property specifies a port number that the user program can use to receive messages from the *Controller* program. Each program should use a unique *ackPort*. The *Controller* will read the simple CARC-sequence in file *Node1_channel-replay.txt* and force this sequence to occur during execution. The simple M-sequences of the monitors are replayed as described in Chapter 4.

The feasibility of a CARC-sequence is determined by running the *Controller* and each user program in *test* mode:

java-Dmode=test -DprocessName=Node1 Controller
java-Dmode=test -DstartID=1-DprocessName=process0-DackPort=3030
distributedMutualExclusion0
java-Dmode=test -DstartID=5-DprocessName=process1-DackPort=3032
distributedMutualExclusion1
java-Dmode=test -DstartID=9-DprocessName=process2-DackPort=3034
distributedMutualExclusion2
java-Dmode=test -DstartID=13-DprocessName=process3-DackPort=3036
distributedMutualExclusion3

The *Controller* will read the CARC-sequence in file *Node1_channel-test.txt* and attempt to force this sequence to occur during execution. If the CARC-sequence is infeasible, the *Controller* will issue a diagnostic and terminate. The feasibility of the M-sequence is determined as described in Chapter 4. If the mode is not specified, the default value for the *mode* property will turn tracing, replay, and testing off.

Figure 6.27*a* shows a CARC-sequence of the DME program in which each process enters its critical section once. We traced an execution and then grouped, reordered, and commented the events to make the sequence easier to understand. The M-sequence for the monitor in *process1* is shown in Fig. 6.27*b*.

6.5.5 Other Approaches to Replaying Distributed Programs

Multithreaded and distributed Java applications can be replayed by extending the Java Virtual Machine (JVM). Section 4.10.3 described a system called DejaVu [Choi and Srinivasan 1998] that provides deterministic replay of multithreaded Java programs on a single JVM. DejaVu has been extended to support distributed Java applications. Distributed DejaVu [Konuru et al. 2000] uses a modified Java Virtual Machine that records and replays nondeterministic network operations in the Java TCP and UDP Socket API. Some of these operations are *accept, connect, read, write, available, bind, listen*, and *close*. Multithreaded and distributed Java applications can be traced and replayed using Distributed DejaVu without any modifications to the source code.

// Connect events issued by p0:
(connect,1,RequestsFor1,1), (connect,1,RepliesFor1,2),
(connect,1,RequestsFor2,3),
(connect,1,RepliesFor2,4), (connect,1,RequestsFor3,5), (connect,1,RepliesFor3,6),
// Connect events issued by p1:
(connect,5,RequestsFor0,1), (connect,5,RepliesFor0,2),
(connect,5,RequestsFor2,3),
(connect,5,RepliesFor2,4), (connect,5,RequestsFor3,5), (connect,5,RepliesFor3,6),
// Connect events issued by p2:
(connect,9,RequestsFor0,1), (connect,9,RepliesFor0,2),
(connect,9,RequestsFor1,3), (connect,9,RepliesFor1,4)
(connect,9,RequestsFor3,5), (connect,9,RepliesFor3,6),
// Connect events issued by p3:
(connect,13,RequestsFor0,1),(connect,13,RepliesFor0,2),
(connect,13,RequestsFor1,3),
(connect,13,RepliesFor1,4),(connect,13,RequestsFor2,5),
(connect,13,RepliesFor2,6),

(arrival,5,RequestsFor0,8), (arrival,9,RequestsFor0,8), (arrival,13,RequestsFor0,8)

// All three requests have arrived at p0.

(arrival,1,RequestsFor1,8), (arrival,9,RequestsFor1,9), (arrival,13,RequestsFor1,9)

// All three requests have arrived at p1.

(arrival,1,RequestsFor2,9), (arrival,5,RequestsFor2,9),
(arrival,13,RequestsFor2,10)
// All three requests have arrived at p2.

(arrival,1,RequestsFor3,10),
(arrival,5,RequestsFor3,10),(arrival,9,RequestsFor3,10)
// All three requests have arrived at p3.
// Now each process has had a request arrive from all the other processes.

(receive,8,RequestsFor1,1)	// p1's helper receives p0's request and replies
(arrival,8,RepliesFor0,3)	// p1's helper's reply arrives at p0
(receive,12,RequestsFor2,1)	// p2's helper receives p0's request and replies
(arrival,12,RepliesFor0,3)	// p2's helper's reply arrives at p0
(receive,16,RequestsFor3,1)	// p3's helper receives p0's request and replies
(arrival,16,RepliesFor0,3)	// p3's helper's reply arrives at p0

// Replies from all the processes have arrived at p0.

Figure 6.27   (*a*) Feasible CARC-sequence for the distributed mutual exclusion program
in Listing 6.19.

(receive,12,RequestsFor2,4)   // p2's helper receives p1's request and replies
(arrival,12,RepliesFor1,6)   // p2's helper's reply arrives at p1
(receive,16,RequestsFor3,4)   // p3's helper receives p1's request and replies
(arrival,16,RepliesFor1,6)   // p3's helper's reply arrives at p1
// Replies from p2 and p3 have arrived at p1.

(receive,16,RequestsFor3,7)   // p3's helper receives p2's request and replies
(arrival,16,RepliesFor2,9)   // p3's helper's reply arrives at p2
// Reply from p3 has arrived at p2

(receive,4,RequestsFor0,1)   // p0 receives requests from p1, p2, and p3
(receive,4,RequestsFor0,3)   // but defers all replies since p0 has priority
(receive,4,RequestsFor0,5)

(receive,1,RepliesFor0,11)   // p0 receives replies from p1, p2, and p3
(receive,1,RepliesFor0,12)   // and enters/exits its critical section
(receive,1,RepliesFor0,13)

(arrival,1,RepliesFor1,15)   // p0 sends all of its deferred replies
(arrival,1,RepliesFor2,16)
(arrival,1,RepliesFor3,17)

(receive,8,RequestsFor1,4)   // p1's helper receives requests from p2 and p3 but
(receive,8,RequestsFor1,6)   // defers replies since p1 has priority over p2 and p3

(receive,12,RequestsFor2,7)   // p2's helper receives rqst from p3, but defers reply

(receive,5,RepliesFor1,11)   // p1 receives all replies and enters/exits CS
(receive,5,RepliesFor1,12)
(receive,5,RepliesFor1,13)

(arrival,5,RepliesFor2,15)   // p1 sends its deferred replies to p2 and p3
(arrival,5,RepliesFor3,16)

(receive,9,RepliesFor2,11)   // p2 receives all replies and enters/exits CS
(receive,9,RepliesFor2,12)
(receive,9,RepliesFor2,13)

(arrival,9,RepliesFor3,15)   // p2 sends its deferred reply to p3

(receive,13,RepliesFor3,11)   // p3 receives all replies and enters/exits CS
(receive,13,RepliesFor3,12)
(receive,13,RepliesFor3,13)

Figure 6.27   (a) (continued)

// Close events issued by p0:
(close,1,RequestsFor1,18), (close,1,RepliesFor1,19), (close,1,RequestsFor2,20),
(close,1,RepliesFor2,21), (close,1,RequestsFor3,22), (close,1,RepliesFor3,23),
// Close events issued by p1:
(close,5,RequestsFor0,17), (close,5,RepliesFor0,18), (close,5,RequestsFor2,19),
(close,5,RepliesFor2,20), (close,5,RequestsFor3,21), (close,5,RepliesFor3,22),
// Close events issued by p2:
(close,9,RequestsFor0,16), (close,9,RepliesFor0,17), (close,9,RequestsFor1,18),
(close,9,RepliesFor1,19), (close,9,RequestsFor3,20), (close,9,RepliesFor3,21),
// Close events issued by p3:
(close,13,RequestsFor0,15), (close,13,RepliesFor0,16),
(close,13,RequestsFor1,17),
(close,13,RepliesFor1,18), (close,13,RequestsFor2,19), (close,13,RepliesFor2,20).

Figure 6.27   (*a*) (*continued*)

(exit,5,Coordinator:chooseNumberAndSetRequesting,NA)
(entry,8,Coordinator:decideAboutDeferral,NA)
(exit,8,Coordinator:decideAboutDeferral,NA)
(entry,8,Coordinator:decideAboutDeferral,NA)
(exit,8,Coordinator:decideAboutDeferral,NA)
(entry,8,Coordinator:decideAboutDeferral,NA)
(exit,8,Coordinator:decideAboutDeferral,NA)
(entry,5,Coordinator:resetRequesting,NA)
(exit,5,Coordinator:resetRequesting,NA)

Figure 6.27   (*b*) Feasible M-sequence for the monitor of *process1*.

Distributed DejaVu does not try to address the feasibility problem. It would
be difficult for users to specify test sequences in DejaVu format since DejaVu
traces contain low-level implementation details about the network operations. By
contrast, the CARC-sequences used by our mailbox classes are at a higher level
of abstraction. Combining the precise and transparent control that is enabled at
the JVM level with the expressiveness of working at the source-code level is
probably the best approach.

FURTHER READING

Distributed programming paradigms are discussed in [Raynal 1988], [Andrews
2000], and [Garg 2002]. Several TCP libraries for Windows are described in [Pee
2001], [Smerka 2001], [Sobczak 2001], and [Schmidt and Huston 2002]. C++
classes for socket programming are described in [Smerka 2001] and [Sobczak
2001]. The Windows.NET framework provides a socket interface similar to the
Java library. It is not difficult to create C# and .NET versions of our tracing,
testing, and replay solutions.

REFERENCES

Andrews, Gregory R. (2000). *Foundations of Multithreaded, Parallel, and Distributed Programming*. Reading, MA: Addison-Wesley.

Baldoni, R., and M. Raynal (2002). Fundamentals of distributed computing: a practical tour of vector clock systems. IEEE Distributed Systems Online, http://dsonline. computer.org.

Bartlet, K. A., R. A. Scantlebury, and P. T. Wilkinson (1969). A note on reliable full-duplex transmission over half duplex lines. *Communications of the ACM*, Vol. 12, No. 5 (May), pp. 260–261.

Bechini, Alessio, and K. C. Tai (1998). Timestamps for programs using messages and shared variables. *Proc. International Conference on Distributed Computing Systems*, pp. 266–273.

Brzezinski, Jerszy, Jean-Michel, Helary, and Michel Raynal (1993). Distributed termination detection: general models and algorithms. *Proc. 13th IEEE International Conference on Distributed Computing Systems*.

Choi, J., and H. Srinivasan (1998). Deterministic replay of Java multithreaded applications. *Proc. ACM Sigmetrics Symposium on Parallel and Distributed Tools*, pp. 48–59.

Fidge, C. (1991). Logical time in distributed computing systems. *IEEE Computer*, Vol. 24, August, pp. 8–33.

Fidge, C. (1996). Fundamentals of distributed system observation. *IEEE Software*, Vol. 13, No. 6 (November), pp. 77–83.

Garg, Vijay K. (2002). *Elements of Distributed Computing*. Hoboken, NJ: Wiley.

Gleason, Mike (2001). The ephemeral port range. http://www.ncftpd.com/ncftpd/doc/ misc/ephemeral_ports.html#Windows

Hartley, Steven J. (1998). *Concurrent Programming: The Java Programming Language*. New York: Oxford University Press.

Konuru, R., H. Srinivasan, and J. -D. Choi (2000). Deterministic replay of distributed Java applications. *Proc. 14th International Parallel and Distributed Processing Symposium (IPDPS'00)*, pp. 219–228.

Lamport, L. (1978). Time, clocks, and the ordering of events in a distributed system. *Communications of the ACM*, Vol. 21, No. 7 (July), pp. 558–565.

Mattern, F. (1989). Virtual time and global states of distributed systems. In M. Cosnard et al. (Eds.), *Proc. International Workshop on Parallel and Distributed Algorithms*. Amsterdam: Elsevier North-Holland, pp. 215–226.

Netzer, R. B., and B. P. Miller (1993). Optimal tracing and replay for debugging shared-memory parallel programs. *Proc. 3rd ACM/ONR Workshop on Parallel and Distributed Debugging*, pp. 1–11.

Pee, James (2001). Guidelines for wrapping sockets in classes. *C/C++ Users Journal*, December, pp. 10–16.

Plouzeau, N., and M. Raynal (1992). Elements for a course on the design of distributed algorithms. *SIGCSE Bulletin*, Vol. 24, No. 2, pp. 35–40.

Raynal, M. (1988). *Distributed Algorithms and Protocols*. New York: Wiley.

Ricart, G., and A. K. Agrawala (1981). An optimal algorithm for mutual exclusion in computer networks. *Communications of the ACM*, Vol. 24, No. 1 (January), pp. 9–17.

Schmidt, Douglas C., and Stephen D. Huston (2002). *C++ Network Programming: Mastering Complexity Using ACE and Patterns*. Reading, MA: Addison-Wesley.

Schwarz, R., and F. Mattern (1994). Detecting causal relationships in distributed computations: in search of the Holy Grail. *Distributed Computing*, Vol. 7, No. 3, pp. 149–174.

Smerka, Richard (2001). Two classes for simple socket programming. *C/C++ Users Journal*, May, pp. 34–41.

Sobczak, Maciej (2001). An IOStream compatible socket wrapper. *C/C++ Users Journal*, December, pp. 18–27.

EXERCISES

6.1. For a given execution, let e_i be an event in thread T_i and e_j be an event in a different thread T_j, $i\ != j$. If only asynchronous communication is used, then $e_i \Rightarrow \varepsilon_j$ if and only if $VT(e_i)[i] \leq VT(e_j)[i]$. Give a rule that can be used to determine when events e_i and e_j are concurrent.

6.2. Show that if event e_1 occurs before event e_2 in real time, it is possible that the integer timestamp for e_1 is greater than the integer timestamp for e_2 [i.e., $IT(e_1) > IT(e_2)$]. (The real-time order of events e_1 and e_2 may not be possible to know, but assume that e_1 occurs before e_2 in real time.) Now consider vector timestamps. If $VT(e_1) > VT(e_2)$, is it possible that e_1 occurred before e_2 in real time?

6.3. Figure 6.28 shows a computation of processes P, Q, and R using asynchronous communication. The messages in this computation are $p1 \rightarrow q1$, $r1 \rightarrow q2$, $q3 \rightarrow p2$, $p3 \rightarrow q4$, and $r2 \rightarrow q5$.

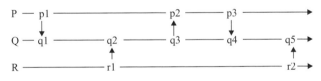

Figure 6.28   A distributed computation.

(a) Determine the integer timestamp of each event in the computation above.

(b) Determine the vector timestamp of each event in the computation above. Each vector timestamp has three elements, with the first, second, and third elements indicating logical clock values for P, Q, and R, respectively.

(c) Indicate all of the events that are concurrent with P3.

(d) Indicate all of the events that are concurrent with R2.

6.4. The Alternating Bit Protocol (ABP) in Section 6.4.3 handles lost messages but assumes that messages are not corrupted, duplicated, or reordered.

Show that reordered messages are not handled correctly by ABP. Messages are considered to be reordered when the order in which they are received is not the same as the order in which they were sent.

6.5. The following is a description of a token-based distributed mutual exclusion algorithm.

There is a single token shared by n threads. A thread cannot enter its critical section unless it holds the token. A thread holding the token may send it to any other thread:

- The token has a vector [E1, E2, ... , En], where Ei indicates the number of times thread Ti has entered its critical section.
- When thread Ti wants to enter its critical section for the (Mi)th time, it sends the message "request(Ti,Mi)" to all the other threads in the system. It then waits until it receives the token. At that time, it modifies the token vector by setting Ei = Mi and enters its critical section.
- After exiting the critical section, Ti examines the incoming request queue:

  - If the request queue is empty, Ti continues execution (i.e., Ti continues entering and exiting its critical section) until it receives a request message.
  - If the request queue is nonempty, Ti does the following:

    do {
        remove the first request message (Tj,Mj);
        if (Mj > Ej) // Ej is the vector value in the token that Ti is holding
            Ti sends the token to Tj and exits the loop;
        else Ti discards this useless request;
    } until (the request queue is empty);

(a) Implement this algorithm using the same structure used in the permission-based *distributedMutualExclusion* algorithm in Section 6.4.1 of the notes. For this exercise, you may want to use the channel classes from Chapter 5 instead of the TCP mailbox classes.

(b) This algorithm contains the statement

    if (Mj > Ej) // Ej is the vector value in the token that Ti is holding
        Ti sends the token to Tj and exits the loop;
    else Ti discards this request;

If the comparison (Mj > Ej) is replaced with (Mj == Ej+1), is the resulting algorithm correct?

(c) Based on this algorithm, a thread deletes old messages in its request queue only when the thread has the token. But is it possible for a thread to delete old messages when the thread does not have the token? If you believe that it is possible, show how to delete as many old messages as possible when a thread does not have the token. Your solution cannot involve a thread making a copy of the token before sending it to another thread.

6.6. Suppose that there are two communicating processes. Process P1 sends three messages to process P2, which receives all three messages. The sends are nonblocking, and the order in which messages are received is not necessarily the order in which they are sent. Figure 6.29 shows an incomplete space-time diagram (i.e., the arrows are missing) that describes such a scenario. Assume that each si and rj event is timestamped with a vector timestamp. Is it possible to use the timestamps to complete the space-time diagram by drawing arrows between matching send and receive events? For example, if we determine from the timestamps that the message sent by s1 must have been received by receive event r5, we would draw an arrow between s1 and r5: s1 → r5. Describe how to use the timestamps to draw the arrows, or show that this cannot be done (i.e., that we cannot always be certain how to draw the arrows based on the information in the timestamps alone).

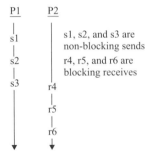

Figure 6.29   Distributed computation.

6.7. Show how to convert vector timestamps into integer timestamps. The integer timestamps that you generate do not have to have the values that would be produced by the algorithm in Section 6.3.5. Just make sure that if event s happens before event t, the integer timestamp of s is less than the integer timestamp of t.

6.8. *Distributed parking lot* [Plouzeau and Raynal 1992]. Implement a distributed algorithm for the case where two gate threads (Gate$_1$ and Gate$_2$) control access to a parking lot (Fig. 6.30). The gate threads must communicate by using message passing; no shared variable communication is allowed between the gates. The automobile threads (Auto) call the gates to enter and exit the parking lot. The size of the parking lot is 3. Denote the number of automobiles that have entered the parking lots as "in," and the number of automobiles that have exited the parking lot as "out." Then the following global condition must always be true: in − out ≤ 3.

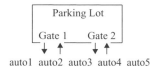

Figure 6.30   Distributed parking lot.

The Gate threads exchange messages about the count of automobiles that have entered and exited through them. These messages are never lost and they arrive in the order sent. The counters used by the Gates are:

- in_1 = number of automobiles that have entered through Gate$_1$
- in_2 = number of automobiles that have entered through Gate$_2$
- out_1 = number of automobiles that have exited through Gate$_1$
- out_2 = number of automobiles that have exited through Gate$_2$

Then the global condition above becomes $in_1 + in_2 - (out_1 + out_2) \leq 3$. Note that each gate has exact knowledge only about the value of its own counters (e.g., Gate$_1$ knows in_1 and out_1 but not Gate$_2$'s counters). Thus, neither Gate can evaluate the global condition exactly. Each Gate can, however, maintain a "safe" approximation for the other Gate's values. (For example, if the value that Gate$_1$ uses for in_2 is always greater than or equal to Gate$_2$'s actual value of in_2, Gate$_1$ is safe from making errors.) Use a simple request/reply protocol to make sure that each Gate maintains a safe value for the other's variables. (That is, the Gates will need to exchange messages to coordinate their counters and to make sure that their messages have been seen by the other Gate.)

Make sure you consider the case where the Gates have both sent a request message. Is a deadlock possible in your program? Should one Gate cancel its request? What if the both Gates cancel their requests? How can a tie be broken? For this exercise, you may want to use the channel classes from Chapter 5 instead of the TCP mailbox classes.

6.9. Implement classes *TCPEntryClient* and *TCPEntryServer*. Together, they should provide the same interface as class *Entry* in Chapter 5, and support client–server communication through methods *call()*, *accept()*, and *reply()*.

Class *TCPEntryClient* encapsulates a *socket* and the stream-based code for communicating with the server. A client creates a *TCPEntryClient* object and uses it to send a serialized *request* object to the server and receive a serialized *reply* object from the server:

```
TCPEntryClient requestAndReply = new
    TCPEntryClient(serverHost,serverPort);
...
Message reply = (Message) requestAndReply.call(request);
```

No connection is made with the server until a *call()* occurs. Class *TCPEntryServer* encapsulates a *ServerSocket* and the stream-based code for communicating with clients. A server creates a *TCPEntryServer* object and executes *accept()* to receive a message and *reply()* to send a reply:

TCPEntryServer requestAndReply = new TCPEntryServer(serverPort);
request = (Message) requestAndReply.accept();
requestAndReply.reply(result);

6.10. For diagram D5 in Fig. 6.13, determine the causal relation between the following pairs of events: (n, o), (b, r), (p, z), (a, z), (a, n), (b, n), (c, n), b, z), (n, w). For a given pair (e1, e2), indicate either e1 $\Rightarrow$ e2, e2 $\Rightarrow$ e1, or e1 $\|$ e2. Justify your answers using rules (HB1)–(HB3) in Section 6.3.5.

6.11. *Distributed mutual exclusion.* The following questions refer to Listing 6.16:

(a) Suppose that method *resetRequesting()* is not in the *Coordinator* monitor (i.e., remove the calls to *enterMonitor()* and *exitMonitor* from this method). Suppose further that method *deferrMessage()* returns the *boolean* value *deferMessage* immediately before the if-statement, so that the statement "deferred[m.ID] = true;" is executed by the *helper* thread whenever it receives a *true* return value from *deferMessage()*. Show that a deadlock is possible.

(b) Suppose that process *m* decides to enter its critical section and sends a request message to process *n*. Process *n* sends a reply to process *m* indicating that process *n* does not want to enter its critical section. Suppose further that process *n* later decides to enter its critical section and sends a request message to process *m* (and to all the other processes). What happens if process *n*'s request message is received by process *m* before process *n*'s earlier reply message is received by process *m*?

7

TESTING AND DEBUGGING CONCURRENT PROGRAMS

Software development is a complex activity. Requirements are collected from users and then analyzed to create a specification of what the software is expected to do. Programs are designed and coded to satisfy the specification and then maintained after they are delivered to the customer. The life cycle of a program also includes testing and debugging phases. In fact, there are many development activities that can produce executable programs of one sort or another: prototypes, specifications, and designs all may be targeted for testing.

- The purpose of testing is to find program failures.

A successful test is a test that causes a program to fail. Ideally, tests are designed *before* the program is written. Designing good tests is not easy, but the thought that goes into test design can find and fix potential failures before they are written into the software.

The conventional approach to testing a program is to execute the program with each test input selected once and then compare the test results with the expected results. Performing this comparison manually is usually tedious, time consuming, and error-prone, and is the hardest part of testing. The term *failure* is used when a program produces unexpected results.

- A failure is an observed departure of the external result of software operation from software requirements or user expectations [IEEE90].

Modern Multithreading: Implementing, Testing, and Debugging Multithreaded Java and C++/Pthreads/Win32 Programs, By Richard H. Carver and Kuo-Chung Tai
Copyright © 2006 John Wiley & Sons, Inc.

In earlier chapters we saw several special ways in which concurrent programs can fail, including deadlock, livelock, starvation, and data races. Failures can be caused by hardware or software faults.

- A software *fault* (or "bug") is a defective, missing, or extra instruction, or a set of related instructions that is the cause of one or more actual or potential failures.

Faults are the result of human errors. For example, an error in writing an `if`-`else` statement may result in a fault that causes an execution to take a wrong branch. If this execution produces the wrong result, it is said to fail; otherwise, the result is coincidentally correct, and the internal state and path of the execution must be examined to detect the error.

If a test input causes a program to fail, the program is executed again, with the same input, in order to collect debugging information.

- *Debugging* is the process of locating and correcting faults.

Since it is not possible to anticipate the information that will be needed to pinpoint the location of a fault, debugging information is collected and refined over the course of many executions until the problem is understood.

After the fault has been located and corrected, the program is executed again with each of the previously tested inputs to verify that the fault has been corrected and that in doing so, no new faults have been introduced. Such testing, called *regression testing*, is also needed after the program has been modified during the maintenance phase.

This cyclical process of testing, followed by debugging, followed by more testing, is commonly applied to sequential programs. Together, testing and debugging account for at least half of the cost of developing large software systems [Beizer 1979]. Unfortunately, this cyclical process breaks down when it is applied to concurrent programs.

Let CP be a concurrent program. Multiple executions of CP with the *same* input may produce *different* results. This nondeterministic execution behavior creates the following problems during the testing and debugging cycle of CP.

Problem 1   When testing CP with input X, a single execution is insufficient to determine the correctness of CP with X. Even if CP with input X has been executed successfully many times, it is possible that a future execution of CP with X will fail.

Problem 2   When debugging a failed execution of CP with input X, there is no guarantee that this execution will be repeated by executing CP with X.

Problem 3   After CP has been modified to correct a fault detected during a failed execution of CP with input X, one or more successful executions of CP with X during regression testing does not imply that the detected fault has been corrected.

Our general framework for understanding and solving these three problems focuses on the synchronization behavior of CP. We assume that CP consists of two or more concurrent processes or threads that communicate and synchronize with each other via constructs such as semaphores, monitors, shared variables, and message passing. An execution of CP is characterized by CP's inputs and the sequence of synchronization events that CP exercises, referred to as the *synchronization sequence* (or *SYN-sequence*) of the execution. The definition of a SYN-sequence is based on the programming language and the synchronization constructs used in the program. We intentionally avoid dealing with implementation-level concerns, such as the compiler, the virtual machine, or the operating system, to keep our framework as abstract and as portable as possible. Defining various types of SYN-sequences is the focus of Section 7.1. In later sections, the general issues and problems that are encountered during testing and debugging are discussed in terms of SYN-sequences. SYN-sequences are used in Section 7.2 to define the paths of a concurrent program and in Section 7.3 to define program correctness and the types of faults in concurrent programs. Section 7.4 describes several approaches to testing concurrent programs. One of these approaches, reachability testing, is described in detail in Section 7.5. All of these approaches were illustrated in earlier chapters.

7.1 SYNCHRONIZATION SEQUENCES OF CONCURRENT PROGRAMS

The definition of a SYN-sequence can be *language-based* or *implementation-based*, or a combination of both. A *language-based definition* is based on the concurrent programming constructs available in a given programming language. An *implementation-based definition* is based on the implementation of these constructs, including the interface with the run-time system, virtual machine, and operating system. In this section we discuss language-based definitions of SYN-sequences. In the following discussion, it is assumed that a concurrent program has no real-time constraints and that all nonsynchronization constructs are deterministic.

Threads in a concurrent program synchronize by performing synchronization operations on synchronization objects, or *SYN-objects*. For example, threads may perform *P()* and *V()* operations on semaphore objects, or *send()* and *receive()* operations on channel objects. A synchronization event, or *SYN-event*, refers to the execution of one of these operations. Thus, an execution of a concurrent program consists of concurrent threads performing SYN-events on SYN-objects. The order in which SYN-events are executed is nondeterministic.

7.1.1 Complete Events vs. Simple Events

Consider the program in Listing 7.1, which uses the synchronous mailboxes defined in Chapter 5. The order in which the messages sent by Thread1 and Thread4 will arrive at mailboxes C1 and C2 is unpredictable. Also, the order in mailbox C1, C2; // synchronous mailboxes

Thread1	Thread2	Thread3	Thread4
C1.send(msg1);	msg = C1.receive();	msg = C1.receive();	C1.send(msg1);
C2.send(msg2);	msg = C2.receive();	msg = C2.receive();	C2.send(msg2);

Listing 7.1   Message passing using synchronous mailboxes.

which Thread2 and Thread3 will receive messages from these mailboxes is unpredictable. In general, a complete characterization of an execution of a concurrent program requires information to be recorded about the SYN-events exercised during this execution. This information can be used to replay an execution or to determine whether a particular SYN-sequence can or cannot occur.

For a concurrent programming language or construct, its *complete SYN-event set* is the set of all types of SYN-events. For example, for the monitor construct in Chapter 4, the types of SYN-events included entering and exiting a monitor and executing a `wait` or `signal` operation. The *complete SYN-event format* is the format used for recording information about each type of SYN-event. The complete SYN-event set and SYN-event format are not necessarily unique, but they must provide sufficient information to describe the synchronizations between threads. In general, the complete SYN-event format contains the following information:

(thread name(s), event type, object name, additional information)

which indicates that a specific thread, or a pair of synchronizing threads, executes a SYN-event of a specific type on a specific SYN-object. Some additional information may be recorded to capture important details about the event, such as the event's vector timestamp (see Section 6.3.6).

Notice that the information recorded about a SYN-event may not include the values of the messages that are received or the values of the shared variables that are read or written. These values may or may not be needed for a particular task. For example, they are not needed for program replay, since they will be (re)computed during the normal course of execution. Omitting these values from SYN-events reduces the amount of space required for saving traces. On the other hand, we may need to know something about these values in order to assess the correctness of an execution. In this case, some representation of these values can be included as part of the additional information recorded about SYN-events.

Example 1   The SYN-events for the program in Listing 7.1 involve sending and receiving messages through *mailboxes* and are called SR-events. Assume that we list all of the SYN-events of an execution as a single linear sequence. Then the complete format of an SR-event is

(sending thread, receiving thread, mailbox name, event type).

One possible complete SR-sequence of this program is

(Thread1, Thread2, C1, SendReceive-synchronization),
(Thread4, Thread3, C1, SendReceive-synchronization),
(Thread1, Thread2, C2, SendReceive-synchronization),
(Thread4, Thread3, C2, SendReceive-synchronization).

SR-sequences for *links, ports*, and *mailboxes* were defined in Section 5.5.1.

   The *complete SYN-sequence* of an execution of program CP is the sequence of SYN-events exercised during this execution, where the information recorded about each SYN-event appears in the complete SYN-event format. The complete SYN-sequence of an execution of CP provides sufficient information to resolve any sources of nondeterminism during execution. For example, if two threads send messages at the same time to the same mailbox, the SYN-sequence specifies the order in which the messages will be received. Consequently, the result of an execution of CP is determined by CP and the input and complete SYN-sequence of this execution. In Section 7.3 we also see that the input and complete SYN-sequence of an execution together determine the path exercised by the execution.
   Some of the information recorded in a complete SYN-event is not needed for program replay. Since the SYN-sequences that we use for replay tend to be simpler than other types of SYN-sequences, we use the term *simple SYN-sequence* to refer to a SYN-sequence that is used for replay. Just as complete SYN-sequences do, a simple SYN-sequence of CP provides sufficient information to resolve any sources of nondeterminism during execution. Thus, the result of an execution of CP is determined by CP and the input and simple SYN-sequence of this execution.

Example 2   For the program in Listing 7.1, the format of a simple SR-event is

(Sender, Receiver).

The simple SR-sequence corresponding to the complete SR-sequence in Example 1 is

(Thread1, Thread2),
(Thread4, Thread3),
(Thread1, Thread2),
(Thread4, Thread3).

Simple SR-sequences were defined in Section 5.5.2.

   Notice that the first simple SR-event in Example 2 does not specify which channel is accessed by Thread1 and Thread2. During replay, the first channel that Thread1 and Thread2 access is guaranteed to be C1, assuming that we have not made any changes to the program in Listing 7.1. Since the particular channel accessed by a thread does not need to be controlled or checked during replay, the channel name "C1" does not appear in the first simple SR-event. However, during replay there is a need to control which pair of threads, Thread1 and Thread2 or Thread4 and Thread3, access channel C1 first. Thus, thread names appear in the simple SR-events recorded during an execution. During replay, the threads are forced to access the channels in the order given in the recorded sequence.

The situation is different during testing. When we test the program in Listing 7.1, we need to determine whether the threads are synchronizing on the correct channels, in the correct order. In this case, whether Thread1 and Thread2 can and should synchronize on channel C1 is a question that we need to answer. To check this, we use complete SR-events, which specify the threads and the channel name for each synchronization event, and a complete SR-sequence, which specifies a synchronization order. During execution, we try to force the threads to synchronize in the specified order, on the specified channels. If the results are not as expected, either there is a problem with the program or we made a mistake when we generated the test sequence.

In general, it takes less information to replay an execution than to determine whether an execution is allowed by a program. But information that is ignored during both of these activities may be important when we are performing others. Thus, we define different types of SYN-sequences for the various activities that occur during testing and debugging.

7.1.2   Total Ordering vs. Partial Ordering

A SYN-sequence can be a *total* or *partial* ordering of SYN-events. The SYN-sequences in Examples 1 and 2 were totally ordered. A totally ordered SYN-sequence of a program is a single, linear sequence of complete or simple SYN-events. Such a sequence contains all the events exercised by all the threads in the program. When a concurrent program is tested or debugged using totally ordered SYN-sequences, events must be executed one by one, in sequential order, which can have a significant impact on performance. This problem can be alleviated if a partially ordered SYN-sequence is used instead.

A partially ordered SYN-sequence is actually a collection of sequences—there is one sequence for each thread or SYN-object in the program. In a partially ordered sequence, SYN-events that are concurrent are unordered. This means that concurrent events can be executed at the same time, which speeds up execution. Assume that a concurrent program CP consists of threads $T_1, T_2, \ldots, T_m$, $m > 0$, and SYN-objects $O_1, O_2, \ldots$, and O_n, $n > 0$. A partially ordered SYN-sequence of CP may be thread- or object-based:

Thread-Based Sequences   The general format of a partially ordered thread-based SYN-sequence of CP is $(S_1, S_2, \ldots, S_m)$, where sequence S_i, $1 \le i \le m$, denotes a totally ordered sequence of SYN-events of thread T_i. Each event in S_i has thread

T_i as the executing thread and has the general format (object name, object order number, event type, other necessary information). An object's order number is used to indicate the relative order of this event among all the events executed on the object. That is, an event with object order number i is the ith event executed on the object.

Object-Based Sequences   The general format of an partially ordered object-based SYN-sequence of CP is $(S_1, S_2, \ldots, S_n)$, where sequence S_j, $1 \leq j \leq n$, denotes a totally ordered sequence of SYN-events on object O_j. Each event in S_j has object O_j as the SYN-object and has the general format (thread name(s), thread order number(s), event type, other necessary information). A thread's order number is used to indicate the relative order of this event among all the events executed by the thread.

Thread-based sequences are a natural way to visualize message-passing programs. The space-time diagrams in Chapter 6 are partially ordered thread-based sequences. Object-based sequences are helpful for understanding the behavior of an individual SYN-object. For example, object-based M-sequences were defined in Chapter 4 for monitors. Program replay can be implemented using either thread- or object-based sequences. Implementation details and the desired user interface may favor one approach over the other.

Example 3   For the program in Listing 7.1, the synchronization objects are synchronous *mailboxes*. The format of an SR-event in an object-based sequence is

(sending thread, receiving thread, sender's order number, receiver's order number, eventType)

where

- the *sending thread* executed the send operation.
- the *receiving thread* executed the receive operation.
- the *sender's order number* gives the relative order of this event among all of the sending thread's events.
- the *receiver's order number* gives the relative order of this event among all of the receiving thread's events.
- *eventType* is the type of this send–receive event.

One feasible object-based SR-sequence of this program is

Sequence of mailbox C1: (Thread1, Thread2, 1, 1, SendReceive-synchronization), (Thread4, Thread3, 1, 1, SendReceive-synchronization).

Sequence of mailbox C2: (Thread1, Thread2, 2, 2, SendReceive-synchronization), (Thread4, Thread3, 2, 2, SendReceive-synchronization).

A thread-based SR-event for thread T is denoted by

(channel name, channel's order number, eventType)

where

- the *channel name* is the name of the channel.
- the *channel order number* gives the relative order of this event among all the channel's events.
- *eventType* is the type of this send–receive event.

The thread-based SR-sequence corresponding to the object-based sequence above is

Sequence of Thread1: (C1, 1, SendReceive-synchronization),
                                     (C2, 1, SendReceive-synchronization).
Sequence of Thread2: (C1, 1, SendReceive-synchronization),
                                     (C2, 1, SendReceive-synchronization).
Sequence of Thread3: (C1, 2, SendReceive-synchronization),
                                     (C1, 2, SendReceive-synchronization).
Sequence of Thread4: (C2, 2, SendReceive-synchronization),
                                     (C2, 2, SendReceive-synchronization).

Thread- and object-based SR-sequences were defined in Section 5.5.

Totally ordered SYN-sequences can be converted into partially ordered object- and thread-based SYN-sequences. Object- and thread-based sequences can be converted into each other. Note that the totally and partially ordered SYN-sequences of an execution should have the same happened-before relation. Chapter 6 described how to use integer timestamps to translate a partially ordered sequence into a totally ordered sequence.

7.2 PATHS OF CONCURRENT PROGRAMS

In this section we address the relationship between the paths and SYN-sequences of a concurrent program. First we define what a path is in a concurrent program. Based on this definition, we then provide a brief overview of path-based test coverage criteria for sequential programs and describe several path-based criteria for concurrent programs.

7.2.1 Defining a Path

An execution of a sequential program exercises a sequence of statements, referred to as a *path* of the program. The result of an execution of a sequential program is determined by the input and the sequence of statements executed during the port M; // synchronous port

Thread1	Thread2	Thread3
(1) M.send(A);	(2) M.send(B);	(3) X = M.receive();
		(4) Y = M.receive();
		(5) output the difference (X − Y) of X and Y

Listing 7.2   Program CP using synchronous communication.

execution. However, this is not true for a concurrent program. Consider program CP in Listing 7.2, which uses synchronous communication.

Assume that an execution of CP with input $A = 1$ and $B = 2$ exercises the totally ordered sequence of statements (1), (2), (3), (4), (5). Since this sequence does not specify whether the message sent at statement (1) is received at statement (3) or at statement (4), it does not provide sufficient information to determine the output of the execution. Note that this same problem exists if we consider partially ordered sequences. That is, every execution of CP executes the following partially ordered sequence of statements:

Sequence of Thread1: (1)
Sequence of Thread2: (2)
Sequence of Thread3: (3), (4), (5)

But this partially ordered sequence does not provide enough information to determine the result of the execution.

Based on this discussion, we now define a proper definition of a path. A totally ordered path of a concurrent program is a totally ordered sequence of statements plus additional information about any synchronization events that are generated by these statements. For example, a totally ordered path of program CP in Listing 7.2 is

((1), (2), (3, Thread1), (4, Thread2), (5)).

Events (3, Thread1) and (4, Thread2) denote that the receive statements in (3) and (4) receive messages from Thread1 and Thread2, respectively.

Of course, information about the synchronization events of a path can be specified separately in the form of a SYN-sequence. Thus, a totally ordered path of CP is associated with a SYN-sequence of CP, referred to as the SYN-sequence of this path. Assume that CP contains threads $T_1, T_2, \ldots,$ and T_n. A partially ordered path of CP is $(P_1, P_2, \ldots, P_n)$, where P_i, $1 \le i \le n$, is a totally ordered path of thread T_i. A partially ordered path of CP is associated with the partially ordered SYN-sequence of this path. In the following discussion, unless otherwise specified, SYN-sequences of CP are thread-based and totally or partially ordered.

A path (SYN-sequence) of CP is said to be *feasible for CP with input X* if this path (SYN-sequence) can be exercised by some execution of CP with input

X. A path (SYN-sequence) of CP is said to be *feasible for CP* if this path (SYN-sequence) can be exercised by some execution of CP. The *domain* of a path or SYN-sequence S of CP is a set of input values. Input X is in the domain of a path or SYN-sequence S if S is feasible for CP with input X. The domain of an infeasible path or SYN-sequence is empty.

The following relationships exist between the paths and SYN-sequences of CP:

1. If a path is feasible for CP with input X, the SYN-sequence of this path is feasible for CP with input X.

2. If a partially ordered SYN-sequence S is feasible for CP with input X, there exists only one partially ordered feasible path of CP with input X such that the partially ordered SYN-sequence of this path is S. Thus, there exists a one-to-one mapping between partially ordered feasible paths of CP with input X and partially ordered feasible SYN-sequences of CP with input X.

3. If a totally ordered SYN-sequence S is feasible for CP with input X, there exists at least one totally ordered feasible path of CP with input X such that the totally ordered SYN-sequence of this path is S.

4. If two or more totally ordered feasible paths of CP with input X have the same totally or partially ordered SYN-sequence, these paths produce the same result and thus are considered to be equivalent.

5. The domains of two or more different partially ordered feasible paths of CP are not necessarily mutually disjoint. This statement is also true for two or more totally ordered feasible paths of CP. The reason is that CP with a given input may have two or more different partially or totally ordered feasible SYN-sequences.

6. If two or more different partially ordered feasible paths of CP have the same partially ordered SYN-sequence, their input domains are mutually disjoint. However, this statement is not true for totally ordered feasible paths of CP (see Exercise 7.11).

We will illustrate relationship 5 with an example. Consider the following program:

Thread1	Thread2	Thread3
(1) p1.send();	(1) p2.send();	(1) input(x);
		(2) if (x)
		(3) output(x);
		(4) select
		(5) p1.receive();
		(6) p2.receive();
		(7) or
		(8) p2.receive();
		(9) p1.receive();
		(10) end select;

One partially ordered path of this program is

Thread1: (1)
Thread2: (1)
Thread3: (1), (2), (3), (5,Thread1), (6,Thread2)

and another path is

Thread1: (1)
Thread2: (1)
Thread3: (1), (2), (3), (8,Thread2), (9,Thread1)

These paths are different, but the value of input x is *true* in both paths, so their input domains are not disjoint. In sequential programs, paths that are different have disjoint domains.

7.2.2   Path-Based Testing and Coverage Criteria

A number of test coverage criteria have been developed for sequential programs. Coverage criteria are used to determine when testing can stop and to guide the generation of input values for test cases. Structural coverage criteria focus on the paths in a program. The *all-paths* criterion requires every path to be executed at least once. Since the number of paths in a program may be very large or even infinite, it may be impractical to cover them all. Thus, a number of weaker criteria have been defined [Myers 1979]. The minimum structural coverage criterion is *statement coverage*, which requires every statement in a program to be executed at least once.

Some stronger criteria focus on the predicates in a program. The predicates in `if-else` and `loop` statements divide the input domain into partitions and define the paths of a program. Simple predicates contain a single condition which is either a single Boolean variable [e.g., if (B)] or a relational expression [e.g., if (e1 < e2)], possibly with one or more negation operators (!). Compound predicates contain two or more conditions connected by the logical operators AND ($\wedge$) and OR ($\vee$) [e.g., if ((e1 < e2) $\wedge$ (e2 < e3))]. Predicate coverage criteria require certain types of tests for each predicate:

- *Decision coverage* requires every (simple or compound) predicate to evaluate to `true` at least once and to `false` at least once. Decision coverage is also known as *branch coverage*.
- *Condition coverage* requires each condition in each predicate to evaluate to `true` at least once and to `false` at least once. Note that decision coverage can be satisfied without testing both outcomes of each condition in the predicate. For example, decision coverage for the predicate $(A \wedge B)$ is satisfied by two tests, the first being $(A = \text{true}, B = \text{true})$ and the second

being (A = true, B = false). But neither of these tests causes A to be false. Condition coverage requires A to be false at least once.

- *Decision/condition coverage* requires both decision coverage and condition coverage to be satisfied. Note that condition coverage can be satisfied without satisfying decision coverage. For example, for the predicate ($A \vee B$), condition coverage is satisfied by two tests: (A = true, B = false) and (A = false, B = true). But neither of these tests causes the predicate to be false. Decision/condition coverage requires the predicate to be false at least once.

- *Multiple-condition coverage* requires all possible combinations of condition outcomes in each predicate to occur at least once. Note that for a predicate with N conditions, there are 2^N possible combinations of outcomes for the conditions.

These criteria can be compared based on the *subsumes* relation [Frankl and Weyuker 1988]. A coverage criterion C_1 is said to *subsume* another criterion C_2 if and only if any set of paths that satisfies criterion C_1 also satisfies criterion C_2 [Taylor et al. 1992]. For example, decision coverage subsumes statement coverage since covering all decisions necessarily covers all statements. This does not mean, however, that a coverage criterion that subsumes another is always more effective at detecting failures. Whether or not a failure occurs may also depend on the particular input values that are chosen for a test. Figure 7.3 shows a hierarchy of criteria based on the subsumes relation. A path from criterion X to Y indicates that X subsumes Y.

Instead of focusing on the control characteristics of a program, other structural coverage criteria focus on the patterns in which data is defined and used. The *all-du-paths* criterion requires tests for *definition–use* (du) *pairs*: If a variable is defined in one statement and used in another, there should be at least one test path that passes through both statements. Uses may occur in predicates or in computations. Under certain assumptions, all-du-paths subsumes decision coverage [Parrish and Zweben 1995].

Structural coverage criteria are often defined with respect to a flowgraph model of a program. In a flowgraph, each circular node represents a statement or a collection of sequential statements that will be executed as a block. That is, if

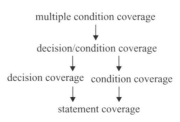

Figure 7.3 Hierarchy of sequential, structural coverage criteria based on the subsumes relation.

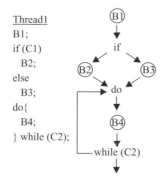

```
Thread1
B1;
if (C1)
    B2;
else
    B3;
do{
    B4;
} while (C2);
```

Figure 7.4 A thread and its control-flow graph.

the first statement in the block is executed, all the statements in the block will be executed. The edges between the nodes represent the flow of control from one block of code to the next. Figure 7.4 shows an example flowgraph for a thread that contains an if-else statement and a do-while loop. Note that some paths through a flowgraph may represent program paths that are not executable. The predicates in the if-else and loop statements must be examined to determine which paths are executable.

In a flowgraph model, statement coverage is achieved by covering *all-nodes*. Note that when a node is executed, each statement in the block represented by that node is guaranteed to be executed. Decision coverage is achieved by covering *all-edges* of the flowgraph. These structural criteria can be applied during unit testing to the individual threads in a concurrent program. Consider again program CP in Listing 7.2. None of the threads in CP contain any branches. Thus, any single execution of the program will cover all the statements in CP and all the paths in each of the threads. (Each thread has one path.) However, based on the definition of a path in Section 7.2.1, there are two partially ordered paths of CP: one path in which T3 receives T1's message first, and one path in which T3 receives T2's message first. Path-based coverage criteria for concurrent programs should consider the statements exercised within threads and also the synchronization between threads, since both are used to define the paths of a concurrent program.

The paths of a concurrent program can be presented by a graph structure called a *reachability graph*. There are several ways to build reachability graphs. They differ in their cost and the completeness and accuracy of the resulting graph model. Taylor [1983] showed how to use the flowgraphs of individual threads to build a reachability graph of a program. In this case, the flowgraph constructed for a thread contains only the nodes and edges necessary to capture the thread's synchronization activity (e.g., sending and receiving messages, selecting alternatives in a selective wait). Thus, the flowgraphs of individual threads are simplified by ignoring thread activities unrelated to synchronization. Flowgraphs of the individual threads are analyzed to derive a *concurrency graph* of the program. A concurrency graph contains nodes that represent the concurrency states of the

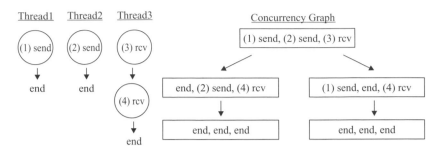

Figure 7.5   Concurrency graph for the program in listing 7.2.

program and edges representing transitions between the states. A concurrency state specifies the next synchronization activity to occur in each of the program's threads. Figure 7.5 shows the flowgraphs for the threads in Listing 7.2 and the concurrency graph for the program. Note that the concurrency graph captures both paths in the program.

Since concurrency graphs ignore statements that are unrelated to synchronization, a path through a concurrency graph corresponds to a SYN-sequence of a program, not a path of the program. This is because two or more different program paths may exercise the same SYN-sequence. In general, the concurrency graph of program CP may not be an accurate representation of the feasible SYN-sequences of CP because the concurrency graph may have been constructed without considering all of CP's semantics. For example, some paths in the graph might not be allowed if the predicates in selective wait and if-else statements were taken into consideration. Building accurate graph models of programs is hard to do. Also, reachability graph models are limited by the state explosion problem, which refers to the rapid increase in the number of states as the number of threads increases.

Based on the concurrency graph model, Taylor et al. [1992] defined structural coverage criteria for synchronous message-passing programs analogously to the criteria for sequential programs:

- *all-concurrency-paths* requires all paths through the concurrency graph (i.e., all SYN-sequences) to be exercised at least once. This criterion is impossible to satisfy if cycles exist in the concurrency graph.
- *all-proper-concurrency-paths* requires all proper paths through the concurrency graph to be exercised at least once. A proper path is a path that does not contain any duplicate states, except that the last state of the path may be duplicated once. Thus, proper paths have a finite length.
- *all-edges-between-concurrency-states* requires that for each edge E in the concurrency graph there is at least one path along which E occurs.
- *all-concurrency-states* requires that for each state S in the concurrency graph there is at least one path along which S occurs.

all-concurrency-paths
↓
all-proper-concurrency-paths
↓
all-edges-between-concurrency-states
↓
all-concurrency-states
↓
all-possible-rendezvous

Figure 7.6   Subsumes hierarchy of structural coverage criteria for concurrent programs.

- *all-possible-rendezvous* requires that for each state S in the concurrency graph that involves a rendezvous between threads there is at least one path along which S occurs.

The subsumes hierarchy for these criteria is shown in Fig. 7.6.

Once a coverage criterion is chosen, a set of SYN-sequences can be selected from the concurrency graph to satisfy the criterion selected. The deterministic testing process, which was illustrated in Section 5.5 for message-passing programs and is described in Section 7.4, can be applied with the test sequences selected.

7.3 DEFINITIONS OF CORRECTNESS AND FAULTS FOR CONCURRENT PROGRAMS

The purpose of testing is to find failures (i.e., show that a program is incorrect). This raises two important questions: How should the correctness of a concurrent program be defined? What types of failures and faults can be found when testing concurrent programs? In this section we present general definitions of correctness, failure, and fault for concurrent programs and illustrate these definitions with the help of a channel-based program. We then formally define three common types of failures, which are known as deadlock, livelock, and starvation. Definitions of these terms are usually informal and often inconsistent, which makes it difficult to discuss the issues involving this important class of failures.

7.3.1 Defining Correctness for Concurrent Programs

Let CP be a concurrent program. A SYN-sequence is said to be *feasible* for CP with input X if this SYN-sequence can be exercised during an execution of CP with input X. Due to nondeterministic execution behavior, there may be several feasible SYN-sequences for CP with input X.

Feasible(CP,X) = the set of feasible SYN-sequences of CP with input X.

A SYN-sequence is said to be valid for CP with input X if, according to the specification of CP, this SYN-sequence is expected to be exercised during an execution of CP with input X. Since nondeterministic execution behavior is expected, there may be several valid SYN-sequences for CP with input X.

Valid(CP,X) = the set of valid SYN-sequences of CP with input X.

These definitions permit some flexibility in how we define the inputs and outputs of a concurrent program. CP could be a stand-alone program (i.e., it reads data from and writes data to files) or a program that interacts with other processes. In the latter case, the inputs and outputs of CP may involve communications with other processes. Also, these definitions assume that synchronization events in the implementation of CP are also events in the specification of CP. If some of the events in the specification of CP are more abstract than the corresponding events in the implementation of CP, specification events must be transformed into implementation events, and there may not be a one-to-one mapping between specification and implementation events. Several other possible relationships between specifications and implementations are discussed below.

Although the sets *Feasible* and *Valid* are, in general, impossible to determine, they are still useful for defining the correctness of concurrent programs, classifying the types of failures in concurrent programs, and comparing various validation techniques for concurrent programs. CP is said to be correct for input X (with respect to the specification of CP) if:

(a) Feasible(CP,X) = Valid(CP,X).
(b) Every possible execution of CP with input X produces the correct (or expected) result. The result of an execution includes the output and termination condition of the execution. The possible types of abnormal termination include divide-by-zero errors, deadlock, and expiration of allocated CPU time, among others.

CP is said to be correct (with respect to the specification of CP) if and only if CP is correct for every possible input. For some concurrent programs, it is possible that the valid/feasible SYN-sequences are independent of the values of the program inputs. This was true for all of the programs in the previous chapters.

Condition (a) specifies a strict equivalence relation between specifications and their implementations. Nonetheless, it is an appropriate relationship for the deterministic testing techniques described in this book. When other validation techniques are being used, condition (a) can be relaxed. Several possible modifications of condition (a) are given below.

(a1) Feasible(CP,X) is a proper subset of Valid(CP,X). This condition is used when the specification of CP uses nondeterminism to model design decisions that are to be made later. That is, a choice that is to be made during the design process is modeled in the specification as a nondeterministic selection between design alternatives. Making design decisions amounts to a *reduction* of the nondeterminism in the specification [Chung et al. 2000]. In this context, specifications and implementations are relative notions in a series of system descriptions, where one description is viewed as an implementation of another description, the specification [Vissers et al. 1991].

(a2) Valid(CP,X) is a proper subset of Feasible(CP,X). This condition is used when the specification of CP is incomplete and thus is *extended* by the implementation. In this case, the implementation adds information that is consistent with the specification.

(a3) Valid(CP,X) = Feasible(CP,X)\S, where S is a set of implementation events that are *not* mentioned in the specification of CP. Feasible(CP,X)\S is obtained from Feasible(CP,X) by deleting from each sequence in Feasible(CP,X) any events that are in S. This condition is used when the events in CP's specification are a proper subset of those in CP's implementation. An example of this appeared in Section 4.10.3, where specification-based communication events and sequences were defined for monitor-based programs. A specification may contain communication events such as "deposit" and "withdraw" while abstracting away implementation events such as entering or executing a monitor or executing a `wait` or `signal` operation.

These alternative equivalence relations can be used by other verification techniques and may be more appropriate at certain phases of the life cycle. In such cases, the foregoing definitions of feasibility, validity, and correctness for a concurrent program can be modified according to the required relationship between a specification and its implementation. At some point, the reductions or extensions made to a specification can be used to generate a new specification, and the valid SYN-sequences of this new specification can be expected to be equivalent to the feasible sequences of the implementation.

When checking the correctness of an execution, it may be convenient to annotate each event in a SYN-sequence with a label that provides an abstract representation of the event (e.g., the label of a receive event can convey information about the value of the message that was received or that is expected to be received). These abstract labels are especially useful for mapping between (abstract) specifications and their implementations and for determining whether or not a feasible sequence of the implementation is also a valid sequence of the specification [Koppol et al. 2002].

7.3.2   Failures and Faults in Concurrent Programs

Based on our earlier definition of correctness, CP is incorrect for input X if and only if one or more of the following conditions hold:

(a) Feasible(CP,X) is not equal to Valid(CP,X). Thus, one or both of the following conditions hold:

(a1) There exists at least one SYN-sequence that is feasible but invalid for CP with input X.

(a2) There exists at least one SYN-sequence that is valid but infeasible for CP with input X.

(b) There exists an execution of CP with input X that exercises a valid (and feasible) SYN-sequence but computes an incorrect result.

The existence of condition (a) is referred to as a *synchronization failure*. (This term has several commonly used synonyms, such as *timing error* and *data race*.) The existence of condition (b) is referred to as a *computation failure*. Note that a sequential program may have computation failures but not synchronization failures.

After an execution of CP with input X completes, it is necessary to determine whether any synchronization or computation failures exist. Assume that an execution exercises a SYN-sequence S and produces a result R. Then one of the following conditions holds: (1) S is valid and R is correct; or (2) S is valid and R is incorrect; or (3) S is invalid and R is incorrect; or (4) S is invalid and R is correct. Condition (2) implies that a computation failure has occurred, while conditions (3) and (4) imply that a synchronization failure has occurred. Note that in condition (4) a correct result R is produced from an incorrect SYN-sequence S, a condition also known as *coincidental correctness*. If the programmer checks only the correctness of R, the invalidity of S will go undetected and might cause condition (3) to occur in the future for the same input or a different input. Thus, when CP is executed, it is important to collect the SYN-sequences that are exercised and determine the validity of each collected SYN-sequence. (As we have already mentioned, the collected SYN-sequences are also needed for regression testing and debugging.)

To illustrate these types of failures, consider the faulty bounded buffer solution in Listing 7.7. Assume that the capacity of the buffer is 2 and that a single producer and a single consumer execute *deposit.call()* and *withdraw.call()* three times, respectively. Note that the set of feasible SR-sequences and the set of valid SR-sequences of this program are independent of the program's inputs.

Thread *boundedBuffer* contains a fault. The guard for the *deposit* alternative:

deposit.guard (fullSlots <= capacity);

is incorrect because it uses the wrong relational operator <=. (The operator should be <.) This fault causes a synchronization failure since it allows an item to be deposited when the buffer is full. Consider an execution of *boundedBuffer* in which the producer deposits items A, B, and C, and the following invalid SR-sequence is exercised:

(producer, boundedBuffer, deposit, rendezvous),
(producer, boundedBuffer, deposit, rendezvous),

```
final class boundedBuffer extends TDThread {
    private selectableEntry deposit, withdraw;
    private int fullSlots=0; private int capacity = 0;
    private Object[] buffer = null; private int in = 0, out = 0;
    public boundedBuffer(selectableEntry deposit, selectableEntry withdraw,
            int capacity) {
        this.deposit = deposit; this.withdraw = withdraw; this.capacity = capacity;
        buffer = new Object[capacity];
    }
    public void run() {
        try {
            selectiveWait select = new selectiveWait();
            select.add(deposit);              // alternative 1
            select.add(withdraw);             // alternative 2
            while(true) {
                deposit.guard (fullSlots <= capacity); // *** (fullSlots < capacity)
                withdraw.guard(fullSlots > 0);
                switch (select.choose()) {
                case 1:  Object o = deposit.acceptAndReply();
                         buffer[in] = o; in = (in + 1) % capacity; ++fullSlots;
                         break;
                case 2:  withdraw.accept();
                         Object value = buffer[out]; withdraw.reply(value);
                         out = (out + 1) % capacity; --fullSlots;
                         break;
                }
            }
        } catch (InterruptedException e) { }
          catch (SelectException e) {
              System.out.println("deadlock detected"); System.exit(1);
          }
    }
}
```

Listing 7.7   Faulty bounded buffer.

```
// deposit into a full buffer
(producer,  boundedBuffer,  deposit,   rendezvous),
(consumer,  boundedBuffer,  withdraw,  rendezvous),
(consumer,  boundedBuffer,  withdraw,  rendezvous),
(consumer,  boundedBuffer,  withdraw,  rendezvous).
```

The SR-sequence above starts with three consecutive rendezvous at *deposit*, followed by three consecutive rendezvous at *withdraw*. (Each rendezvous is actually two events: the start of an entry call followed by the end of an entry call.) The output of this execution is (C,B,C), not the expected output (A,B,C). This is an example of failure condition (3) above, since this SR-sequence is invalid and the output (C,B,C) is incorrect.

If an execution of *boundedBuffer* with input (C,B,C) exercises the invalid SR-sequence above, the output of this execution is (C,B,C). This is an example of failure condition (4) above, since this SR-sequence is invalid but the output (C,B,C) is correct. Note that an execution of *boundedBuffer* that does not exercise the foregoing SR-sequence will not produce an invalid SR-sequence nor will it produce an incorrect result.

Finally, assume that the incorrect guard for *deposit* is modified to

deposit.guard (fullSlots+1 < capacity);

Now thread *boundedBuffer* allows at most one character in the buffer. In this case, the set of feasible SR-sequences of *boundedBuffer* is a proper subset of the set of valid SR-sequences of *boundedBuffer* (i.e., *boundedBuffer* has a missing path). Thus, *boundedBuffer* still has a possible synchronization failure. However, this failure cannot be detected by a nondeterministic execution of *boundedBuffer* since such an execution will always exercise an SR-sequence that is feasible and valid, and will always produce a correct result.

7.3.3 Deadlock, Livelock, and Starvation

Deadlock, livelock, and *starvation*, and other terms, such as *deadness errors, infinite wait, global blocking, indefinite blocking*, and *indefinite postponement*, have been used to describe failures involving threads that are permanently blocked or not making any progress. Deadlock and livelock are important failures since the absence of deadlock and livelock is usually an implicit requirement of all programs. Informal definitions of deadlock, livelock, and starvation were given in Chapter 2. In this section we provide formal definitions of deadlock, livelock, and starvation in terms of the reachability graph of a concurrent program [Tai 1994].

Reachability graphs were introduced in Section 7.2.2. The reachability graph of program CP, denoted by RG_{CP}, contains all the reachable states of CP. We assume that a state of RG_{CP} contains the number of the next statement to be executed by each of the threads in CP, and the values of the variables in CP. A path of RG_{CP} corresponds to a sequence of statements and SYN-events in CP. In this section we also present algorithms for detecting deadlock, livelock, and starvation. These algorithms assume that the reachability graph of CP contains a finite number of states.

Let CP be a concurrent program containing threads $T_1, T_2, \ldots, T_r$, where $r > 1$. A state of CP is denoted as $(S_1, S_2, \ldots, S_r,$ other information), where S_i, $1 \leq i \leq r$, is the atomic action or the set of atomic actions that can possibly be executed next by thread T_i. The "other information" in a state may include the values of local and global variables, the contents of message queues, and so on. Let $S = (S_1, S_2, \ldots, S_r,$ other information) be a state of CP. If action S_i, $1 \leq i \leq r$, is a blocking synchronization statement, and executing S_i blocks thread

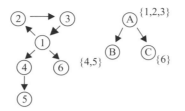

Figure 7.8   Directed graph G and condensed(G).

T_i in state S, thread T_i is said to be blocked in state S. If thread T_i, $1 \leq i \leq r$, is neither terminated nor blocked in state S, then S has one or more outgoing transitions for thread T_i resulting from the execution of S_i. If S_i is an if, while, or assignment statement, S has exactly one outgoing transition for T_i. If S_i is a nondeterministic statement, such as a selective wait statement, S may have multiple outgoing transitions for T_i. If S_i is an input statement for one or more variables, S may have one outgoing transition for each possible combination of values of the input variables.

The algorithms that we present below first find the strong components of a reachability graph. A strong component G' of a directed graph G is a maximal subgraph of G in which there is a path from each node of G' to any other node of G' [Baase 1988]. Let the condensation of graph G, denoted as Condensed(G), be G modified by considering each strong component as a node. Condensed(G) is cycle-free and has a tree structure. A leaf node in Condensed(G) is a node without child nodes. Figure 7.8 shows a directed graph and the condensation of the graph. Nodes B and C are leaf nodes. Beside each node N in Condensed(G), we show the nodes of G that N contains.

Deadlock   A deadlock requires one or more threads to be blocked permanently. A thread is blocked if it is not running and it is waiting for some event to occur. *Sleep* statements block a thread for a specified amount of time, but only temporarily. A blocking receive statement permanently blocks the thread that executes it if a message never arrives.

Assume that at the end of some execution of program CP there exists a thread T that satisfies these conditions:

- T is blocked due to the execution of a synchronization statement (e.g., waiting for a message to be received).
- T will remain blocked forever, regardless of what the other threads do.

Thread T is said to be *deadlocked* and CP is said to have a *deadlock*.

As an example, assume that CP contains Thread1 and Thread2 and the following execution sequence is possible:

- Thread1 is blocked waiting to receive a message from Thread2.
- Thread2 is blocked waiting to receive a message from Thread1.

Both Thread1 and Thread2 will remain blocked forever since neither thread is able to send the message for which the other thread is waiting.

Let CP be a concurrent program and S be a state in RG_{CP}:

- If a thread T in CP is blocked in S and all states reachable from S, then T is deadlocked in S and S is a deadlock state of T.
- S is a deadlock state if at least one thread of CP is deadlocked in S. A deadlock state S is a global deadlock state if every thread is either blocked or terminated in S; otherwise, S is a local deadlock state.
- CP has a deadlock if RG_{CP} contains at least one deadlock state.

Algorithm for Detecting Deadlock   Let CP be a concurrent program containing threads $T_1, T_2, \ldots, T_r$. For each node N in the condensed reachability graph, algorithm *DeadlockTest* computes two sets of threads:

- Blocked(N) is the set of threads that are blocked in every state in node N. (Remember that all the states in N are in the same strong component of the reachability graph.)
- Deadlock(N) contains i, $1 \leq i \leq r$, if and only if thread T_i is deadlocked in every state in node N.

Program CP contains a deadlock if Deadlock(N) is not empty for some node N. Algorithm *DeadlockTest* is as follows:

(a) Construct the condensation of RG_{CP}, denoted as Condensed(RG_{CP}). A node in Condensed(RG_{CP}) is a set of states in RG_{CP}.

(b) Perform a depth-first traversal of the nodes in Condensed(RG_{CP}). For each node N in Condensed(RG_{CP}), after having visited the child nodes of N:

- Blocked(N) = {i| thread T_i is blocked in every state in N}.
- If N is a leaf node of Condensed(RG_{CP}), Deadlock(N) = Blocked(N), else Deadlock(N) = the intersection of Blocked(N) and the Deadlock sets of N's child nodes.

Figure 7.9 shows four threads and the reachability graph for these threads. (The reachability graph and the condensed graph are the same.) The state labels show the next statement to be executed by each thread. Algorithm *DeadlockTest* proceeds as follows:

- Node (2,2,2,end) is a leaf node. Since Thread1, Thread2, and Thread3 are blocked, Deadlock(2,2,2,end) = {Thread1, Thread2, Thread3}.
- In node (2,2,1,1), Thread1 and Thread2 are blocked. The only child node of (2,2,1,1) is node (2,2,2,end), where Deadlock(2,2,2,end) was just computed to be {Thread1, Thread2, Thread3}. Thus, Deadlock(2,2,1,1) = {Thread1, Thread2} ∩ {Thread1, Thread2, Thread3} = {Thread1, Thread2}.

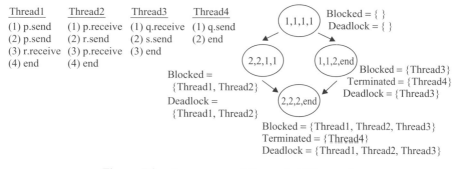

Figure 7.9 A program and its reachability graph.

- In node (1,1,2,end), thread Thread3 is blocked. The only child node of (1,1,2,end) is node (2,2,2,end). Thus, Deadlock(1,1,2,end) = {Thread3} ∩ {Thread1, Thread2, Thread3} = {Thread3}.
- In node (1,1,1,1), there are no blocked threads. Thus, Deadlock(1, 1, 1, 1) = { }.

Hence, *DeadlockTest* has detected a deadlock in the program. States (2,2,1,1) and (1,1,2,2) are both local deadlock states, and state (2,2,2,end) is a global deadlock state.

Let n be the number of transitions in RG$_{CP}$. Since RG$_{CP}$ has only one initial state, the number of states in RG$_{CP}$ is less than or equal to n + 1. The running time of step (a) is at most O(n) [Baase 1988] and that of step (b) at most O(n*r). So the time complexity of algorithm *DeadlockTest* is at most O(n*r).

Livelock   We assume that some statements in CP are labeled as *progress statements*, indicating that the threads are expected eventually to execute these statements. Statements that are likely to be labeled as progress statements include the last statement of a thread, the first statement of a critical section, or the statement immediately following a loop or a synchronization statement. If a thread executes a progress statement, it is considered to be *making progress*.

Assume that there is an execution of CP that exercises an execution sequence S, and at the end of S there exists a thread T that satisfies the following conditions, regardless of what the other threads will do:

- T will not terminate or deadlock.
- T will never make progress.

Thread T is said to be livelocked at the end of S, and CP is said to have a livelock. Livelock is the busy-waiting analog of deadlock. A livelocked thread is running (or ready to run), not blocked, but it can never make any progress.

Incorrect solution 2 in Section 2.1.2 (reproduced below) has an execution sequence that results in a violation of the progress requirement for solutions to the critical section problem. (The progress requirement defined specifically for the critical section problem should not be confused with the more general requirement to "make progress" that we introduced in this section. The latter is used to indicate the absence of livelock and is a requirement for all programs.) The first statement of the critical section is designated as a progress statement.

int turn = 0;

Thread0		Thread1	
while (true) {		while (true) {	
while (turn != 0){ ; }	(1)	while (turn != 1){ ; }	(1)
critical section	(2)	critical section	(2)
turn = 1;	(3)	turn = 0;	(3)
noncritical section	(4)	noncritical section	(4)
}		}	

Below is a prefix of the execution sequence that violates the progress requirement of the critical section problem.

- Thread0 executes (1), (2), and (3). Now *turn* is 1.
- Thread1 executes (1), (2), and (3) and then terminates in its noncritical section. Now *turn* is 0.
- Thread0 executes (4), (1), (2), (3), (4), and (1). Now *turn* is 1.

At the end of this sequence, Thread0 is stuck in its busy-waiting loop at (1) waiting for *turn* to become 0. Thread0 will never exit this busy-waiting loop and enter its critical section (i.e., make any progress). Thus, Thread0 is livelocked.

Let CP be a concurrent program and S a state of RG_{CP}:

- A thread in CP is said to make progress in S if S contains a progress statement for this thread.
- If a thread T in CP is not deadlocked, terminated, or making progress in S or any state reachable from S, T is livelocked in S and S is a livelock state for T.
- S is a livelock state of RG_{CP} if at least one thread is livelocked in S. A livelock state S is a global livelock state if every thread in S is either livelocked or terminated; otherwise, S is a local livelock state.
- CP has a livelock if RG_{CP} contains at least one livelock state.

Algorithm for Detecting Livelock   Let CP be a concurrent program containing threads $T_1, T_2, \ldots, T_r$. For each node N in the condensed reachability graph, algorithm *LivelockTest* computes two sets of threads:

- NoProgress(N) is the set of threads that are not deadlocked, terminated, or executing a progress statement in any state in N.

- Livelock(N) contains i, $1 \leq i \leq r$, if and only if thread T_i is livelocked in every state in N.

Program CP contains a livelock if Livelock(N) is not empty for some node N. Algorithm *LivelockTest* is as follows:

(a) Construct Condensed(RG_{CP}).
(b) Perform a depth-first traversal of the nodes in Condensed(RG_{CP}). For each node N in Condensed(RG_{CP}), after having visited the child nodes of N:

- NoProgress(N) = {i| thread T_i is not deadlocked, terminated, or executing a progress statement in any state in N}.
- If N is a leaf node of Condensed(RG_{CP}), Livelock(N) = NoProgress(N), else Livelock (N) = the intersection of NoProgress(N) and the NoProgress sets of N's child nodes.

Algorithm *LivelockTest* has the same time complexity as algorithm *DeadlockTest*.

Starvation   We assume that the scheduling policy used in executing a concurrent program CP is fair (i.e., a thread ready for execution will eventually be scheduled to run). A cycle in RG_{CP} is said to be a fair cycle if for every thread T in CP, either this cycle contains at least one transition for T, or T is blocked or terminated in every state on this cycle.

Informally, CP is said to have a starvation if CP can reach a state on a fair cycle such that some thread in CP is not deadlocked, livelocked, or terminated in this state, but this thread may not make any progress in any state on this cycle. Incorrect solution 3 in Section 2.1.3 (reproduced below) has an execution sequence that results in a violation of the bounded waiting requirement for critical sections. We will show that solution 3 also has a starvation.

boolean intendToEnter0=false, intendToEnter1 = false;

Thread0		Thread1	
while (true) {		while (true) {	
intendToEnter0 = true;	(1)	intendToEnter1 = true;	(1)
while (intendToEnter1) {	(2)	while (intendToEnter0) {	(2)
intendToEnter0 = false;	(3)	intendToEnter1 = false;	(3)
while(intendToEnter1) {;}	(4)	while(intendToEnter0) {;}	(4)
intendToEnter0 = true;	(5)	intendToEnter1 = true;	(5)
}		}	
critical section	(6)	critical section	(6)
intendToEnter0 = false;	(7)	intendToEnter1 = false;	(7)
noncritical section	(8)	noncritical section	(8)
}		}	

Denote a state of Thread0 and Thread1 as (S0, S1), where $S0$ and $S1$ are the next statements to be executed by Thread0 and Thread1, respectively. State (4,2) is not a livelock state for Thread0 since the following execution sequence allows Thread0 to enter its critical section:

(a) Thread1 executes (2) and (6), enters and exits it critical section, and then executes (7).
(b) Thread0 executes (4), (5), and (2), and then enters its critical section at (6).

State (4,2) has a cycle to itself that contains one transition for Thread0 [representing an iteration of the busy-waiting loop in (4)] and no other transitions. This cycle is not a fair cycle since it does not contain a transition for Thread1. State (4,2) has another cycle to itself that represents the following execution sequence:

(c) Thread1 executes (2) and (6), enters and exits it critical section, and then executes (7), (8), and (1).
(d) Thread0 executes (4) and stays in its busy-waiting loop.

This cycle is fair. After state (4,2) is entered, if this cycle is repeated forever, Thread0 never enters its critical section. State (4,2) is called a *starvation state* for Thread0.

Let CP be a concurrent program and S a state of RG_{CP}:

- A cycle in RG_{CP} is said to be a *no-progress cycle* for a thread T in CP if T does not make progress in any state on this cycle. (Assume that some statements are labeled as *progress statements*.)
- A cycle in RG_{CP} is said to be a *starvation cycle* for a thread T in CP if (1) this cycle is fair, (2) this cycle is a no-progress cycle for T, and (3) each state on this cycle is not a deadlock, livelock, or termination state for T.
- A starvation cycle for thread T is said to be a *busy-starvation cycle* for T if this cycle contains at least one transition for T, and is said to be a *blocking-starvation cycle* for T otherwise (i.e., T is blocked in each state on this cycle).
- If state S is on a starvation cycle for thread T, then S is a *starvation state* for T. A starvation state is a global starvation state if every thread in S is either starved or terminated; otherwise, it is a local starvation state.
- CP is said to have a *starvation* if RG_{CP} contains at least one starvation state.

If contention for a critical section is low, as it is in many cases, starvation is unlikely, and solutions to the critical section problem that theoretically allow starvation may actually be acceptable [Tarski 1991]. This is the case for the first hardware solution in Section 2.3.

Algorithm for Detecting Starvation Let CP be a concurrent program containing threads $T_1, T_2, \ldots, T_r$. For each node N in the condensed reachability graph, algorithm *StarvationTest* computes two sets of threads:

- NoProgress(N) is the set of threads that do not terminate in N and for which N contains a fair, no-progress cycle.
- Starvation(N) contains i, $1 \le i \le r$, if and only if a starvation cycle for thread T_i exists in N.

Program CP contains a starvation if Starvation(N) is not empty for some node N. Algorithm *StarvationTest* is as follows:

(a) Construct Condensed(RG_{CP}).
(b) Perform a depth-first traversal of the nodes in Condensed(RG_{CP}). For each node N in Condensed(RG_{CP}), after having visited the child nodes of N:

- If N does not contain any fair cycles, Starvation(N) = empty.
- Else NoProgress(N) = {i|thread T_i does not terminate in N, and N contains a fair, no-progress cycle for T_i} and Starvation(N) = NoProgress(N) − Deadlock(N) − Livelock(N).

To compute NoProgress(N), we need to search for fair cycles in N. We must consider cycles of length at most $(1 + \#\text{Transitions})$ where #Transitions is the number of transitions in N. The number of cycles with length less than or equal to $(1 + \#\text{Transitions})$ is at most $O(2^{\#\text{Transitions}})$. Let n be the number of transitions in RG_{CP}. The time complexity of algorithm *StarvationTest* is at most $O(r*2^n)$.

Other Definitions Local deadlock has been referred to as a *deadness error* [German 1984; Helmbold and Luckham 1985] and *permanent blocking* [Avrunin et al. 1991]. Global deadlock has been referred to as *infinite wait* [Taylor 83], *global blocking* [German 1984; Helmbold and Luckham 1985], *deadlock* [Avrunin et al. 1991], and *system-wide deadlock* [Karam and Buhr 1991].

One special type of deadlock, called a *circular deadlock*, refers to a circular list of two or more threads such that each thread is waiting to synchronize with the next thread in the list. A circular deadlock is similar to a circular wait condition, which arises during resource allocation (see Section 3.10.4). *Circular wait* refers to a list of two or more processes such that each process is waiting for a resource that is held by the next process in the list. A circular wait condition is a necessary condition for deadlock during resource allocation. According to our definition, a deadlock in a concurrent program is different from a deadlock during resource allocation, since the former is not necessarily a circular deadlock. Several definitions of deadlock for concurrent programs require the existence of a circular wait condition among a set of threads [Cheng 1991; Masticola and Ryder 1991; Silberschatz et al. 1991].

Andrews [1991] defined a *livelocked thread* as one that is spinning (i.e., executing a loop) while waiting for a condition that will never become true. Holzmann [1991] defined *livelock* as the existence of an execution sequence that can be repeated infinitely, often without ever making effective progress. *Starvation* (or *indefinite postponement*) has been defined in several ways. Deitel [1984] said that starvation occurs when a process, even though not deadlocked, waits for an event that may never occur. Silberschatz et al. [1991] defined starvation as a situation in which processes wait indefinitely, and Tannenbaum [1992] defines starvation as a situation in which processes continue to run indefinitely but fail to make any progress.

Our definitions of deadlock, livelock, and starvation have the following characteristics: They are independent of the programming language and constructs used to write the program; they are formally defined in terms of the reachability graph of a program; they cover all undesirable situations involving blocking or not making progress; they define deadlock, livelock, and starvation as distinct properties of concurrent programs; and they provide a basis for developing detection algorithms.

In Chapter 2 we defined the mutual exclusion, progress, and bounded waiting requirements for solutions to the critical section problem. These requirements can be defined in terms of deadlock, livelock, and starvation, as some of the examples above showed [Tai 1994]. Thus, the correctness of a solution to the critical section problem can be verified automatically.

7.4   APPROACHES TO TESTING CONCURRENT PROGRAMS

Typically, a concurrent program CP, like a sequential program, is subjected to two types of testing:

- *Black-box testing.* Access to CP's implementation is not allowed during black-box testing. Thus, only the specification of CP can be used for test generation, and only the result (including the output and termination condition) of each execution of CP can be collected.
- *White-box testing.* Access to CP's implementation is allowed during white-box testing. In this case, both the specification and implementation of CP can be used for test generation. Also, any desired information about each execution of CP can be collected.

White-box testing may not be practical during system or acceptance testing, due to the size and complexity of the code or the inability to access the code. Following is a third type of testing, which lies somewhere between the first two approaches:

- *Limited white-box testing.* During an execution of CP, only the result and SYN-sequence can be collected. Thus, only the specification and the SYN-sequences of CP can be used for test generation. Also, an input and a

SYN-sequence can be used to control the execution of CP deterministically. Deterministic testing is described below.

The remainder of this section describes several approaches to testing concurrent programs and discusses the relationships they have with the types of testing described above.

7.4.1   Nondeterministic Testing

Nondeterministic testing of a concurrent program CP involves the following steps:

1. Select a set of inputs for CP.
2. For each selected input X, execute CP with X many times and examine the result of each execution.

Multiple, nondeterministic executions of CP with input X may exercise different SYN-sequences of CP and thus may detect more failures than a single execution of CP with input X. This approach can be used during both (limited) white-box and black-box testing.

The purpose of nondeterministic testing is to exercise as many distinct SYN-sequences as possible. Unfortunately, experiments have shown that repeated executions of a concurrent program do not always execute different SYN-sequences [Hwang et al. 1995]. In the absence of significant variations in I/O and network delays, or changes in the system load, programs tend to exhibit the same behavior from execution to execution. Furthermore, the probe effect, which occurs when programs are instrumented with testing and debugging code, may make it impossible for some failures to be observed (see Sections 1.8.1 and 7.4.2).

There are several techniques that can be used to increase the likelihood of exercising different SYN-sequences during nondeterministic testing. One is to change the scheduling algorithm used by the operating system (e.g., change the value of the time quantum that is used for round-robin scheduling and vary the order that ready processes are selected for execution). This may have the desired affect on program executions [Hwang et al. 1995]; however, in many commercial operating systems, this is simply not an option.

The second technique is to insert `Sleep` statements into the program with the sleep time chosen randomly [Yang and Pollock 1997; Stoller 2002]. Executing a `Sleep` statement forces a context switch and affects thread scheduling indirectly. The objective of this technique is to ensure a nonzero probability for exercising an arbitrary SYN-sequence while minimizing the number of delays or removing redundant delays, since each delay adds to the execution time.

Even though both of these techniques increase the number of SYN-sequences that are exercised during nondeterministic testing, some sequences are likely to be exercised many times, which is inefficient, and some may never be exercised at all. In general, nondeterministic executions are easy to perform; however, each execution creates additional work since the result of the execution must be checked. If a formal specification exits, the checking can be partially automated [Koppol et al. 2002]. Otherwise, checking must be done manually, which creates a lot of work for the programmer and effectively restricts the number of nondeterministic executions that can be performed.

Certain types of failures can be detected automatically. The lockset algorithm in Chapter 3 checks that all shared variable accesses follow a consistent locking discipline in which every shared variable is protected by a lock. Data races are detected automatically and reported as they occur. Deadlocks can also be detected automatically using techniques such as the one described in Section 3.10.4.

7.4.2   Deterministic Testing

Deterministic testing of a concurrent program CP involves the following steps:

1. Select a set of tests, each of the form (X, S), where X and S are an input and a complete SYN-sequence of CP, respectively.
2. For each test (X, S) selected, force a deterministic execution of CP with input X according to S. This forced execution determines whether S is feasible for CP with input X. (Since S is a complete SYN-sequence of CP, the result of such an execution is deterministic.)
3. Compare the expected and actual results of the forced execution (including the output, the feasibility of S, and the termination condition). If the expected and actual results are different, a failure is detected in the program (or an error was made when the test sequence was generated). A replay tool can be used to locate the fault that caused the failure. After the fault is located and CP is corrected, CP can be executed with each test (X,S) to verify that the fault has been removed and that in doing so, no new faults were introduced.

Note that for deterministic testing, a test for CP is not just an input of CP. A test consists of an input and a SYN-sequence and is referred to as an *IN-SYN test*. Deterministic testing is similar to the concept of forcing a path, mentioned in [Taylor et al. 1992].

Deterministic testing provides several advantages over nondeterministic testing:

- Nondeterministic testing may leave certain paths of CP uncovered. Several path-based test coverage criteria were described in Section 7.2.2. Deterministic testing allows carefully selected SYN-sequences to be used to test specific paths of CP.
- Nondeterministic testing exercises feasible SYN-sequences only; thus, it can detect the existence of invalid, feasible SYN-sequences of CP, but not the existence of valid, infeasible SYN-sequences of CP. Deterministic testing can detect both types of failures.

- After CP has been modified to correct an error or add some functionality, deterministic regression testing with the inputs and SYN-sequences of previous executions of CP provides more confidence about the correctness of CP than does nondeterministic testing of CP with the inputs of previous executions.

The selection of IN-SYN tests for CP can be done in different ways:

- Select inputs and then select a set of SYN-sequences for each input
- Select SYN-sequences and then select a set of inputs for each SYN-sequence.
- Select inputs and SYN-sequences separately and then combine them.
- Select pairs of inputs and SYN-sequences together.

Chapters 1 through 6 dealt with various issues that arise during deterministic testing and debugging. These issues are summarized below:

Program Replay   Repeating an execution of a concurrent program is called *program replay*. The SYN-sequence of an execution must be traced so that the execution can be replayed. Program replay uses simple SYN-sequences, which have a simpler format than the complete sequences used for testing. Definitions of simple SYN-sequences for semaphores, monitors, and message passing were given in Chapters 3 to 6. A *language-based* approach to replay uses a concurrency library that supports various types of thread and synchronization objects and contains embedded code for program tracing and replay. Alternatively, replay code can be inserted into a program automatically by a source transformation tool [Tai et al. 1991]. An implementation-based approach to replay involves modifying the compiler, debugger, run-time system, virtual machine [Choi and Srinivasan 1998; Konuru et al. 2000], or operating system. In Chapters 1 to 6 we presented a library of Java and C++ classes supporting threads, semaphores, monitors, and several types of message-passing channels. Our synchronization library also supports replay, but it does not have the benefit of being closely integrated with a source-level debugger. However, it does serve as a high-level design for an effective implementation-based testing and debugging tool.

Program Tracing   Chapters 2 to 6 showed how to trace simple and complete SYN-sequences for shared variables, semaphores, monitors, and various types of message channels.

An observability problem occurs when tracing a distributed program because it is difficult to determine accurately the order in which actions occur during an execution. In Chapter 6 we saw how to use vector timestamps to ensure that an execution trace of a distributed program is consistent with the actual execution.

For long-running programs, storing all the SYN-events requires too much space. Netzer and Miller [1994] developed an adaptive tracing technique that records the minimal number of SYN-events required to replay an execution exactly. Netzer's technique makes run-time decisions about which events to trace by detecting and tracing certain race conditions during execution. Experiments show that for some programs it is possible to achieve a reduction in trace size of two to four orders of magnitude over techniques that trace every event.

Sequence Feasibility   A sequence of events that is allowed by a program is said to be a *feasible sequence*. Program replay always involves repeating a feasible sequence of events. This is because the sequence to be replayed was captured during an actual execution and thus is known to be allowed by the program. (Replay assumes that the program has not been changed.) Testing, on the other hand, involves determining whether or not a given sequence is feasible or infeasible. Valid sequences are expected to be feasible, whereas invalid sequences are expected to be infeasible. For example, feasibility becomes an issue when a synchronization failure is discovered. Testing is required to determine whether the invalid but feasible sequence that exposed the failure is still feasible after the program is changed in an attempt to fix the fault.

The information and the technique used to determine the feasibility of a SYN-sequence are different from those used to replay a SYN-sequence. The techniques illustrated in Chapters 4 to 6 check the feasibility of complete SYN-sequences of monitors and message channels. Selecting valid and invalid SYN-sequences for program testing is a difficult problem. One approach is simply to collect the feasible SYN-sequences that are randomly exercised during nondeterministic testing. These SYN-sequences can be used for regression testing when changes are made to the program. Another approach is to generate sequences that satisfy one of the coverage criteria described in Section 7.2.2 or that are adequate for the mutation-based testing procedures described in Section 7.4.3.2. Mutation testing has the advantage that it requires both valid and invalid sequences to be generated. This is helpful since there are usually a huge number of invalid sequences to choose from.

Sequence Validity   A sequence of actions captured in a trace is definitely feasible, but the sequence may or may not be valid. The goal of testing is to find valid sequences that are infeasible and invalid sequences that are feasible; such sequences are evidence of a program failure. A major issue then is how to check the validity of a sequence. If a formal specification of valid program behavior is available, checking the validity of a SYN-sequence can be partially automated. Without such a *test oracle*, manually checking validity becomes time consuming, error prone, and tedious.

Probe Effect   Modifying a concurrent program to capture a trace of its execution may interfere with the normal execution of the program [Gait 1985; LeDoux and Parker 1985]. Working programs may fail when instrumentation is removed, and failures may disappear when debugging code is added. As we mentioned in Section 7.4.1, executions can be purposely disturbed during nondeterministic testing in order to capture as many different SYN-sequences as possible. Instrumentation at least offers the prospect of being able to capture and replay the failures that are observed. One approach to circumventing the probe effect is to generate all the possible SYN-sequences systematically, which leaves no place for faults to hide. This approach can be realized through reachability testing if the number of sequences is not too large (see Sections 3.10.5, 4.11.4, 5.5.5, and 7.5).

The probe effect is different from the observability problem described in Section 6.3. The observability problem is concerned with the difficulty of accurately tracing an execution of a distributed program. In Section 6.3.6 we saw how to use vector timestamps to address the observability problem. The probe effect is concerned with the ability to perform a given execution at all. Deterministic testing addresses the probe effect partially by allowing us to choose a particular SYN-sequence that we want to exercise. As we've already seen, reachability testing goes one step further and attempts to exercise all possible SYN-sequences. The observability problem and the probe effect are different from the replay problem, which deals with repeating an execution that has already been observed.

Real Time   The probe effect is a major issue for real-time concurrent programs. The correctness of a real-time program depends not only on its logical behavior, but also on the time at which its results are produced [Tsai et al. 1996]. A real-time program may have execution deadlines that will be missed if the program is modified for tracing. Instead, tracing is performed by using special hardware to remove the probe effect or by trying to account for or minimize the probe effect. Real-time programs may also receive sensor inputs that must be captured for replay. Some of the techniques we have covered may be helpful for testing and debugging the logical behavior of real-time systems, but we have not considered the special issues associated with timing correctness.

Tools   The synchronization library that we presented in Chapters 1 to 6 demonstrates that tracing, replay, and feasibility can be applied to a wide range of synchronization constructs. Our library is a simple but useful programming tool; however, it is no substitute for an integrated development environment that supports traditional source-level debugging as well as the special needs of concurrent programmers. Commercial debugging tools that are integrated with compilers and operating systems can accomplish much more than the library presented in this book. Access to the underlying virtual machine, compiler, operating system, or run-time system maximizes the ability of a tool to observe and control program executions.

On the other hand, testing and debugging tools should allow programmers to work at a level of abstraction that is appropriate for the task at hand. For example, program replay can be accomplished by counting the number of instructions that each thread executes during each of its time quantums [Mellor-Crummey and LeBlanc 1989]. However, instruction counts provide little help for understanding an execution or determining its validity. (Of course, instruction counts can be used to replay an execution and collect additional information.) Different levels of abstraction are appropriate for different activities.

Life-Cycle Issues   Deterministic testing is better suited for the types of testing that occur early in the software life cycle. Feasibility checking and program replay require information about the internal behavior of a system. Thus, deterministic testing is a form of white-box or limited white-box testing. This is not always possible during later stages, such as system and user-acceptance testing, where knowledge about internal behavior may not be available, or the system may just be too large. Nevertheless, deterministic testing can be applied during early stages of development allowing concurrency bugs to be found as early as possible, when powerful debugging tools are available and bugs are less costly to fix.

7.4.3 Combinations of Deterministic and Nondeterministic Testing

Although deterministic testing has advantages over nondeterministic testing, it requires considerable effort for selecting SYN-sequences and determining their feasibility. This effort can be reduced by combining deterministic and non-deterministic testing. Below are four possible strategies for combining these approaches:

1. First, apply nondeterministic testing with random delays to collect random SYN-sequences and detect failures. Then apply deterministic regression testing with the sequences collected. No extra effort is required for generating SYN-sequences since they are all randomly selected during nondeterministic executions.

2. Apply nondeterministic testing until test coverage reaches a certain level. Then apply deterministic testing to achieve a higher level of coverage. This strategy is similar to the combination of random and special value testing for sequential programs. Theoretical and experimental studies of random testing for sequential programs show that random testing should be supplemented with the use of carefully selected inputs [Duran and Ntafos 1984]. In [Vouk et al. 1986], six Pascal programs were randomly tested against the same specification. Random testing rapidly reached steady-state values for several test coverage criteria: 60% for decision (or branch) coverage, 65% for block (or statement) coverage, and 75% for definition-use coverage, showing that special values (including boundary values) are needed to improve coverage.

3. The SYN-sequences collected during nondeterministic testing can be modified to produce new SYN-sequences for deterministic testing. This is easier than generating sequences from scratch.

4. Apply deterministic testing during module and integration testing and nondeterministic testing during system and acceptance testing.

Prefix-Based Testing   Another interesting combination of nondeterministic and deterministic testing is called *prefix-based testing*. The purpose of prefix-based testing is to allow nondeterministic testing to start from a specific program state other than the initial one. Prefix-based testing uses a *prefix sequence*, which contains events from the beginning part of an execution, not a complete execution.

Prefix-based testing of CP with input X and prefix sequence S proceeds as follows:

1. Force a deterministic execution of CP with input X according to S. If this forced execution succeeds (i.e., it reaches the end of S), then go to step 2; otherwise, S is infeasible.
2. Continue the execution of CP with input X by performing nondeterministic testing of CP.

If S is feasible for CP with input X, prefix-based testing replays S in step 1. The purpose of step 1 is to force CP to enter a particular state (e.g., a state in which the system is under a heavy load), so that we can see what happens after that in step 2.

Prefix-based testing is an important part of a general testing technique called *reachability testing*. Assume that every execution of CP with input X terminates and the number of distinct feasible SYN-sequences of CP with input X is finite. Reachability testing is a systematic way of exercising all possible SYN-sequences of CP with input X. By doing so, reachability testing can determine the correctness of CP with input X. In Chapters 3, 4, and 5, we described the results of applying reachability testing to programs that use semaphores, monitors, and/or message passing. Details about reachability testing are described in Section 7.5.

Mutation-Based Testing   To illustrate the combination of deterministic and non-deterministic testing, we will now show how to apply both approaches during mutation-based testing [Hamlet 1977; DeMillo et al. 1979]. Mutation-based testing helps the tester create test cases and then interacts with the tester to improve the quality of the tests. Mutation-based testing is interesting since it subsumes the coverage criteria in Fig. 7.3. That is, if mutation coverage is satisfied, the criteria in Fig. 7.3 are also satisfied [Offutt and Voas 1996]. Furthermore, mutation-based testing also provides some guidance for the generation of invalid SYN-sequences, unlike the criteria in Fig. 7.3.

Mutation-based testing involves the construction of a set of *mutants* of the program under test. Each mutant differs from the program under test by one *mutation*. A mutation is a single syntactic change made to a program statement, generally inducing a typical programming fault. For example, the *boundedBuffer* thread in Listing 7.7 was created by making a single mutation to the correct version in Listing 5.10. The relational operator $<$ in the guard for deposit was changed to $<=$, creating a fault.

Test cases are used to cause a mutant to generate an output which is different from that of the program under test. If a test case causes a mutant program to produce output different from the output of the program under test, that test case is strong enough to detect the faults represented by that mutant, and the mutant is considered to be distinguished from the program under test. The goal of mutation-based testing is to distinguish a large number of mutant programs. Each set of

```
(1)    Generate mutants (m₁,m₂,...,mₙ) from P;
(2)    repeat {
(3)        Execute P with test input X producing actual result Actualₚ;
(4)        Compare the actual result Actualₚ with the expected result Expectedₚ;
(5)        if (Expectedₚ != Actualₚ)
(6)            Locate and correct the error in P and restart at (1);
(7)        else
(8)            for (mutant mᵢ, i<=i<=n) {
(9)                Execute mᵢ with test input X producing actual result Actualₘᵢ;
(10)               if (Actualₚ <> Actualₘᵢ)
(11)                   mark mutant mᵢ as distinguished;
(12)           }
(13)   }
(14)   until (the mutation score is adequate);
```

Figure 7.10   Mutation-based testing procedure for a sequential program P.

test cases is used to compute a mutation score. A score of 100% indicates that the test cases distinguish all mutants of the program under test and are adequate with respect to the mutation criterion. (Some mutants are functionally equivalent to the program under test and can never be distinguished. This is factored into the mutation score.)

Figure 7.10 shows a mutation-based testing procedure for a *sequential* program P. This testing procedure encounters problems when it is applied to a concurrent program CP. In addition to the three general problems 1 to 3 described at the beginning of this chapter, nondeterministic execution behavior creates the following problem:

Problem 4   In line (10), the condition $Actual_p <> Actual_{mi}$ is not sufficient to mark mutant m_i as distinguished. Different actual results may be a product of nondeterminism and not the mutation.

Problems 1 to 4 can be solved by using a combination of deterministic testing and nondeterministic mutation-based testing. Below we outline a two-phase procedure for deterministic mutation testing (DMT). In phase one, SYN-sequences are randomly generated using nondeterministic testing, until the mutation score has reached a steady value. In phase two, we select IN_SYN test cases and apply deterministic testing until we achieve an adequate mutation score.

Figure 7.11 shows a phase one test procedure using nondeterministic testing to select SYN-sequences randomly for mutation-based testing. In line (4), if SYN-sequence S_{CP} and actual result $Actual_{CP}$ were produced by an earlier execution of CP with input X, we should execute CP again until a new SYN-sequence or actual result is produced. In line (16), deterministic testing is used to distinguish mutant programs by differentiating the output *and the feasible SYN-sequences* of the mutants from those of the program under test. If the SYN-sequence randomly

(1)   repeat {
(2)   Generate mutants $(m_1, m_2,...m_n)$ from CP;
(3)   Apply non-determ. testing to randomly execute CP with test input X;
(4)   Assume execution exercises new SYN-sequence S_{CP}, or produces a new
             actual result $Actual_{CP}$.
(5)   Check which of the following conditions holds:
(6)   (a) S_{CP} is valid and $Actual_{CP}$ is correct
(7)   (b) S_{CP} is valid and $Actual_{CP}$ is incorrect
(8)   (c) S_{CP} is invalid and $Actual_{CP}$ is correct
(9)   (d) S_{CP} is invalid and $Actual_{CP}$ is incorrect;
(10)   if (condition (b), (c), or (d) holds) {
(11)   Locate and correct the error in CP using program replay; apply
(12)   Apply det. testing to validate the correction by forcing an execution
                of CP with IN_SYN test case (X, S_{CP}); and restart at (1);
(13)   } else
(14)   for (mutant m_i, $i<=i<=n$) {
(15)   Apply deterministic testing to m_i with IN_SYN test case (X, S_{CP})
                   producing actual result $Actual_{mi}$;
(16)   if ((S_{CP} is infeasible for m_i) or
                     (S_{CP} is feasible and $Actual_{CP} <> Actual_{mi}$))
(17)   mark mutant m_i as distinguished;
(18)   }
(19)   }
(20)   until (the mutation score reaches a steady value);

Figure 7.11 Deterministic mutation testing using nondeterministic testing to generate SYN-sequences.

exercised by CP during nondeterministic testing is infeasible for the mutant program, or this sequence is feasible but the mutant program produces results that are different from CP's, the mutant is marked as distinguished.

Although nondeterministic testing reduces the effort needed to select SYN-sequences for testing, it may not be possible to distinguish some of the mutants if nondeterministic testing alone is applied to CP in line (3). To distinguish a mutant m_i, we may need to exercise SYN-sequences that are feasible for mutant m_i but *infeasible* for CP; however, in line (3) only *feasible* SYN-sequences of CP can be exercised using nondeterministic testing.

Example 1 Assume that the program under test is an incorrect version of the bounded buffer that allows at most *one* (instead of two) consecutive *deposits* into the buffer. (In other words, the program under test has a fault.) Call this program boundedBuffer1. A possible mutant of this program is the correct version in Listing 5.10. Call this correct version boundedBuffer2. Mutant *boundedBuffer2* is distinguished by an SR-sequence that exercises *two* consecutive *deposits*, as this sequence differentiates the behaviors of these two versions. But this SR-sequence is a *valid, infeasible* SR-sequence of *boundedBuffer1* that cannot be exercised when nondeterministic testing is applied to *boundedBuffer1* in line (3).

Example 2 Assume that the program under test is *boundedBuffer2*, which correctly allows at most *two* consecutive *deposit* operations. A possible mutant of this program is *boundedBuffer3*, representing the mutation shown in Listing 7.7. Mutant *boundedBuffer3* is distinguished by an SR-sequence that exercises *three* consecutive *deposits*. But this SR-sequence is an *invalid, infeasible* SYN-sequence of *boundedBuffer2* that cannot be exercised when nondeterministic testing is applied to *boundedBuffer2* in line (3).

These examples suggest that upon reaching a steady mutation score, we should select IN_SYN test cases and apply deterministic testing (DT) to CP in line (3) in order to distinguish more mutants. As Examples 1 and 2 showed, the SYN-sequences selected for deterministic testing may need to be infeasible for CP. Also, both valid and invalid SYN-sequences should be selected. A phase two test procedure using selected IN_SYN test cases in line (3) is shown in Fig. 7.12.

We now describe the results of applying deterministic mutation testing to the correct version of the bounded buffer program, denoted as *boundedBuffer2*. The *boundedBuffer* thread was mutated manually using the mutation operators of the Mothra mutation system [King and Offutt 1991]. (Statements that involved accesses to the buffer or to the buffer indices *in* and *out* were not mutated.) Since Mothra was developed for Fortran 77, a few of the mutations were not applicable or they needed to be modified slightly for our program. For example, some of the mutations resulted in errors that were caught by the compiler. The result was a set of 95 mutants. Since 14 of the mutations resulted in mutants that were equivalent to *boundedBuffer2*, this left 81 live mutants.

The DMT testing procedures in Figs. 7.11 and 7.12 were applied to *boundedBuffer2* and the 81 mutant programs: In phase one we used nondeterministic testing to generate SR-sequences of *boundedBuffer2*. Random delays were inserted into *boundedBuffer2* to increase the chances of exercising different SR-sequences during nondeterministic testing. The mutation score leveled off at 71%. At this point, all four valid and feasible sequences of *deposit* (D) and *withdraw* (W) events had been exercised:

- (D,D,W,W,D,W)
- (D,W,D,D,W,W)
- (D,W,D,W,D,W)
- (D,D,W,D,W,W)

It was not possible to distinguish any more mutants using nondeterministic testing to select SR-sequences of *boundedBuffer2*.

Two of the SR-sequences exercised using nondeterministic testing were modified to produce two new invalid SR-sequences:

(1)   repeat {
(2)   Generate mutants $(m_1, m_2, ... m_n)$ from CP;
(3)   Apply *DT* to deterministically execute CP with a selected IN_SYN test
                case (X,S);
(4)   Compare the actual and expected results of this forced execution:
(5)   (a) The results are identical. Then no error is detected by the test (X,S).
(6)   (b) The results differ in the feasibility of S.
(7)   (c) The results agree on the feasibility of S, but not on the termination
                condition of CP.
(8)   (d) The results agree on the feasibility of S and the termination
                condition, but not on the output of CP.
(9)   if (condition (b), (c), or (d) holds) {
(10)   Locate and correct the error in CP using program replay;
(11)   Apply *DT* to validate the correction by forcing an execution of CP
                    with IN_SYN test case (X,S); and restart at (1);
(12)   } else
(13)   for (mutant m_i, i<=i<=n) {
(14)   Apply *DT* to m_i with IN_SYN test case (X,S);
(15)   Compare the actual results of the forced executions of CP and
                        mutant m_i;
(16)   if (the results differ in the feasibility of S, the termination
                        condition, or the output)
(17)   mark mutant m_i as distinguished;
(18)   }
(19)   }
(20)   until (the mutation score is adequate);

Figure 7.12 Deterministic mutation testing using deterministic testing with selected IN_SYN test cases.

- (D,D,D,W,W,W)   //invalid: three consecutive deposits into a two-slot buffer
- (W,D,D,W,D,W)   //invalid: the first withdrawal is from an empty buffer

These sequences were used to create IN_SYN tests for phase two. Both of these invalid SR-sequences were shown to be infeasible for *boundedBuffer2*, but feasible for the remaining mutants. Thus, all of the remaining mutants were distinguished. This example illustrates the need for deterministic testing with carefully selected SYN-sequences to distinguish mutants. It also shows that both valid and invalid SYN-sequences should be generated during testing.

7.5   REACHABILITY TESTING

In Section 7.4 we described several approaches to testing concurrent programs. Nondeterministic testing is easy to carry out, but it can be very inefficient. It is possible that some behaviors of a program are exercised many times while others are never exercised at all. Deterministic testing allows a program to be tested with carefully selected valid and invalid test sequences. Test sequences are usually selected from a static model of the program or of the program's design. Several coverage criteria for reachability graph models were defined in Section 7.2.2. However, accurate static models are difficult to build for dynamic program behaviors.

Reachability testing is an approach that combines nondeterministic and deterministic testing. It is based on prefix-based testing, which was described in Section 7.4.3.1. Recall that prefix-based testing controls a test runup to a certain point and then lets the run continue nondeterministically. The controlled portion of the test run is used to force the execution of a prefix SYN-sequence, which is the beginning part of one or more feasible SYN-sequences of the program. The nondeterministic portion of the execution randomly exercises one of these feasible sequences.

A novel aspect of reachability testing is that it uses prefix-based testing to generate test sequences dynamically. That is, test sequences are derived automatically and on the fly as the testing process progresses. In this framework, the SYN-sequence traced during a test run is analyzed to derive prefix SYN-sequences that are *race variants* of the trace. A race variant represents the beginning part of a SYN-sequence that definitely could have happened but didn't, due to the way that race conditions were resolved arbitrarily during execution. The race variants are used to conduct more test runs, which are traced and then analyzed to derive more race variants, and so on. If every execution of a program with a given input terminates, and the total number of possible SYN-sequences is finite, reachability testing will terminate and every partially ordered SYN-sequence of the program with the given input will be exercised.

7.5.1   Reachability Testing Process

In this section we introduce some basic concepts of reachability testing and illustrate the reachability testing process by applying it to a message-passing solution to the bounded buffer program. Assume that an execution of some program CP with input X exercises SYN-sequence Q represented by the space-time diagram in Fig. 7.13. Send events *s1* and *s2* in Q have a race to see which message will be received first by Thread2. While *s1* wins the race this time, by analyzing Q we can see that there exists at least one execution of CP with input X in which the message sent at *s2* is received by *r1*. Thus, we say that the message sent by *s2* is in the *race set* for r1.

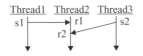

Figure 7.13   Sequence Q.

Computing race sets is one of the major tasks of reachability testing. Race sets are used to identify alternative paths that an execution could have executed. Later we will see how to compute race sets. For now, note that race sets are computed by analyzing execution traces, not by analyzing programs. Although program analysis might allow us to perform reachability testing more efficiently, an accurate static analysis of source code is difficult to do; hence, we do not rely on static analysis to compute race sets. As we will see below, we can and do use program information that is captured through dynamic analysis (i.e., while the program is running). This information is recorded in execution traces and used to perform race analysis.

An analysis of sequence Q in Fig. 7.13 allows us to guarantee that $s2$ can be received at r1. It does not, however, allow us to guarantee that $s1$ can be received at $r2$ since we cannot guarantee that Thread2 will always execute two receive statements. For example, the code in *Thread2* that generates $r1$ and $r2$ could be:

Thread2

```
x = port.receive();      //generates event r1 in Q
if (x > 0)
    y = port.receive();  //generates event r2 in Q
```

If $r1$ receives the message sent by $s2$ instead of $s1$, the condition $(x > 0)$ may be false, depending on the value of $s2$'s message. But if the condition $(x > 0)$ is false, the second *receive* statement will not be executed, and since we do not examine CP's code during race analysis, it is not safe to put $s1$ in the race set of $r2$.

The second major task for reachability testing is to use race sets to generate the *race variants* of an execution trace. A race variant represents the beginning part of one or more alternative program paths (i.e., paths that could have been executed if the message races had been resolved differently). When a race variant is used as a prefix sequence during prefix-based testing, one of these alternative paths will be selected nondeterministically.

Figure 7.14 shows the race variant produced for sequence Q in Fig. 7.13. When this variant is used for prefix-based testing, Thread2 will be forced to receive its first message from Thread3, not Thread1. What Thread2 will do after that is unknown. Perhaps Thread2 will receive the message sent at $s1$, or perhaps Thread2 will send a message to Thread1 or Thread3. The dashed arrow from $s1$ indicates that $s1$ is not received as part of the variant, although it may be received later. In any event, whatever happens after the variant is exercised will

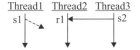

Figure 7.14   Race variant for sequence Q in Fig. 7.13.

be traced, so that new variants can be generated from the trace and new paths can be explored.

Next, we illustrate the reachability testing process by applying it to a solution for the bounded buffer program. Pseudocode for threads *Producer, Consumer,* and *Buffer* is shown below. The *Buffer* thread uses a selective wait statement (see Section 5.3) to accept entry calls from the *Producer* and *Consumer* threads. The guards on the `accept` alternatives control whether an entry call can be accepted for one or both of entries *deposit* and *withdraw*.

Producer	Consumer	Buffer
(s1) deposit.call(x1);	(s4) item = withdraw.call();	loop
(s2) deposit.call(x2);	(s5) item = withdraw.call();	select
(s3) deposit.call(x2);	(s6) item = withdraw.call();	when (buffer is not full) =>
		item = deposit.acceptAndReply();
		/* insert *item* into buffer */
		or
		when (buffer is not empty) =>
		withdraw.accept();
		/* remove *item* from buffer */
		withdraw.reply(*item*);
		end select;
		end loop;

The reachability testing process for this bounded buffer program proceeds as follows. First, assume that sequence Q0 is recorded during a nondeterministic execution. Sequence Q0 and the three variants derived from Q0 are shown in Fig 7.15. [The labels on the arrows for the send events match the labels on the send statements in the *Producer* (P) and *Consumer* (C) threads.] The variants are derived by changing the order of *deposit* (D) and *withdraw* (W) events whenever there is a message race. If the message for a receive event *r* is changed, all the events that happened after *r* are removed from the variant (since we cannot guarantee that these events can still occur). Notice that there is no variant in which the first *receiving event* is for a *withdraw*. Run-time information collected about the guards will show that the guard for *withdraw* was false when the first *deposit* was accepted in Q0. Thus, we do not generate a variant to cover this case.

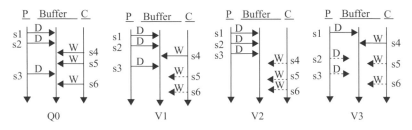

Figure 7.15 Sequence Q0 and its variants.

To create variant V1 in Fig. 7.15, the outcome of the race between s3 and *s5* in Q0 is reversed. During the next execution of CP, variant V1 is used for prefix-based testing. This means that variant V1 is replayed, and afterward, the execution proceeds nondeterministically. Sequence Q1 in Fig. 7.16 is the only sequence that can be exercised when V1 is used as a prefix. No new variants can be derived from Q1.

To create variant V2 in Fig. 7.15, the outcome of the race between *s3* and *s4* in Q0 is reversed. During the next execution of CP, variant V2 is used for prefix-based testing and sequence Q2 in Fig. 7.16 is the only sequence that can be exercised. No new variants can be derived from Q2.

To create variant V3 in Fig. 7.15, the outcome of the race between *s2* and *s4* in Q0 is reversed. During the next execution of CP, variant V3 is used for prefix-based testing. Assume that sequence Q3 in Fig. 7.17 is exercised. Variant V4 can be derived from Q3 by changing the outcome of the race between *s3* and *s5*. Notice that there is no need to change the outcome of the race between *s2* and *s5* in Q3 since the information collected about the guard conditions will show that a withdraw for *s5* cannot be accepted in place of the deposit for *s2*. During the next execution of CP, variant V4 is used for prefix-based testing, and sequence Q4 in Fig. 7.17 is the only sequence that can be exercised. Reachability testing stops at this point since Q0, Q1, Q2, Q3, and Q4 are all the possible SYN-sequences that can be exercised by this program.

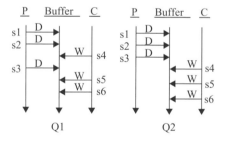

Figure 7.16   Sequences Q1 and Q2.

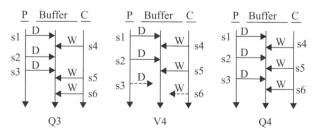

Figure 7.17   Sequences Q3 and Q4 and variant V4.

7.5.2 SYN-Sequences for Reachability Testing

To perform reachability testing we need to find the race conditions in a SYN-sequence. The SYN-sequences defined for replay and testing were defined without any concern with identifying races. Together, a program, an input, and a complete or simple SYN-sequence contain sufficient information to identify the path and determine the result of an execution, but they do not contain sufficient information to identify the alternative paths of an execution. For example, a (simple) M-sequence of a monitor-based execution records the sequence in which threads entered a monitor, which determines the result of an execution, but it does not contain any monitor call events, which are the events that must be analyzed to determine the alternative order(s) in which threads could have entered the monitor. Similarly, a PV-sequence for a semaphore-based program records the order in which threads completed their P and V operations, but there are no events representing calls to these operations. To compute the races in an execution, we need to capture this new type of execution event.

For reachability testing, an execution is characterized as a sequence of event pairs:

- For asynchronous and synchronous message-passing programs, an execution is characterized as a sequence of *send* and *receive* events. (For the execution of a synchronous *send* statement, the *send* event represents the start of the *send*, which happens before the message is received.)
- For programs that use semaphores or locks, an execution is characterized as a sequence of *call* and *completion* events for P, V, *lock*, and *unlock* operations.
- For programs that use monitors, an execution is characterized as a sequence of monitor *call* and monitor *entry* events.

We refer to a *send* or *call* event as a *sending event*, and a *receive, completion*, or *entry* event as a *receiving event*. We also refer to a pair $< s, r >$ of sending and receiving events as a *synchronization pair*. In the pair $< s, r >$, s is said to be the sending partner of r, and r is said to be the receiving partner of s. An arrow in a space-time diagram connects a sending event to a receiving event if the two events form a synchronization pair.

An event descriptor is used to encode certain information about each event:

- A descriptor for a sending event s is denoted by *(SendingThread, Destination, op, i)*, where S*endingThread* is the thread executing the sending event, D*estination* is the destination thread or object (semaphore, monitor, etc.), *op* is the operation performed (P, V, *send*, *receive*, etc.), and i is the event index indicating that s is the ith event of the *SendingThread*.
- A descriptor for a receiving event r is denoted by *(Destination, OpenList, i)*, where *Destination* is the destination thread or object and i is the event index indicating that r is the ith event of the *Destination* thread or object.

The *OpenList* contains program information that is used to compute the events that could have occurred besides r. For example, the *OpenLists* for the *receive* events in the example bounded buffer program above capture run-time information about the guard conditions (i.e., the list of accept alternatives that are open when a *deposit* or *withdraw* alternative is selected). This information enabled us to determine, for example, that a *withdraw* event could not be executed in place of the first *deposit* event. More *OpenList* examples are given below.

The individual fields of an event descriptor are referenced using dot notation. For example, operation *op* of sending event s is referred to as *s.op*. Tables 7.1 and 7.2 summarize the specific information that is contained in the event descriptors for the various synchronization constructs. Although the information is construct-specific, the format and general meaning of the fields in the event descriptors are the same for all constructs. This will allow us to present a single race analysis algorithm that operates on event descriptors and thus works for any construct. The values for most of the fields in the event descriptors are straightforward, except for the *OpenList* in receiving events. Below we describe how to compute *OpenLists* and provide examples of event descriptors for the various constructs.

Descriptors for Asynchronous Message Passing Events   For asynchronous message passing, the *OpenList* of a receive event r contains a single port, which is the source port of r. A send event s is said to be open at a receive event r if port *s.Destination* is in the *OpenList* of r, which means that the ports of s and r match. For a sending event s to be in the race set of receive event r, it is necessary (but not sufficient) for s to be open at r. The race analysis algorithm presented in the next section can be used to determine whether s is involved in a race condition that could allow s to be the send partner of r.

Figure 7.18 shows a space-time diagram representing an execution with three threads. Thread *T2* receives messages from ports *p1* and *p2*. Thread *T1* sends two messages to port *p1*. Thread *T3* sends its first message to port *p1* and its second message to port *p2*. Event descriptors are shown for each of the events.

TABLE 7.1   Event Descriptors for a Sending Event *s*

Synchronization Construct	SendingThread	Destination	Operation	i
Asynchronous message passing	Sending thread	Port ID	Send	Event index
Synchronous message passing	Sending thread	Port ID	Send	Event index
Semaphores	Calling thread	Semaphore ID	P or V	Event index
Locks	Calling thread	Lock ID	Lock or unlock	Event index
Monitors	Calling thread	Monitor ID	Method name	Event index

TABLE 7.2   Event Descriptors for a Receiving Event *r*

Synchronization Construct	Destination	OpenList	*i*
Asynchronous message passing	Receiving thread	Port of *r*	Event index
Synchronous message passing	Receiving thread	List of open ports (including the port of *r*)	Event index
Semaphores	Semaphore ID	List of open operations (*P* and/or *V*)	Event index
Locks	Lock ID	List of open operations (lock and/or unlock)	Event index
Monitors	Monitor ID	List of the monitor's methods	Event index

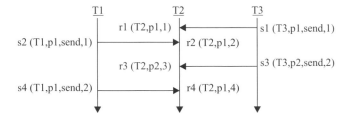

Figure 7.18   Sequence of asynchronous send/receive events.

Descriptors for Synchronous Message Passing Events   Synchronous message passing may involve the use of selective waits. The *OpenList* of a receive event *r* is a list of ports that had open receive alternatives when *r* was selected. Note that this list always includes the source port of *r*. For a simple receive statement that is not in a selective wait, the *OpenList* contains a single port, which is the source port of the receive statement. Event *s* is said to be open at *r* if port *s.Destination* is in the *OpenList* of *r*.

Figure 7.19 shows a space-time diagram representing an execution with three threads. Thread *T1* sends two messages to port *p1*, and thread *T3* sends two messages to port *p2*. Thread *T2* executes a selective wait with receive alternatives for *p1* and *p2*. Assume that whenever *p2* is selected, the alternative for *p1* is open, and whenever *p1* is selected, the alternative for *p2* is closed. This is reflected in the *OpenLists* for the receive events, which are shown between braces {...} in the event descriptors. Note that each solid arrow is followed by a dotted arrow in the opposite direction. The dotted arrows represent the updating of timestamps when the synchronous communication completes. Timestamp schemes are described in Section 7.5.4.

Descriptors for Semaphore Events   Figure 7.20 shows an execution involving threads *T1* and *T2* and semaphore *s*, where s is a binary semaphore initialized

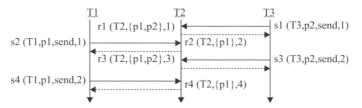

Figure 7.19   Sequence of synchronous send/receive events.

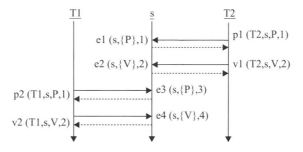

Figure 7.20   Sequence of *P* and *V* operations.

to 1. There is one time line for each thread and each semaphore. A solid arrow represents the completion of a *P()* or *V()* operation. The open lists for the completion events model the fact that *P* and *V* operations on a binary semaphore must alternate. This means that the *OpenList* of a completion event for a binary semaphore always contains one of *P* or *V* but not both. *OpenLists* for binary and counting semaphores can easily be calculated at run time based on the semaphore invariant (see Sections 3.1 and 3.4.1). A call event *c* for a *P* or *V* operation is open at a completion event *e* if *c* and *e* are operations on the same semaphore (i.e., *c.Destination* = *e.Destination*, and operation *c.op* of *c* is in the *OpenList* of *e*).

Descriptors for Lock Events   If a lock is owned by some thread *T* when a completion event *e* occurs, each operation in the *OpenList* of *e* is prefixed with *T* to indicate that only *T* can perform the operation. (Recall that if a thread *T* owns lock *L*, only *T* can complete a *lock()* or *unlock()* operation on *L*.) For example, if the *OpenList* of a completion event *e* on a lock *L* contains two operations *lock()* and *unlock()*, and if *L* is owned by thread *T* when *e* occurs, the *OpenList* of *e* is {*T* : *lock*, *T* : *unlock*}. A call event *c* on lock *L* that is executed by thread *T* is open at a completion event *e* if (1) *c.Destination* = *e.Destination*; (2) operation *c.op* is in the *OpenList* of *e*, and (3) if *L* is already owned when *e* occurs then *T* is the owner.

Figure 7.21 shows a space-time diagram representing an execution with two threads and a mutex lock *k*. Thread *T2* performs two *lock()* operations followed by two *unlock()* operations, and thread *T1* performs one *lock()* operation followed

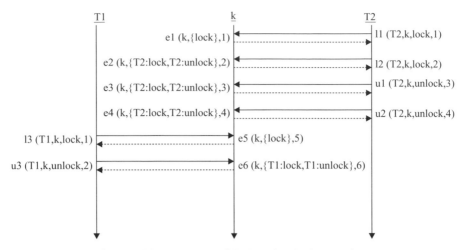

Figure 7.21 Sequence of *lock* and *unlock* operations.

by one *unlock()* operation. The *OpenList* for *e2* reflects the fact that only thread *T2* can complete a *lock()* or *unlock()* operation on *k* since *T2* owns *k* when *e* occurs.

Descriptors for Monitor Events   The invocation of a monitor method is modeled as a pair of monitor-call and monitor-entry events:

- *SU monitors.* When a thread *T* calls a method of monitor *M*, a monitor-call event *c* occurs on *T*. When *T* eventually enters *M*, a monitor-entry event *e* occurs on *M*, and then *T* starts to execute inside *M*.
- *SC monitors.* When a thread *T* calls a method of monitor *M*, a monitor-call event *c* occurs on *T*. A call event also occurs when *T* tries to reenter a monitor *M* after being signaled. When *T* eventually (re)enters *M*, a monitor-entry event *e* occurs on *M*, and *T* starts to execute inside *M*.

In these scenarios, we say that *T* is the calling thread of *c* and *e*, and *M* is the destination monitor of *c* as well as the owning monitor of *e*. A call event *c* is open at an entry event *e* if the destination monitor of *c* is the owning monitor of *e* (i.e., *c.Destination = e.Destination*). The *OpenList* of an entry event always contains all the methods of the monitor since threads are never prevented from entering any monitor method (although they must enter sequentially and they may be blocked after they enter).

Figure 7.22 shows a space-time diagram representing an execution involving three threads *T1, T2,* and *T3*, an *SC* monitor *m1* with methods *a()* and *b()*, and an SC monitor *m2* with a single method *c()*. Thread *T1* enters *m1.a()* first and executes a *wait* operation. The second call event performed by *T1* occurs when *T1* reenters *m1.a()* after being *signaled* by *T2*. Note that if *m1* were an *SU*

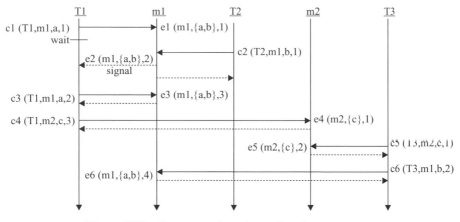

Figure 7.22   Sequence of monitor call and entry events.

monitor, there would be no *c3* event representing reentry. After *T1* exits from *m1*, *T1* enters and exits *m2*. This is followed by thread *T3* entering and exiting *m2* and then entering and exiting *m1*.

7.5.3   Race Analysis of SYN-Sequences

In this section we show how to perform race analysis on SYN-sequences. Section 7.5.2 showed a common event descriptor format for a variety of synchronization constructs. To illustrate race analysis, we will first consider a program CP that uses asynchronous ports. We assume that the messages sent from one thread to another may be received out of order. To simplify our discussion, we also assume that each thread has a single port from which it receives messages.

Let Q be an SR-sequence recorded during an execution of CP with input X. Assume that $a \rightarrow b$ is a synchronization pair in Q, c is a send event in Q that is not a, and c's message is sent to the same thread that executed b. We need to determine whether sending events a and c have a race (i.e., whether $c \rightarrow b$ can happen instead of $a \rightarrow b$ during an execution of CP with input X). Furthermore, we need to identify races by analyzing Q, not CP.

To determine accurately all the races in an execution, the program's semantics must be analyzed. Fortunately, for the purpose of reachability testing, we need only consider a special type of race, called a *lead race*. Lead races can be identified by analyzing the SYN-sequence of an execution (i.e., without analyzing the source code).

Definition 6.1   Let Q be the SYN-sequence exercised by an execution of a concurrent program CP with input X. Let $a \rightarrow b$ be a synchronization pair in Q and let c be another sending event in Q. There exists a *lead race* between c and $< a, b >$ if $c \rightarrow b$ can form a synchronization pair during some other execution of CP with input X, provided that all the events that happened before c or b in Q are replayed in this other execution.

Note that Definition 6.1 requires all events that can potentially affect c or b in Q to be replayed in the other execution. If the events that happened before b are replayed, and the events that happened before c are replayed, we can be sure that b and c will also occur, without having to analyze the code.

Definition 6.2   The *race set* of $a \to b$ in Q is defined as the set of sending events c such that c has a (lead) race with $a \to b$ in Q.

We will refer to the receive event in Q that receives the message from c as receive event d, denoted by $c \to d$. (If the message from c was not received in Q, d does not exist.) To determine whether $a \to b$ and c in Q have a message race, consider the 11 possible relationships that can hold between a, b, c, and d in Q:

(1) $c \Rightarrow d$ and $d \Rightarrow b$.

(2) $c \Rightarrow d$, $b \Rightarrow d$, and $b \Rightarrow c$.

(3) c is send event that is never received and $b \Rightarrow c$.

(4) $c \Rightarrow d$, $b \Rightarrow d$, $c||b$, and a and c are send events of the same thread.

(5) $c \Rightarrow d$, $b \Rightarrow d$, $c||b$, and a and c are send events of different threads.

(6) $c \Rightarrow d$, $b \Rightarrow d$, $c \Rightarrow b$, and a and c are send events of the same threads.

(7) $c \Rightarrow d$, $b \Rightarrow d$, $c \Rightarrow b$, and a and c are send events of different threads.

(8) c is a send event that is not received, $c||b$, and a and c are send events of the same thread.

(9) c is a send event that is not received, $c||b$, and a and c are send events of different threads.

(10) c is a send event that is not received, $c \Rightarrow b$, and a and c are send events of the same thread.

(11) c is a send event that is not received, $c \Rightarrow b$, and a and c are send events of different threads.

The happened before relation $e \Rightarrow f$ was defined in Section 6.3.4. Recall that it is easy to examine a space-time diagram visually and determine the causal relations. For two events e and f in a space-time diagram, $e \Rightarrow f$ if and only if there is no message $e \leftrightarrow f$ or $f \leftrightarrow e$ and there exists a path from e to f that follows the vertical lines and arrows in the diagram.

Figure 7.23 shows 11 space-time diagrams that illustrate these 11 relations. Each of the diagrams contains a curve, called the *frontier*. Only the events happening before b or c are above the frontier. (A send event before the frontier may have its corresponding receive event below the frontier, but not vice versa.) For each of diagrams (4) through (11), if the send and receive events above the

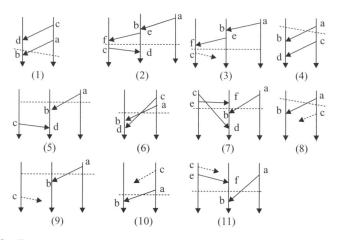

Figure 7.23 For message $a \to b$ and send event $c \to d$ in Q, the eleven possible relations between a, b, c, and d.

frontier are repeated, events b and c will also be repeated and the message sent by c could be received by b. This is not true for diagrams (1), (2), and (3).

Based on these diagrams, we can define the race set of $a \to b$ in Q as follows:

Definition 6.3 Let Q be an SR-sequence of a program using asynchronous communication and let $a \to b$ be a synchronization pair in Q. The race set of $a \to b$ in Q is $\{c|c$ is a send event in Q; c has b's thread as the receiver; not $b \Rightarrow c$; and if $c \to d$, then $b \Rightarrow d\}$.

Figure 7.24a shows an asychronous SR-sequence and the race set for each receive event in this SR-sequence. Consider send event $s8$ in Fig. 7.24a. Send event $s8$ is received by Thread2 and is in the race sets for receive events $r1$ and $r2$ of Thread2. Send event $s8$ is not in the race set for receive event $r6$ since $r6$ happens before $s8$. Send event $s8$ is not in the race set for receive event $r7$ since $s8 \to r8$ but $r8 \Rightarrow r7$. Thus, $s8$ is in the race sets for receive events of Thread2 that happen before $r8$ but do not happen before $s8$.

The asynchronous ports and mailboxes used in Chapters 5 and 6 are FIFO ports, which means that messages sent from one thread to another thread are received in the order that they are sent. With FIFO ordering, some of relations (1) through (11) above must be modified:

- Relations (4) and (8) no longer have a race between message $a \to b$ and c.
- Relations (6) and (10) are not possible.
- Relations (5), (7), (9), and (11) have a race between $a \to b$ and c if and only if all the messages that are sent from c's thread to b's thread before c is sent are received before b occurs.

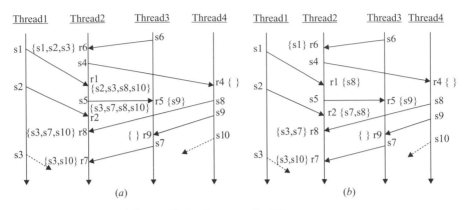

Figure 7.24   Race sets for SR-sequences.

Thus, the definition of race set must also be modified for FIFO asynchronous SR-sequences.

Definition 6.4   Let Q be an SR-sequence of a program using FIFO asynchronous communication, and let $a \rightarrow b$ be a message in Q. The race set of $a \rightarrow b$ in Q is $\{c \mid c$ is a send event in Q; c has b's thread as the receiver; not $b \Rightarrow c$; if $c \rightarrow d$, then $b \Rightarrow d$; and all the messages that are sent from c's thread to b's thread before c is sent are received before b occurs$\}$.

Figure 7.24b shows a FIFO asynchronous SR-sequence and the race set for each receive event in this SR-sequence. (Since the asynchronous SR-sequence in Fig. 7.24a satisfies FIFO ordering, it is also used in Fig. 7.24b.) Consider the nonreceived send event s3 in Fig. 7.24b. Send event s3 has Thread2 as the receiver and is in the race sets for receive events r7 and r8 in Thread2. Thread2 executes r2 immediately before executing r8. Since r2 has the same sender as s3 and s2 is sent to Thread2 before s3 is sent, s2 has to be received by Thread2 before s3 is received. Thus, s3 is not in the race set for receive event r2. (Note that in Fig. 7.24a, s3 is in the race sets for receive events r6, r1, r2, r8, and r7.)

In some parallel programs, nondeterminism is considered to be the result of a programming error [Empath et al. 1992]. If an execution of CP with input X is expected to be deterministic, the race set for each receive event in Q should be empty. If the race set for each receive event in Q is empty, all executions of CP with input X exercise the same SR-sequence and produce the same result.

In general, sending and receiving events may involve constructs such as semaphores, locks, and monitors, not just message passing. The following definition describes how to compute the race set of a receiving event assuming that all the constructs use FIFO semantics.

Definition 6.5   Let Q be a SYN-sequence exercised by program CP. A sending event s is in the race set of a receiving event r if (1) s is open at r; (2) r does not happen before s; (3) if $< s, r' >$ is a synchronization pair, r happens before r'; and (4) s and r are consistent with FIFO semantics (i.e., all the messages that were sent to the same destination as s, and were sent before s, are received before r).

Following are some examples of race sets:

- *Asynchronous message passing.* The race sets for the receive events in Fig. 7.18 are as follows: $race(r1) = \{s2\}$ and $race(r2) = race(r3) = race(r4) = \{\}$. Note that $s3$ is not in the race set of $r1$ because $s3$ is sent to a different port and thus $s3$ is not open at $r1$. For the same reason, $s4$ is not in the race set of $r3$. Note also that $s4$ is not in the race set of $r1$, because FIFO semantics ensures that $s2$ is received before $s4$.

- *Synchronous message passing.* The race sets of the receive events in Fig. 7.19 are as follows: $race(r1) = \{s2\}$, $race(r2) = \{\}$, $race(r3) = \{s4\}$, and $race(r4) = \{\}$. Since the receive alternative for port $p2$ was open whenever thread $T2$ selected the receive alternative for port $p1$, the race set for $r1$ contains $s2$ and the race set for $r3$ contains $s4$. On the other hand, since the receive alternative for $p1$ was closed whenever thread $T2$ selected the receive alternative for $p2$, the race set for $r2$ does not contain $s3$.

- *Semaphores.* The race sets of the completion events in Fig. 7.20 are as follows: $race(e1) = \{p2\}$ and $race(e2) = race(e3) = race(e4) = \{\}$. Note that since $P()$ is not in the *OpenList* of $e2$, the race set for $e2$ does not contain $p2$. This captures the fact that the $P()$ operation by $T1$ could start but not complete before the $V()$ operation by $T2$ and hence that these operations do not race.

- *Locks.* The race sets of the completion events in Fig. 7.21 are as follows: $race(e1) = \{l3\}$ and $race(e2) = race(e3) = race(e4) = race(e5) = race(e6) = \{\}$. Note that since $T2$ owned lock k when the operations for events $e2$, $e3$, and $e4$ were started, the race sets for $e2$, $e3$, and $e4$ are empty. This represents the fact that no other thread can complete a $lock()$ operation on k while it is owned by $T2$.

- *Monitors.* The race sets of the entry events in Fig. 7.22 are as follows: $race(e1) = \{c2\}$, $race(e2) = race(e3) = \{\}race(e4) = \{c5\}$, and $race(e5) = race(e6) = \{\}$. Sending event $c3$ is not in the race set of $e2$ since $c3$ happened after $e2$. (Thread T2 entered monitor m at $e2$ and executed a signal operation that caused $T1$ to issue the call at $c3$.)

7.5.4 Timestamp Assignment

As we just saw, the definition of a race between sending events is based on the happened-before relation, which was defined in Section 6.3.3. In this section we present thread-centric and object-centric timestamp assignment schemes for capturing the happened-before relation during race analysis. A *thread-centric* timestamp has a dimension equal to the number of threads involved in an execution. An *object-centric* timestamp has a dimension equal to the number of synchronization objects involved. Therefore, a thread-centric scheme is preferred when the number of threads is smaller than the number of synchronization objects, and an object-centric scheme is preferred otherwise.

Thread-Centric Scheme The vector timestamp scheme described in Section 6.3.5 is thread-centric by our definition and can be used for race analysis. Recall that in this scheme each thread maintains a vector clock. A vector clock is a vector of integers used to keep track of the integer clock of each thread. The integer clock of a thread is initially zero and is incremented each time the thread executes a send or receive event. Each send and receive event is also assigned a copy of the vector clock as its timestamp.

Let $T.v$ be the vector clock maintained by a thread T. Let $f.ts$ be the vector timestamp of event f. The vector clock of a thread is initially a vector of zeros. The following rules are used to update vector clocks and assign timestamps to the send and receive events in asynchronous message passing programs:

1. When a thread T_i executes a nonblocking send event s, it performs the following operations: (a) $T_i.v[i] = T_i.v[i] + 1$; (b) $s.ts = T_i.v$. The message sent by s also carries the timestamp $s.ts$.
2. When a thread T_j executes a receive event r with synchronization partner s, it performs the following operations: (a) $T_j.v[j] = T_j.v[j] + 1$; (b) $T_j.v = \max(T_j.v, s.ts)$; (c) $r.ts = T_j.v$.

Figure 7.25*a* shows the timestamps for the asynchronous message passing program in Fig. 7.18. A timestamp scheme for synchronous message passing was also described in Section 6.3.5, but this scheme must be extended before it can be used for race analysis. The scheme in Section 6.3.5 assigns the same timestamp to send and receive events that are synchronization partners:

1. When a thread T_i executes a blocking send event s, it performs the operation $T_i.v[i] = T_i.v[i] + 1$. The message sent by s also carries the value of vector clock $T_i.v$.

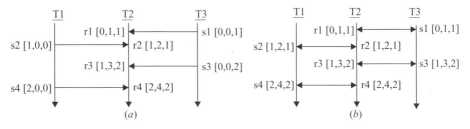

Figure 7.25   Traditional timestamp schemes for asynchronous and synchronous message passing.

2. When a thread T_j executes a receiving event r that receives the message sent by s, it performs the following operations: (a) $T_j.v[j] = T_j.v[j] + 1$; (b) $T_j.v = \max(T_j.v, T_i.v)$; (c) $r.ts = T_j.v$. Thread T_j also sends $T_j.v$ back to thread T_i.

3. Thread T_i receives $T_j.v$ and performs the following operations: (a) $T_i.v = \max(T_i.v, T_j.v)$; (b) $s.ts = T_i.v$.

The exchange of vector clock values between threads T_i and T_j represents the synchronization that occurs between them; their send and receive operations are considered to be completed at the same time. Figure 7.25b shows the timestamps for the synchronous message passing program in Fig. 7.19. In our execution model for synchronous message passing, a send event models the start of a send operation, not its completion. This allows us to identify synchronous send operations that start concurrently, which is essential for race analysis. For send and receive events that are synchronization partners, the start of the send is considered to happen before the completion of the receive, which means that the timestamps for sending and receiving partners should not be the same. Thus, when a synchronization completes, we use the timestamp of the receive event to update the vector clock of the sending thread, which models the synchronization that occurs between the threads. But we do not use the timestamp of the receive event to update the timestamp of the send event, since the start of the send is considered to happen before the completion of the receive.

The timestamp scheme synchronous message passing is as follows:

1. When a thread T_i executes a blocking send event s, it performs the following operations: (a) $T_i.v[i] = T_i.v[i] + 1$; (b) $s.ts = T_i.v$. The message sent by s also carries the value of vector clock $T_i.v$.

2. When a thread T_j executes a receiving event r that receives the message sent by s, it performs the following operations: (a) $T_j.v[j] = T_j.v[j] + 1$; (b) $T_j.v = \max(T_j.v, T_i.v)$; (c) $r.ts = T_j.v$. Thread T_j also sends $T_j.v$ back to thread T_i.

3. Thread T_i receives $T_j.v$ and performs the operation $T_i.v = \max(T_i.v, T_j.v)$.

Figure 7.26 shows the timestamps that are assigned so that race analysis can be performed on the synchronous message passing program in Fig. 7.19. Note that the dashed arrows represent the application of rule 3. The timestamps for $s1$ and $s2$ indicate that these send events were concurrent even though the synchronization between T1 and T2 happened after the synchronization between T3 and T2.

Below we describe a thread-centric timestamp scheme for semaphores, locks, and monitors. We refer to semaphores, locks, and monitors generally as *synchronization objects*. In this scheme, each thread and synchronization object maintains a vector clock. (As before, position i in a vector clock refers to the integer clock of thread T_i; synchronization objects do not have integer clocks and thus there are no positions in a vector clock for the synchronization objects.) Let $T.v$ (or

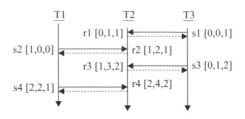

Figure 7.26 Timestamp scheme for race analysis of synchronous message passing programs.

$O.v$) be the vector clock maintained by a thread T (or a synchronization object O). The vector clock of a thread or synchronization object is initially a vector of zeros. The following rules are used to update vector clocks and assign timestamps to events:

1. When a thread T_i executes a sending event s, it performs the following operations: (a) $T_i.v[i] = T_i.v[i] + 1$; (b) $s.ts = T_i.v$.
2. When a receiving event r occurs on a synchronization object O, the following operations are performed: (a) $O.v = \max(O.v, s.ts)$; (b) $r.ts = O.v$, where s is the sending partner of r.
3. *Semaphore/Lock.* When a thread T_i finishes executing an operation on a semaphore or lock O, it updates its vector clock using the component-wise maximum of $T_i.v$ and $O.v$ [i.e., $T_i.v = \max(T_i.v, O.v)$].
   SU monitor. When a thread T_i finishes executing a method on a monitor O, it updates its vector clock using the component-wise maximum of $T_i.v$ and $O.v$ [i.e., $T_i.v = \max(T_i.v, O.v)$].
   SC monitor. When a thread T_i finishes executing a method on a monitor O, or when a thread T_i is signaled from a condition queue of O, it updates its vector clock using the component-wise maximum of $T_i.v$ and $O.v$ [i.e., $T_i.v = \max(T_i.v, O.v)$].

Figure 7.27a and b show the thread-centric timestamps assigned for the executions in Figs. 7.20 and 7.22, respectively. Again, dotted arrows represent application of the third rule. Thread-centric timestamps can be used to determine the happened-before relation between two arbitrary events, as the following proposition shows:

Proposition 6.1 Let CP be a program with threads $T_1, T_2, \ldots, T_n$ and one or more semaphores, locks, or monitors. Let Q be a SYN-sequence exercised by CP. Assume that every event in Q is assigned a thread-centric timestamp. Let $f.tid$ be the (integer) thread ID of the thread that executed event f, and let f_1 and f_2 be two events in Q. Then, $f_1 \rightarrow f_2$ if and only if (1) $<f1, f2>$ is a synchronization pair; or (2) $f_1.ts[f_1.tid] \leq f_2.ts[f_1.tid]$ and $f_1.ts[f_2.tid] < f2.ts[f2.tid]$.

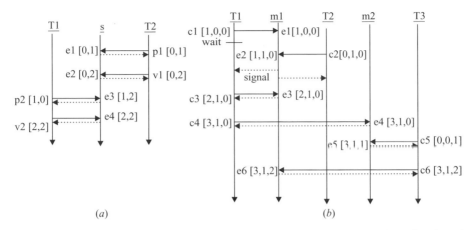

(a)   (b)

Figure 7.27 Timestamp scheme for race analysis of semaphore-based and monitor-based programs.

Object-Centric Scheme   In an object-centric scheme, each thread and synchronization object (port, semaphore, lock, or monitor) maintains a version vector. A version vector is a vector of integers used to keep track of the version number of each synchronization object. The version number of a synchronization object is initially zero and is incremented each time a thread performs a sending or receiving event. Each sending and receiving event is also assigned a version vector as its timestamp.

Let $T.v$ (or $O.v$) be the version vector maintained by a thread T (or a synchronization object O). Initially, the version vector of each thread or synchronization object is a vector of zeros. The following rules are used to update version vectors and assign timestamps to events:

1. When a thread T executes a sending event s, T assigns its version vector as the timestamp of s (i.e., $s.ts = T.v$;).
2. When a receiving event r occurs on a synchronization object O, letting s be the sending partner of r, the following operations are performed: (a) $O.v = \max(O.v, s.ts)$; (b) $r.ts = O.v$.
3. *Semaphore/Lock.* When a thread T finishes an operation on a semaphore or lock O, T updates its version vector using the component-wise maximum of $T.v$ and $O.v$ [i.e., $T.v = \max(T.v, O.v)$].
   SU monitor. When a thread T finishes executing a method on a monitor O, T updates its version vector using the component-wise maximum of $T.v$ and $O.v$ [i.e., $T.v = \max(T.v, O.v)$].
   SC monitor. When a thread T finishes executing a method on a monitor O, or when a thread T is signaled from a condition queue of O, T updates its version vector using the component-wise maximum of $T.v$ and $O.v$ [i.e., $T.v = \max(T.v, O.v)$].

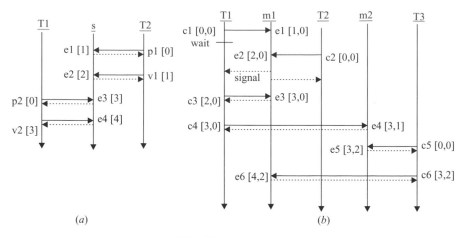

Figure 7.28   Object-centric timestamps.

Timestamps assigned using the rules above are called object-centric timestamps. Note that this scheme is preferred only if the number of synchronization objects is smaller than the number of threads. Considering that in a message-passing program, each thread usually has at least one port, we do not expect that this scheme will frequently be used for message-passing programs. Figure 7.28 shows object-centric timestamps assigned for the executions in Fig. 7.27.

Object-centric timestamps cannot be used to determine the happened-before relation between two arbitrary events. However, they can be used to determine the happened-before relation between two events if at least one of the events is a receiving event, which is sufficient for our purposes.

Proposition 6.2   Let CP be a program that uses synchronization objects O_1, O_2, ..., O_m, and let Q be a SYN-sequence exercised by CP. Assume that every event in Q is assigned an object-centric timestamp. Let e be a receiving event on O_i and f be a receiving event on O_j, where $1 \le i, j \le m$. Then $e \rightarrow f$ if and only if $e.ts[i] \le f.ts[i]$ and $e.ts[j] < f.ts[j]$.

Proposition 6.3   Let CP be a program that uses synchronization objects O_1, O_2, ..., O_m, and let Q be the SYN-sequence exercised by CP. Assume that every event in Q is assigned an object-centric timestamp. Let r be a receiving event on O_i and s be a sending event on O_j, where $1 \le i, j \le m$. Then $r \rightarrow s$ if and only if $r.ts[i] \le s.ts[i]$.

In Fig. 7.28b, monitor entry e_3 happens before entry e_4 since $e_3.s[1] \le e_4.ts[1]$ and $e_3.ts[2] < e_4.ts[2]$. Monitor entry e_3 happens before call c_6 since $e_3.ts[1] \le c_6.ts[1]$.

7.5.5   Computing Race Variants

The race variants of a SYN-sequence Q are computed by constructing a *race table*, where every row in the race table represents a race variant of Q. Each race variant V of Q is required to satisfy the following three conditions: (1) If we create V by changing the sending partner of receiving event *r*, the new sending partner of *r* must be a sending event in the race set of *r*; (2) if we create V by changing the sending partner of receiving event *r*, any event *e* that happens after *r* must be removed from V if *e's* execution can no longer be guaranteed; and (3) there must be at least one difference between Q and V. As an example, consider the race table for sequence Q0 of the bounded buffer program in Section 7.5.1. Sequence Q0 and its variants are reproduced in Fig. 7.29. The receiving events in Q0 are numbered and shown with their race sets.

Table 7.3 is the race table for sequence Q0. The three columns represent the three receiving events whose race sets are nonempty. Each row represents a race variant of Q0. Consider the second row, which is (0, 1, −1). Each value indicates how the sending partner of the corresponding receiving event in Q0 is changed to create variant V2. The value 0 indicates that the sending partner of receiving event r_2 will be left unchanged. The value 1 indicates that the sending partner of receiving event r_3 will be changed to s_3, which is the first (and only) send event in $race(r_3)$. The value −1 indicates that receiving event r_4 will be removed from V2. In general, let *r* be the receiving event corresponding to column *j*, V the race variant derived from row *i*, and *v* the value in row *i* column *j*. Value *v* indicates how receiving event *r* is changed to derive variant *V*:

1. $v = -1$ indicates that *r* is removed from V.

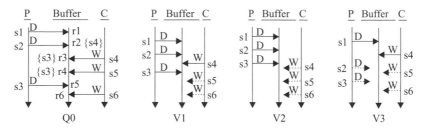

Figure 7.29   Reachability testing for the bounded buffer program.

TABLE 7.3   Race Table for Q0

	r_2	r_3	r_4
1	0	0	1
2	0	1	−1
3	1	−1	−1

2. $v = 0$ indicates that the sending partner of r is left unchanged in V.

3. $v > 0$ indicates that the sending partner of r in V is changed to the vth (sending) event in $race(r)$, where the sending events in $race(r)$ are arranged in an arbitrary order and the index of the first sending event in $race(r)$ is 1.

The receiving events with nonempty race sets are arranged across the columns in left-to-right order with respect to the happened-before relation. (If receiving event a happens before receiving event b, the column for a appears to the left of the column for b.) Conceptually, a race table is a number system in which each row is a number in the system and each column is a digit in a number. In Table 7.3, each receiving event has a race set of size 1. Thus, the base of the number system is 2 and each digit (i.e., column value) has the value 0 or 1. (In general, the race sets of the receiving events may have different sizes.) The significance of the digits increases from right to left.

The rows in the race table are computed iteratively. Starting with the number 0, all the numbers in the number system are enumerated by adding 1 at each iteration. Each new number (not including 0) becomes the next row in the table. Observe that the addition of 1 to a number can be accomplished by incrementing the least significant digit g whose value is less than the value of its base minus 1 and then setting all the digits that are less significant than g to 0. For the binary (base 2) system in Table 7.3, the first row of the race table is 001. Adding 1 to this row generates the second row 010, adding one to the second row generates the third row 011, and so on. This process generates variants representing all the possible combinations of outcomes of the race conditions. There is a slight complication, however, for dealing with the case where the value of a digit is, or becomes, -1. The value -1 is used to ensure that each row represents a variant that is a feasible prefix of the program being tested, as described below.

To compute the next row in the race table for a SYN-sequence Q, we increment the least significant digit whose value is less than the value of its base minus 1 and whose value is not -1. Let $t[]$ be an array representing the next row in the race table. We use the following rules to ensure that $t[]$ represents a valid race variant V of sequence Q:

1. Whenever we change digit $t[i]$ from 0 to 1, which means that the sending partner of receiving event r_i will be changed to create V, we set $t[j] = -1, i < j \leq n$, if r_i happens before r_j and r_j is no longer guaranteed to occur. (Recall that changing the sending partner of r_i may affect the execution of the events that happen after r_i.) This removes receiving event(s) r_j from V and ensures that V represents a feasible prefix of one or more executions.

2. Let b_i be the base of digit $t[i]$. Whenever we change digit $t[i]$ from b_i to 0, which means that the sending partner of r_i will be changed back to r_i's original sending partner in Q, we set $t[j] = 0, i < j \leq n$, if the current value of $t[j]$ is -1 and there no longer exists an index k, $1 \leq k < j$, such that $t[k] > 0$ and r_k happens before r_j. In other words, if r_i is the only

event causing $t[j]$ to be set to -1 [due to the application of rule (1)] and we change r_i's sending partner back to its original sending partner in Q, we need to change $t[j]$ to 0 so that r_j is no longer removed from V.

3. Whenever we increment $t[i]$, we need to determine whether there exists an index j such that $t[j] = m$, $m > 0$, and $r_i \rightarrow s$, where s is the mth send event in $race(r_j)$. Array $t[]$ is added to the race table as the next row if and only if such an index j does not exist. If such an index j does exist, the sending partner of receiving event r_j was previously changed to s but since $r_i \rightarrow s$ and the sending partner of r_i has just been changed, we can no longer guarantee that send event s will occur.

As an example, consider how to add 1 to the number represented by row 1 in Table 7.3. First, we increment the value in the second column (i.e., the column for r_3), which is the rightmost column whose value is less than its base minus 1 and is not -1. (The base of the third column is 2, which is one more than the number of send events in the race set of r_4. The value 1 in the third column is not less than 2 minus 1; hence we do not increment the value in the third column.) We then apply rule 1, changing the value in the third column to -1 since r_3 happens before r_4 in sequence Q0. Rule 2 is not applicable since we did not change the second column from 1 to 0. For rule 3, observe that no other column has a value greater than 0; hence, changing the sending partner of r_3 does not affect the sending partners of any other receiving events.

Notice that when we change $t[i]$ from 0 to 1 or from b_i to 0, we need only check the values of $t[k]$, $i < k \leq n$, which are the values in the columns to the right of $t[i]$. This is because receiving events are ordered from left to right based on the happened-before relation. This ordering also ensures that the value represented by $t[]$ increases at each iteration. Therefore, this iterative process of computing rows will eventually terminate.

Every row in a race table represents a unique, partially ordered variant, which means that totally ordered sequences are not considered during race analysis. As a result, race analysis never produces two sequences that differ only in the order of concurrent events (i.e., two different totally ordered sequences that have the same partial ordering). To see this, consider a race table that has columns for two concurrent receiving events r_1 and r_2. Three variants will be generated: one in which the sending partner of r_1 is changed, one in which the sending partner of r_2 is changed, and one in which the sending partners of both r_1 and r_2 are changed. No variants are generated to cover the two orders in which r_1 and r_2 themselves can be executed (r_1 followed by r_2, and r_2 followed by r_1). The order in which r_1 and r_2 are executed is not specified by the variants. This avoids the "test sequence explosion problem" that would result if test sequences were to be generated to cover all the possible interleavings of concurrent events.

7.5.6 Reachability Testing Algorithm

In the preceding section we described how to generate race variants for a single SYN-sequence. The reachability testing process, however, is iterative. A sequence is collected and its race variants are derived and used to collect more sequences, which are used to derive more variants, and so on. The objective of this process is to exercise every (partially ordered) SYN-sequence exactly once during reachability testing. However, if a newly derived race variant V is a prefix of a SYN-sequence Q that was exercised earlier, prefix-based testing with V could exercise Q again. Reachability testing algorithms must deal with this potential for collecting duplicate sequences.

One approach to preventing duplicates is to save all the SYN-sequences that are exercised. Then a newly derived variant can be used for prefix-based testing only if it is not a prefix of a SYN-sequence that has already been exercised. For large programs, the cost of saving all of the sequences can be prohibitive, both in terms of the space to store the sequences and the time to search through them. As a result, the scalability of this approach is limited.

In this section we describe an alternative approach that does not save any exercised sequences. The idea is to identify variants that may cause duplicates and prevent them from being generated. Some of these variants, however, cannot be prevented, since the best we can say before we execute these variants is that they *might* produce duplicates. In such cases, we allow the suspect variants to be executed, but we prevent duplicate sequences from being collected from them.

To understand this alternative approach, it is helpful to consider reachability testing from a graph-theoretic perspective. Let CP be a concurrent program. All the possible SYN-sequences that could be exercised by CP with input X can be organized into a directed graph G, which we refer to as the *Sequence/Variant graph* of CP, or simply the *S/V-graph*. For example, Fig. 7.30a is the S/V-graph for the bounded buffer example in Section 7.5.1.

Each node n in S/V-graph G represents a SYN-sequence that could be exercised by CP with input X. Each edge represents a race variant. An edge labeled V from node n to node n' indicates that sequence n' could be exercised by prefix-based testing with the variant V derived from sequence n. Note that a node n may have multiple outgoing edges that are labeled by the same variant of n. The reason for this is that prefix-based testing with a race variant forces the variant to be exercised at the beginning of the test run and then lets the run continue nondeterministically; this nondeterministic portion can exercise different sequences in different test runs. For example, in Fig. 7.30a node Q0 has two outgoing edges that are both labeled V3 since prefix-based testing with variant V3 may exercise

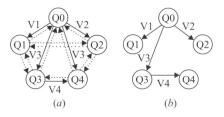

(a)   (b)

Figure 7.30   SV-graph and spanning tree for the bounded buffer program.

Q3 or Q4. Note also that an S/V-graph is strongly connected, which means that there is a path in the graph from each node to every other node.

From a graph-theoretic perspective, the goal of reachability testing is to construct a spanning tree of the S/V-graph. A spanning tree of S/V-graph G is a subgraph of G that is a tree (i.e., a graph with no cycles) and that connects the n nodes of G with $n - 1$ edges (i.e., each node, except the root, has one and only one incoming edge.). Since S/V-graphs are strongly connected, reachability testing can start from an arbitrary node, which explains why the reachability testing process begins by collecting a sequence during a nondeterministic execution. Also note that each variant is used to conduct a single test run. Therefore, in a spanning tree that represents the reachability testing process, no two edges should be labeled with the same variant. Figure 7.30*b* shows the spanning tree representing the reachability testing process that was illustrated in Section 7.5.1.

A reachability testing algorithm must constrain the way variants are generated so that every sequence is exercised exactly once (i.e., so that the reachability testing process represents a spanning tree of the SV-graph). Of course, the SV-graph is not known when reachability testing begins, so we are only using SV-graphs and spanning trees as a device to guide the implementation of, and demonstrate the correctness of, our reachability testing algorithm. Below, we describe several constraints that are implemented in the reachability testing algorithm and show how they relate to SV-graphs and spanning trees. Details about the algorithm can be found in the references at the end of this chapter.

Let G be the S/V graph of program CP with input X. If we can find some constraints on the paths through G such that given two arbitrary nodes n and n' in G there is exactly one acyclic path from n to n' that satisfies these constraints, we can construct a spanning tree of G by enforcing these constraints. If the reachability testing algorithm implements these constraints, the reachability testing process will exercise every sequence once. We will refer to node n and n' as the source node and target node, or the source sequence and target sequence, respectively. The two constraints we present next constrain the path between n and n' such that there is exactly one path H that satisfies the constraints.

Constraint C1 *The sending partner of a receiving event can be changed only if the receiving event exists in the target sequence and can be changed at most once along a path.* This constraint ensures that path H between n and n' is acyclic. Consider again the S/V-graph in Fig. 7.30*a*. A reachability testing process involving the cyclic path Q0Q1Q0 would not represent a spanning tree of the S/V-graph since trees cannot have cycles. Such a path would represent a reachability testing process in which sequence Q0 was exercised twice. Note that receiving event *r4* has a different sending partner in Q0 and Q1. Indeed, variant V1 changes *r4* so that its sending partner is *s3* instead of *s5*. Therefore, the edge from Q1 to Q0 must change the sending partner of *r4* back to *s5*. This is, however, impossible due to Constraint C1, since the sending partner of *r4* was already changed once in V1 and is not allowed to be changed again. Therefore, the cyclic path Q0Q1Q0 cannot occur during reachability testing.

Constraint C1 can be implemented during reachability testing by associating each receiving event r in variant V with a color that is either black or white. If the sending partner of r is changed to derive variant V, r's color is set to black, and this color is inherited by r in any sequences collected from V. Black receiving events are excluded from race tables (even though they may have nonempty race sets), which prevents the sending partners of black receiving events from being changed again. For example, in Fig. 7.30a, variant V1 was derived by changing the sending partner of $r4$ (see Fig. 7.29). Therefore, the color of $r4$ in V1 will be black, and this color will be inherited by $r4$ in Q1. Thus, $r4$ will be excluded from the heading of Q1's race table, preventing the sending partner of $r4$ from being changed again when deriving race variants from Q1.

Constraint C2   Each edge along a path must reconcile as many differences as possible. A difference between source sequence n and target sequence n' refers to a receiving event r that exists in both sequences but has different sending partners in each sequence. In terms of these differences, reachability testing can be viewed as the process of transforming, through one or more variants, sequence n into sequence n'. Each variant resolves one or more differences between n and n'. Constraint C2 says that if there are differences that can be reconciled by an edge (e.g., the sending partner of r in n' is in the race set of r in n), these differences should be reconciled by this edge. This means that when deriving a variant V, if there are receiving events whose sending partners can be changed but are not changed, these unchanged receiving events cannot be changed afterward in any sequences derived from V. Recall that it is common for a variant to leave some receiving events unchanged since all combinations of changed and unchanged receiving events are enumerated in the race table. Constraint C2 ensures that a particular set of changes occurs in only one variant.

To illustrate Constraint C2, consider sequence Q0 and its three variants in Fig. 7.31. A variant and the sequence that was collected from it are shown in the same space-time diagram, with the variant above the dashed line and the rest of the sequence below it. The SV-graph and spanning tree for these sequences are also shown in Fig. 7.31. Notice that the SV-graph contains paths Q0Q2Q3 and Q0Q3, both of which are paths from Q0 to Q3. Constraint C2 excludes path Q0Q2Q3 from the spanning tree. To see this, observe that receiving events $r2$ and $r4$ exist in Q0 and also in Q3, but the messages they receive in Q0 are different from the messages they receive in Q3. Also observe that edge V2 along the path Q0Q2Q3 only changes the sending partner of $r4$, leaving the sending partner of $r2$ unchanged. The sending partner of $r2$ is changed afterward by the edge from Q2 to Q3. Thus, path Q0Q2Q3 violates Constraint C2, which prohibits $r2$ from being changed in any sequences derived from V2 since $r2$ could have been changed in V2 but wasn't. Note that edge V3 of path Q0Q3 can be included in the spanning tree since it changes the sending partners of both $r2$ and $r4$.

Constraint C2 can be implemented during reachability testing by removing *old* sending events from the race sets of *old* receiving events before variants are derived. A sending or receiving event in a SYN-sequence VQ is an old event if it

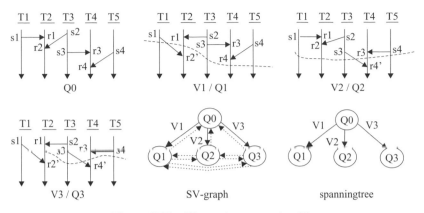

Figure 7.31   Illustrating constraint C2.

also appears in the variant V that was used to collect VQ. For example, consider SYN-sequence Q2 in Fig. 7.31. Events *r1* and *s2* are old events because they appear in both V2 (the variant that was used to collect Q2) and Q2. Therefore, *s2* will be removed from the race set of *r1* in Q2, which means that the sending partner of *r1* cannot be changed to *s2* when the race variants of Q2 are derived. As a result, path Q0Q2Q3 cannot be generated during reachability testing, as in order to reach Q3 from Q2, the sending partner of *r1* must be changed from *s1* to *s2*.

Implementing Constraints C1 and C2 is complicated by the possibility that a receiving event may be removed from a variant and then recollected when the variant is used for prefix-based testing. Figure 7.32 shows a variant V containing a receiving event *r1* that happens before receiving event *r2*. Suppose that variant V is used to collect sequence VQ, which is also shown in Fig. 7.32. Suppose further that some thread executes a sending event *s* that is received by Thread2 and is in the race set of *r1* in VQ. When the sending partner of *r1* is changed from *s1* to *s* in order to derive variant VQV of VQ, *r2* will be removed from VQV since *r1* happens before *r2* in VQ. Notice, however, that *r2* will be recollected when VQV is used for prefix-based testing since Thread3 will definitely execute *r2* again. In this case, changing the sending partner of *r1* to *s* does not affect the flow of control in Thread3 *before* the point where Thread3 executes *r2* (though possibly after that point). This can be determined by examining VQ, which allows

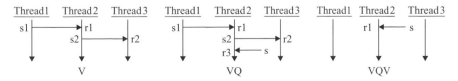

Figure 7.32   Recollected events.

us to guarantee that Thread3 will execute *r2* in the sequence collected from variant VQV.

Recollected events such as *r2* must be handled carefully. There are two cases to consider:

1. Event *r2* in V is a black receiving event, indicating that the sending partner of *r2* was changed earlier in the reachability testing process. When *r2* is recollected during prefix-based testing with VQV, it will be recollected as a new (i.e., white) event. The send partners of white receiving events can be changed. However, Constraint C1 would be violated if we allowed *r2*'s sending partner to be changed when deriving variants of VQV since it was already changed earlier. To prevent a violation of Constraint C1, when *r2*'s color is set to black in V, receiving event *e*'s color in *V* is also set to black for any receiving event *e* that happened before *r2*, such as *r1*. This prevents *r1*'s sending partner from being changed when deriving variants from VQ, which in turn prevents *r2* from being removed from any variant derived from VQ or from any sequence collected afterward. [Recall that if event *e* is colored black in a variant, *e* inherits that color in any sequence(s) collected from that variant.]

2. Event *r2* in V is a white receiving event, indicating that the sending partner of *r2* has not yet been changed. When *r2* is recollected during prefix-based testing with VQV, it will be recollected as a white receiving event, but *r2* will also be an old receiving event. This means that old sending events must be pruned from *r2*'s race set in the sequences collected from variant VQV; otherwise, Constraint C2 would be violated when we changed the sending partner of *r2* to an old sending event. Recollected white receiving events such as *r2* are handled as follows. When the race table of a sequence such as VQ is built, *r2* should not be removed (i.e., set to −1) when variants such as VQV are created, since *r2* will definitely be recollected. Furthermore, in a variant such as VQV, which has recollected event *r2* in it, we allow *r2*'s sending partner to be changed just like the other receiving events in the race table. If r2's sending partner is changed, nothing special must be done when the variant is used for prefix-based testing. If, however, the sending partner of *r2* is not changed, the sending partner of *r2* must be left unspecified in the variant, since the original sending partner of r2 must be removed. (For example, the sending partner *s2* of *r2* in VQ happens after *r1* in VQ, so *s2* must be removed when the sending partner of *r1* is changed to derive VQV.) In this case, *r2* must be prevented from receiving a message from any old sending events when the variant is used for prefix-based testing. This prevents Constraint C2 from being violated.

Figure 7.33 shows the algorithm that drives the reachability testing process. Algorithm *Reachability-Testing* starts with a SYN-sequence Q0 that is collected from a nondeterministic test run. It then applies Constraints C1 and C2 and builds the race table of Q0 to generate the race variants of Q0. Each of these race

ALGORITHM *Reachability-Testing (CP: a concurrent program; I: an input of CP)* {
> let *variants* be an empty set;
> collect *SYN*-sequence *Q0* by executing *CP* with input *I* nondeterministically;
> compute race variants of *Q0*, *variants(Q0)*, by constructing the race table of
> > *Q0* and enforcing Constraints C1 and C2;
> *variants = variants(Q0);*
> while (*variants* is not empty) {
> > withdraw a variant *V* from *variants*;
> > collect a SYN-sequence *Q* by performing prefix-based testing with V;
> > compute the race variants of *Q*, *variants(Q)*, by constructing the race table
> > > of *Q* and enforcing Constraints C1 and C2;
> > *variants = variants ∪ variants(Q);*
> }
}

Figure 7.33   Reachability testing algorithm.

variants is used for prefix-based testing to collect a new SYN-sequence. This process is then repeated for each newly collect SYN-sequence until no more race variants can be generated. The results of applying algorithm *Reachability-Testing* to semaphore, monitor, and message passing programs were described in Sections 3.10.5, 4.11.4, and 5.5.5, respectively.

7.5.7   Research Directions

In this section we suggest several interesting ways in which it may be possible to improve or extend the results of reachability testing.

Coverage-Based Reachability Testing   Reachability testing is inherently an exhaustive testing approach. Exhaustive testing, however, may take too much time or may be unnecessary for some applications. To strike a balance between the cost and coverage of testing, reachability testing can be modified to exercise a set of SYN-sequences selectively. Sequence selection can be guided by test coverage criteria or by heuristics designed to expose bugs as early as possible. The goal of coverage-based reachability testing is to shorten the testing phase and produce meaningful results when exhaustive testing is impractical.

Coverage-Preserving Reductions   Exercising every possible SYN-sequence may be impractical, but it may also be unnecessary. In Section 3.10.5 we suggested several ways to reduce the number of sequences exercised by reachability testing without reducing its ability to detect failures. The results in Section 3.10.5 suggest that significant reductions are possible.

The number of sequences can be reduced based on the semantics of synchronization operations. For example, the semantics of *P* and *V* operations on a semaphore can be used to identify race conditions whose outcomes have no effect on the rest of the execution. For instance, the order of two consecutive *V* () operations on a semaphore *s* has no effect on the operations that follow. Thus, if an *s.V* () operation by Thread1 is followed immediately by an *s.V* () operation by Thread2, we can ignore the race variant that reverses the order of these *V* () operations.

The number of sequences can be reduced based on the symmetry of program threads. For example, the number of possible test sequences for a solution to the readers and writers problem is greatly reduced if you avoid generating test sequences that differ only in the order in which two or more readers perform the same operation (e .g., start reading), or the order in which two or more writers perform the same operation (e .g., start writing). Notice that three readers can start reading in six different ways, but exercising more than one of these six orders may not increase test coverage in any useful way.

The number of sequences can be reduced based on properties of the application. Sometimes, two or more sequences are equivalent in terms of some application-level property. Perhaps this equivalence can be expressed and verified formally, and perhaps it can be discovered automatically by analyzing the code. Otherwise, the programmer can simply assert this equivalence based on his or her intuition about the program. As an example, consider the distributed mutual exclusion (DME) program in Section 6.4.1. A process that wishes to gain mutually exclusive access to some resource requests and waits for permission from all the other processes. The code that the processes use for receiving replies is as follows:

```
public void waitForReplies() { // wait for all the other processes to reply
    while (true) {
        messageParts m = (messageParts) receiveReplies.receive();
        // the value of m is not used
        replyCount++;
        if (replyCount == numberOfProcesses-1)
            break; // all replies have been received
    }
}
```

Exercising all the possible orders in which replies can be received accounts for a large number of the sequences that can be exercised by the DME program. For three processes there are 4032 possible sequences. Note, however, that the behavior of a process does not depend on the values received in the replies, on the identities of the senders, or on the order in which the replies are received; it depends only on the number of replies (*replyCount*) that are received. If we only require reachability testing to exercise one of the possible orders of receiving replies, the total number of sequences for three processes drops from 4032 to 504.

Run-Time Monitoring and Failure Detection Analyzing the large number of sequences exercised during reachability testing must be automated at least partially. In Chapter 3 we described techniques for detecting data races and deadlocks automatically. Since reachability testing provides some guarantees about the completeness of testing, it can be used to bridge the gap between testing and verification. Run-time verification techniques are needed for specifying and verifying correctness properties against the individual sequences generated during reachability testing.

Formal Methods and Model Checking There is growing interest in combining formal methods and testing. Some formal methods are model based, which means that a finite-state model must be extracted from a program before the program can be verified. Static analysis methods for model extraction have difficulty handling dynamic objects such as threads, heaps, and data structures. These objects ought to be easier to handle in a dynamic framework. Since reachability testing is dynamic and can be exhaustive, it is possible to extract complete models of behavior from concurrent programs and then verify the extracted models. As we mentioned above, correctness properties can also be verified as the program is running, without building a finite-state model. However, model-based formal methods are supported by a variety of powerful state-reduction techniques, model checkers, and specification languages, which makes this approach attractive.

FURTHER READING

Hwang et al. [1995] presented a reachability testing algorithm that exercises all possible interleavings of read and write operations on shared variables. A reachability testing algorithm for asynchronous message-passing programs was reported by Tai [1997]. Tai's algorithm constructs a race variant of an SR-sequence by changing the outcome of a single race condition and then uses the race variant for prefix-based testing. Eventually, this process produces race variants that represent changes to the outcomes of two or more race conditions. Lei and Tai [2002] developed an improved algorithm, which generates all the race variants of an SR-sequence at once. Lei and Carver [2004a,b; 2005] and Carver and Lei [2004] developed the reachability testing models and algorithms presented in this chapter.

REFERENCES

Andrews, Gregory R. (1991). *Concurrent Programming: Principles and Practice.* Redwood City, CA: Benjamin-Cummings.

Avrunin, G. A., U. A. Buy, J. C. Corbett, L. K. Dillon, and J. C. Wileden (1991). Automated analysis of concurrent systems with the constrained expression toolset. *IEEE Transactions on Software Engineering*, Vol. 17, No. 11 (November), pp. 1204–1222.

Baase, Sara (1988). *Computer Algorithms: Introduction to Design and Analysis*, 2nd ed. Reading, MA: Addison-Wesley.

Beizer, B. (1979). *Software Testing Techniques*, 2nd ed. New York: Van Nostrand Reinhold.

Carver, Richard H., and Y. Lei (2004). A general model for reachability testing of concurrent programs. *Proc. International Conference on Formal Engineering Methods*, pp. 76–98.

Cheng, J. (1991). A survey of tasking deadlock detection methods. *ACM Ada Letters*, Vol. 11, No. 1 (January–February), pp. 82–91.

Choi, J., and H. Srinivasan (1998). Deterministic replay of Java multithreaded applications. *Proc. ACM Sigmetrics Symposium on Parallel and Distributed Tools*, pp. 48–59.

Chung, I. S., B. M. Kim, and H. S. Kim (2000). A new approach to deterministic execution testing for concurrent programs. *Proc. ICDS Workshop on Distributed System Validation and Verification*, pp. E59–E66.

Deitel, H. M. (1984). *An Introduction to Operating Systems*. Reading, MA: Addison-Wesley.

DeMillo, R. A., R. J. Lipton, and F. G. Sayward (1979). Program mutation: a new approach to program testing. In E. F. Miller (Ed.), *Software Testing, Vol. 2, Invited Papers*. Infotech International, Maidenhead, England, pp. 107–128.

Duran, J. W., and S. Ntafos (1984). An evaluation of random testing. *IEEE Transactions on Software Engineering*, Vol. SE-10, pp. 438–444.

Empath, P. A., S. Ghosh, and D. A. Padua (1992). Detecting nondeterminacy in parallel programs. *IEEE Software*, Vol. 9, No. 1, pp. 69–77.

Frankl, P. and E. Weyuker (1988). An applicable family of data flow testing criteria. *IEEE Transactions on Software Engineering*, Vol. 14, No. 10 (October), pp. 1483–1498.

Gait, J. (1986). A probe effect in concurrent programs. *Software: Practice and Experience*, Vol. 16, No. 3, pp. 225–233.

German, S. M., (1984). Monitoring for deadlock and blocking in Ada tasking. *IEEE Transactions on Software Engineering*, Vol. 10, No. 6 (November), pp. 764–777.

Hamlett, R. G. (1977). Testing programs with the aid of a compiler. *IEEE Transactions on Software Engineering*, Vol. 3, No. 4, pp. 279–290.

Helmbold, D., and D. Luckham (1985). Debugging Ada tasking programs. *IEEE Software*, Vol. 2, No. 2 (March), pp. 47–57.

Holzmann, G. J. (1991). *Design and Validation of Computer Protocols*. Englewood Cliffs, NJ: Prentice Hall.

Hwang, G., K. C. Tai, and T. Huang (1995). Reachability testing: an approach to testing concurrent software. *Journal of Software Engineering and Knowledge Engineering*, Vol. 5, No. 4, pp. 493–510.

IEEE90 (1990). STD 610.12–1990, *IEEE Standard Glossary of Software Engineering Terminology*. New York: IEEE Press.

Karam, G., and R. J. A. Buhr (1991). Temporal logic-based deadlock analysis for Ada. *IEEE Transactions on Software Engineering*, Vol. 17, No. 10 (October), pp. 1109–1125.

King, K. N., and A. J. Offutt (1991). A Fortran language system for mutation-based software testing. *Software: Practice and Experience*, Vol. 21, No. 7 (July), pp. 685–718.

Konuru, R., H. Srinivasan, and J. -D. Choi (2000). Deterministic replay of distributed Java applications. *Proc. 14th International Parallel and Distributed Processing Symposium (IPDPS'00)*, pp. 219–228.

Koppol, Pramod V., Richard H. Carver, and Kuo-Chung Tai (2002). Incremental integration testing of concurrent programs. *IEEE Transactions on Software Engineering*, Vol. 28, No. 6, pp. 607–623.

Ledoux, C. H., and D. Stott Parker (1985). Saving traces for Ada debugging. *Proc. 1985 International Ada Conference*, pp. 97–108.

Lei, Yu, and Richard H. Carver (2004a). Reachability testing of semaphore-based programs. *Proc. 28th Computer Software and Applications Conference (COMPSAC)*, pp. 312–317.

Lei, Yu, and Richard H. Carver (2004b). Reachability testing of monitor-based programs. *Proc. 8th IASTED International Conference on Software Engineering and Applications*, pp. 312–317.

Lei, Yu, and Richard H. Carver (2005). A new algorithm for reachability testing of concurrent programs. Technical Report GMU-CS-TR-2005-1.

Lei, Yu, and Kuo-Chung Tai (2002). Efficient reachability testing of asynchronous message-passing programs. *Proc. 8th IEEE International Conference on Engineering for Complex Computer Systems*, pp. 35–44.

Masticola, S. P., and B. G. Ryder (1991). A model of Ada programs for static deadlock detection in polynomial time. *Proc. Workshop on Parallel and Distributed Debugging*, pp. 97–107.

Mellor-Crummey, J., and T. LeBlanc (1989). A software instruction counter. *Proc. 3rd Symposium on Architectural Support for Programming Languages and Operating Systems*, pp. 78–86.

Myers, Glenford (1979). *The Art of Software Testing*. New York: Wiley.

Netzer, R. B., and B. P. Miller (1994). Optimal tracing and replay for debugging message-passing parallel programs. *Journal of Supercomputing*, Vol. 8, No. 4, pp. 371–388.

Offutt, A. Jefferson, and Jeffrey M. Voas (1996). *Subsumption of Condition Coverage Techniques by Mutation Testing*. Technical Report ISSE-TR-96-01. Department of Information and Software Systems Engineering, http://www.isse.gmu.edu/techrep/1996.

Parrish, A. S., and S. H. Zweben (1995). On the relationships among the all-uses, all-du-paths, and all-edges testing criteria. *IEEE Transactions on Software Engineering*, Vol. 21, No. 12 (December), pp. 1006–1009.

Silberschatz, A., J. L. Peterson, and P. Galvin (1991). *Operating Systems Concepts*. Reading, MA: Addison-Wesley.

Stoller, S. D. (2002). Testing concurrent Java programs using randomized scheduling. *Proc. 2nd Workshop on Runtime Verification (RV)*, Vol. 70, No. 4. *Electronic Notes in Theoretical Computer Science*. Amsterdam: Elsevier.

Tai, K. C. (1994). Definitions and detection of deadlock, livelock, and starvation in concurrent programs. *Proc. 1994 International Conference on Parallel Processing*, pp. 69–72.

Tai, K. C. (1997). Reachability testing of asynchronous message-passing programs. *Proc. 2nd International Workshop on Software Engineering for Parallel and Distributed Systems*, pp. 50–61.

Tai, K. C., R. H. Carver, and E. Obaid (1991). Debugging concurrent Ada programs by deterministic execution. *IEEE Transactions on Software Engineering*, Vol. 17, No. 1 (January), pp. 45–63.

Tannenbaum, A. S. (1992). *Modern Operating Systems*. Englewood Cliffs, NJ: Prentice Hall.

Turski, W. M. (1991). On starvation and some related issues. *Information Processing Letters*, Vol. 37, No. 3, pp. 171–174.

Taylor, R. N. (1983). A general-purpose algorithm for analyzing concurrent programs. *Communications of the ACM*, Vol. 26, No. 5, pp. 362–376.

Taylor, R. N., D. L. Levine, and C. D. Kelly (1992). Structural testing of concurrent programs. *IEEE Transactions on Software Engineering*, Vol. 18, No. 3, pp. 206–215.

Tsai, J., Y. Bi, S. Yang, and R. Smith (1996). *Distributed Real-Time Systems: Monitoring, Debugging, and Visualization*. New York: Wiley.

Vissers, C. A., G. Scollo, Mv. Sinderen, and E. Brinksma (1991). Specification styles in distributed systems design and verification. *Theoretical Computer Science*, Vol. 89, pp. 179–206.

Vouk, M. A., M. L. Helsabeck, D. F. McAllister, and K. C. Tai (1986). On testing of functionally equivalent components of fault-tolerant software. *Proc. COMPSAC'86*, October, pp. 414–419.

Yang, C., and L. L. Pollock (1997). The challenges in automated testing of multithreaded programs. *Proc. 14th International Conference on Testing Computer Software*, pp. 157–166.

EXERCISES

7.1 Suppose that CP is a nondeterministic concurrent program. Must it be true that there are two or more different possible outputs for an execution of CP with some input X?

7.2 Create several mutations of the message-passing solution to the readers and writers program in Section 5.4.1. List your mutations and indicate whether the sequence that distinguishes the mutant from the correct solution is a valid or an invalid sequence.

7.3 Show a sequential program for which a set of test sequences that satisfies decision coverage may not detect a failure that is detected by a set of test sequences that satisfies statement coverage but not decision coverage.

7.4 Figure 7.34 shows a sequence of call and completion events for semaphores $s1$ and $s2$. Semaphore $s1$ is a counting semaphore initialized to 2. Semaphore $s2$ is a binary semaphore initialized to 1.

(a) Based on the semaphore invariant, compute the *OpenList* for each completion event ei, $1 \leq i \leq 10$.

(b) Compute a timestamp for each call and completion event using the object-centric timestamp scheme.

(c) Compute the race set for each completion event.

(d) Compute the race table for this sequence.

7.5 It is possible to reduce the number of sequences exercised during reachability testing by considering the semantics of P and V operations.

(a) Show how to perform such a reduction by modifying the definition of an *OpenList* for P and V operations. For example, if operation V is

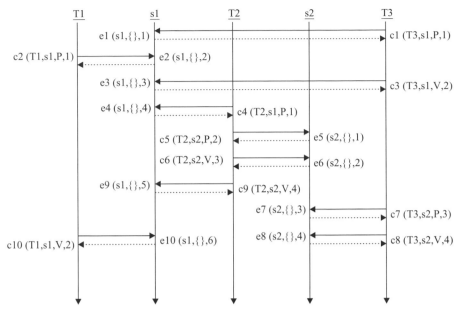

Figure 7.34   Sequence of P and V operations.

excluded from the *OpenList* of completed *V* operations, race analysis will not consider an alternative order of two *V* operations on the same semaphore since *V* operations will never race with each other.

(b) Given your answer to part (a), how many sequences would be exercised during reachability testing for the bounded-buffer program in Listing 3.17?

7.6 In Sections 3.10.5 and 4.11.4 we reported the results of applying reachability testing to semaphore and monitor solutions for the bounded-buffer problem. It was reported that with reductions based on thread symmetry and the semantics of *P* and *V* operations (see Exercise 7.5), reachability testing of the semaphore solution with two producers and two consumers exercised only two sequences. With reductions based on thread symmetry, reachability testing of the SU monitor solution with two producers and two consumers exercised 20 sequences. Why is the reduction greater for the semaphore program? The SU monitor was implemented using semaphores. Would it help to apply reachability testing directly to the semaphore implementation?

7.7 Suppose that we apply reachability testing to a monitor-based bounded-buffer program with three producers and three consumers. Suppose that in the first sequence exercised, Producer1 enters the monitor first, Consumer2 enters the monitor second, and the other Producers and Consumers enter after that. Based on the notion of thread symmetry, what are the variants of this sequence? You only need to consider the first entry into the monitor. That is, should we generate variants in which some other Producer or Consumer enters the monitor first?

7.8 The beginning of Section 7.5 says: "If every execution of a program with a given input terminates, and the total number of SYN-sequences is finite, reachability testing will terminate and every partially ordered SYN-sequence of the program with the given input will be exercised."

(a) Write a program or point out one in the text that terminates for every input but does not have a finite number of possible SYN-sequences. *Hint:* Consider programs that have a loop that makes an undetermined number of iterations.

(b) Does the program really have an infinite number of possible sequences? If not, is it possible to put an upper bound on the number of sequences?

7.9 Draw a concurrency graph for the following program:

port p1, p2; // synchronous ports

Thread1	Thread2	Thread3	Thread4
p1.send(x);	x = p1.receive();	p2.send(y);	y = p2.receive();
end;	end;	end;	end;

(a) How many states and transitions does your concurrency graph have?

(b) Would it be possible to reduce the number of states in your graph without losing any information about the program?

7.10 Suppose that a thread has a loop, which could be a for -loop or a while -loop. Will the concurrency graph for the thread include a cycle? Under what conditions would the concurrency graph not have a cycle?

7.11 In Section 7.2.1 we mentioned the following relationship between the paths and SYN-sequences of a concurrent program: "If two or more different partially ordered feasible paths of CP have the same partially ordered SYN-sequence, their input domains are mutually disjoint." The input domain of a path T is the set of inputs for which T is feasible. If the input domains of a path are mutually disjoint, there is no input that appears in the domains of both paths. For example, here is a simple sequential program with two feasible paths:

```
int main() {
1. int x;
2. std::cout << "Enter an integer:";
3. std::cin >> x;
4. if (x%2==0)
5.     std::cout << x << "is even."<< std::endl;
```

6. else

7.   std::cout << x << "is odd."<< std::endl;

8. return 0;

9. }

The feasible paths are (1,2,3,4,5,8,9) and (1,2,3,4,6,7,8,9). The input domain of the first path is {even integers}, and the input domain of the second path is {odd integers}. The input domains of these paths are mutually disjoint. Explain why this statement is not true for totally ordered feasible paths of concurrent program CP. That is, show that if different totally ordered feasible paths of CP have the same totally ordered SYN-sequence, their input domains may have a nonempty intersection. Remember, in a totally ordered path, concurrent events from different threads are interleaved in an arbitrary order.

7.12 Can reachability testing be used to detect livelock and starvation? Explain your answer.

7.13 In Fig. 7.31, explain how Constraint C1 and/or Constraint C2 in Section 7.5.6 prevents path Q0Q1Q2 from being included in the spanning tree for the SV-graph.

INDEX

*Modern Multithreading: Implementing, Testing, and Debugging Multithreaded Java
and C++/Pthreads/Win32 Programs*, By Richard H. Carver and Kuo-Chung Tai
Copyright © 2006 John Wiley & Sons, Inc.